Highwire Act

Daniel Gawthrop is the author of *Affirmation: The AIDS Odyssey of Dr. Peter*. He lives in Vancouver.

HIGHWIRE ACT

Power, Pragmatism, and
the Harcourt Legacy

Daniel Gawthrop

NEW STAR BOOKS
VANCOUVER
1996

Published by New Star Books Ltd., 2504 York Avenue, Vancouver, BC V6K 1E3.
All rights reserved. No part of this work may be reproduced or used in any form or
by any means – graphic, electronic or mechanical – without the prior written permis-
sion of the publisher. Any request for photocopying or other reprographic copying
must be sent in writing to the Canadian Copyright Licensing Agency (CANCOPY),
6 Adelaide Street East, Suite 900, Toronto, ON M5C 1H6.

Publication of this book is made possible by grants from the Canada Council
and the Cultural Services Branch, Province of British Columbia.

Editing and production by Rolf Maurer
and Audrey McClellan
Cover by Val Speidel
Printed and bound in Canada by Imprimerie Gagné ltée
1 2 3 4 5   00 99 98 97 96

Canadian Cataloguing in Publication Data
Gawthrop, Daniel, 1963-
Highwire Act
Includes bibliographical references and index.
ISBN 0-921586-48-5
1. British Columbia – Politics and government – 1991-*
2. New Democratic Party of British Columbia.
I. Title.
FC3829.2.G38 1995   971.1'04   C95-911019-4
F1088.G38 1995

CONTENTS

for Celso

PREFACE

IN MANY WAYS, THE PROCESS OF WRITING THIS BOOK HAS BEEN like the metaphor that inspired its title. The "highwire act" — for me, at least — began in September, 1995 as I was completing the manuscript for an early November release. As New Star began production of the book, Mike Harcourt was seriously considering a fall election date that would have all but killed the project. Given how much I had sacrificed in order to tell this tale — countless hours of research, interviews and writing, not to mention all those turned-down job opportunities and other book ideas — my feelings toward the NDP at this point were less than charitable.

But fate intervened. On October 12 — one week after I had written the first draft of this preface — the RCMP raided NDP offices in Burnaby and six other locations, brandishing search warrants that accused a prominent former New Democrat of theft and fraud involving nearly $1 million. The next day — appropriately enough, Friday the 13th — a BC Supreme Court judge ordered the release of a long-awaited report on a festering scandal that had plagued the government for three years. From this report, the media learned that the NDP had concealed a repayment of $60,000 to a party-connected non-profit society that was about to be convicted of defrauding charities. Needless to say, all bets for a fall election were off and – though it would require some revisions – my book once again had a life.

By the time this book went to press, the NDP was preparing to select BC's fourth premier in five years. All polls suggested that the winning candidate would soon be succeeded by a fifth premier, Liberal leader Gordon Campbell. Here's hoping that *Highwire Act*, at the very least, offers some food for thought before voters make that a reality.

THIS BOOK WOULD NOT HAVE BEEN WRITTEN IF NOT FOR A friendly challenge by Stan Persky. Stan, who has informed and entertained many with his unofficial New Star trilogy on BC politics (*Son of Socred*, *Bennett II* and *Fantasy Government*), was hoping to pick up where *Fantasy Government* left off – with Bill Vander Zalm expecting to face the electorate some time in 1990. The idea was for me to do the research and provide some of the writing for what would basically be another Persky opus, this time on the NDP's first government since Dave Barrett's 1972-75 administration.

Unfortunately, a series of scheduling conflicts and lack of funding – not to mention Stan's trip to Berlin in the spring – prevented us from doing it together. I agreed to carry on with the project at my own pace, while Stan provided valuable advice on ideas, the manuscript and politics in general. Persky's broad, pragmatic socialist perspective was a big influence during my undergrad years in political science – though I never studied at Capilano College – and that influence continues to this day.

Highwire Act is the product of several months' sweat and the good will of everyone who put up with me while I wrote it. Above and beyond the call of duty was Michael Geoghegan in Victoria, who went out of his way to provide contact sources, advice and much-needed background. I also received ongoing support and sustenance from Kevin Griffin, Don Larventz, Warren O Briain, Eric Kyle, Tom Sandborn, Harry Grunsky, Bernard and Catherine von Schulmann, members of my immediate family, and the Cutting Edges hockey team.

I'm also grateful to Chris Gainor, Geoff Meggs, George Stanley, Terry Glavin, Tara Todd-Macdonald, Colin Welch, Marc Piché, Peter

McCue, Cindy Filipenko and Michele Green. And special thanks to my dad, Paul Gawthrop, for generously providing a new fax machine, his old 386 computer, and a small loan.

Highwire Act was compiled mostly through secondary sources, including hundreds of newspaper articles and government documents. But I'm also grateful to several people who offered their time through interviews. This includes the premier, Mike Harcourt, who was willing to subject himself to several hours of questioning – before and after his resignation – despite daily bombardment by the media. (Patti Haire and Michelle Purdon in the Premier's Office were more than flexible, given the circumstances.)

Thanks also to Moe Sihota, Tom Perry, Bill Barlee, Jean Greatbatch, Ken Georgetti, Bill Tieleman, Joe Gosnell, George Watts, barbara findlay, Dennis Dahl, Libby Davies, Gideon Rosenbluth, Gerry Stoney, Dave Stupich, Brian Smith, Bill Duncan, Frank Murphy and others who asked not to be named.

I should especially thank New Star for tempting fate by publishing a book about a government as it approached the fifth year of its mandate. Rolf Maurer was never too busy to take my calls, talk about hockey, or reassure me that there wouldn't be a fall election, and he was tremendously flexible and helpful with the manuscript. Thanks again to Audrey McClellan, who will be sorely missed at New Star, and to Carolyn Stewart.

Finally, the biggest thank you goes to Celso Rivera – a true believer in my "sustainable development". Without him, this book would have remained an idea.

DANIEL GAWTHROP
VANCOUVER
DECEMBER, 1995

Politics is not the art of the possible. It is the art of choosing between the abhorrent and the disastrous.

JOHN KENNETH GALBRAITH

Falling Off

VICTORIA, NOVEMBER 15, 1995

MIKE HARCOURT'S MORNING PRESS CONFERENCE WAS NOT expected to be a blockbuster. The media's coverage of the most recent NDP scandal had peaked a few days earlier, and there was no indication that the premier would have anything important to announce — unless, that is, he really found it necessary to comment on the government's proposed changes to BC Transit. Not likely.

In fact, there was so little anticipation of the conference that the regional CBC office didn't even bother sending a camera to the press theatre. Within minutes, however, Canada's national broadcaster would be scrambling for good footage of the event.

"I wish to inform you that I have made a decision not to seek the leadership of the New Democratic Party at the upcoming convention of the party," a nervous Harcourt began. "Nor will I be seeking re-election as a member of the legislature at the next provincial election. I will continue as premier and leader until the party picks a new leader at the next convention."

Given that he had just declared his intention a few days earlier to fight the next election, the news was something of a shock for the assembled reporters. Here was Harcourt, who had confounded his critics for several weeks by vowing to endure the storm of an NDP scandal, suddenly struck by the cold, hard facts. The NDP had no choice but to renew itself, he said; that task would "best be carried on by a new leader who will be free of some of the baggage that I have been harnessed with as I have undertaken to clean up some of the problems of the past."

Harcourt's decision to quit was prompted by a damning, government-appointed forensic audit of an NDP-connected non-profit society. But his tone was hardly that of a premier resigning in disgrace. Indeed, much of his statement focussed on the NDP's achievements since the party came to power in 1991:

> When I look back at the work we've done in forest renewal, protecting and renewing our forests and natural wilderness ... I take great pride. I said we needed to bring about a reconciliation between aboriginal and non-aboriginal people and I believe we're on track in doing so ... I said we needed a plan to invest in BC that involved building for the future instead of engaging in a race to the bottom. I said we needed to clean up the fiscal mess we inherited. We've done that – eliminating the deficit, bringing in a debt management plan, and ensuring that BC has the lowest per capita debt and best credit rating of any province in Canada. I believe the province is in good shape ...

For all his upbeat talk, however, there was something sadly familiar about Harcourt's press conference. Had it been only four and a half years since another BC premier stood at that very same podium to announce his resignation? For those who followed BC politics closely, there were few similarities between Mike Harcourt's New Democrats and the party and premier that preceded them. But five years is a long time in BC politics: memories fade, distinctions get blurred, and before long, if you're not paying attention, it's easy to dismiss real accomplishments – and even easier to equate a marginal case of "scandal", "conflict", or "sweetheart deal" with the genuine article.

To understand how Mike Harcourt found himself in the position he was in on this day – indeed, to arrive at a fair assessment of the NDP's entire term in office – one must first examine the circumstances that led to his party's victory in 1991. This requires one more look at the final, ignominious chapter of Social Credit – a party whose corruption and greed paved the way for a New Democrat government.

PART I

Cleaning House

This hasn't been a government, it's been a roller-coaster ride through hell.
                    Vancouver *Province* editorial assessing the
                    Vander Zalm years, October 13, 1991.

I became leader because people saw that we had to become more main-stream and broaden our base and get rid of a lot of the old dusty policies that were out of date.
                    NDP leader Mike Harcourt, on his party's
                    decision to move to the right.

April Fool

VANCOUVER, AUGUST 4, 1990
SOME TIME AFTER 3 AM, IN A CORNER SUITE OF THE WESTIN
Bayshore hotel, a group of business people were closing a deal on a
valuable piece of real estate. All the major players were present: the
host, a Taiwanese billionaire, who had flown in from Taipei a few
days earlier; the local businessman whose theme park was up for sale;
his wife; the real estate broker who arranged the deal; her husband.
Toward the end of the meeting, the billionaire turned to the real estate
broker and asked her to retrieve a brown envelope from his safety
deposit box downstairs.

When she returned, she approached him with the envelope but he
would not take it, gesturing toward her husband. The real estate broker's husband then took the envelope, ripped open the seal and pulled
out a wad of US hundred dollar bills. As he counted the money, he
placed each bill on a table, forming twenty stacks of ten. Then he
turned to the park owner.

"Bill, come over," he said. "You count the money." The park owner
stepped forward and repeated the procedure, nodding his head when
he was done. "Twenty thousand dollars," he said, confirming the figure. "Now you count it, you take it," said the real estate broker's hus-

band. With that, the theme park owner picked up the stacks of bills, put them back in the envelope and stuffed the envelope in his jacket pocket.

The transaction may have been routine by most business standards, but for one important detail: the man who stuffed the US$20,000 into his pocket was the premier of British Columbia, Bill Vander Zalm.

As far as the premier was concerned, there was nothing unusual or unethical about his meeting with Taiwanese billionaire Tan Yu. Months later he would explain that he was merely divesting himself of a valuable private asset that had gradually become a liability to his government. Fantasy Garden World Inc., the Biblical theme park he had purchased six years earlier as a private citizen, had made him a great deal of money in a short time. The problem was, he had made most of that money while he was premier, leading to charges that he had used his influence to benefit the business and was therefore in a conflict of interest.

Most politicians anticipate this kind of problem by selling their assets before they run for office. Bill Vander Zalm's problem – and it was about to become a huge one – was that he waited until long after he became premier before he sold his. By getting involved in the sale directly, he had just violated his own government's conflict of interest guidelines.

The Fantasy's Over

THE MEDIA HAD LONG SUSPECTED THAT VANDER ZALM WAS AT possible risk for conflict. From the day he announced his candidacy for the leadership of the governing Social Credit Party in 1986, he appeared to be doing everything possible to avoid selling Fantasy Gardens, which had become a highly profitable business since he purchased the 8.5 hectare property in July 1984 for $1.7 million. Before he was done, Vander Zalm received fifteen separate approvals from Richmond municipal council to expand his commercial enterprise into a veritable Disneyland of tourist attractions.

Located at the corner of No. 5 Road and Steveston Highway in Richmond, Fantasy Gardens was previously the Bota Garden Centre, a botanical garden and low-key tourist attraction for horticulturalists. Under Bill Vander Zalm's management it became a monument to Christian kitsch. There were little bridges and ponds, a Dutch clock tower with chimes, a windmill, and dozens of small signs with cloying aphorisms like "Kill Nothing But Time, Leave Nothing But Footprints." There was a children's playground, including a Noah's Ark with nothing inside it but a taperecorded story. And behind the ten-foot hedge surrounding the garden there was a biblical theme park featuring fifteen life-size statues in scenes depicting the life of Christ. It was, as Vander Zalm's biographer Alan Twigg put it, "a wasteland of uninventive hucksterism, so wholesome it's sterile, so unoriginal it's frightening."

The day before Vander Zalm was sworn in as premier on August 6, 1986, he resigned as officer and director of Fantasy Gardens. Shortly afterward, Richmond municipal council granted approval to lease shops in the complex, raising the assessed value of the land and buildings from $800,000 to $4.7 million by the spring of 1987. In essence, the premier had made a $3 million profit from his initial investment. When Fantasy Gardens reorganized its share structure in April 1989, the premier continued to own 83 percent of shares, while his wife, Lillian, owned the balance.

Mike Harcourt, leader of the Opposition New Democratic Party, had called for an investigation into Fantasy Gardens as early as May 1988. The premier, he argued, had misled the legislature by failing to disclose his financial stake in the property. But despite Harcourt's efforts, and those of the media, the issue never caught on with the public until September 7, 1990. That's when an offshore investment conglomerate known as the Asiaworld International Group publicly announced its intention to purchase the biblical theme park.

On that day, British Columbians received their first glimpse of the Taiwanese billionaire who would finally take Fantasy Gardens off the premier's hands. Unbeknownst to the public, the premier had been in active negotiations with Tan Yu since the previous March 31, when local real estate broker Faye Leung told him about the Taiwanese group's interest in the property. On June 2 Vander Zalm signed his acceptance of an interim agreement with Tan Yu, with an understanding that the billionaire would visit BC in early August to inspect Fantasy Gardens and work out the final details.

On September 6, the day before the official announcement of the sale, the premier asked Lieutenant Governor David Lam to play host to the Asiaworld Group with a luncheon at Government House. But Vander Zalm neglected to inform the Queen's representative that the government's special guests were also his personal clients, and the unsuspecting Mr. Lam did not learn he had been hoodwinked until he saw the news the next day.

As the media continued to hound him about his role in the Fantasy Gardens sale, Vander Zalm was soon engaged in a private battle of wits with Faye Leung. The real estate broker claimed that Vander Zalm had not paid her the agreed commission on the sale. In October she began to harrass the premier with letters and phone calls, threatening to go public about his role in the sale.

These were not empty threats. During a complex series of legal proceedings against her, the real estate broker told the court that – contrary to Vander Zalm's claim that Fantasy Gardens was "Lillian's business" – she had dealt directly with the premier in the sale and had taken instructions from him during the negotiations. By confirming the premier's role in business dealings with Asiaworld, Faye Leung revealed to the public that the premier had used his office for his own financial gain. By now it was obvious that he would have to be held accountable for the conflict. Obvious to everyone but Vander Zalm, that is. Even at this point, the premier refused to recognize the trouble he was in – or was confident that he would get away with it.

On January 29 he went on live television to contradict Leung's claims. It was a foolish gesture: two weeks after the premier's latest denial, Leung's solicitor released a letter from Lillian Vander Zalm to Tan Yu that not only confirmed the premier's involvement in the sale but cheerfully explained his efforts to acquire property next to the Gardens for his new Asian friend. The premier had personally telephoned Petro Canada chief executive officer Wilbert Hopper to help arrange the sale of land adjacent to Fantasy Gardens, property eventually purchased by Tan Yu along with the Gardens. Other documents

filed in court included hand-written memos by the premier acknowledging two separate payments by Tan Yu totalling $3 million.

On Valentine's Day the premier finally announced that BC conflict
of interest commissioner Ted Hughes would conduct a thorough
investigation of the Fantasy Gardens sale. Hughes was perhaps the
ideal candidate to play Pontius Pilate in Vander Zalm's final passion
play. Unlike the premier, Hughes, a former Saskatchewan high court
judge who had been BC's deputy attorney general, was a modest,
rational figure respected by his peers for his measured but firm
approach to controversial issues. Appointed the previous September
as BC's first conflict of interest commissioner, he was primarily
responsible for determining the political liability of each MLA's financial holdings, as well as those of each MLA's spouse. Although he had
previously looked into the premier's business relationship with Delta
businessman Peter Toigo, this was his first major inquiry.

Vander Zalm was confident he would be vindicated by the investigation. What he didn't realize was that Hughes planned to conduct
the inquiry according to the 1987 conflict guidelines, which had a
much broader definition of conflict of interest than the Members'
Conflict of Interest Act, proclaimed in December 1990. According to
the 1987 rules, even the appearance of conflict was considered an
offense. The premier was much more likely to be found guilty under
this definition.

Vander Zalm's failure to step aside as premier during the investigation was not well received by everyone in the Socred caucus. The first
to show his displeasure was Finance Minister Mel Couvelier, who
resigned in protest on March 6. He had good reason to be angry, given
the premier's treatment of him the previous summer. In July, Couvelier had dutifully provided the premier with briefing materials for
Faye Leung, regarding the establishment of a trust fund in BC. Vander
Zalm never told him that Leung was representing Tan Yu's group in
the Fantasy Gardens sale. On September 6, the same day the lieutanant
governor held the state luncheon, Couvelier and his deputy minister
met with Tan Yu in the premier's office, not knowing that Lillian Vander Zalm would be present. For Couvelier, the premier's failure to
resign was unforgivable.

Vander Zalm was beginning to crack under the pressure. On March 19 he lashed out at his critics. "It's terrible because it's like a bunch of vigilante action and you have to sort of prove your innocence," he said, in a statement typical of the martyr stance he adopted whenever his credibility was questioned. "It's very depressing ... I don't know what investigation is taking place. I'm simply saying it's reminiscent of Nazi Germany ... It's not the sort of justice I thought we had in this country."

For all his criticism of the justice system, however, Vander Zalm had no defense when it came to his own behaviour. During his first interview with Ted Hughes on March 1, the premier said nothing about a US$20,000 payment from Tan Yu. But on March 21 Faye Leung dropped a bombshell on the proceedings when her lawyers released to the media a 25-minute cassette of taped phone conversations, between herself and Vander Zalm. In the December 3 and 4 conversations the premier and his real estate broker can be heard discussing, among other things, the $20,000 payment. In the recording, a defensive and conciliatory Vander Zalm can barely be heard above the high-pitched, mile-a-minute ranting of Faye Leung.

> LEUNG: Do you think I got a penny? Do you think I got any money out of it? Anything out of it? And I was supposed to get 10 percent out of that IAA was assigned over when Taiwan, when Tan Yu, came with the 10 percent for the Petro lands and all those other lands. Why I haven't a penny? I turned the $20,000 ... Tan Yu got a good deal, you got a good deal. Everybody got a good deal but I get the bum rap. I am the underdog ...

Later, Leung threatens Vander Zalm with legal action.

> VANDER ZALM: Faye, Faye, you've got six lawyers. I've only got one.
> LEUNG: You'll need a litigation lawyer tomorrow!
> VANDER ZALM: No, I don't want any more lawyers.

Leung continues shouting at the premier, before he interrupts.

VANDER ZALM: Faye, don't, don't get upset yet.

Not surprisingly, these tapes provided comic relief for thousands of radio listeners throughout BC. With widespread airplay on various stations, including caricatures on CBC's "Double Exposure" radio show, the Bill and Faye tapes became, for a short time, B.C's hottest political soap opera.

Much of the comic appeal lay in the contrast between two extreme characters. In one corner, the eternally optimistic, gladhanding premier for whom style was substance; in the other, the flamboyant broker with the colourful hat collection and fiery temper, whose credibility as a witness was dismissed by one Supreme Court judge , who called her self-serving and manipulative.

The Bill and Faye tapes were no joke to Ted Hughes. The tapes only confirmed his worst suspicions that in order to save himself, the premier was intentionally suppressing information during the course of a public inquiry. When the two met again in late March, Hughes made it clear that Vander Zalm was in deep trouble. Finally, on Good Friday, March 29, the premier announced his decision to resign as soon as the Social Credit Party could elect a successor.

The wording of this announcement implied that not even the release of Hughes's report would force him to quit sooner, but Vander Zalm's immediate departure was already a foregone conclusion in the party. "As soon as the albatross is off our necks, we'll be able to get the debate back on our agenda," one anonymous Socred told the Vancouver *Sun*'s Vaughn Palmer. "We've got three or four candidates, any one of whom could beat invisible Mike," said another, glibly dismissing the NDP leader.

The anti-Zalm dissidents appeared to have forgotten that most of the caucus had supported Vander Zalm's leadership at four successive annual conventions after 1986. But none of this appeared to matter as the Easter weekend approached. Vander Zalm was fond of comparing himself to Jesus Christ, and he might well have asked seven of his disciples why they had forsaken him as he neared his final hours as premier. Peter Dueck, Lyall Hanson, Norm Jacobsen, Ivan Messmer, Dan Peterson, Claude Richmond and Bruce Strachan had never publicly criticized Vander Zalm. Indeed, they had either supported the premier or silently endured his ethical lapses for the past four years. Only now, when his political capital appeared to be spent, were they all more than willing to join forces against him. Advanced Education Minister Strachan, for one, implied that the cabinet would force Vander Zalm out if he didn't voluntarily resign immediately instead of waiting for a leadership convention. To the NDP, the media, and much of the public, it was hard not to interpret this action as opportunistic. The Socred caucus was waiting until the last minute to reject Bill Vander Zalm's leadership — not because his conflicts of interest and frequent abuse of government ethics were unacceptable, but because he had finally been caught and was no longer electable.

There was at least one dissenter in the cabinet, though. Despite having told the press that the Hughes report would decide the premier's fate, longtime loyalist Rita Johnston defended Vander Zalm's decision to stay on as leader and voiced her confidence that the report would exonerate her beleaguered friend. "Bill Vander Zalm asked for that review," a defiant Johnston told the legislative press gallery. "Would a person ask for a review of his private activities if he felt something was wrong? I suggest that he wouldn't."

VICTORIA, APRIL I, 1991
TWENTY-FOUR HOURS BEFORE TED HUGHES'S REPORT WAS released to the media, the unflappable premier was still trying to convince the public that there would be nothing serious enough in its contents to affect his political future. "I don't have anything to be ashamed of, or I don't have anything to worry about in the sense that I've not taken a dime from anyone in the province and I've not cheaten or done anything unfairly," he told one radio station.

But the premier's April Fool's Day declaration of innocence seemed rather foolish itself the next day. At 11:15 on the morning of April 2, Ted Hughes presented Vander Zalm and Mike Harcourt with copies of his 60-page report. Two and a half hours later the premier told his caucus he was quitting, and the report was released to the media; half an hour after that he went public with his resignation. His decision to quit immediately was no surprise, given some of Ted Hughes's findings.

Vander Zalm had broken at least three of his own government's conflict of interest guidelines. First, he created the appearance of conflict
by combining his personal financial interests with the use of his
office, public officials and facilities; second, he compromised his ability to exercise his duties and responsibilities objectively when he
accepted $20,000 in cash from Tan Yu; finally, he had telephoned the
CEO of Petro-Canada to arrange a land sale that would benefit him
personally. "The premier's problem," concluded Hughes, "stems not
just from his inability to draw a line between his private and public
life but in his apparently sincere belief that no conflict existed so long
as the public wasn't aware of what was going on."

The suggestion of a coverup – and the premier's belief that such an
approach was entirely appropriate – was one of the more shocking
aspects of the Fantasy Gardens affair. Until this moment, many British
Columbians had assumed that their political system was free of such
corruption.

At his final press conference, Vander Zalm gave the impression that
his mistake was little more than a minor clerical error. "During my
time as premier, I believe I have always served and acted in the public
interest … In that respect, I stand by my record," he said, blaming his
cracking voice on a cold he had picked up from Lillian the day before.
He wouldn't answer questions, and was quickly ushered away by a
group of handlers. His final act as premier was a trip to Government
House, but this time there was no lavish spread for preferred clients.
Instead Vander Zalm quietly handed in his resignation to Lieutenant
Governor David Lam, whose trust he had abused by serving up the
red carpet treatment for Tan Yu at the taxpayers' expense.

As he left Government House and approached his car, Vander Zalm
was met for a final time by the throng of reporters he had once considered his allies. Even in disgrace the premier couldn't resist one last
Nixonian statement to the media. "You see those flowers?" he said,
pointing to a small garden. "Those are forget-me-nots. Don't forget
me." And with that, British Columbia's most famous gardener drove
off into political oblivion and a $50,000 a year pension.

A Fresh Start, A Sour Finale

THE FANTASY GARDENS FIASCO MAY HAVE BEEN THE SOLE responsibility of Bill Vander Zalm, but in the context of Social Credit it was only the final insult in a long process of public disillusionment. In fact, the electorate had already lost patience with Socred philosophy by 1986, when it was prepared to reject the confrontational government of Bill Bennett. Under the restraint programs of 1983-84, the Socreds had badly eroded education, health care and social services, attacked unions and spent billions of dollars on megaprojects while the province was accumulating deficits of more than $1 billion a year, and its citizens were facing double-digit unemployment.

By 1986 Social Credit had also compiled a legacy of ethical scandals and conflicts of interest that was beginning to wear on the public patience. Not even Bennett's promotion of Expo 86 – the Vancouver world's fair that promised to attract millions of tourist dollars to the province – was considered enough to save the party at the next election. When he finally resigned on May 22, 1986, Bill Bennett's approval rating was lower than that of any other premier in BC history. The party's selection of a new leader that summer was supposed to mark a fresh start for Social Credit – an end to confrontation and a new era of responsible, open government. The choice of the charismatic Bill Vander Zalm did signal a new era in BC politics, but that era proved to be more damaging to the party than any one before it.

Before 1986, Christian fundamentalism had never been much of a problem, politically speaking, for Social Credit. Although the party maintained a strong level of support among Protestant evangelicals, most Socred power brokers knew that a religious platform of any kind did not translate into broad, popular appeal in a province like BC. Thus, while the party maintained its fringe element of religious eccentrics (the right-wing equivalent of the NDP's disgruntled Trotskyite element), not even W.A.C. Bennett, a devout Protestant himself, was willing to adopt the missionary zeal of Alberta's Social Credit mentor, William "Bible Bill" Aberhart.

Social Credit under its first BC premier was a business-first, free-enterprise party. It assumed the dominant Christian values typical of North America in the 1950s without actively promoting religious orthodoxy in its political program. This was even more the case when Bill Bennett succeeded his father as leader in 1973. With a pluralistic, multicultural society taking shape on Canada's west coast, religion was simply not a winning platform for any BC party to adopt – not even Social Credit.

Despite this lesson, the party came out of the 1986 Whistler leadership convention with a new premier whose religious grandstanding and bigotry had the editorial cartoonists drooling.

Within months of taking office, Bill Vander Zalm made it clear that Roman Catholicism and white suburban "family values" were things he wanted all British Columbians to share. When he wasn't reducing the role of women to that of the 1950s housewife (Lillian was too busy washing his socks to join him on a campaign stop), he was criticizing legalized abortion at every turn (too many women were using it for birth control), defending homophobic remarks by his ministers (AIDS was a "self-inflicted wound" according to Forests Minister Dave Parker, who also said the NDP's theme song should be "Sodomy Forever"), comparing himself to Jesus Christ ("He never had a UBC education. He would have been low in the polls. But he left a tremendous impression on the world") and condoning anti-Semitic insults (Socred dissident Michael Levy was verbally abused by delegates at the 1989 party convention when he questioned a clause in its constitution committing the Socreds to "Christian principles." Instead of apologizing for the incident at the next morning's breakfast meeting, Vander Zalm told a joke about a Jewish rabbi and suggested that Levy and the media should lighten up).

His messianic complex was also evident in his method of governing. With Vander Zalm at the helm, deputy ministers were often expected to go over their ministers' heads and report directly to the premier. Throughout his reign there were countless stories of ministers learning about key legislation through the media or at a press conference called by the premier. In the case of Bill 19, the Industrial Relations Act which wiped out the province's 1973 Labour Code and prompted a one-day general strike throughout the province, Labour Minister

Lyall Hanson was left on the sidelines. Vander Zalm's decision to hire a group of lawyers to draft a new labour law containing his own ideas seemed to defeat the purpose of his stated campaign promise, to provide more open government and consultation.

If the messiah complex wasn't enough to kill Social Credit during Bill Vander Zalm's reign, the legacy of scandal and corruption certainly was. Vander Zalm was by no means alone in the conflict of interest/ethical lapses department. During his five-year reign, a long list of ministers were cited for various forms of misconduct: Stephen Rogers failed to divulge forest company shareholdings, Stan Hagen failed to resign as president of a cement company which had a contract with the University of BC, Cliff Michael offered to sell private property to an individual who sought cabinet approval of other business, Carol Gran intervened on behalf of her son to have BC Hydro bill payments deferred, Bill Reid directed more than $277,000 in grant funding to a company owned by his constituency campaign chairman, John Savage voted on Delta council for a zoning favourable to his brother-in-law's housing development, Peter Dueck accepted free food and hotel accommodation from a major European supplier of medical equipment to the Ministry of Health, Russ Fraser accepted a bid on a contract to privatize computer services in his ministry from a company already under contract to the ministry, Harry De Jong lobbied the Matsqui mayor to obtain $104,000 for an irrigation project that would benefit no farm but his own, Jack Kempf misused MLA travel expenses, Walter Davidson counselled a printing company to commit forgery, Bud Smith obstructed justice with a partisan attack on a lawyer, and Lyall Hanson condoned a lie to defend a party supporter's application for a pub licence.

This litany of sleaze was well-documented in a 1991 book by Graham Leslie, the former deputy minister of Labour. Leslie, who quit the public service four years earlier when Vander Zalm realigned his ministries, provides a chilling assessment of the 1986-91 government in *Breach of Promise*, a book Vaughn Palmer referred to as "a veritable cornucopia of Socred squalor." Indeed, the chapter titles of the book's revised edition read like a reform school detention list for chronic delinquents. The book includes at least 16 confirmed cases of conflict of interest, 12 examples of ethical breaches, 70 pages devoted to institutional neglect and abuse of the legislature and another 75 pages to financial mismanagement. In case readers miss the point, there's also a section titled "Socred Boorishness and Insensitivity."

As Leslie concludes in *Breach of Promise*, the failure of the Vander Zalm government was a failure shared by the entire Social Credit Party. The book, published in early 1991 with an updated version released just before the fall election campaign, was a ravaging indictment of Social Credit as a political phenomenon. It was by no means the only critical assessment of the Vander Zalm years, but given that the messenger was a former civil servant appointed by Bill Bennett and coming, as it did, in the final year of Social Credit's mandate, Leslie's analysis was far more damning in its impact. This was no dyed-in-the-wool socialist or scandal-hungry reporter talking; Leslie was a disillusioned free enterpriser who had voted Social Credit in nearly every election for the past three decades.

In passing sentence on both Vander Zalm's leadership and the Social Credit party in general, Leslie's book confirmed the prophecy of Kim Campbell, later to become Canada's first female prime minister. Campbell had placed last in a field of twelve candidates at the 1986 Socred leadership convention, but her speech to the delegates proved a fitting epitaph for both Social Credit and the political career of Bill Vander Zalm. "In this day and age," she said, "a leader cannot deceive the public with a simplistic vision of a past that can never be recaptured. Even the slickest salesmanship cannot sell for long a vision that is essentially empty, a vision that is really only a memory. It is fashionable to speak of leaders in terms of their charisma. But charisma without substance is a dangerous thing."

Given that six of the ministers cited in Leslie's book had served under Bill Bennett, and a seventh, Bud Smith, was Bennett's former principal secretary, it was hard to pretend that the sleaze was entirely the product of Bill Vander Zalm's leadership. The so-called fresh start that Vander Zalm promised did not take long to sour with the public: in addition to the 12 cabinet resignations from 1986-91, even former premier Bill Bennett — who had managed to avoid legal scrutiny throughout his years in office — embarrassed the party during Vander

Zalm's leadership. In January 1989, he, brother Russell and forest magnate Herb Doman were charged with insider trading in a case that dragged on for more than six years.

Running On Empty

WITH VANDER ZALM OUT OF THE PICTURE, THE NEW SOCRED premier would face the unenviable prospect of an election before year's end. With a host of polls showing the Socreds far behind the NDP in popular support, a mainstream media that had grown increasingly hostile toward the government, and widespread criticism from both labour and business, Vander Zalm's successor would first have to deal with a leadership race that promised to be much more sobering than the 1986 version. Who on earth would want to steer this sinking ship?

As Vander Zalm prepared his resignation statement to the media on the morning of April 2, the Socred caucus held a closed-door meeting to decide an interim successor. Four hours after the Hughes report was made public, and following a narrow fourth-ballot victory over Attorney General Russ Fraser, Vander Zalm loyalist Rita Johnston was sworn in as BC's 28th premier and Canada's first female provincial leader.

The interim premier got off to a rough start when she refused to apologize for the sins of her predecessor. Johnston told her first press conference that Vander Zalm had done the honourable thing by resigning and that the media had paid far too much attention to Fantasy Gardens. "When history is written," she said, "the period of 1986 to '91 is going to be one that most British Columbians will look back upon with pride."

The next day, when the Social Credit Party announced a leadership convention for July 18-20 at the Vancouver Trade and Convention Centre, Johnston faced rumours of a bloodbath because of the caucus decision to name a Vander Zalm loyalist as interim premier.

She was able to silence her critics momentarily. First she called the House into session for May 7; then she announced a cabinet shuffle.

The new premier's choice of ministers appeared to be an attempt to distance herself from Vander Zalm's leadership. Mel Couvelier was returned to the Ministry of Finance in a clear vindication of his earlier decision to resign on principle; scandal-tainted Bud Smith and Cliff Michael were dropped from the cabinet; two prominent anti-Vander Zalm backbenchers, David Mercier and Graham Bruce, were named to the ministries of Environment and Municipal Affairs respectively.

Shortly afterward, Johnston announced a get-tough stance on ethics. "I expect the very highest standards of personal and public conduct from all members of the executive council at all times," she boldly pronounced. "There will be no exceptions for anyone at any time. There will be no second chances." She appeared to be serious; within days of reinstating Couvelier as Finance minister, Johnston accepted his resignation after a review by the attorney general's office concluded that he breached the confidentiality section of the Financial Institutions Act. (Couvelier had sent a confidential memo to the premier's office which revealed that Faye Leung was under investigation by the RCMP.)

At the end of April Johnston announced her intention to retain the Social Credit leadership. On July 20 she won the contest after a bitter two-ballot fight with the grande dame of Social Credit, Grace McCarthy. There was little else to do now but call the long-awaited election. From all appearances, Social Credit was headed for its worst defeat in history. "Let's go. We're ready," an upbeat Mike Harcourt told reporters. "We want an election and I think the people of this province want an election." Harcourt's enthusiasm was well-founded. Never before in the history of BC politics had an Opposition leader gone into an election campaign so far ahead in the polls that he could afford to coast through it.

BY THE FALL OF 1991, THE VERY WORDS "SOCIAL CREDIT" HAD been reduced to a pejorative epithet that could prompt embarrassment or ridicule, depending on the company. For those who embraced the free market principles of the party, the word "Socred" was now a sad reminder of Bill Vander Zalm, conflict of interest, kickbacks, lying under oath and other forms of corruption. In future years, those who included themselves among the free-enterprise vote found more comfort under Liberal or Reform banners – although both parties contained many of the same members who had turned a blind eye to such corruption under Social Credit.

For many other British Columbians it was the policy, not the scandals, that made "Socred" a dirty word. For those who recalled the restraint budget and abolition of the Human Rights Branch in 1983, the public service firings and the continual cutbacks in education, health care and social services, or the eviction of impoverished downtown eastside Vancouver residents to make way for Expo 86, the word "Socred" was already burdened with so much negative connotation that it didn't matter how many ministers were cited for official breach of ethics. For these people, "Socred" had long been synonymous with callous or selfish, and described someone who embraced the most heartless or cruel social policies in order to ensure maximum profits.

The members of Vander Zalm's cabinet provided easy targets for denunciation, and Mike Harcourt's shadow cabinet took full advantage in the House and in the media. The result was that ethics became a major focus of political debate in the province, and NDP piety caused the public to expect superhuman behaviour from party members. As the election campaign got under way, Mike Harcourt faced the considerable challenge of convincing voters to endorse NDP policies, not just reject Socred sleaze.

2

Mikey
Milquetoast

TO DESCRIBE MIKE HARCOURT IN 1991 AS THE "PREMIER IN waiting" was stating the obvious. Apart from the scandals and blundering of the Socreds which assured his party of victory, the 48-year-old NDP leader's bland, consensus-building style was a refreshing departure from the flamboyant, one-man government and fundamentalist vision of Bill Vander Zalm. "I'm a political leader, not an entertainer," Harcourt frequently told the media. "I'm not an Elmer Gantry kind of populist. I'm a populist in the sense that I believe in gaining consensus."

Unlike many of his NDP colleagues, whose left-wing politics had softened over the years, Harcourt had always been a Liberal with social democratic leanings. His parents were both Liberals; Frank Harcourt was a Great West Life insurance salesman, his mother Stella a prairie schoolteacher and United Church activist for social justice. Young Mike developed his sense of citizenship while attending Magee high school in Vancouver, where he served as student council president and played on the basketball team. His game was good enough to win him a scholarship to the University of British Columbia. Like many undergraduates on university campuses in the 1960s, he opposed the Vietnam War – and didn't mind being ribbed by conservative friends, who called him "Ho Chi" Harcourt.

After graduating from law school he worked as a storefront lawyer and was a founding member of the Vancouver Community Legal Assistance Society. In the early 1970s, his firm advised then-federal Justice minister John Turner on how to set up legal aid clinics across Canada. In 1972, 29-year-old Harcourt began his political career by joining The Electors Action Movement (TEAM) – a coalition of moderate Conservatives, Liberals and New Democrats formed in the late 1960s to counter the bias toward real estate speculators at city hall. Elected to council on his first attempt, he chaired the city's housing and environment committee which worked with the Dave Barrett government's Human Resources Department to increase social assistance rates, extend social services and build public housing for the downtown eastside poor.

Harcourt's only setback in city politics occurred in 1976, when he decided to take an early run at the mayor's seat. As it turned out, the power struggle that ensued from his candidacy had a lasting impact on party politics in Vancouver. By the mid-70s, the ideological agenda of TEAM had more in common with the right-wing, development-friendly Non Partisan Association (NPA), than with the progressive, neighbourhood-first party Harcourt had joined in 1972. When TEAM councillor Jack Volrich decided to run for mayor on an anti-tax platform that also promised to ban Sunday shopping, Harcourt surprised and offended his conservative TEAM colleagues by contesting the nomination several months after Volrich had assumed his coronation was guaranteed.

The 47-year-old Volrich – none too pleased by the challenge of a 33-year-old upstart – launched a partisan attack on his former colleague. In the weeks before the nomination meeting, Volrich accused Harcourt of trying to destroy the party by stacking it with New Democrats; Harcourt accused him of selling out the progressive policies of TEAM by leaving the party "in the clutches of landlords, real estate speculators and corporate interests who want back Vancouver, their plaything, their Monopoly game." By the end of the bitter nomination meeting, Volrich beat Harcourt by a narrow 612-487 margin. Harcourt declined TEAM's conciliatory offer of a spot on their slate of council candidates, choosing instead to run as an independent. He regained his seat on council, and served two more terms as an alderman before going head-to-head against his old foe Volrich in 1980, with the mild endorsement of the leftist Committee of Progressive Electors (COPE). According to the pre-election analysis of longtime civic politics watcher Stan Persky, Harcourt's leftist credentials were better than some of his more cynical critics in COPE were willing to admit. "To give Harcourt his due," said Persky, "he has not attempted to represent himself as other than what he is – a relatively moderate, slightly left of centre social democrat. While those to the left of him have every right to criticize his failings, it would be one-sided of them not to recognize that during an eight-year period in public office Harcourt has consistently advocated and voted for progressive measures to solve problems of housing and transportation and to enhance the democratic process."

Nine years later – after three terms as Vancouver mayor followed by a jump to provincial politics – Persky's portrait of Harcourt had changed very little. In his 1989 appraisal of the Vander Zalm years, *Fantasy Government*, the Vancouver political pundit described the new NDP leader as "a reasonably typical Yuppie with a left-of-centre, but unthreatening, social conscience … His critics accused him of being wishy-washy, but when he got something done, such as ensuring a 'fair wage' package on civic projects, they were frustrated because his evident moderation made it impossible to dub him a radical."

As Vancouver mayor, Harcourt was popular and accessible to a wide variety of citizens, joining anti-nuke demonstrators on peace marches one day and doing lunch with chambers of commerce the next. Somehow he managed to maintain the grudging respect of the business community despite his opposition to such megaprojects as Expo 86 and the rapid transit "Skytrain," the latter of which was introduced by a Socred cabinet minister named Bill Vander Zalm.

The future Socred premier turned out to be one of Mike Harcourt's easiest political victims when he challenged him for the Vancouver mayor's seat in 1984. Vander Zalm, who had quit the Bennett government in disgust the previous year when his "gutless" cabinet colleagues failed to support his Land Use Act amendments, was now seeking a back door to the Socred leadership – a position everyone knew would soon be vacant, given Bill Bennett's sagging popularity. The problem with running for Vancouver mayor, however, was that Vander Zalm knew next to nothing about the city or its politics.

Harcourt portrayed Vander Zalm as a cynical opportunist who just wanted the job for the high profile he would be guaranteed during Expo 86. Harcourt also took advantage of several gaffes which revealed that the former Socred cabinet minister was totally out of touch with the political culture of BC's biggest city: his opposition to Vancouver's nuclear-free status and his criticism of a civic grant for the Downtown Eastside Residents Association, which both civic parties supported.

Unlike many of his fellow New Democrats, Harcourt's friendships were not governed by party loyalties. Before his conversion to the NDP (while working on a CN train during the 1960s, he met Tommy Douglas, and was inspired by their chat to join the party), he had worked for Liberal candidates. Much later in his political life he would count Liberal senator Jack Austin among his tennis partners, have his hair cut by a Liberal barber, and brag about a group of friends who called themselves "Tories for Harcourt." He saw nothing contradictory in this; if anything, these relationships gave him a more rounded perspective of the issues. "I don't understand people who get stand-offish with people who have different politics than them," Harcourt told the Vancouver *Sun* in 1991. "I run into people who say, 'How can you talk to that person because he's Socred or he's Liberal' or whatever? I sort of shake my head and say, 'Why would you not want to? Why cut off half the people in the province?'"

This flirtation with the Liberal Party was not unusual for a potential New Democrat leader. Bob Rae, NDP premier of Ontario from 1990 to 1995, had a Liberal pedigree; his father, Saul Rae, was a career civil servant under Liberal governments who once served as special assistant to the secretary of state for External Affairs under Lester Pearson. Rae's oldest brother John was an ally of Jean Chrétien, and his sister Jennifer once dated Pierre Trudeau. Like Harcourt, Bob Rae cultivated many friendships among Liberals, and found common political ground on several issues. But here the similarities end.

Harcourt's social democrat beliefs were the product of experience, not the youthful idealism of a student. Rae wrote passionate essays criticizing Pierre Trudeau's abandonment of Keynesian economics and sought the approval of campus radicals at the University of Toronto – only to be rebuffed as hopelessly bourgeois; Harcourt embraced pragmatism as a political virtue from the beginning and showed little interest in abstract principle. While Bob Rae's decision to enter politics was precipitated by a career crisis (he was convinced to join the NDP after returning from studies at Oxford, England, where he was suffering from depression and had lost his sense of purpose), Harcourt's entry into politics was the logical result of his work as a storefront lawyer and community activist. While Bob Rae impressed the intellectual left with his speeches and ideas, Mike Harcourt impressed advocacy groups with his legal aid for the poor and his opposition to development projects that threatened neighbourhoods. While Bob Rae lacked the common touch and struggled with small talk, Mike Harcourt had no difficulty soliciting votes in a gay bar.

Throughout his career, Harcourt's moderate political stance was lampooned by editorial cartoonists who enjoyed poking fun at his bland accountant image. A tall, imposing man with a balding dome, wire-rimmed glasses and Groucho Marx moustache, he seemed dull compared to more flamboyant BC politicians like Vander Zalm and Dave Barrett. Despite his finesse at mediation, his grasp of the issues and his ability to gladhand in a crowd, most of his political skills were invisible in the soundbite world of television. And his speeches seemed over-rehearsed, clichéd or, as Vaughn Palmer put it, "a great cure for insomnia." To his supporters, Harcourt was a no-nonsense pragmatist; to his critics, he was "Mikey Milquetoast."

'1000 Days' and the Art of Compromise

THE BC NDP'S EXPERIMENT IN THE POLITICS OF PRAGMATISM began in May 1984, six months before Harcourt won his third term as Vancouver mayor by beating Bill Vander Zalm. The party was choosing its first new leader in fifteen years. Dave Barrett, BC's only NDP premier and the party's longest serving leader, was considered washed up and volunteered to quit after enduring three consecutive election defeats since 1975. In many ways, the leadership convention of 1984 was symptomatic of an existential crisis the NDP was suffering everywhere else in Canada by the mid-1980s; should the party go back to its socialist roots as laid out in the Regina Manifesto, or become a slick machine focussed on winning votes from the middle in order to gain power?

There were six candidates for the leadership, but delegates were torn between two men who represented the conflicting views of the party's future. Hardline socialist Bill King was a party veteran and longtime union activist who represented the former vision. He had plenty of support in the caucus, having served in the Barrett cabinet of 1972-75. Victoria lawyer David Vickers was a former Liberal who had been deputy attorney general for the Socreds as well as the NDP. Vickers had come to the party only recently, was friendly toward business, and represented the latter vision. Those who supported Vickers cited his experience as a deputy AG during the Barrett years, arguing further that his slick media profile would make him an ideal alternative to Bill Bennett. Indeed, he was the only candidate the Socreds feared. Vickers's selection as leader would have been entirely in keeping with the kind of mainstream, urban professional left that was already taking control of the Ontario NDP under the youthful leadership of Bob Rae.

But the BC New Democrats were not ready for change in 1984. With Vickers ahead of King after the first two ballots, delegates began to murmur about his unproven socialist credentials. After the fourth ballot, King dropped out and passionately urged delegates to "vote for the true socialist," a compromise candidate named Bob Skelly. Most of King's supporters backed the 41-year-old Port Alberni MLA, who was considered a reliable environment critic and native issues expert, and he emerged the victor on May 20, 1984.

Notwithstanding his strengths as an MLA, the party's choice of Bob Skelly as leader was a major strategic blunder, perhaps more devastating to the party than Barrett's decision to introduce back-to-work leg-

islation in the strike-filled summer of 1975. Skelly was a strong intellectual presence in the party, but he was not a natural leader. He
lacked the media charisma and political assertiveness to revive a party
that had lost three consecutive elections and had been out of power
for nearly a decade. Worst of all, he had trouble anticipating the strategy of his opponents. For the two years following his selection as
leader, he hammered away at Bill Bennett's Socreds, carefully planning the NDP's election strategy by watching the premier's every
move. But Skelly's plan went out the window when Bennett retired
from politics on May 22, 1986.

Against Bill Vander Zalm, who succeeded Bennett as Socred premier
during a record tourist season, Bob Skelly didn't have a hope of winning an election. In 1985 he told *Equity* magazine that charisma was
not in his nature, that he was a grey-sweater-and-blue jeans kind of
guy. But the charisma issue came back to haunt Skelly when Vander
Zalm became Social Credit leader in the summer of 1986.

First, the new Socred premier pulled off a major public relations
coup designed to create the impression that Social Credit was entering
a new era of cooperation with organized labour. On August 20, the
34,000-member BC Government Employees Union (BCGEU) reached
agreement on a 33-month contract with the government. Negotiations
had gone so smoothly that BCGEU chief John Shields couldn't help
sweetening the day for the new premier by offering him a compliment
through the media. "The atmosphere and direction I believe that Mr.
Vander Zalm brought to the talks was a catalyst to push the talks to a
successful conclusion," Shields commented. "In a single ten-second
sound clip," wrote the *Sun*'s Gary Mason and Keith Baldrey, "Shields
gave Vander Zalm the key victory he needed to take into an election
campaign. So much for the NDP's strategy to portray him as a confrontational flake."

By the time Vander Zalm called the election for October 22, there
was no question of who the frontrunner was. Putting Skelly's sober
campaign platform of jobs and the environment up against the razzle
dazzle of Bill Vander Zalm — particularly in the euphoric afterglow of
Expo 86, and with the BCGEU settlement so fresh in people's minds —
was like the Monty Python sketch where an aging Sir Kenneth Clark is

placed in a boxing ring to face an actual heavyweight boxer. (Sir Kenneth begins reading from a lecture but barely finishes a sentence before being knocked to the floor with a single punch, thus losing his "title" as the Oxford chair of Art History.)

The NDP executive realized it was in trouble, but waited too long to act. Only two weeks before the election was called, a group of veteran MLAs led by Bob Williams and Colin Gabelmann presented a motion of non-confidence in Skelly's leadership at a top-secret caucus meeting. Skelly emerged from the vote victorious, but only barely — eleven caucus members voted for him, seven against, while three abstained. With so many knives in his back before he even had a chance to face the voters, it was no wonder he was feeling a bit nervous when Vander Zalm set the election date on September 24. As he began his first press conference of the campaign, Skelly was suddenly paralyzed by an attack of nervous anxiety. With the cameras and microphones of every major media outlet awaiting his words, Skelly's throat constricted and his hands began to shake. Stammering his way through a prepared statement, he clutched the podium and looked up to face reporters with a plea, "Can I stop this?" Skelly's moment of nerves was noted by most of the media, but by none more than BCTV, which referred to his weakness as "ominous" and subsequently set up a "death watch" on his campaign.

Sadly, he didn't help matters in his few attempts to recover from his misfortune. Even his casual attempt at self-deprecation, "I think I went out for lunch and ate the wrong kind of tulip bulbs," was perceived as a cruel jab at his opponent's childhood in Holland during World War II. Although he did manage to regain his composure over the course of the campaign, and gained some ground on Vander Zalm on the issues, Skelly was further burdened by Vander Zalm's refusal to engage in a leader's debate, where Skelly would have excelled. In the end, the NDP leader's election platform of better education and higher employment could not compete with the feelgood rhetoric of Bill Vander Zalm. The Socreds won in a landslide, 47 seats to 22. Despite Skelly's respectable showing in the popular vote, he wasn't about to stick around for more backstabbing. Three weeks after the election, he announced his resignation.

Bob Skelly's two-and-a-half-year term as NDP leader was a sobering lesson for the party. Faced with a choice between a traditional socialist and a slick moderate, they had chosen the apparently safe alternative in Skelly. Now there seemed to be a cynical acknowledgement among the party's left that perhaps they should have gone for the sure winner in David Vickers. After its fourth consecutive defeat at the polls, the party was ready to shift to the right. At this point, there appeared to be only one candidate people were willing to consider. Two days after the party's defeat, former Nelson-Creston MLA Lorne Nicholson said the NDP members had a "diamond right under their noses" with Mike Harcourt, the party's newly elected MLA in Vancouver-Centre. "It doesn't take someone with fourteen years experience in the legislature to recognize that," Nicolson told the *Sun*.

Shortly after he was sworn in as MLA on November 18, 1986 — about the same time a 38-year-old former developer named Gordon Campbell defeated COPE's Harry Rankin to recapture the Vancouver mayor's seat for the NPA — Harcourt confirmed his intention to seek the NDP leadership in the spring of 1987. He was not the only contender for the job; federal MPs Jim Fulton (Skeena) and Nelson Riis (Kamloops) were also mentioned, as was IWA chief Jack Munro. But no one seriously considered challenging Harcourt, and his installation as leader during the April 10-12, 1987 convention was practically a coronation.

In making such a unanimous choice, the party executive was acknowledging its final break with the interventionist solutions the party had prescribed since the 1950s. After more than a decade of uninterrupted Social Credit rule, the socialist party finally had to make its peace with big business if it wanted to control the purse strings of British Columbia. Now that Skelly had failed, the door was wide open for a right-wing New Democrat like Harcourt to experiment with the party's agenda.

Or so the argument went. For his part, Harcourt rejected the notion that there was a "lose-lose dynamic" to the NDP — that the party either had to appeal to its traditional supporters (trade unionists and socialists) and therefore lose the 20 percent considered moderate or "swing" votes, or lose the main core of support and be accused of running away from the principles of social democracy. "I never accepted that," Harcourt recalled later. "I've always worked from the assumption that we have strong values about people and society, that we're not a market place, we're a community. We represented ordinary working people, and [that's] broadly defined."

The real problem, according to Harcourt, was that the NDP's economic policy was out of date, "On social policy and medicare and education, social services and environmental issues – great. People liked those values but didn't feel we paid enough attention to the really hard world of economics, budgets and deficits. The better part of the 1980s and 90s was a mean streak world we were in. So it took a much more, I wouldn't use the word 'hardnosed' social democracy, but we had to live in the real world. You couldn't ignore the globalization of the economy, you couldn't ignore the need to be competitive. It didn't mean you had to buy into the right-wing rhetoric, but it meant you had to convince people that you understood the economy, understood how jobs were created ... that you understood the need for balancing the books.

"I think there was an intuitive understanding among our people that we were setting up phoney battles. And some of it was, either you're a socialist or you're not, which was kind of a false bravado and a false premise to begin with. There are certain values that social democrats share, like representing the working people, like community is important, the market can't determine certain key values, and there's a limit to what the market can do."

One of the biggest challenges Harcourt faced, as he said often between 1987 and 1991, was to convince the public to vote *for* the NDP instead of merely voting against Social Credit. To that end, Harcourt was already preparing an election platform within a year of assuming the leadership, and even factored in Vander Zalm's possible resignation. He also set up a transition team, a committee that prepared a plan for the smooth transfer of power from the Socreds to the NDP after the expected election victory. (The team was so well prepared by 1989 that its plan was used by Ontario NDP leader Bob Rae when his New Democrats won a surprise victory the following year.) "Events and polls of the day suggested there was a good chance of the

NDP forming government," recalled one member of Harcourt's personal staff. "There was a certain sense of opportunity, if not inevitability. It appeared to have been extended by Vander Zalm stepping down."

The transition planning committee was chaired by former Barrett cabinet minister Bob Williams, with caucus input from Colin Gabelmann, Anita Hagen and Lois Boone. While a separate committee worked on policy papers, this group concentrated on structural and organizational issues such as cabinet committee structure, departmental organization, and the role and prerogatives of the premier. The latter document, which outlined the constitutional role and sources of the premier's power and leverage, was considered necessary because of the abuses of power during Vander Zalm's reign as premier. There were other discussions, which did not appear in the documents, about the premier's relationship with the media; questions like "How do you structure relations with the media so that it's not always a scrum on the way to the office every day?"

In terms of policy, Harcourt took pains to assert his moderate stance from the very beginning. Shortly after becoming leader and launching his "thousand days" campaign (the length of time the NDP expected it would take to become government), Harcourt was confronted by reporters who wanted to know what he'd do in the event of an illegal strike. "I will not break the law, nor will New Democrats who are elected members of the legislature break the law, because we're patient people," he replied, in the first of many statements that would reassure the business sector. By the spring of 1991, as the Socreds were self-destructing under Bill Vander Zalm, the NDP had prepared its election platform with a 48-point plan, "A Better Way for British Columbia."

As election platforms go, it was a fairly safe document. While there were a few innovations bearing a distinctly NDP stamp – wilderness preservation, aboriginal rights, community health centres, for example – much of it was a direct response to Socred incompetence. Among its promises was a measure to ensure more open government by enacting a freedom of information law, toughening disclosure requirements for MLAs, providing an open tender process for government contracts and encouraging community involvement in lottery fund distribution.

The NDP also promised to reintroduce a tough anti-pollution law vetoed by the Socreds; amend the Industrial Relations Act; increase capital expenditures for schools and hospitals, an area left dormant by the Socreds; and impose a minimum corporate tax, a measure the Socreds would never have introduced. The environmental section was the most detailed policy in the entire document, with promises to double the park space and protected wilderness area to 12 percent of the provincial land base by the year 2000; and resolve land use conflicts through environment and job accords at the community level.

A Liberal Lazarus

AS HARCOURT WAS BUSY PREPARING THE NDP'S LONG-AWAITED return to power, another leader was about to bring his party out of the wilderness after twelve years in political hibernation. Given the history of coalition politics in BC since World War II, the Liberal Party was bound to return to its former relevance once Social Credit was on its way out. What was surprising, however, was how quickly that process occurred in 1991.

Although the BC Liberal Party had remained invisible for most of the previous twelve years, it had maintained an awkward relationship with the Socreds based on a kind of mutual pact to keep "the socialist hordes" out of office. Even during the 1930s – long before the emergence of Social Credit – the governing Liberals were openly contemptuous of coalitions. That position changed, however, when they were reduced to minority status in the 1941 election. Following that setback, the party dumped its leader, Duff Pattullo, who was opposed to coalitions, and joined forces with the Conservatives.

W.A.C. Bennett's defection from the Conservatives to the newly formed Social Credit Party once again affected the Liberal Party's status in the legislature. After the Socreds formed their first government in 1952 – reducing both the Liberal and Conservative parties to a rump presence in the House – the Liberals spent the 1950s and 1960s as a party of the middle, rejecting both the leftist Co-operative Commonwealth Federation and the right-wing Socreds. By 1972, however, the party was more than willing to abandon the middle ground it had claimed so righteously for two decades. With the Socreds finally defeated by the Dave Barrett New Democrats, Liberal MLAs Pat McGeer, Allan Williams and Garde Gardom crossed the floor to join the Socreds in 1975. The free-enterprise coalition was affirmed once again.

As the Bill Bennett Socreds (including their Liberal recruits) introduced union-bashing, fiscal restraint and social service cutbacks from 1975 to 1986, the remnants of the BC Liberal Party toiled in obscurity, never gaining more than six or seven percent of the popular vote in the 1979, 1983, and 1986 elections. By the time outgoing leader Art Lee handed the keys to Gordon Wilson on Hallowe'en 1987, few British Columbians were aware that a provincial Liberal Party even existed. And Wilson didn't exactly have to struggle to win the leadership; aside from former Yukon cabinet minister Clive Tanner – who eventually withdrew from the race because of a broken leg – no one else wanted it.

Wilson, a 38-year-old college geography instructor, was something of an enigmatic outsider. Born in Vancouver and raised in Kenya, where his father established a market research and polling company and his mother worked in the public service, young Gordon witnessed the Mau Mau uprising and remained in Kenya to complete his elementary and secondary schooling before returning to North America for his post-secondary study. Unlike most aspirants to Liberal Party leadership, Wilson did not have big money connections. His interest in politics was inspired largely by unsexy issues like government reform, the constitution, and local environmental concerns like water protection. During the public sector strike of 1983, Wilson was part of the faculty association at Capilano College that worked with Operation Solidarity, the provincewide coalition of labour and social justice groups established in response to the Socred restraint budget's cuts to education, health care and the social safety net. Like many others involved in the Solidarity movement, Wilson was disillusioned by the Kelowna Accord, the agreement between government and labour leaders that ended the protest. Convinced that "the unions were in

Solidarity for what they could gain for themselves" rather than to effect "significant reform to the system of government," Wilson decided to enter politics in a formal way. First he was elected as a Liberal Party regional representative for MacKenzie district on the Sunshine Coast. Then he sought the Liberal Party leadership.

The fact that Wilson was able to win the leadership so easily is a testament to the Liberal Party's irrelevance in 1987. Despite being an outsider to partisan party politics, Wilson required no support from "hybrid" Liberals — those who supported the federal Liberals but voted Socred provincially — and he was ignored by Vancouver's corporate business community. With his rather owlish, professorial demeanor, he was also not the kind of politician to inspire electoral mania, as the Vancouver *Sun* later observed. Unlike his hero, Pierre Trudeau, Wilson was "more a double-breasted-suit, Preston Manning kind of guy. Serious. Pleasant-looking, but not one to stand out in a crowd."

And, unlike Trudeau, Wilson never had a particularly strong grasp of the Liberal leadership. The federal group that included former BC leader Gordon Gibson and Jean Chrétien's BC organizer, Ross Fitzpatrick, refused to embrace him. Within months of winning the leadership, Wilson found himself struggling to defend it from the handful of hybrid Liberals and well-connected Vancouver business types determined to take it away from him.

In September 1988, as Bill Vander Zalm was alienating Socred supporters near and far, various media outlets reported that $1 million had been set aside to finance anyone who wished to head up a free-enterprise coalition in BC. At the same time, Gordon Gibson was trying to convince an old friend, Vancouver developer Jack Poole, to challenge Wilson for the Liberal leadership — he even asked Wilson to step aside, assuming, perhaps, that the cash-strapped, professorial underdog would recognize he was a lightweight compared to the well-connected developer from Vancouver. But Wilson refused to play Gibson's power game. Instead, he called a leadership convention and challenged Poole to take him on. Poole eventually backed off and Wilson cancelled the convention. Having made his point, he stayed on as unpaid leader.

The following spring, Wilson's first attempt to win a seat in the legislature ended in failure when he lost the Vancouver-Point Grey by-election to the NDP's Tom Perry. In 1990, Wilson was so convinced that Bill Vander Zalm would call a summer election that he committed his poverty-stricken party to a $160,000 television and radio advertising campaign. Wilson told his executive that he would find a private donor to pick up the costs, but no donor materialized and the leader nearly landed his party in court over its failure to pay debts. In the controversy that followed, he dismissed several calls for his resignation and prevailed in a leadership vote at the March 1991 party convention. By this point, however, a deep rift had developed within the Liberal ranks; most of Wilson's detractors abandoned him and the provincial party in favour of the federal Liberals.

One week after the Liberal convention in late March, Bill Vander Zalm resigned as premier and the Liberals turned their attention to the upcoming election. On April 1, the day before Vander Zalm quit, the Vancouver *Sun* raised the possibility of a Liberal renaissance in another of its frequent calls for a three-party system. "It seems like a perfect time to be a provincial Liberal," the editorial said. "The election that must come by year end should offer the perfect chance for a third party to reassert itself between the two poles in provincial politics."

Bogus Polling + Instant Fame = New Opposition

HAVING RETAINED THE SOCRED LEADERSHIP WITH HER JULY victory over Grace McCarthy, Premier Rita Johnston had little time to prove herself to the public before the government's mandate ran out. And the news didn't get much better once she did call the election on September 19; with the latest poll putting the Socreds fifteen points behind the NDP in popularity, much of the premier's time during the 28-day campaign was consumed by damage control and attempts to reassure depressed Socred campaign workers.

Johnston, in her attempts to distance herself from Bill Vander Zalm's record, failed to realize just how hopeless a task it was. The New Democrats immediately put the premier on the defensive by hammering the Socreds on the litany of scandals that plagued the goverment and by implying that Rita Johnston, through her silence, had condoned Bill Vander Zalm's abuses of power. Johnston could do very little but reply earnestly that yes, ethics were indeed a major issue in the campaign. "It is an issue. No question. Ethics is right up there."

If that weren't enough, Johnston's own election team – including three cabinet ministers – was beginning to turn against her. Stan Hagen backed away from Johnston's commitment to transfer the Comox ferry's base of operations outside his riding; Howard Dirks opposed the premier's decision to use benefits of the Columbia River treaty to reduce the provincial debt, arguing that some of the money should go to the affected communities; and Attorney General Russ Fraser criticized the conflict of interest law for being too restrictive. Another Socred candidate, Marilyn Baker, openly disputed the Socred's wage restraint legislation, and longtime MLA Jack Kempf refused to give up his party candidacy after being charged with breach of trust and theft over the use of constituency funds.

The Kempf situation was particularly embarrassing for Johnston. The long-serving Socred had been dumped from cabinet in 1987 and had sat in the House as an independent for three years before rejoining the party. Two days after he was charged, the party suspended his lifetime Socred membership and revoked his nomination, but his fight to remain a Socred candidate once again raised the spectre of corruption in the party. Johnston tried to convince Kempf's campaign manager to run in his place, but the manager refused to file nomination papers after winning the candidacy and told the Vancouver *Sun* that she would manage Kempf's campaign as an independent. As if losing a candidate for one riding wasn't bad enough, Johnston's get-tough stance with Kempf was criticized by Mike Harcourt as a belated conversion to the politics of ethics. "She has movable morals," Harcourt told reporters, clearly relishing the premier's discomfort. "She has not been consistent in her treatment of Jack Kempf and her treatment of her friends Bill Vander Zalm and Bill Reid."

Johnston's campaign strategists also failed to warn her about a number of potential scandals. The most notable involved the candidacy of Richmond East Socred John Ball. For some reason known only to a select group of party insiders, Ball's connection to neo-Nazi organizations was apparently not deemed to be scandalous until it was reported in the media; only after the coverage was Ball forced to withdraw. "On a couple of occasions, I haven't been as quickly informed about things as I would have liked to have been – the Ball situation was one," said Johnston, in what must have been the understatement of her campaign.

Finally, even the Socreds' standard criticism of the NDP – that "socialist" economics are dangerous – was falling on deaf ears. Earlier that year, Johnston tried to discredit NDP policy by calling attention to the Ontario government's first budget, a $9.7-billion shortfall that was triple the previous year's deficit. By the mid-way point of her campaign, however, Johnston's Chicken Little predictions were ringing rather hollow. In one of the party's most glaring mistakes, a Socred document called "The Harcourt Hoax: A $15 Billion New Debt Plan" – which was meant to imply that the NDP platform would be far too expensive – was filled with arithmetic errors and quoted NDP figures in the billions where they should have been in the thousands. The mistake was picked up by the press, leaving some of the Socreds' cheekier critics to wonder whether British Columbia's free-enterprise party no longer know the difference between $1.5 and $15 billion.

As if that wasn't enough bad news for the government, a third party was about to burst into the race. In retrospect, Socred strategists could not possibly have realized they were wasting valuable energy focussing their attack on the NDP when it was the Liberals they should have been worrying about. In the six months since his reaffirmation as leader, Gordon Wilson had quietly canvassed the province in a grassroots campaign that seemed anything but threatening. Working without a salary, Wilson could not depend on the chartered planes, campaign buses, hotel rooms and entourage of advisors and reporters that Rita Johnston and Mike Harcourt took for granted. With no money in the party coffers, Wilson travelled the province by car, spending money out of his own pocket to spread the Liberal message. Even after the election call, Wilson often had to introduce himself to reporters when making an official statement outside the legislature.

For all his lack of big money clout, however, the Liberal leader was a feisty campaigner. If Sharon Carstairs could do it in Manitoba, he declared, then why couldn't his Liberals make a comeback in BC? (Manitoba Liberal leader Carstairs managed, albeit briefly, to turn one seat into a 21-member Opposition.) Borrowing a page from Preston Manning's Reform plan for Canada, Wilson tried to engage voters in a discussion of tax reform, government reform and the Constitution. It didn't seem like the kind of platform that would catch on in BC, but none of this mattered by October 8. By then, Wilson's fortunes, and those of his party, were transformed literally overnight.

On October 1, sixteen days before the election, the Liberals had no seats in the legislature and were running at 7 percent in public opinion polls. For these reasons, Gordon Wilson was not considered important enough to participate in a pre-election leaders' debate to be broadcast live by CBC television on October 8.

Wilson responded to the snub with a passionate critique of the two-party system that was quoted by most media outlets. At the same time, his supporters picketed the CBC, bombarded it with faxes, letters and phone calls, and threatened to take the publicly funded broadcaster to court. A Vancouver *Sun* editorial urged the CBC to include Wilson, pointing out that the Liberals were running candidates in 70 of 75 ridings. Even Liberal senator Ray Perrault wrote a letter to CBC regional director John Kennedy, urging him to change his mind. Critics pointed out that Saskatchewan Liberal leader Linda Haverstock was invited to participate in the television debate in that province, even though the Liberals had no seats in the legislature. BCTV then got in on the act, proposing a second debate and inviting Wilson. Finally, late in the evening on October 2, the debate format was changed and Wilson was allowed in.

Like most live television events designed to boost ratings, the three-party discussion on CBC was not so much a debate as a battle of insults between a couple of frontrunners. It was Johnston and Harcourt's battle, with newcomer Wilson standing on the sidelines. Johnston — who later said she behaved like a "fishwife" — was constantly on the attack, calling her NDP opponent "gutless," and accusing Harcourt of lying to voters about the cost of NDP programs. "Why don't you stop scaring the senior citizens of British Columbia with your lies? You're afraid," she said. "You said you would tell us how much your programs would cost and you haven't. You are afraid of the truth and you're afraid to be honest with the people because you know if you are it will cause you to lose the election."

Harcourt was eager not to engage in the mudslinging, but there was no strategy to improve his on-camera demeanor, which was wooden, uptight. He missed an opportunity to score major points when Johnston repeated her party's mistaken $15 billion estimate of the NDP's $1.5 billion program costs. And instead of responding directly to a question about the constitution, he awkwardly pulled out his BC CareCard in one hand and an American Express card in the other, warning voters that the Socreds planned to introduce "an Americanized health system." To the voters of BC, this was the first indication that television performance was not one of Harcourt's great strengths.

Wilson, on the other hand, needed only to be seen on camera to gain political points. The Liberal leader knew his debate appearance was his maiden speech to most of the BC public, and he capitalized on the opportunity. As Johnston shouted "wishy-washy!" at Harcourt and the NDP leader pulled off his credit card gimmick, Wilson shook his head sadly and explained how his opponents' behaviour demonstrated the need for a third party in BC. "It is time that British Columbians recognized that the two-party polarized system ... has kept this province in constant confrontation virtually every day of the year, every year between elections," he said.

Wilson's posturing as the rational, moderate uncle figure presiding over two spoiled children struck a big chord among voters. In yet another testimony to the power of television, his performance caused a tidal wave of "instant Liberals" who had no affiliations before October 8 but were willing to vote for the party now. The morning after the debate, campaign workers at BC Liberal headquarters fielded 400 calls, and the Vancouver-Langara Liberal office gave out the last 100 of the 400 party signs it had printed. Some callers offered support and requested signs, while others walked into party offices to write out cheques.

Two days after the debate, a Vancouver *Sun*-Angus Reid poll showed that 76 percent of those surveyed felt that Wilson performed best in the debate, with only 9 percent supporting Johnston and 8 percent supporting Harcourt. A separate poll on vote prediction, however, showed the New Democrats in front with 40 percent of post-debate support, with the Socreds and Liberals running neck and neck in the high 20s.

BC's largest private broadcaster had a different version of reality. BCTV began experimenting with the murky world of public opinion-making when it introduced its own polling service, "Voice of BC," on September 24. By presenting different sets of results every night for the remainder of the election campaign, assistant news director Keith Bradbury said BCTV's intention was to "show what's going on," not to set any kind of agenda (although, if he were more frank, he could have admitted that daily polling was a good way to boost BCTV's ratings).

The brain behind "Voice of BC" was former BCTV news director Cameron Bell, who was described by various New Democrat insiders as having "a legendary hate-on for the NDP." Bell and pollster Les Storey, a former NDP organizer and executive director of the BC Wildlife Federation, faced immediate charges by other pollsters that the daily disclosure of polling information during a campaign had potential to cause a bandwagon effect. Storey estimated that his findings, like those of most professional pollsters, were accurate within plus or minus 3.5 percent, 19 times out of 20.

In the first week of polling, "Voice of BC" had the NDP lead over the Socreds yo-yoing from 8 percent to 17 percent, then back down to 7 percent. But those numbers went out the window after the television debate. The new series of questions the pollsters asked respondents began by focussing on the performance of the candidates, gradually moving toward a logical conclusion; "Who do you think won the debate?" was followed by "Who do you think is the best leader?" and finally, "If an election were held today, who would you vote for?"

The emergence of the Liberals as BCTV's party of choice was a self-fulfilling prophecy under this format. Sure enough, the final "Voice of BC" poll – released only two days before the election – put the Liberals in the lead with 35 percent support, followed by the NDP with 33 percent and the Socreds with 19. The *Province* newspaper, meanwhile, showed the NDP in front with 42 percent, followed by the Liberals with 33 and Social Credit with 22.

Several pollsters dismissed the BCTV methodology, saying the figures were distorted by questions about the debate. "This is known in polling as priming the pump," said Dave Gotthilf, a partner in Winnipeg-based Viewpoints Research. "This is known as a disreputable technique." But BCTV ignored the criticism, and dismissed NDP officials who complained about the figures. "Quibble, quibble, quibble. They don't like the numbers," said Les Storey. To Keith Bradbury, the NDP's complaints were based on "esoterica."

Meanwhile, BCTV's failure to secure a second debate was becoming a story in itself. Initially, the Liberals and Greens were the only parties confirmed for the October 14 debate, but Johnston later agreed to participate on the condition that Harcourt was also there. When Harcourt refused, saying he did not want to debate in the last week of the campaign, BCTV reporters grilled the frontrunning NDP leader on his decision. "I think this is now getting to harassment," a visibly angry Harcourt snapped at reporter Brian Coxford during one media scrum. "I've said no. I've said that three days ago, I said it two days ago, I'm saying it today. And I think that your station had a chance to participate in the [first] debate and it didn't. I think this is going way beyond inter-station competition, taking away from the election itself ... My concern is not inter-station rivalry, which led to one of the stations not participating in [the CBC] debate."

Wilson's meteoric rise in the polls took the Liberal leader so much by surprise that he was forced to put his entire platform on hold. Only two days before the election, he reduced to three the 262 campaign initiatives he had announced the previous summer. This move, and his sudden shift to criticism of the NDP, roused suspicion that Wilson's agenda was perhaps not as moderate as his debate performance suggested. "It's no wonder that stock promoter Murray Pezim rushed to embrace Mr. Wilson on the weekend," Vaughn Palmer wrote on October 14, skewering Wilson's plan for a universal income tax rate of 25 percent. "The Liberal leader is suggesting millionaire Murray should pay the same tax rate as the average citizen."

Given his plan to cut sales taxes, offer a three-year tax holiday for businesses, and cut government spending by 5 percent, Wilson's rightward moving platform was hard to reconcile with his earlier campaign commitments to spend more money, not less. But according to NDP finance critic Glen Clark, this flip-flop was to be expected from a leader who "writes his policies on the backs of envelopes." Like many politicians in the legislature, Clark considered Wilson's team of political rookies "a group of unknown and untried candidates with a platform of dubious quality." But this criticism proved irrelevant for many voters, as the election results soon demonstrated.

As the election date grew nearer and an NDP victory appeared imminent, the business pages shifted their attention from Social Credit's problems to Mike Harcourt's campaign platform. As if on cue, the business pages trotted out the Dave Barrett government of 1972-75 as a warning flag of socialist excess. (One of their favourite anecdotes was Barrett's admission, in the fall of 1974, that "an unidentified person in the Human Resources Department" – namely the minister, Norman Levi – had made a "clerical error" of $102.8 million in that year's budget.)

Whether or not one agreed with NDP ideology, using Dave Barrett to dismiss the 1990s party made no sense at all. The Barrett regime inherited the latter stages of a boom economy, and both the economy and the party had changed drastically since then. But this was of no consequence to Howe Street. The NDP had "screwed the economy" once; there was no reason to believe they wouldn't do it again.

Harcourt could easily have gone on the attack, refusing to accept Howe Street's assessment of the Barrett government. Instead, he took pains to assure the business community that his NDP government would be a fiscally responsible one. "We're a 1990s New Democratic Party focussed on the realities of a global economy and trade, deficits and tax, tax, tax," Harcourt told the *Sun*. "The options that were open for previous governments to choose from just aren't there any more. There is more discipline needed now and I think we are more sensitive to the mainstream." To appease the party's critics in the business community, Harcourt, along with Colin Gabelmann, Glen Clark, and other caucus members, took their message of fiscally responsible socialism

to board of trade meetings, chambers of commerce and any other business organization that would hear them.

But the "new" New Democrats were careful not to be too enthusiastic in their criticism of Barrett. Gabelmann, the long-serving Vancouver Island MLA and former Barrett caucus member, conceded that the
Barrett government tried to introduce far too much legislation too
soon. "We came to power with a shopping list that was a mile long – a
50-year agenda," said Gabelmann, a member of the Communist Party
of Canada in his youth. "It was not thought through clearly." Harcourt reminded reporters that for all his apparent spending lust, Barrett was responsible for a wealth of progressive legislation that
managed to survive every Socred government. "There is a perception
that Dave Barrett was bad for the province. Most of that is just a bum
rap," Harcourt told the *Sun*. The Socreds, he added, had plenty of
opportunities to get rid of such socialist innovations as the Insurance
Corporation of BC (ICBC), the agricultural land reserve and Pharmacare. But they didn't.

This strategy appeared to be a good one, as many observers dismissed attempts to use the Barrett government's record to discredit
the current crop of New Democrats. "If you're going to blame the NDP
for the mini-recession of 1974, then you have to blame the Socreds for
the even deeper recession of 1982," University of Victoria political scientist Norman Ruff told a *Sun* reporter. Doug Ward, the reporter, also
quoted George Woodcock's history of BC to make the same point
about Barrett. "The brief NDP government," Woodcock had written,
"did no more to shift British Columbia in the direction of a balanced
socialist economy than its predecessor [Socred W.A.C. Bennett's
administration] had done."

But Harcourt's campaign in the business community was far more
calculated than a simple wooing of Howe Street, as the media liked to
characterize it. He may indeed have been "wooing" the business community by saying all the right things about deficits and fiscal responsibility, but that's not where the votes were. If anything, Harcourt
was "playing to Surrey" by proving to unaffiliated, white collar
workers in the suburbs that his NDP could rub shoulders with the
financial elite. In the post-Barrett, post-Skelly NDP, this eagerness to

broaden the middle-class support base was what separated Harcourt from more traditional left New Democrats.

He also knew he could score big points by targeting corruption in the stock market. During the campaign, the NDP leader had praise for everyone from Vancouver Stock Exchange president Don Hudson and the superintendant of brokers, to BC Securities Commission chair Doug Hyndman, all of whom he credited with working hard to rid the exchange of "shysters." Harcourt's enthusiasm for expanding the scope of exchange business appeared to be genuine. "I think we can create a lot more business for the exchange by utilizing union pension funds as sources for investment in entrepreneurial capital, and helping small businesses get venture capital funding," he said.

Like Skelly before him, Harcourt also took pains to assure investors that his government would be a lot kinder to the mining industry than the Barrett government was. There would be no super-royalties or succession duties on mineral production, he promised. Another concession to business (although few were convinced he was serious) was a pledge that he would put a muzzle on two of his most outspoken caucus members, Moe Sihota and Glen Clark, who in 1988 and 1989 had launched a series of assaults on the VSE and some of Howe Street's most powerful brokers.

Sihota and Clark had spent hours in the legislature outlining fraudulent VSE listings and naming promoters who had breached securities regulations, pointing fingers at then-VSE chairman John Mathers and well-known Socred Peter Brown. But they gradually eased off on their assault, according to Vancouver *Sun* reporter David Baines, because Harcourt did not want to create the impression that the NDP was "anti-VSE or anti-business." As well, the BC Securities Commission was making progress in its reform program and the VSE was eager to "introduce itself to the NDP and explain its side of the story."

By the eve of the election, the Vancouver business community was softening its criticism of the NDP. "I don't think Michael Harcourt is by any stretch of the imagination a hardline socialist," said securities lawyer Bill Rand. "He's more of a German-style social democrat." Global Securities senior vice-president David Levi, one of the few NDP activists on Howe Street and a past-president of Harcourt's constituency (his father, Norm Levi, was a minister in the Barrett cabinet), concurred with this view. "We have been talking to people in the VSE who were rabidly anti-NDP in the past, but feel they can work with a Harcourt government. I think there's a general view that Mike understands business."

Still, there was some skepticism at the Vancouver *Sun*. Even as they endorsed his party, editorial writers damned Harcourt with faint praise. "Mr. Harcourt has made a career out of being a dull pragmatist," the October 11 editorial said. While his conciliatory nature and sincerity "might convince some wavering right-wingers that he can find the compromise between social sensitivity and fiscal responsibility," Harcourt nonetheless carried the baggage of opposing Expo 86 and failing to convince critics that he was serious about reining in caucus pitbulls Sihota and Clark.

But the *Sun* knew which way the wind was blowing. "Mike Harcourt and the 1991 breed of New Democrats are less radical than the version that swept to power in 1972 ... As mayor of Vancouver ... he proved to be a cautious politician not given to rash undertakings." On the condition that voters send a large pack of Liberals to Victoria to keep the NDP in check, the *Sun* judiciously concluded, "we suggest Mr. Harcourt be given his chance to lead the province."

Down the hall, the *Province* was much more explicit, preferring to annoint the NDP by condemning the Socreds to eternal damnation. "This hasn't been a government, it's been a roller-coaster ride through hell. Social Credit cannot distance itself from the poisonous stew it served up to the people of this province under Bill Vander Zalm. Its track record, unique in Canadian history, is a complete disgrace ... What BC needs most is stable, responsible, responsive government. The New Democrats are the only hope."

Within months, it would be hard to imagine that Vancouver's morning tabloid could ever have offered the NDP such an unqualified endorsement.

3

Retooling
the Shop

OCTOBER 17, 1991

THE NDP'S FIRST VICTORY PARTY IN NINETEEN YEARS WAS A jubilant affair. While Dixieland jazz combos wearing Bavarian outfits were playing downbeat versions of "Put on a Happy Face" for the losing Socreds next door at the Hotel Vancouver, the scene at NDP headquarters was more like a beer garden chatfest following a lively policy convention.

While same-sex couples danced to recorded music in Robson Square's underground ballroom, a rogue's gallery of leftie establishment figures greeted each other like old friends at a class reunion. Jack Munro leaped down the stairs to savour the victory with Ken Georgetti. Party communications wizard Bill Tieleman showed off the badge he'd been saving for years ("Laugh now, but one day we'll be in charge"), native leader Bill Wilson looked pleased, and the BC Government Employees Union's Sheila Fruman was still in shock. Vancouver-Burrard's long-serving MLA Emery Barnes greeted everyone with a giant bear hug, and Coquitlam-Maillardville MLA John Cashore embraced Burnaby MP Svend Robinson, who showed up just before Mike Harcourt's victory speech to share the great moment with his provincial comrades.

On his way to the stage Harcourt was approached by Vancouver *Sun* reporter Keith Baldrey, who thrust a first-edition copy of the next morning's paper in his hands. Acknowledging the cheers of the party faithful, the premier-elect flashed the *Sun*'s banner headline to the jubilant crowd: "NDP SWEEPS IN." Until this moment, Social Credit had seemed like a monolithic beast that could never be destroyed; the NDP's last election victory in 1972 was like a century ago. Not any more. The official scorecard read: NDP 51 seats, Liberals 17, Socreds 7.

Within a few hours on October 17, the free-enterprise machine that had controlled the purse strings of BC for most of the past 40 years was reduced to a rump party with no clout in the legislature, while a third party had come out of nowhere to become the official Opposition. All the Socred heavyweights had gone down in flames: Rita Johnston, Russ Fraser, Bruce Strachan, John Jansen, John Reynolds, Dave Parker and Carol Gran were defeated. The only survivors were former Health Minister Peter Dueck in Matsqui, Harry De Jong in Abbotsford, Richard Neufeld in Peace River North, Jack Weisgerber in Peace River South, Len Fox in Prince George-Omineca, Lyall Hanson in Okanagan-Vernon, and Cliff Serwa in Okanagan West.

The NDP captured 41 percent of the popular vote, the Liberals were second with 33 percent and Social Credit third with 24 percent. These figures made a mockery of BCTV's pre-election "Voice of BC" poll, which predicted the Liberals would finish with 41 percent and the NDP with 37. Perhaps, someone joked, this election was merely the one time out of twenty that a poll result was completely out to lunch.

Nevertheless, Gordon Wilson felt like the real winner as he celebrated with supporters at Liberal Party headquarters. On the strength of his debate performance, his party was back in the legislature for the first time since 1979. And the rebirth exceeded even his own expectations: with seventeen new MLAs, including himself, the Liberals won twice the number of seats they predicted when the campaign began. The emergence of a new free-enterprise party, however ill-defined, did not go unnoticed by former Socreds. Among those who attended the Liberal victory celebrations were Bill Vander Zalm's former driver Bill Kay, now working for newly elected West Vancouver-Garibaldi

MLA David Mitchell, an author and historian best known for his sympathetic biography of W.A.C. Bennett. Also there was Jim Bennett (no relation), formerly a Grace McCarthy aide who was also working for Mitchell, and Gord Robson, another Socred who managed former Finance Minister Mel Couvelier's run at the Socred leadership in 1986.

The new premier was not surprised by Gordon Wilson's coterie of Socred hangers-on. "I think Murray Pezim put it succinctly when he handed over a six-figure cheque to Gordon Wilson," Harcourt wryly commented to a reporter. "He said, 'Gordon, we're all Socreds underneath it all.'" The beast may have been dead, but its ghosts would remain indefinitely on BC's political landscape.

The date chosen for the transition was ironic. November 5 is Guy Fawkes Day, the anniversary of an English Catholic's attempt to blow up the British parliament. The events of BC politics in 1991 were hardly explosive, but the NDP's swearing-in ceremony could be described as revolutionary, given the political makeup of this province since 1952. November 5, 1991, would bring the first New Democratic cabinet in sixteen years, the most women appointed to a BC cabinet, the first Indo-Canadian cabinet minister in the country, and the cabinet with the most university degrees in BC history.

With Mike Harcourt's first official announcement as BC's 29th premier, women moved from the backbenches to the inner circles of power. Eileen Dailly was the only woman in Dave Barrett's cabinet, but times had changed and women in the Harcourt administration were not tokens. Seven of eighteen ministries, four of eight positions on Planning Board, and five of eight positions on Treasury Board – the two most powerful committees of cabinet – would be occupied by women. All told, women would control about 80 percent of the provincial budget.

The most prominent of these appointments went to 60-year-old Anita Hagen, an ex-schoolteacher representing New Westminster. Hagen was named deputy premier, chair of the Planning Board, minister of Education and minister responsible for Multiculturalism and Human Rights. Elizabeth Cull, the 39-year-old upstart who stole the conservative riding of Oak Bay from the Socreds in a 1989 by-election, was put in charge of Health; Kootenay MLA Anne Edwards, 55, was given Energy, Mines and Petroleum Resources; Penny Priddy, the newcomer who defeated Premier Rita Johnston in Surrey-Newton, received the new, high-profile Women's Equality Ministry; Joan Smallwood, a strong critic of the Socreds on Social Services, was rewarded with that ministry. Lois Boone, who had been on the transition team, was appointed Government Services minister. And Darlene Marzari, Harcourt's old friend and colleague from Vancouver city council days, was put in charge of Tourism and Culture.

Another prominent position went to 45-year-old Joan Sawicki, a land use consultant who was designated to take the post of Speaker once the house resumed sessions the following spring. Sawicki was the first rookie MLA to be named Speaker since 1952, and the job would not be easy. The chamber included a record number of neophytes – 49 of 75 MLAs, including the entire 17-member Liberal caucus. Sawicki's appointment surprised Vancouver New Democrats, many of whom had expected Harcourt to give the job to Emery Barnes.

The men appointed to cabinet were a mixed bag of longtime New Democrats (Colin Gabelmann as attorney general, Robin Blencoe in Municipal Affairs, Dan Miller in Forests), and ambitious young turks (Glen Clark in Finance, Moe Sihota in Labour and Consumer Services, Andrew Petter in Aboriginal Affairs). Most of these appointments were well-received in the press, as Harcourt appeared determined to match as many ministers as possible with the portfolios they held as Opposition critics.

This was especially the case with the 33-year-old Clark, a meticulous researcher who had made a habit of embarrassing the Socred Finance minister at every available opportunity. Clark, a protégé of Bob Williams – the acerbic former Vancouver-East MLA and backroom troubleshooter for Dave Barrett – was the leading member of the NDP's Rat Pack, a group of bright, ambitious young MLAs including Sihota, Cull and Petter that formed the nucleus of Harcourt's shadow cabinet. Clark's appointment to the position of government house leader seemed a logical move. His relentless pursuit of Vancouver Stock Exchange fraud artists, and his frequent revelations of Socred mismanagement, had earned him praise before the election even from former rivals. "By virtue of his dedication as a critic I have to believe that he has a willingness to work hard at mastering the operation of government and the management of money," said Mel Couvelier. "I think he has a bright future, and he is capable."

Andrew Petter, 37, was something of a child prodigy whose experience in government began with BC's previous NDP government. At eighteen he served as executive assistant to Housing Minister Lorne Nicholson. After the NDP's defeat in BC, he went on to work as a special assistant to Saskatchewan Premier Allan Blakeney.

But not all of the NDP's bright lights received their logical appointments. Sihota, a cocky young lawyer from Esquimalt and one of the NDP's most impressive debaters, looked like he was aiming for the attorney general's job for most of his five years in Opposition. But Sihota was seen as far too aggressive and partisan to be named top law enforcement officer for the province. Critics were sure he would politicize the AG's office and alienate the Law Society of BC, which was already investigating his business practice. It was Sihota's role in the Bud Smith tapes scandal of 1990, however, that all but destroyed any chance he had of getting the job. Although the cellular phone conversations between then-Attorney General Smith and a television reporter were a serious enough breach of trust to force Smith's resignation from cabinet, Sihota's disclosure of the tapes was also considered a breach of ethics. Sihota was given responsibility for Labour and Consumer Services, with the added responsibility of Constitutional Affairs, while non-lawyer Colin Gabelmann was given the attorney general's job. Similarly, Tom Perry was rumoured to be a candidate for minister of Health. Perry, who had served as health critic after winning the 1989 Vancouver-Point Grey by-election, was one of those rare commodities: a doctor with impeccable socialist credentials. An attending physician at Vancouver's University Hospital, he had served as past-president of the BC chapter of Canadian Physicians for the Prevention of Nuclear War, had won the Roderick Haig-Brown Award for his efforts to preserve the Skagit Valley, and was also active on preservation campaigns in the Stein Valley, the Valhalla Wilderness and the Queen Charlotte Islands. But Perry was never under consideration for the Health minister's job. Being "qualified" for the position meant that Perry would be in a conflict of interest every time he dealt with the BC Medical Association. He was also a strong supporter of euthanasia, which didn't make him a neutral observer of health issues. In fact, in the week before the swearing-in ceremony, questions were raised about Perry's role in administering morphine to his dying father. Instead of becoming Health minister, he was appointed minister of Advanced Education, Training and Technology.

Apart from Environment minister John Cashore — a progressive United Church minister, anti-poverty activist and native affairs consultant who was part of the NDP's green caucus before the election — the remainder of cabinet was made up of pragmatists and small businessmen not known for doctrinaire left-wing ideology.

Bill Barlee (Agriculture) was a conservative small businessman who wouldn't have looked out of place in the Liberal Party. Barlee, 58, had worked as a placer miner and was currently a partner in a gold and platinum mining company in the Similkameen area. His expertise in gold panning and knowledge of the area led to two bestselling books, a magazine (*Canada West*) and a TV program carried on four networks nationwide. As a spokesperson for farmers, ranchers and growers in a traditionally conservative pocket of the province, he proved to be a major factor in Harcourt's plan to broaden the NDP's appeal in the Okanagan.

David Zirnhelt (Economic Development, Small Business and Trade), was a 43-year-old rancher from Williams Lake who also practised selective logging. Before winning the Cariboo South by-election in 1989, Zirnhelt worked in the federal public service on a project to establish the Ministry of State for Urban Affairs, and later headed a federal youth employment program for BC and the Yukon. Also considered moderate enough to be a Liberal, Zirnhelt actually ran for that party as a 21-year-old in 1969, but was badly beaten by Socred heavyweight Alex Fraser. Late in the NDP's first term, Liberals in the Cariboo tried to convince him to cross the floor, but Zirnhelt declined.

Finally there was Art Charbonneau (Transportation and Highways), a 51-year-old, self-employed civil engineering consultant. Charbonneau, who developed and marketed computer software, was also co-founder of the Principal Group Investors' Association which led the fight for recovering seniors' investment money following the 1988 collapse of the Principal Group trust company. Charbonneau was a pragmatist who led by quiet example and eschewed the headline-grabbing tactics of Clark and Sihota.

The Harcourt cabinet was truly an indication that a new generation was taking over in Victoria. The average age, 45, was much younger than that of recent Socred governments, and as the first premier born in the 1940s, Harcourt was also the first premier whose political perspective was not informed by the harsh realities of the Depression or World War II. Presumably, the intellectual quotient of government was higher with the New Democrats in office; fourteen of the eighteen ministers had university educations, and nine had more than one degree. The Harcourt New Democrats were more like the Clinton Democrats, who swept to power in Washington a year later, than the Dave Barrett socialists who provided such an ideological foil for the free-enterprise vision of the Bennett family.

The swearing-in ceremony, which took place before a crowd of 1,200 invited guests at the University of Victoria, was notable for the speech by Lieutenant Governor David Lam. Lam, a Chinese immigrant who made his fortune in real estate, had become one of the most popular Queen's representatives in BC, and ended up serving more than six years in Government House. On this day, he received a standing ovation when he called for "the healing of wounds" after years of confrontation and corrupt government.

There was much pomp and ceremony on November 5. After the UVic event, about 9,000 visitors filed into the legislature for a three-hour open house commemorating the transition. Harcourt was beaming as the crowds walked by. "It's your house," said the new premier. "I'm just a temporary employee here." It was quite the love-in. Moe Sihota was mobbed by adoring locals asking for his autograph. Even federal NDP leader Audrey McLaughlin shared the limelight, accepting the congratulations of well-wishers on her provincial colleagues' behalf, and down the hall, MuchMusic veejay Terry David Mulligan captured an accordion-and-fiddle duo playing tunes outside the old Socred caucus office.

In the cabinet room, visitors couldn't help noticing a red light attached to a panel alongside the cabinet table. The light – a warning signal installed by the Bill Bennett Socreds to alert cabinet ministers whenever an angry mob of socialist hordes was gathering in protest outside the legislature – seemed a fitting tribute to the old regime. Recalling the days of restraint and the draconian budgets of the early 1980s, one could almost imagine a harried Grace McCarthy or a fumbling Hugh Curtis scrambling down the backstairs exit at the first flicker of that light.

But according to an already skeptical media, the light could just as easily be a warning signal for Mike Harcourt. "The New Democrats might want to wait a year or two before deciding it is safe to have the warning light disconnected," Vaughn Palmer wryly commented the next day. "The new premier and his ministers can be forgiven for basking in glory, but they also [have] to be aware of the expectations they [are] creating."

For that matter, they would also have to be aware of the media vultures in their midst. As the goverment was welcoming the public to the legislature November 5, one of the new premier's staff members was sitting in a nearby hotel restaurant, where he overheard *Province* columnist Brian Kieran chatting with a radio reporter. Later, the staffer told Harcourt about the conversation. "I'll give the NDP six months' honeymoon," Kieran is reported to have said. "Then I'm gonna make sure they're defeated. What Marjorie Nichols did to Dave Barrett was nothing compared to what I'm gonna do to Harcourt."

After the Party, the Hangover

THE NEW GOVERNMENT DIDN'T WAIT LONG TO GET BUSY. ON November 6, the day after the NDP cabinet officially took office, Agriculture Minister Bill Barlee announced, as he walked into the first cabinet meeting, that the government would rescind the June 1988 order-in-council that permitted golf courses and other developments on Agricultural Land Reserve (ALR) farm land. Within two weeks, the order was rescinded.

With a single move, the NDP strengthened an institution (the ALR) its one previous government had created in 1973, defending the average farmer while inhibiting the growth of a yuppie sport. Applications for new developments had increased dramatically and property values had mushroomed once the Socreds cleared the way for golf courses, restaurants and pro shops to be included within the ALR. Even the family of John Savage – the Agriculture minister who signed the order – tried to sell its 20-hectare Delta cornfield for more than six times what it paid in 1985 (the Savages later took the land off the market when the minister was accused of conflict). Under the terms of the new decision, announced ten days after the cabinet's first meeting, all 181 applications for golf courses on the ALR were put on hold pending a review by the Agricultural Land Commission (ALC). The move was an early indication that NDP-created government bodies would regain the clout they had lost when the party was defeated in 1975.

Harcourt was also eager to leave a good first impression on foreign investors. Ten days after being sworn into office the premier was in Tokyo, schmoozing with the Japanese business community in an attempt to improve relations with BC's second-largest trading partner. The five-day visit was intended to boost trade and tourism with Japan, and to restore BC's image. "This is the first visit of a BC premier in four years," Harcourt told a reporter. "That's ridiculous. The last government cancelled two trips by the premier and one by the Finance minister. It sends such a terrible signal, one that is embarassing and insulting. That's not the way to do business here. You've got to come back again and again. Things don't even get serious until the third or fourth visit."

In the following weeks the government acted on several of its promises. In December, cabinet accepted a BC First Nations Council report that recognized aboriginal title and the inherent right to native self-government. It also introduced a provincewide get-tough policy on law-breaking drivers.

But even as ministers were settling into their portfolios and getting on with the business of running BC, the ominous shadow of Social Credit continued to haunt the province. At every turn, NDP ministers and senior bureaucrats were met by a series of nasty surprises left behind by the previous government. At the Insurance Corporation of BC it was revealed that rates hadn't kept up with the costs of overhead and accident claims. Because the Socreds repeatedly rejected senior management's recommendations to raise insurance rates more than a minimal amount, ICBC was facing a massive deficit unless the new government acted immediately. That was Labour Minister Moe Sihota's justification for announcing the unpopular 19 percent rate hike on December 13.

The NDP was also left with the bills for major Socred megaprojects — some of which the NDP supported in Opposition. There was a continuing need for cash infusions for the newly established University of Northern BC, the TRIUMF Kaon project at UBC, and the BC Ferry Corporation's commitment to a $200 million expansion plan for its "superferries."

But this was pocket change compared to the surprise that greeted Glen Clark when the Finance minister sat down with the books left by the previous administration. The Socreds had hidden more than $3 billion in government debt from the taxpayers during their final fiscal year in power. For the current year alone, the provincial deficit was $500 million higher than previously disclosed. "Glen came into my office and his face was white as a sheet," Harcourt remembered. "He couldn't believe the numbers he was reading."

On November 13, Clark held a press conference at which a group of senior Finance officials released a briefing that outlined the province's outlook up to the 1993-94 fiscal year. At least two of their findings would significantly alter the course the government was planning to take. First, the $395 million deficit figure that outgoing Finance Minister John Jansen used throughout the election campaign was far too low. Second, revenue projections for 1991-92 had dropped $218 million below budget while expenditures were expected to go up by $272 million.

"I guess at this point all that's fair to say is that it [eliminating the deficit] will be much more difficult to accomplish, given the numbers we were operating under were not real numbers," said Clark. The following day, he ordered an independent investigation into the financial operations of all key government agencies and departments during the Socred reign. The probe, conducted by the firms Peat Marwick, Stevenson & Kellogg and Deloitte & Touche, was supervised by a steering committee led by Auditor General George Morfitt.

Morfitt's final report, released on January 30, 1992, was a damning indictment of Social Credit accounting practices. Not only had the previous government lied about the state of provincial finances, it also broke the law several times. Specifically, the Vander Zalm Socreds had twice violated the Financial Administration Act by transfering $773 million from the now-defunct Budget Stabilization fund to the general fund, without signing an order-in-council. They also violated the Lottery Act by doling out cash through the BC Lottery Corporation without going through the normal review process applied by the Attorney General's Ministry, and failed to report the payments as Lottery Fund "special transactions" (nor did they record whether the money went to charities, as required). And Socred financial statements did not include the $450 million in "underfunded" pension benefits the government had accumulated over twenty years and still owed its employees.

In short, Bill Vander Zalm had decided early in 1990 that the best way to get reelected was to go on a spending spree. In one example unearthed by the auditors, the premier himself had met with the principals of a company in his home riding that had been turned down for a government loan. Soon afterward, the firm received $2.5 million in public funds, interest free, with no terms of repayment. Rita Johnston continued this system of handouts, running up the tab to more than $300 million in questionable advances to private corporations.

Many of these "loans" would later be written off as grants. Similarly, the Socreds recorded about $7.4 billion in "loans" to be repaid by crown corporations, even though $2.8 billion of that money for colleges, universities, hospital and school districts was non-refundable." By the spring of 1991 the books were so cooked, you could have served them for breakfast," noted Vaughn Palmer.

While these revelations may have vindicated the NDP's criticism of the Socreds while in Opposition, they didn't make the new government's job any easier. Faced with a growing debt, Harcourt ordered all ministries to cut the next year's spending by 15 percent. Transportation, Energy and Economic Development were singled out for cutbacks so that essential social ministries like Health, Social Services and Education would be spared major cuts.

But the cutbacks had only just begun. In order to control spending and cut 10 percent from the budget, all ministers were asked to identify at least three programs their ministries could do without. Tax increases were also on the horizon. Clark knew he was inviting accusations of a radical shift to the right, so he put his dilemma in terms that the average voter could appreciate. "Would the people like to see us raise the sales tax one point, or would they like to see us reduce the property tax grant, or would they like to see us shut down some schools and some hospitals?"

To some observers, Clark's tough talk sounded like a father withholding allowance from a wayward teenager. But his born-again deficit bashing was a source of amusement in the press gallery. Some pundits delighted in referring to the socialist union man as "the most right-wing Finance minister in Canada." Only with his announcement of the budget would Clark escape this label for good.

Taking Care of Business

MARCH 17, 1992
WITH THE OPENING OF THE LEGISLATURE AND THE NEW GOVernment's first Speech from the Throne, the NDP formally introduced the province to its financial and political program. The speech blasted the federal Conservative government for its "failure to shoulder its responsibility" to maintain social programs, and for its monetary policy which resulted in 15,000 lost jobs and contributed to the provincial deficit. It also served notice that the new government would waste little time acting on its social policy promises.

One of its first legislative actions made it easier for women to have abortions outside of hospitals. Under the Vander Zalm government, the Medical Services Plan would fund abortions only in hospitals or doctors' offices, leaving the decision entirely to medical authorities. As of April 1, however, MSP funding would now extend to procedures carried out at BC's two freestanding abortion clinics as well.

And that wasn't the only good news for BC women. Along with increased funding for child support programs ($17 million) and victim assistance and violence prevention programs for women and children ($6 million), the government also announced its plan to introduce pay equity in the public sector. "With all the talk of fiscal restraint and deficits left them by the Socreds, I'm glad they're holding to their promises right away," said Trisha Joel of Vancouver Status of Women.

Another major announcement was the long-awaited amendment to the Human Rights Act which banned discrimination on the basis of sexual orientation. Throughout the 1980s, the political culture in BC was such that homophobic Socred ministers could afford to make bigoted remarks about gays and lesbians without fear of reprisal from their premier. Like Bill Vander Zalm, they cheerfully assumed that all British Columbians shared their quaint view of the province as an oasis of tractor pull aesthetics and *100 Huntley Street* religion. Gays and lesbians aren't real British Columbians, the reasoning went, so who cares if we insult them? During the height of the AIDS crisis, when approval of new treatments was delayed despite the fact that hundreds of people were dying, Health Minister Peter Dueck defended his government's dismal efforts to contain the disease by distinguishing the majority of people living with AIDS – gay or bisexual men and intravenous drug users – from those he described as "innocent, [who] did not go out and wilfully or very carelessly through their lifestyle, contract that disease." Dueck was later reprimanded by a BC Supreme Court judge who described his remark as "unnecessary, inflammatory and reflect[ing] a regrettable ignorance of the disease that one would not expect from a minister of health."

With the NDP's rise to power, gays and lesbians no longer had to worry about being treated like lepers. One reason for the party's willingness to act on gay rights was its frequent consultation with community activists while in Opposition. The NDP had accepted submissions from a gay and lesbian caucus formed in early 1990. According to gay human rights lawyer Dennis Dahl, who supported Vancouver-Burrard MLA Emery Barnes's bid for renomination that year despite challenges from a gay man and a lesbian, the party assured the gay and lesbian caucus that it was committed to Human Rights Act amendments, increased AIDS funding and homophobia training – a promise that Barnes and his colleagues would deliver on over several sessions.

The Human Rights Act amendment banned discrimination against gays and lesbians in housing, employment and basic public services. And this apparently radical development in provincial law passed through the House with about as much resistance as a highway improvement project in the North. ("They were smart about it," said Dahl. "They brought it in during the first session, before they were criticized about anything else.")

Social policy was relatively easy to sell to the public, but tax increases were another story. Even after the NDP was sworn in, Harcourt had promised there would be no new taxes – leaving the impression that there would be no tax increases, period. But that was before the full extent of the Socreds' financial mismanagement was revealed to the public. With the budget announcement of March 26 – a $17.98 billion document that projected a $1.7 billion deficit – British Columbians were told that they would have to pay an additional $800 million in taxes on top of what they had paid the previous year. Business was expected to pay an additional $300 million. Taxpayers with incomes of more than $60,000 would pay a 10 percent surtax, while those earning more than $86,500 would pay a higher surtax. One of the most controversial measures was the elimination of the supplemental homeowners' grant, which provided municipal tax rebates on a sliding scale according to the assessed property value of a home. This change was designed to hit owners of more expensive homes the hardest; under the new system, a $360,000 west-side Vancouver home would lose $420 in supplemental benefits, while a $75,000 Prince George home would lose $80.

Other budget measures included a cap on the amount doctors could bill for services, and the cancellation of a doctors' pension plan, approved by the Socreds, that would have been paid entirely by taxpayers; a 6 percent sales tax on legal fees, which were exempt from sales tax under the Socreds (this measure alone brought in $32 million for the 1993 fiscal year); and a corporate capital tax for companies with more than $1 million in paid-up capital (this included crown corporations for the first time).

These tax increases, argued Clark, would help to cover the estimated $60 million the province expected to lose from reductions in
federal transfer payments – money that normally went toward health
and education – as well as cover the spiralling cost of welfare payments. With more British Columbians out of work and increased
immigration from other provinces, welfare funding would require an
additional $231 million in the coming fiscal year – a 19 percent
increase over the previous year's levels. These spending increases
were necessary, despite the fact that welfare and unemployment
insurance rates would be frozen.

To Glen Clark, the compromises facing his government seemed
obvious. "Some tough decisions have to be made," he said. "Should
we cut highway spending to, say, feed hungry school kids in Vancouver? I think that's what the people who elected us want us to do."
Even with the tax increases, the NDP's first budget maintained a tax
rate that was second lowest in the country next to Alberta's. And as
Harcourt had promised all along, most of the increases would affect
the wealthier members of society. This approach appeared to be consistent with the idea of social democracy which most British
Columbians knew they were getting when the NDP was elected.

In spite of this moderate approach, the business lobby remained in
election mode, unwilling to cut the NDP a bit of slack on its first budget. "The government talks about this being the road map to recov-
ery. But frankly, we think it's the road map taking us in the wrong
direction," said Kathy Sanderson, BC director of the Canadian Federation of Independent Business. "We understand that they have to
increase taxes, but we expect a quid pro quo. We saw easy cuts on
things like highways, but where they needed to take a tougher line on
things like education and health care, there was nothing."

Then there were the partisan political reactions. Vancouver Mayor
Gordon Campbell called the budget a "war on taxpayers," Liberal
finance critic Fred Gingell called it a "tax grab" that would hurt middle-income earners, and Socred leader Jack Weisgerber called it "a
vicious assault" (leaving one to wonder how he would describe the
effect of Socred economics on the poor). While the business lobby

griped about the NDP's first budget, a tri-partisan committee of government, labour and business representatives was busy canvassing the province for input on the new labour code.

Three Amigos and a New Labour Code

FOR A PARTY SO STRONGLY IDENTIFIED WITH THE TRADE UNION movement, it should have been no surprise that the NDP would move quickly to introduce new labour laws in the province. The ranks of organized labour in BC had been demoralized since 1983, when the IWA's Jack Munro and Socred Premier Bill Bennett signed the Kelowna Accord, a negotiated settlement in which the government forfeited almost none of its key anti-labour legislation. (This included public sector wage controls and the right to fire employees without cause upon expiry of the collective bargaining agreement.) In the next four years, union membership decreased dramatically, particularly in construction, where the increase in non-union contractors forced labour leaders to accept wage rollbacks.

By 1987, the trade union movement was sufficiently vulnerable that Bill Vander Zalm introduced a labour law more sweeping in its attempts to stifle unions than anything attempted during the restraint era. Bill 19, known as the Industrial Relations Act, effectively wiped out the provincial Labour Code which had been the standard for collective bargaining in BC since the Dave Barrett NDP introduced it in 1973. The new legislation gave cabinet the power to impose a settlement in a labour dispute, and send workers back to the job by signing a cabinet order, even if the legislature wasn't in session; allowed unionized companies to develop non-union divisions ("doublebreasting"); prohibited union members outside construction from refusing to work beside non-union workers; prohibited union members from refusing to handle "hot" goods from struck or non-union employers; outlawed secondary picketing; forced unions to vote on an employer's final offer, even if the union executive thought the offer was bad; and included a host of other measures designed to weaken unions.

The Industrial Relations Act also established the Industrial Relations Council (IRC), a provincially appointed labour watchdog headed by Ed Peck, the man chosen by Bill Bennett to administer the Socreds' mid-1980s wage control program. The IRC gave Peck the authority to intervene and end any labour-management dispute deemed to be a threat to the public interest – a condition only Peck had the right to define. Aside from the obvious effect of weakening the rights of workers and enhancing those of employers, the Industrial Relations Act gave government greater power over the collective bargaining process than it had ever previously enjoyed, and handed over unprecedented power to an appointed official. The brainchild of Bill Vander Zalm himself, the 1987 labour legislation was widely regarded as a vindictive act by a small businessman who wanted "vengeance for all the woes unions had ever caused small businessmen everywhere." (Vander Zalm may also have been suffering from his failure to settle a woodworkers' strike the previous fall – the only blemish on an otherwise sunny election campaign.)

The legislation was attacked by most people left of the Fraser Institute. Deputy minister of Labour Graham Leslie (who later expressed his frustration with the Socreds in his book *Breach of Promise*) quit the government in protest and called Bill 19 "an act of legislated violence," a thinly veiled attempt to de-unionize the province that would only lead to more confrontation. Jim Matkin of the BC Business Council said it threatened the collective bargaining process. Even the Vancouver *Sun* opposed it.

The Socreds' rhetoric surrounding the new Act reached such proportions that even normally level-headed Brian Smith was carried away by it all. On June 1, 1987, as 300,000 unionized workers across the province staged a one-day general strike, the attorney general went to the Supreme Court to apply for an injunction forbidding further job action against Bill 19. What Smith neglected to tell the public was that the wording of the writ he filed in court was lifted verbatim from a Criminal Code section dealing with sedition – the revolutionary overthrow of government. Among other things, Smith was seeking to have the act of "pointing out errors in the government" declared a crime. The courts later threw out the writ, but the effect of Smith's action and Vander Zalm's legislation was well-noted in the press; BC was beginning to look like "an unnerving version of South Africa."

It was this kind of arrogance and contempt for unionized workers that the NDP was determined to redress once it came to power. The promise to introduce a new labour code – or at least to return to something similar to the 1973 version – was a key reason for the labour movement's support of the NDP before the election. On February 3, 1992, Labour Minister Moe Sihota introduced a nine-member committee that would shape the new labour law and plan a long-term strategy for industrial labour relations that would, he hoped, bring a healthier labour relations climate, as well as more investment, to the province.

Committee members included Graham Leslie (an appropriate choice, given his two decades of experience in labour relations and his insider's view of the ministry during the Bill 19 debacle), Vancouver mediator Vince Ready, and labour lawyers Thomas Roper and John Baigent. Ready, Roper and Baigent (who were subsequently referred to as the "three amigos") headed a subcommittee responsible for recommending final changes to the new labour code. While some of the changes were expected as early as June, Sihota gave the team no fixed timetable.

As it turned out, the 125-page consensus report required eight months to complete, and the new labour code was not tabled in the legislature until October 27. The new Labour Relations Code represented 98 percent agreement among labour and management. Only four key items remained to be resolved by the government.

Sectoral bargaining – which would have opened up the small business sector to unionization – was not included in the code, Sihota explained at the time, because such a measure would limit an employer's ability to negotiate a distinctive collective agreement. Sectoral bargaining would have been the "scariest" part of the labour code, explained the BC Federation of Labour's Bill Tieleman, because it would have created a domino effect in the service sector. "You could take any geographical area and take the fast food sector like a burger joint or a 7-11, and get unionized," Tieleman explained. "You could get a master bargaining contract at one gas station, then go down to another station and get an automatic certification with a 55 percent signup. Once you get one, you can start rolling them in. You'd soon have a highly unionized sector, where you didn't have it at all."

The government, convinced that the small business community would "go absolutely berserk" if such a measure was introduced, was not willing to risk that level of confrontation. "We had a mandate, being a left-of-centre party, to bring in a new labour code ... that made it easier to unionize," Sihota recalled. "[But] we made a conscious decision not to swing the pendulum so far so as to create a dynamic where another government could come in and subsequently reverse it."

The government also ruled that secondary picketing would continue to be restricted, although the Labour Relations Board retained the right to decide whether workers could picket their own worksite, even if third parties were affected; replacement workers or "scabs" would be prohibited (the government argued that this measure would reduce the length of disputes and reduce the levels of tension that so often lead to picket line violence); and the government restored the freedom to negotiate terms to allow secondary boycotts in a collective agreement. (For example, employees could opt not to use or handle products of a struck employer, or require that dealings be with unionized companies.)

The decision to prohibit replacement workers was never in doubt. "We worked very hard on anti-scab [legislation]," recalled Sihota. "There was just no chance that the government was going to back off, because the memory of Peter Pocklington at Gainers – even though it was in Alberta – was so sharp in my mind. You didn't want to create a situation where you could have violence."

The new code was generally perceived as a big improvement over Vander Zalm's Industrial Relations Act, but it was not without its compromises. The NDP's decision not to introduce sectoral bargaining (which, after all, would have allowed tens of thousands of workers to unionize) was considered as much a concession to employers as the compulsory certification vote (if union support was between 45 and 55 percent) was to the unions. By most accounts, the "Three Amigos" process was about as broad a consultation on labour law as it's possible to have without consulting every shopowner and political science undergrad in the province. The subcommittee heard more than 200 oral submissions and received nearly 300 written submissions after visiting eleven communities throughout the province.

Despite the involvement of business at every stage of the process, a few determined members of the BC Chamber of Commerce made a concerted effort to derail the new legislation. Within weeks of Sihota's announcement of the Labour Relations Code, the Chamber – which represents about 13,000 large and small businesses in BC – mobilized its members to line up and take shots at it. Chief among its objections were the Code's elimination of secret ballots on certification drives, the inclusion of secondary boycott rights, and the anti-scab legislation.

Sihota scoffed at the criticism. "If we were to compete with them on the basis of labour matters, we would probably have to undo our code, considerably weaken our workers' compensation provisions, and eliminate many of our social programs," said the minister. "We would have to pretty well rescind our Employment Standards Act and decrease our minimum wage. I don't think most British Columbians want that."

The Chamber argument was hardly surprising. This was the same organization, after all, that gave the government a failing grade for cancelling the BC doctors' pension plan, and sought legal advice when the government reviewed the Kemano Completion Project and agreed to the concept of aboriginal title prior to negotiations on native land claims. It was hardly an ally to begin with.

The Chamber of Commerce, along with the Canadian Federation of Independent Business, may have felt they were being left out of the labour code consultations because Tom Roper – the business representative in the Three Amigos process – came from the BC Business Council, whose member employers are predominantly unionized. These employers are often in the position of fighting unions, explained Tieleman, but "they're not fighting the existence of unions. Whereas the small-business sector is predominantly non-unionized and they wanted to stay that way. So they started agitating."

As for the Chamber's claim that business would pack its bags and move south to Washington and Oregon, Sihota's response was typically blunt. "What a bunch of crap," Sihota said nearly three years after the Labour Relations Code was introduced. "The criticisms that were levelled at the Code were more rhetorical than substantive. [Liberal house leader] Gary Farrell-Collins said if we bring in this code, there won't be any investment in British Columbia. He said that in 1992, correct? And we've got the best performing economy in the country."

Some trade unionists argue that the NDP could have preempted the assault from small business. If the government had wrapped up the consultation by the end of February in time to draft the new law and introduce it in the spring sitting, the BC Fed's Ken Georgetti contends, "our 'friends' in the anti-union, small-business coalition wouldn't even have woken up from the trance that they were in" to launch a campaign against it. Instead, the Coalition of BC Businesses was formed and Kathy Sanderson was appointed chair, to continue the barrage of criticism begun by the BC Chamber of Commerce and the Vancouver Board of Trade.

According to Tieleman, the small business lobby behaved like a spoiled child. "They liked the book, they didn't like the author. They liked the music, they didn't like the composer. If any other government was doing this, they'd be out trumpeting. If it was a right-wing government, they would say 'Look at the BC economy, it's incredible what this government has done.' But it's an NDP government, so they give it no credit at all."

But the new labour code was by no means the only big issue that the government was grappling with that fall. The Labour Relations Act was introduced in the House on October 27, the day after Canadians had voted in a national referendum on Canada's constitution. By this point, there were quite a few chinks in the NDP's armour.

The Deal That Got Away

IN ITS ORIGINAL FORM, THE CHARLOTTETOWN ACCORD TO amend the Canadian constitution was an unprecedented agreement of federal, provincial, territorial and native leaders. It marked the end of an often exhausting five-year campaign in which Canadian citizens had been canvassed, polled or interviewed on the three remaining issues dividing the country: special status for Québec, a reorganized Senate, and self-government for aboriginal peoples.

The process began in 1987 with the Meech Lake Accord, an agreement that would have declared Québec a "distinct society." But the Meech Lake Accord was scuttled by Clyde Wells's refusal to seek its approval in the Newfoundland legislature and by Elijah Harper's famous "No" vote in the Manitoba legislature. In September 1991, Prime Minister Brian Mulroney appointed a special joint committee of the House of Commons and the Senate to canvass the public for input. By the time it was all over the following March, the committee had received more than 3,000 written submissions and heard testimony from 700 individuals. Five months of closed-door negotiations later, Canadians were asked to amend their constitution in a referendum – despite having only the sketchiest knowledge of the details.

The question put to the public was, "Do you agree that the Constitution of Canada should be renewed on the basis of the agreement reached on August 28, 1992?" For most Canadians, who would not be reading the twenty-page final report on the agreement before casting their votes, the notion of approving or rejecting a constitutional document based on the media's coverage of it was rather like depending on the Coles Notes summary to write an undergrad essay on *War and Peace*.

In the months preceding the final agreement, supporters of the accord were optimistic that, with Québec finally onside and national native leaders in consensus, the Canadian public would put an end to its constitutional woes once and for all. Prime Minister Mulroney and his BC lieutenant, Justice Minister Kim Campbell, were brashly confident of the outcome. What deeply misguided cynicism, they wondered, could possibly get in the way of a "Yes" vote?

Things had looked especially promising on Tuesday, July 7, when the federal government led by negotiator Joe Clark, along with nine premiers and the Native Council of Canada, reached what they thought was the final agreement on a package of constitutional reforms after an all-day session at the Toronto Hilton. The deal included distinct society status for Québec, aboriginal self-government and a reformed Senate. It appeared advantageous for the country as a whole, but particularly for BC. All six of BC's demands were included in the deal: a limited distinct society clause for Québec, a BC veto on future constitutional changes to the House of Commons and the Senate, a reformed and elected Senate, more provincial powers over the economy, protection of social programs and a recognition of aboriginal self-government.

Moe Sihota was almost reverential in his recollection of the premier's backroom bargaining skills. Toward the end of one gruelling, late-night session at the External Affairs building, he recalled, a discussion on the Senate was derailed by Alberta Premier Don Getty. Harcourt, who was co-chairing the meeting with former Prime Minister Joe Clark, prevented Clark and Getty from exploding at each other. "We thought we had a deal on the Senate and we were moving on to other issues," said Sihota. "And Ed Roberts [constitutional minister for Newfoundland] came over to me and told me, 'Look, Don Getty's not going to support the Senate.' And I turned around and told Joe Clark, 'Joe, Alberta's off board right now.' And I remember Clark, he had an earphone in his ear, throws it down on the ground, slams the gavel and says, 'We have to have an adjournment for a few minutes.' And Harcourt and Clark go in the corner and talk to Don Getty, and they revisit all of these issues, and there was a wrinkle. They managed to iron out the wrinkle, Clark comes back with Harcourt, and we have a deal. People have no idea how effective Mike was at that meeting. I've never seen Mike so good."

According to Mel Smith, a former constitutional advisor to the Vander Zalm government (and who would later emerge as an opponent of the Charlottetown Accord), BC had "definitely come out ahead" with the new ten-province veto. "Senate representation ... will set up a new dynamic in the halls of power in Ottawa that could have significant positive spillovers in BC," such as "increasing the representation of BC on major boards and commissions" and, possibly, more federal contracts for the province.

Even CKNW radio talk show host and former Socred cabinet minister Rafe Mair – never a big fan of Québec – supported the deal. As of July 7, all that was needed was Québec's signature to make the deal unanimous. While Liberal Premier Robert Bourassa pondered the document, at least two of his ministers responded favourably.

But the deal was doomed to failure long before the referendum votes were counted, and the Canadian public had no opportunity to hear Bourassa's response. One week after the July agreement was reached, Mulroney returned from an economic summit in Europe and pronounced the deal dead. "Mr. Mulroney had an ego the size of this country," Sihota recalled. "And Mr. Mulroney could not, in my view, accept the fact that Joe Clark had successfully brokered a deal. And much to my horror, I watched the following Tuesday as Benoit Bouchard and Brian Mulroney had a press conference and said that the deal would not be satisfactory to the province of Québec ... Benoit Bouchard, who was sort of his Québec lieutenant, just wasn't on board. And if he wasn't on board, then Mr. Mulroney wasn't going to be on board."

Sihota did next what he does so well: he called the media into his office and said, "Mr. Mulroney has to decide whether he is the prime minister of Québec or the prime minister of Canada." The prime minister was not amused. Only weeks earlier at Sussex Drive, Mulroney had wrapped a paternal arm around Sihota's shoulder and told him what a marvelous job he had done for Canada. Now he was calling Harcourt to get him fired.

It was all downhill after that. When Harcourt and Sihota returned from the final negotiating session in Charlottetown at the end of August with a revised accord, Mel Smith and Rafe Mair were no longer on side, and Liberal leader Gordon Wilson and Social Credit leader Jack Weisgerber accused Harcourt of selling out BC's interests. Both objected to the fact that Québec would have special status and would be guaranteed 25 percent of the seats in the House of Commons, even though its population was falling while BC's was rising.

They also attacked the government for items in the accord that had already been approved by nine out of ten provinces. The Senate, they said, would not represent provincial interests in national decision making, and the amending formula would ensure the federal system was permanently dominated by central Canada. Weisgerber, the former Aboriginal Affairs minister, also opposed any recognition of aboriginal self-government "without any clear indication of its scope, jurisdiction, or costs to the Canadian taxpayer."

The campaign leading up to the October 26 referendum vote was more passionate than the average federal election, but far less partisan when it came to the issues. The "Yes" forces were an eclectic mish-mash of establishment elites including all three mainline federal parties, big business and big labour leaders, economists, and media giants, while the "No"s were populist underdogs – a grassroots movement led by talk show hosts, Reform Party conservatives, the National Action Committee on the Status of Women, and social advocacy groups. With each side so dramatically crossing ideological boundaries, it was impossible to frame the debate in terms of "left" or "right" dualisms.

In BC, the "Yes" campaign was led by the NDP caucus behind Harcourt and Constitutional Affairs Minister Moe Sihota, along with such traditional left supporters as BC Federation of Labour president Ken Georgetti (whose sister later emerged as an organizer for the "No" side) and the First Nations Summit – including representatives from 200 BC Indian bands which had unanimously approved the aboriginal rights component. Other NDP heavyweights in favour of the accord included former Premier Dave Barrett and former MLA Rosemary Brown, along with backroom strategists and communication specialists like Hans Brown, Gerry Scott, Ron Johnson and Sheila Fruman.

But the BC "Yes" campaign was supported, politically and financially, by people who wouldn't normally be caught dead embracing an NDP position. The group of BC business leaders cozying up to Harcourt and Sihota included former Socred Attorney General Brian Smith, who had recently become chair of Canadian National, federal Liberal fundraiser Ross Fitzpatrick, Concord Pacific director Stanley Kwok, Canfor chair and CEO Peter Bentley, Westcoast Energy CEO Michael Phelps and Mitsubishi chair Arthur Hara. Then there were Tory and Socred strategists like Jerry Lampert and Ray Castelli, Jess Ketchum and Owen Lippert. "I'm quite taken aback by the diversity of the coalition," said Georgetti, summing up the amazement of many. "I never thought that Jerry Lampert and Hans Brown would ever be working together in the strategy rooms." The union of such strange bedfellows proved to be a major factor in the public response to Harcourt's "Yes" campaign.

The "No" forces in BC were an equally mixed bag. On the left there was Burnaby-Kingsway MP Svend Robinson and Saul Terry of the Union of BC Indian chiefs. Terry, unlike Ovide Mercredi of the Assembly of First Nations, preferred to pursue native rights through Section 35 of the existing constitution, which the union believed already recognized a broad range of aboriginal and treaty rights, including the inherent right of self-government. Gordon Wilson occupied the centre of the spectrum on the "No" side, with Jack Weisgerber, federal Reform Party leader Preston Manning, and former Social Credit constitutional advisor Mel Smith occupying the right. The "No" campaign later suffered the embarrassing support of a rejuvenated Bill Vander Zalm, speaking on behalf of the Family Coalition Party, and Doug Christie, a lawyer who defended white supremacists and anti-Semites and who had once led the separatist Western Canada Concept party.

But the undisputed champion of the "No" side was radio talk show host Rafe Mair, the former Socred Health minister who joined CKNW radio in 1984 and gradually became famous for his on-air tirades against "big government" and central Canada. Mair seemed to enjoy his notoriety as BC's most celebrated fed-basher. In his interviews, Mair preferred going for the jugular. When Harcourt appeared on the show halfway through the campaign, the premier had barely finished his opening small talk before the host ripped him apart.

One of Mair's greatest objections – and it was echoed by other critics throughout the campaign – was that the "Yes" forces, led by Mulroney but also including premiers like Harcourt, were engaging in fearmongering by predicting the end of Canada if the accord failed. He didn't notice that the "No" forces weren't much better. On September 22, Gordon Wilson predicted that a "Yes" vote would lead to the breakup of Canada. "I fear for the province of BC," he told one crowd, explaining that a successful vote for the Charlottetown Accord would force Canada's westernmost province to build stronger links with Washington and Oregon.

Wilson had far more immediate problems than the breakup of Canada. Thanks to his insistence that all Liberal MLAs oppose Charlottetown, he was now facing the breakup of his caucus. Wilson had made it clear early in the campaign that he wanted a united caucus, but he never did explain how he would deal with dissenters. Yes, those who supported the accord were allowed to speak their minds, but no, they weren't allowed to do so publicly. Yes, MLAs who didn't fall in line with his position would be reprimanded, but no, that did not mean they'd be penalized. By September 18, Wilson had a big problem on his hands; house leader David Mitchell, caucus chair Art Cowie, and MLAs Val Anderson and Clive Tanner had all gone on public record in support of the accord.

Meanwhile, the Accord was dying a slow death. In BC, only 34 percent of people surveyed were inclined to vote "Yes," while 50 percent were leaning toward "No." Opponents of the accord accused the "Yes" side of forcing the issue by saying that Canadians were tired of constitutional debate. They were also offended by Dave Barrett's remark that British Columbians should "hold their noses and vote Yes" because they had no choice.

Nor did Harcourt escape blame. The premier admitted that he was "confused" about the House of Commons seat count when he was preparing the final numbers for restructuring, and that he never expected the criticism the government received for its support of gender equality in the Senate. Vaughn Palmer later described how he heard one NDP strategist complaining about the criticism. Didn't people realize that Nova Scotia and Ontario supported gender balance? "The poor fellow had just discovered people here don't give a damn how they do things in other places," mused Palmer.

Harcourt – who *Province* columnist Brian Kieran was now referring to as "Premier Bonehead" – was contrite about his mistakes. "If I've led to some misinformation or have not been able to express myself as clearly as you'd like, I'll try to do better in the future," he said. Stan Persky, the *Sun*'s media critic, summed up the premier's problems thus: "What the media detected is that Harcourt either didn't do his homework or else he doesn't have a proper grasp of constitutional questions. If true, that's more than a minor flaw. For both politicians and pundits, when you're playing on a stage like this one, the sound and fury had better signify something."

If Harcourt's handling of the debate left the public unsure about his position, the premier only confused matters further on October 2 when he called the legislature into session for October 20. Only two weeks earlier he had maintained that the time for debate about the accord was over, but now he was adamant that British Columbians needed to know their MLAs' positions on the issue. Not only did he intend to debate the constitution with less than a week remaining before the referendum – and wouldn't rule out a house vote on the issue – he planned to begin the debate on the same day the government introduced its long-awaited amendments to the provincial labour code.

Gordon Wilson protested that Harcourt was using the Charlottetown Accord as a smokescreen to sneak through the new labour code with as little discussion as possible. A more likely scenario, however, was that the government was using the accord to exploit the growing division in the Liberal ranks. Surely a free vote in the House would embarrass Wilson, who had been facing a mutiny in his caucus for several days. By Tuesday, October 6, Harcourt's instincts appeared to be right on the mark; both Art Cowie and David Mitchell had broken publicly with Wilson and signed on to the "Yes" campaign. To make matters worse for the Liberal leader, David Mitchell resigned as house leader in the first of several challenges that would plague Wilson's leadership in the coming months.

But the premier soon had his own problem. The same day Cowie and Mitchell made their announcements, Moe Sihota was in the Interior town of Quesnel, talking tough about the accord. Sihota was going out of his way to convince the audience that Québec was not getting more out of the accord than BC, but the timing of his comment couldn't have been worse. Referring to himself in the third person, Sihota recalled the Charlottetown meetings he attended, "[Québec Premier Robert] Bourassa came to that table and ran into a brick wall formed by nine other governments, where particularly people like [New-foundland Premier Clyde] Wells, [Alberta Premier Don] Getty and Sihota said, 'Look, there is no way that you are going to get special status and we are going to keep the equality of the provinces provisions in there.' He lost. Nine governments looked him in the eye and said no." That comment, reported in Québec through a French-speaking reporter who heard Sihota's speech, was used by Québécois opponents of the deal as further evidence that Bourassa sold Québec short. Sihota's remarks received major TV and radio coverage throughout Québec the following day and were the lead referendum story in most major French language newspapers on Thursday. "THE PROVINCES SAY NO TO BOURASSA/Sihota drops a rock on Québec premier's head," screamed a headline in the *Journal de Montréal*, Québec's largest-circulation daily.

For Harcourt, this was the first of many occasions in which he was forced to clarify, defend, back away from, or otherwise explain a "Sihota-ism" − one of those well-intended, refreshingly blunt but strategically embarrassing comments by one of his most popular ministers. In this case, the premier moved swiftly to distance himself from Sihota's remark and even contacted Bourassa to apologize. "I don't think Québec lost, that's the issue," he told reporters. "There wasn't that atmosphere − it wasn't a question of staring anyone down ... I was in the room with Clyde Wells and Robert Bourassa and I can tell you that Robert Bourassa was tough and looking after the interests of Québec and the people of Québec, but he was there for Canada too." Sihota, for his part, was apologetic. "It's embarrassing that the separatists would take a comment and use it for their own political purposes ... I can't control that," he said. "[But] the intention was to point out to people in British Columbia the principle of equality of provinces, the fact that any power Québec had was available for all the provinces."

The following week, Harcourt finally found his footing on the referendum debate. At a Victoria "Yes" rally of about 200 people, he scolded the "No" forces for a series of misleading statements about the meaning of native self-government. Stopping just short of accusing his opponents of racism, Harcourt condemned the "distortions intended to raise fears among British Columbians and Canadians − distortions that are designed to appeal to the worst of emotions." A "Yes" vote would lead to "a partnership based on justice and fairness," he said, while a "No" vote would mean "continued instability and confrontation. We've had far too much of that between aboriginal and non-aboriginal people. It means continuing the welfare state mentality and economic dependency."

Harcourt was optimistic that a "Yes" vote could still happen, that many voters would wait until referendum day before making their decision. His speech amazed Vaughn Palmer, who had waited weeks for Harcourt to show some enthusiasm for the cause. "For the first time, he has a serviceable text. For the first time, he is delivering it with some conviction. For the first time, he has a long list of reasons to vote Yes on Oct. 26 ... I figure he's dreaming but give him credit for at last showing some strength, sincerity and enthusiasm for the cause."

Harcourt had been receiving better reviews of late. New Brunswick Premier Frank McKenna, during a visit to BC in mid-October, told a group of 100 business and labour leaders in Vancouver that he was amazed at complaints that BC had been shortchanged by the deal. "I laughed back home when I heard that the deal was having some trouble in BC and that people were critical of the premier of BC," said the Liberal premier. "How can they be critical of him?" McKenna, echoing earlier praise from John Turner, described Harcourt as "the best chairman that we've had in all of my years in politics ... During the constitutional process there were a couple of times when the federal chairperson seemed incapable of getting any consensus and things started breaking down, where several of the premiers intervened and said 'Look, would it be possible for Premier Harcourt to take over as chairman to try to get this thing back on the rails?'"

McKenna added that Harcourt won larger gains for BC in both the Commons and the Senate than any other province, and won the clause in the accord stating that no province would receive less than 95 percent of the Commons seats it would get based on strict representation by population. "He did all of those things and I walked away by losing four senators and go home to New Brunswick and everybody thinks I've done a pretty good job." Saskatchewan's NDP Premier Roy Romanow agreed with McKenna's assessment. "He teased, he bullied, he pleaded, he schmoozed, he worked the crowd," Romanow said of Harcourt's performance. "He chaired from about 2:30 to about 10:30 with no dinner break and he did it with skill. It was as good as I have seen."

Despite these glowing endorsements, however, the premier was winning few converts among the BC electorate. Ten days before the vote, an Angus Reid poll showed that the "No" side had gained slightly, at 56 percent support in BC, while the "Yes" support remained stuck at about 34 percent. "The problem with the Charlotte-town Accord is that it is serving as a lightning rod for people to say No to a whole range of things," Harcourt conceded. "An unpopular prime minister, the GST, the free trade agreement, what have you." But even if the accord failed, wouldn't the premier support another round of negotiations? Out of the question. "If people say No on October 26, then that's it. It's over," he said. "If I thought we could sweeten the pot for BC and be able to say No to the 25 percent guarantee for Québec, then I would go back. But there is no realistic chance of that happening."

When all the votes were cast on October 26, the final results for the nation were: Yes – 44.7 percent, No – 54.3 percent. The failure of the accord was most dramatic in the western provinces, with BC casting the loudest rejection of all: Yes – 31.9 percent, No – 67.8 percent. While Québec sovereignists declared the result a victory for the sepa-ratist cause (within a couple of years the province elected a Parti Québecois government, and on October 30, 1995 held a second refer-endum on sovereignty that was defeated by a single percentage point), and several native leaders lamented the decision as a repudia-tion of their own sovereignty ("We were looking for parole and we got a further sentence to continued inequality in Canada," said Ron George of the Native Council of Canada), political pundits tried to make sense of the result for Canadians at large.

On a national scale, the result was a rejection of the so-called "elites" – politicians, business and labour leaders, key interest groups and top media commentators – who produced and packaged the accord for the general public. Mulroney especially had underestimated the level of antipathy that many Canadians had developed for him since his first election win in 1984. Within months of the accord's defeat, the former president of Iron Ore Canada would resign in disgrace from the prime minister's office, leaving a trail of scandal which was later explored in meticulous detail by journalist Stevie Cameron in her 1994 book, *On the Take: Crime, Corruption and Greed in the Mulroney Years*.

In BC, the power of Rafe Mair's radio program was credited with shifting the momentum to the "No" side early on, and Gordon Wilson received kudos for his campaign despite the internal discord of his Liberal caucus. Ultimately though, the premier had to accept much of the blame for the "No" victory in BC. Harcourt had remained far too long in the shadows to mount much of a case for the "Yes" forces. He had also underestimated the level of anti-Québec, anti-native sentiment in BC that allowed the "No" forces to pick up speed in the final weeks.

But Harcourt did not agree that the defeat of the accord was a personal setback. "I think most British Columbians had a whole series of issues that made up their minds to vote yes or no," he told reporters, denying that his own leadership was a factor. He also pledged to keep on fighting for native self-government, adding that several provisions from Charlottetown could be saved through separate, non-constitutional agreements among provincial and federal governments.

BY THE FALL OF 1992, THE NDP HAD SPENT MOST OF ITS FIRST year in power trying to walk a tightrope between the expectations of its traditional supporters and the wariness of the business community who feared the government would run up the deficit. In terms of concrete achievements, there was still much to be done, and dozens of items from the party's 48-point platform had yet to see the light of day: pay equity, environmental changes, revisions in health care, and increased access to education were still on the horizon.

Harcourt had quickly discovered that his biggest challenge as premier was in lowering the expectations of longtime supporters who had waited sixteen years for the party to regain power and wanted big changes, fast. "We've had some tough challenges being a rookie government, and the financial situation has made us very cautious financially, which I would have been anyway, in terms of spending," said Harcourt, adding that the party's left would have to be more patient. "Look, anyone who wants instant gratification is not being realistic. We have to deal with some fundamental issues, but we also have to deal with some very real economic considerations."

For the NDP's first year in power, at least, this conflict between "fundamental issues" and "economic considerations" would play itself out most dramatically in the government's handling of provincial health care priorities.

4

New Directions ...
Same Old Turf

PROMISE 39 OF THE NDP'S 48-POINT PLAN FOR BC ENDS WITH one of those optimistic truisms that sounds impressive during an election campaign but are difficult to achieve in gaining power. "A New Democrat government," it says, "will seek the cooperation [of] and work closely with our health professionals and workers in making the health care system work more effectively." Sure, the skeptics replied, and while you're at it, why not try to solve world hunger, restore the ozone layer, and put an end to hostilities in the Middle East? Apart from the environment, health care was the most emotionally charged area of public policy in BC. Making the system work more effectively would require a lot more than good intentions from the new government.

All across Canada during the 1980s, universal medicare appeared to be in jeopardy as politicians, hospital administrators, medical professionals and unionized workers engaged in a neverending tug-of-war for the dwindling health dollar. The process had quietly begun in 1977, when the federal government's creation of the Established Programs Financing Act (EPF) changed the funding system for provincial expenditures on health and post-secondary education from cost-sharing to unconditional grants. This approach, which allocated monies according to the national GDP and provincial population size, was meant to ensure that the federal government would not commit itself to sharing in expenditures "over whose growth it had no control."

With the conservative shift in federal fiscal policy in the early 1980s, the government revised the EPF formula to reduce federal contributions below those produced by the original formula. Six years into office, Brian Mulroney introduced an Expenditure Control Plan that froze the per capita transfer for the five-year period from 1990-91 to 1994-95. It didn't take long for the provinces to feel the effects of this policy; bed closures and hospital waiting lists became the order of the day, while hospital workers faced layoffs and displacement at alarming rates and administrators explored various ways to trim budgets. By the fall of 1991, provincial governments were under increasing pressure to blame "spiralling costs" for the health care crisis. Soon the ominous words "two-tiered, American-style health care" were on everybody's lips.

In BC, the NDP's good intentions from the election campaign were challenged by a major study on the health care system that landed on the premier's desk only a week after the party took office. The Royal Commission on Health Care and Costs, chaired by Justice Peter Seaton, was appointed by Bill Vander Zalm in the wake of Mulroney's 1990 budget. However, the Socreds never got a chance to apply their free-market solutions to the situation in BC.

The Seaton commission's final report, as it turned out, included a number of recommendations that were more consistent with NDP philosophy than that of Social Credit. Titled "Closer to Home," Seaton's report called for increased local management of health services and a shift away from acute care hospitals to long-term care facilities and home care. It also targeted doctors, urging the government to "limit expenditures for physicians' services by imposing an annual global cap on the total billings by physicians."

The report's conclusions appeared to endorse those of a favourite NDP text, *Second Opinion: What's Wrong With Canada's Health Care System and How to Fix It*. Co-authored by Michael Rachlis and Carol Kushner, the book targets extra billing, fee-for-service payments for doctors, and hospital bureaucracies as the major culprits in health care cost overruns. The Seaton report's focus on community-based care was consistent with the grassroots social democratic values the NDP promoted in its campaign literature.

But some of the proposed changes were not universally embraced by the health care community. The NDP was inheriting a system run by people who had no ideological difficulty with the federal government's slash-and-burn approach to health care. Many of the hospital board members, who later voted against an employment security agreement for health care workers, were Socred appointees whose own positions would be wiped out by health care reform. The government also knew that it faced resistance from health care workers whose jobs were also in jeopardy under the new reforms. Thus, Health Minister Elizabeth Cull decided to table the report and launch a year-long consultation process before acting on its conclusions.

'Barking Up a Dead Dog's Ass'

AS THE NDP BEGAN THIS SENSITIVE PROCESS, THE GOVERN- ment was about to experience its first significant challenge on the labour relations front. By the end of March 1992, the 29,000-member Hospital Employees Union had been without a contract for a year and was fully prepared to go on strike. The prospect of major job action by a major health care union was not something Mike Harcourt was look- ing forward to, especially so soon after the election. During the cam- paign, the NDP had made several promises to health care workers, including pay equity and free collective bargaining – principles the party had long embraced in opposition. Based on these promises, the HEU had decided for the first time to commit big money to the NDP's election effort, fully confident that negotiations with the new govern- ment would be smooth and productive.

Within days of the election, however, it was clear that the union had a fight on its hands. First, the Health Labour Relations Association (HLRA), the employer representative for hospitals, rejected HEU goals including a fair wage increase, pay equity and action on workload issues. (The union claimed an increase in back injuries and work-related stress.)

HLRA president Gordon Austin predicted that nothing would change under an NDP government. As far as he was concerned, the bed closures, layoffs and contracting out that began under Social Credit would continue at the same rate under the NDP. "I do not believe that an NDP government, when it looks at the economy in BC, will be able to finance major wage increases for public sector employees," said Austin. For his part, the HLRA president was determined that health care workers should not receive more than a 2 percent wage hike, even though public sector wage settlements were running at 7 percent.

From that point on, it was war between the HEU and HLRA. On December 19, 1991, the government-appointed mediator, Stephen Kelleher, suspended the talks indefinitely. The HEU's provincial executive, realizing that job action might be necessary to force a settlement, decided early in January to hold a strike vote. On February 13, HEU members voted 78 percent in favour of a strike. The HLRA was determined not to bargain, and took advantage of a seldom-used provision in Bill 19 (the Socred labour code which was still in effect while the NDP government was preparing the new labour code), which allowed it to apply to the Industrial Relations Council (IRC) for a new mediator. IRC commissioner Ed Peck appointed veteran mediator Vince Ready as Stephen Kelleher's replacement. The HLRA wanted to prevent the HEU from using its strike mandate to force the employer to bargain a fair contract, and Ready's appointment ensured that any job action by the HEU would be illegal if it were taken before Ready was ready, as it were, to report out. But the new mediator had barely settled into the position when Gordon Austin tabled the HLRA's "final offer" on March 4, 1992. HEU rejected the offer by the same 78 percent vote its members had cast in favour of a strike.

One reason for the NDP's reluctance to conclude a quick and easy wage settlement was the Finance Ministry's discovery of an exploding deficit. Thanks to the widespread media hysteria surrounding the $2 billion projected deficit, the government was beginning to retreat from the bold, pro-union rhetoric its members employed during the election campaign. As the HEU/HLRA battle continued into the spring, cabinet remained out of the dispute, only entering the picture in March when escalating job action and a union rally at the legislature threatened to embarrass it.

On March 10, 500 angry health care workers gathered on the front steps of the legislature to protest the NDP's failure to intervene. The crowd booed as Health Minister Elizabeth Cull repeated that the government would not get involved in the dispute. Harcourt had already met privately in his office with an HEU delegation, and things had not gone well. "It was a very tense meeting," one HEU member recalled. "We brought in a few of our ordinary members to talk about workload issues, just to bring home the flesh and blood humanity of the dispute. Harcourt said, 'We have to stand firm on the budget.' He was clearly frustrated with the way the system was set up, but he said it was 'like turning a supertanker around, and you can't do it on a dime.' I think he said that to everyone that year."

There were many hard feelings when the premier emerged from the twenty-minute meeting to talk with the press. Harcourt was aware of the rally and had heard some of the chants ("We got you elected!" "Make good on your promises!"), but was clearly not contrite. "Who got us elected are the voters of BC ... and we're here to govern for all the people of BC," he told reporters. Then, throwing out one of his oft-quoted election slogans, he added, "We've had far too much under the previous government of 'friends and insiders' and giving special deals to people."

That comment hardly endeared the premier to the HEU. As another unionist recalled, "Basically, what Harcourt was saying about our members was that these people were barking up a dead dog's ass — that was the message. It was a total slap in the face. We felt we were being treated like Socred patronage deals for corporate real estate types, when in fact we were representing some of the lowest paid workers in the province."

How could the premier and Elizabeth Cull kiss off one of the NDP's strongest supporters so easily, and so soon into the government's mandate? It may have had something to do with the HEU's maverick status in the provincial labour movement. The union had remained outside the BC Federation of Labour until 1984, and since that time had remained something of an outcast within the labour mainstream. This alone limited its clout with the government.

There was also bad blood between the HEU and the NDP, much of it the product of NDP red-baiting. Many in the party saw the HEU as a haven for unrepentant Communists and fellow radical travellers; they singled out secretary-business manager Carmela Allevato for attack, despite her solid reputation in the union movement, because she was a Communist. Now these ideological differences were playing themselves out on the provincial stage, as the HEU struggled to get a contract.

But the NDP's cool response to the union was due more to financial panic than partisan resentments. Two weeks after the March 11 rally, the government tabled its first budget and announced that the province was expecting $60 million less from the federal government for health and education costs in the coming year. Along with the Seaton report's much-publicized recommendation to close 1,000 hospital beds across the province, the timing was bad for a quick wage settlement. The last thing Harcourt and Cull needed was to be accused in the media of caving in to the HEU at the expense of the sick and dying.

As bargaining resumed on March 29, the HLRA and HEU were still far apart on pay equity. The HLRA's offer of 4 percent adjustments over three years was still about half of what the BCGEU received, 1 percent less than what CUPE members at UBC negotiated, half the wage adjustment that teachers received and .5 percent less than nurses got. On March 31 – a year to the day after the last contract expired – HEU began escalating, rotating job action. On April 10, 5,000 health care workers from around the Lower Mainland marched to the Plaza of Nations. Five days later, the first picket line went up at Delta General Hospital, and by April 23, there were pickets in every region of the province.

The HLRA responded with an alarmist media attack on the HEU. Among its claims, HLRA said the job action was causing hospitals to close beds, and patients would have to be flown out of the country for treatment. Elizabeth Cull responded to the pressure by offering to fly cardiac and cancer patients out of the province. But the Health minister was left with egg on her face when only two patients required out-of-province care. "She totally bought into the HLRA's publicity stunt," recalled an HEU activist. "Our office was deluged with phone calls from people who were concerned about the situation. So we just gave them Elizabeth Cull's phone number, and that was the end of it!"

By the end of April, the government was shying away from its hard-line stance. Many in the party could recall what happened the last time an NDP government imposed back-to-work legislation – the Barrett New Democrats were badly defeated in the 1975 election. Thus, when Labour Minister Moe Sihota finally sat down with the HEU executive on April 22, there was none of the tough talk that character-ized the March 11 demonstration at the legislature. Instead, Sihota appointed Don Munroe as a special conciliator to report on the dis-pute, and an agreement was finally reached in May. The contract included a provision that would give HEU members wage comparabil-ity with the BC Government Employees Union by October 1994.

'Sweetheart Deals', Part One

THE NDP'S EXPERIENCE WITH THE HEU AGREEMENT WAS A storm signal to the government that more confrontation would occur unless something was done about job security for health care workers. Following recommendations from the Seaton report, the government introduced a funding formula that lowered the rate of hospital services according to population rates. But this policy had a punitive effect on northern communities, where hospitals served as all-purpose health care and social service facilities.

In 1992, the government closed 587 beds and served layoff notices to more than 1,000 health care workers (resulting in the loss or reduc-tion of full-time work) in Terrace, Kitimat, Prince Rupert and other small communities. The outcry was so great that the government was forced to call an inquiry into the funding crisis. More than 60 groups made submissions before the inquiry. Because only a handful of work-ers received job placement assistance or retraining as a result of the layoffs, unions began to demand a more meaningful system to help displaced workers; the government's labour adjustment strategy was simply too vague to adequately address the issue of displacement.

This concern over displacement led to the government's July 1992 appointment of Health Sciences Association executive director Peter Cameron to a post in the Ministry of Health. Cameron, who as an assistant deputy minister took much of his direction from Glen Clark, was a left-wing pragmatist and an ideal appointee for the position which dealt with labour adjustment and trade union relations. The fact that he came from one of the three health care unions helped restore some trust in the government that had been damaged by the HEU's round of negotiations. Early in January 1993, as the government was preparing its budget and long-awaited response to the Seaton report, Cameron held a secret meeting with the three unions to bring them up to date. Using a flip chart, he explained how wage increases would achieve pay equity, but at a price: under the government's health care restructuring plan, 4,500 full-time equivalent jobs would be cut from the acute care sector. This target was later revised to 4,800.

"Cameron told us that from now on we'd have to think of 'employment security' instead of 'job security'," recalled one unionist who attended the meeting. "Basically, this meant that the unions would have to move to a shorter work week and employees would have to accept postings elsewhere in the region." It also meant that the unions would have to reopen their collective agreements. Formal talks began on January 29, with the union bargaining committees sitting down with a government negotiating team led by Cameron. Cabinet ministers like Clark, Sihota and Women's Equality Minister Penny Priddy — who helped out with pay equity issues — were advised of the discussions.

The unions were well prepared for change when Elizabeth Cull finally announced the government's response to the Seaton report on February 2. "New Directions in Health Care" was a reform plan with 38 major health policy changes. Included among the cost-cutting measures was yet another series of bed closures. This time, 2,000 of BC's acute care beds were eliminated, continuing the provincewide trend that had already affected so many jobs in the north.

The first casualty turned out to be the biggest. On February 15, Cull announced the closure of Shaughnessy Hospital, an acute care facility with 250 beds. The government defended the move by arguing that the building was old and had reached the end of its use. Upgrading the site to satisfy earthquake standards was too expensive. However, all Shaughnessy workers would retain their jobs by moving to other facilities within the region.

Vancouver Mayor Gordon Campbell, who sat beside Elizabeth Cull as she made the announcement, supported the decision on the grounds that Grace Women's Hospital and the BC Children's Hospital would now be able to expand (Grace and Children's are on the same site as Shaughnessy). But the announcement sparked angry opposition from health care workers and Shaughnessy-area residents that took weeks to subside. Even the BC Medical Association was able to make political hay out of the issue.

There were also signs that Shaughnessy would not be the only hospital shut down by the government. When the HEU publicly asked Elizabeth Cull to confirm the existence of a list of hospitals slated for closure, the Health minister angrily denied the rumour, accusing the HEU of causing a panic. (Two years later, however, the premier's chief of staff, Chris Chilton, testified under oath that a list had been compiled that included ten more hospitals recommended for closure. The plan was later scrapped thanks to NDP provincial secretary and former party president Hans Brown. According to a union insider, Brown "nearly flipped" when he saw the list, and he advised the Health Ministry that the government would be "committing electoral suicide" if it followed through on the plan.)

Meanwhile, the three unions continued their talks with the government on a proposed employment security agreement. Discussions continued throughout the Shaughnessy controversy for 44 days, finally resulting in a March 12 agreement that was ratified by the unions on April 20. But the HLRA, despite its earlier intention to ratify the new health accord, and despite 55 percent of its membership voting in favour, rejected the deal on April 24.

The HLRA had thrown another obstacle in the way of a deal when it leaked a cost-benefit analysis of the agreement. While the three unions were willing to assist the government's cutback measures, the

HLRA study claimed that reducing the work week was not enough. According to one estimate, the government could have saved $529 million by cutting several jobs altogether. In raising this figure, management was suggesting that issues such as pay equity and the HEU wage comparability adjustments – provisions already won in the 1992 round of bargaining – should be part of the current negotiations. Indeed, the righteous tone adopted by management was so convincing that various media pundits criticized the accord as a "sweetheart deal" for the unions. By July 1995, however, the HLRA's cost-benefit analysis appeared to be groundless; according to HEU calculations there were 4.2 million fewer hours worked in the first two years of the health accord, for a total compounded saving of $179.2 million. The net saving, which subtracted the costs of the Health Labour Adjustment Agency (which finds employment for displaced workers) and other job-related programs that amounted to $37 million, was $142.2 million.

The HLRA's strategy at this point may have been a defensive tactic on behalf of Socred-appointed hospital administrators worried about their own positions. Under the health care reform, hospital boards were to be replaced by community health councils and regional health boards, and the accord obliged hospitals to lay off management in equal proportion to unionized workers. However, by 1995 the rate of downsizing among hospital staff was still much higher than the rate of attrition among management. While Opposition MLAs criticized the deal in the legislature, the unions met with HLRA and government officials to try and salvage the agreement. Once again, mediator Vince Ready was brought in to work out a deal. After identifying 25 issues for clarification, both HLRA and the unions returned to their memberships and the deal was finally ratified by both sides in July 1993. Under the new Health Labour Accord, known to the unions as the Employment Security Agreement, the unions agreed to eliminate 4,800 full-time jobs in acute care facilities while the employers agreed to reduce the work week to 36 hours from 37.5 hours. Management also agreed to refrain from contracting out services, to offer comparable jobs within the facility or region, and to provide voluntary options for early retirement and job sharing. Staff reductions would first be made through attrition, and layoffs would only occur when a displaced worker refused to accept a job with equivalent wages and benefits elsewhere in the public sector. The agreement also established the Healthcare Labour Adjustment Agency, whose first task was to help workers displaced by the Shaughnessy closure.

Management was happy because the government prevented a 3 to 4 percent wage hike while achieving an across-the-board reduction in the acute care workforce. The unions were happy because the shorter work week addressed the workload issue without cutting jobs, and the agreement allowed for a general wage increase of 1.5 percent while keeping the benefits unions had won in earlier contracts. But despite what appeared to be a fair compromise after a lengthy and difficult negotiation process, the Harcourt government was hammered by the Opposition, medical professionals, and most of the media for having caved in to the unions with a sweetheart deal.

Much of the blame for this perception belonged with the NDP itself. According to union insiders, the government's health care strategy was weakened from the start by four familiar flaws: the Harcourt cabinet's refusal to take advice from natural allies in the labour and progressive movements, its tendency to bend over backward to impress its adversaries, its preference for staff advisors with little experience in BC politics, and its lack of an overall communications strategy to promote progressive health policies around the province.

The Health Labour Accord was a perfect example of these problems. "They should have known that administrators wouldn't like it, because it threatened their power," said Jean Greatbatch of the BC Nurses Union. "They should have known the Liberals would make hay out of it, that Vaughn Palmer would do a number on it. There was no plan of communication to promote it as progressive health policy." The Shaughnessy closure was another example: health care unions had advised the government to appoint a task force to set priorities for hospital services instead of closing down Shaughnessy with a unilateral decision. While unions organized a community campaign against the closure, the BCMA managed to exploit the issue in order to bash the government in advance of its own negotiations.

'Sweetheart Deals', Part II

FOR ALL THE MEDIA'S TALK ABOUT A SWEETHEART DEAL FOR health care unions, the same criticism was not raised a month later when the government reached a generous agreement with the province's 6,000 doctors. Elizabeth Cull's August 23, 1993 announcement of a deal with the BCMA marked a reversal of government policy which, in retrospect, seems far more a sweetheart deal than the Health Labour Accord.

The NDP's eighteen-month war with the BCMA was a curious development, given the congenial relationship the BCMA had enjoyed with the previous NDP government of Dave Barrett and Health Minister Dennis Cocke. However, faced with a mounting debt and a royal commission report recommending major cutbacks in the Medical Services Plan, Harcourt, Cull and Finance Minister Glen Clark saw no reason why doctors shouldn't carry some of the health care burden. Their one big mistake was their failure to consult the medical community about the Seaton report, or even to welcome token input during budget deliberations.

This much was evident on March 13, when BCMA president Gur Singh bemoaned the fact that no doctors had been appointed to a 24-member committee dealing with the Seaton report's findings. Singh blasted Elizabeth Cull in the press, calling her "two-faced" and accusing her of squeezing out the BCMA while favouring the HEU, BC Nurses Union and the Registered Nurses Association. "We had hoped for a new era of cooperation," Singh lamented, "but the NDP is going out of its way to pick a fight with us."

The NDP's first budget earned particular scorn from the BCMA. The doctors' main objection was that Bill 13 would limit the global budget for doctor's fees at $1.27 billion for the following year and impose an individual cap on doctors' incomes. This was a "soft cap" which would come into effect, for general practitionners, once they had earned $300,000 in a year, and for specialists once they had earned $360,000. If a family doctor billed the Medical Services Plan for more than $300,000, he or she would receive two thirds of the excess; after

$340,000, doctors would be paid in 50-cent dollars. A similar scale would apply to specialists.

The doctors also objected to Bill 14, which wiped out the controversial pension plan negotiated by the Socreds. Toward the end of his administration, Bill Vander Zalm signed an agreement committing the government to a fully subsidized $25 million pension plan – an agreement reached through collective bargaining, but only after BCMA president and future Liberal MP Hedy Fry had taken the doctors' case directly to the premier.

Doctors' response to the budget was predictable. A Kelowna heart specialist interviewed by the Vancouver *Sun* predicted longer lineups for heart surgery as doctors fled the country to escape the salary cap, while a Vancouver heart surgeon predicted that the cap wouldn't save the system any money. "It will cost the government the same amount of money, whether I do 300 cases or two people do 150 cases. The patients will have to be done, regardless," Robert Miyagishima told the *Sun*. And Gur Singh accused the government of applying a double standard. "They should have negotiated with us, the same way they negotiated with the HEU, the same way they negotiated with nurses," said the BCMA president.

Singh found an unlikely ally in BC Federation of Labour president Ken Georgetti. "If they were our affiliates, we would scream blue murder," said Georgetti, adding that the government was interfering with the doctors' right to free collective bargaining. But Elizabeth Cull refused to take the bait. "I think doctors realize we all have to do our part in hard economic times," Cull told reporters the day after the budget was announced. "We need changes in the health care system, that's pretty obvious. And this is just one of them."

But scrapping the pension plan was much harder to explain. In an interview with the *Sun*'s Vaughn Palmer, Glen Clark said that the NDP's initial plan was to renegotiate the agreement or wait for it to expire. A closer look, however, revealed that neither option was possible. "It's a perpetual agreement," he told Palmer. "The previous government signed something that requires the taxpayers to contribute $25 million a year forever." Since the agreement couldn't be changed, the government simply decided to render it invalid. Hence

Bill 14, the Professional Retirement Savings Plan Agreement Extinguishment Act. The new law extinguished all the government's obligations, including its promise to contribute $25 million per year to the pension plan. "The retirement plan is terminated," said Clause 3. "The BC Medical Association and other persons are not entitled to any entitlement arising from the plan." Furthermore: "No contractual arrangements between the government and the doctors to provide retirement benefits shall be deemed to exist ... and no undertaking by the government to make $25 million available annually shall be deemed to exist."

Vaughn Palmer could barely contain his delight at being handed such delicious column material. "I bet you didn't know your government could do that," he mused. "Deem something right out of existence and deem in addition that it never did exist ... Don't you love the way they use the language? George Orwell himself could not have put it better."

In a final gesture designed to cover all the government's bases, Bill 14 stated that "no action for damages or compensation against the government, the medical commission or any person arises by reason of this act." It was this clause, as much as anything else in the bill, that convinced the BCMA that the NDP was engaging in an ideological assault on the medical profession. As Palmer pointed out, "New Democrats used to denounce this kind of highhanded legislation when they were in Opposition." So what made them think they could get away with it now?

As they soon discovered, doctor-bashing has never been a winning platform for any government. "No reform of our health-care system, however well-motivated, will succeed without the support of the medical profession," wrote Dr. Michael Rachlis, co-author of *Second Opinion*. Former Socred Health Minister Jim Nielsen could vouch for that. Despite his efforts throughout the 1980s, Nielsen tried and failed to restrict the number of billing numbers in the province or regulate where new doctors could practise. Watching the new government with detached amusement, he predicted that the NDP would be in for a rough ride. "Overall, the government does not win this fight," he told the *Sun*. "It's pretty tough to beat the doctors. The problem is that individuals do not think their own doctor is overpaid or anything like that."

Among other things, the NDP had failed to anticipate the dangers of annoying upper-middle-class professionals with clout. Doctors, typically among the most articulate citizens of any society, also tend to be politically well organized. In the months following the introduction of Bills 13 and 14, the BCMA committed a war chest of $3 million to the fight – including $750,000 for an advertising campaign – and hired a team of high-profile consultants to help combat the legislation. Thanks to people like former Socred guru Patrick Kinsella and federal Liberal David McPhee, the campaign was as slick as the well-oiled election machine from the heyday of Social Credit. Within a few weeks, the BC public was subjected to a flurry of full-page newspaper ads, half-hour television programs, letters to patients, leaflets, and posters in every doctor's office in the province. In most cases, the premier and Elizabeth Cull were painted as irrational demagogues; physicians were the noble, helpless victims of a hostile government.

The ads were clever enough. One television spot captured the moment from the 1991 CBC-TV election debate in which Harcourt held up his Medical Services CareCard in one hand and his American Express card in the other as he tried to explain the difference between Social Credit and NDP approaches to health care. The BCMA appropriated the image with the added warning, "This man and his government could be hazardous to your health." Two other ads, meant to embarrass Elizabeth Cull and Labour Minister Moe Sihota, quoted 1990 statements in which both Opposition MLAs expressed their support for negotiations with doctors. "If power doesn't corrupt, it can affect one's memory," said one ad.

Harcourt put on a brave face throughout the media assault, acknowledging that he should have consulted with doctors before introducing Bills 13 and 14. "We had to make a lot of tough decisions fast," he told the Victoria *Times-Colonist*. "We didn't consult as much as we'd have liked to, but we had to cut the deficit while maintaining health care services." He bristled at suggestions that the BCMA should have sat in on the MSP budget deliberations. Whether it was health care, education or highways, he added, it was the government's job to set the budget – not doctors, unions, or any other special interest group. After the kicking he took from the HEU for saying he'd had enough of "friends and insiders" determining budgets, this was a wise move on the premier's part.

But the weight of an expensive media campaign is difficult to counter, and the BCMA's sustained pressure on the government appeared to be having an effect. On June 3, two weeks after a BCMA-commissioned Marktrend poll found that 87 percent of nearly 500 doctors preferred binding arbitration to a government-imposed settlement, Elizabeth Cull announced that Bill 13 would be scrapped. Legislation replacing Bill 13 eliminated the cap on individual doctors' fees while maintaining the global cap, and created a new medical services commission to oversee the health care budget. Membership on the commission would be split evenly among the BCMA, the government and the public.

That announcement alarmed many in the press gallery, who didn't expect the NDP to cave in so quickly. "The minister not only proposes to rewrite the Medical Services Act to set up a new commission to oversee MSP funds," wrote Thomson News Victoria correspondent John Pifer, "she includes three doctors on that commission. Thus, they in effect would be reviewing and setting their own payments. Cull has also agreed to give the doctors an unprecedented 'sneak peek' at the new legislation, something not accorded to any other group or profession. From all this, it is obvious the doctors' anti-government campaign is hurting."

Despite these unprecedented privileges, the BCMA was not about to budge. Adamant that the global cap be removed from the legislation, the new president, Steve Hardwicke, turned up the rhetoric and made several threats as the Medical and Health Care Services Act, Bill 71, was being prepared for final reading. On June 15, Hardwicke faxed a letter to the premier, demanding that Harcourt overrule his Health minister and cancel the bill, or appoint a mediator to resolve the dispute. "If the bill proceeds in its present form, it will be the equivalent of a declaration of legislative war on the medical profession," wrote Hardwicke. Another BCMA spokesperson, John McCaw, claimed that doctors had "lost their trust" in Cull; that dealing with the Health minister was "like talking to the Cheshire Cat – all you're left with is a smile. There's no substance. We've been left in a position of total impotence and cannot believe anything said by the Health minister."

Cull responded with a few missiles of her own. First she got up in the legislature and quoted figures that showed BC doctors earn well above the national average; then she accused the BCMA of blatant fearmongering. "In my riding we have a lot of senior citizens," she told the *Times-Colonist*. "The main public calls we have had, apart from doctors, have been from frightened seniors who have been told by their doctor that they won't be able to see them next year. It's very hard to explain to them that this bill is not going to have that impact on their doctors." Cull added that one North Vancouver physician had needlessly frightened one of his patients by telling the 69-year-old woman that she wouldn't receive bypass surgery – even though she suffered from blockage of the arteries and deteriorating blood vessels – because he had to ration his services.

On June 28, the BCMA pulled out of talks with the government after a marathon round of negotiations. Steve Hardwicke announced that physicians in Prince George and Quesnel would close their offices for two days, and similar actions were promised elsewhere. In rejecting Bill 71, the doctors were rejecting participation in a new medical services commission which would have given the BCMA power to negotiate future budgets. But the doctors were unwilling to contribute to their own pension plan and wanted the government to add $50-100 million over and above the 4.7 percent increase in doctor's fees for 1992-93. To combat the $60 million shortfall they estimated from the current budget, they suggested introducing user fees and deinsuring some items, such as preliminary eye examinations, to increase revenue. Cull balked at the BCMA's demands, pointing out that the global cap was never on the table. "The fundamental issue for us was that the budget was established as non-negotiable," she told reporters. "But they wanted to add on to it … they want it available for their incomes."

In the war of words, Glen Clark went even further in condemning the doctor's lobby. On June 29, the Finance minister stood up in the legislature and delivered a blistering attack on the BCMA executive.

"This dispute between the government and certain aspects of the BCMA has boiled down to money and to universality of our health care system," he began.

> They're not content with what I think will be the second or third largest increase for medical services in the country. Over and above that, they want special provisions for a slush fund; they want special provisions for a northern allowance; they want special provisions for other aspects of the medical profession ... They have asked the government of British Columbia to delete reference in Bill 71 to the Canada Health Act. What does that mean? It would allow medically necessary services to be delisted, or deinsured. It would make it possible for the government to make people pay for medically necessary services. That's what the BC Medical Association demanded last night at eleven o'clock.

But Clark was only warming up for the knockout punch, an accusation of partisanship designed to embarrass the Opposition. Beginning with a history of Liberal support for user fees in Newfoundland, New Brunswick and Québec, and continuing with an overview of the party's objection to Medicare when it was introduced by the Saskatchewan NDP, Clark then moved in for the kill.

> It is clear that the Liberal Party is in the pockets of certain elements of the BC Medical Association, certain elements that are opposed to univeral access to medicare ... the Liberal Party stands up here hour after hour and mouths support for the BCMA. We have to assume they also support deleting the reference to the Canada Health Act, and that's shameful ... We have the pitiful sight of the Liberal Party of British Columbia coddling up to the BCMA executive, an executive in my view not representative of the vast majority of doctors in this province. If you had phoned the BCMA last week or so and asked for Dr. Finlayson [executive director of the BCMA], the staff rep, you'd have got a recorded mes-

sage. That message says they're not in right now, phone this
number; and if you phone the number, you get the Liberal
Party Opposition. Shame on them!

They have staff people from the BC Medical Association,
paid by the BC Medical Association, sitting in their offices
for weeks on end here, telling them what to say in this
House. Their lips move, but it is the staff people from the
BCMA who are sitting there giving them advice day in and
day out ... They have sold their souls to the BC Medical
Association.

Norm Finlayson had indeed been spotted coaching Liberal MLAs in
a caucus meeting room – not only by New Democrats but by HEU staff
member Chris Gainor, who entered the caucus room for a meeting
with Liberal health critic Linda Reid in time to witness a spirited pep
rally by Finlayson. But there was more. Clark produced a May 8 letter,
written by Gordon Wilson for a 9,000-address mailout, in which the
Liberal leader reminded doctors of his party's public defence of physicians and concluded by asking for financial assistance to fight Bill 71.
"The Liberal Opposition is bought and paid for," said Clark.

It is nothing short of scandalous that the Liberal Party would
filibuster a bill in this House and stand up and mouth the
words of the BCMA – and certain elements of the BCMA at
that – while they secretly mail a letter asking for money in
the pockets of their partisan interests. This has nothing to do
with health care. It has to do with vested interest ... It has to
do with them shamelessly using this dispute – the future of
health care – for fundraising.

Clark's speech was a tour de force, reminiscent of his nastier days as
Opposition finance critic. Wilson attempted to dismiss the comments
in partisan terms, calling Clark's address an attempt to deflect criticism from the government. Liberal health critic Linda Reid, meanwhile, offered a lame defence of the BCMA's cozy relationship with
the Liberal caucus. "Our door is open to every single British

Columbian," she said. "Do we treat the BCMA differently? No." But the damage was done. Clark's tirade was a subtle reminder that Liberal Party ethics had changed since the party's return to the legislature. During the election campaign, Wilson had boasted that he accepted no corporate donations with strings attached; now, it seemed, the party saw a major potential sponsor in the BCMA – just as the federal Liberals did.

The BCMA had one more ace up its sleeve that summer. In Nanaimo, seven doctors announced that they would opt out of Medicare and begin to bill their patients directly by September 11, with another 55 physicians considering the same option. "We just don't feel we can deliver the best care to our patients while worrying about the Health minister's budget," said internist Lawrence Winkler, in a BCMA-issued statement. Patients who were billed directly would have to pay at the time they received service (the initial consultation fee was $115.06). They would then receive a receipt with a form they could send to the Medical Services Plan for reimbursement.

This marked the first time since the introduction of Medicare in BC that the province's doctors would bill patients directly – a dubious milestone for the "Hub City" of Nanaimo. "Count on it," said the Vancouver *Sun*'s editorial of August 20, "There will be some, very likely the elderly and the poor, who will put off medical treatment because they cannot face the embarrassment of having to make payment arrangements."

This view was embraced by some members of the medical community. At least two physicians who were not members of the BCMA were willing to go public in their condemnation of direct billing, accusing the organization of undermining universality. One of these physicians, Ambrose Marsh of Sidney, said the BCMA's endorsement of private health insurance would create a two-tiered health care system in BC that would hurt "the working poor, whose health care isn't covered by their jobs." In Williams Lake, the local BCMA action coordinator resigned his post when only 50 percent of his colleagues endorsed opting out of Medicare as a strategy for achieving wage contract goals.

There appeared to be no end to the conflict. The dispute lingered through the fall, with the BCMA rejecting a government offer in December. On February 4, 1993 a group of Prince George doctors began extra billing – charging patients a $10 surcharge, a gesture which the BC College of Physicians and Surgeons preferred to ignore. In March, the BCMA tabled a petition with nearly 330,000 signatures from 130 communities throughout the province that called for the premier to settle the dispute.

The NDP's second budget, tabled in the House at the end of March, was the last straw for the BCMA. For the coming year, the global cap was reduced from $1.27 billion to $1.21 billion, a reduction of $55 million, or 4.3 percent. The Health Ministry also threatened to cancel government-subsidized training and upgrading programs for doctors if the BCMA did not approve its final offer. Hardwicke responded by pulling the BCMA out of the talks and demanding Elizabeth Cull's resignation. With his April 5 letter to association members, Hardwicke finally brought the BCMA's elitist agenda out of the closet. Despite the fact that hospitals and unionized health care workers had done their part to bear the cost of funding cuts, Hardwicke's gloves-off, partisan attack on Elizabeth Cull made it clear that doctors believed they were above the process.

Cull, he said, had "bought off the three major health unions with a sweetheart deal that will cost taxpayers millions"; she had "bull-doz[ed] her New Directions for Health Care, primed with another $100 million to feed her burgeoning bureaucracy"; and she had embarked on an "ideological power trip" that left the BCMA with no option but to form its own union. "Only by becoming a union," wrote Hardwicke, "will the BCMA be properly equipped to represent the profession during the 'reform' process. The future well-being of doctors, in the uncertain times ahead, will best be served if we possess the representation and bargaining rights now reserved for trade unions."

To actual living, breathing trade unionists, Hardwicke's remarks about doctors' need to assert "bargaining rights" during "uncertain times" seemed silly. Somehow, the thought of BMW-driving, $100,000-a-year doctors attending labour conventions and singing "Solidarity Forever" just didn't make sense to the working-class rank and file. The HEU's Carmela Allevato, for one, couldn't hide her amusement. "It's interesting that the group which is at the top of the hierarchy in an industry that's extremely hierarchical is looking to trade unionism to advance its collective rights," she told reporters. "Their strategy – and they're being quite open about this – is that they [want] access to the mediation and arbitration processes in the labour code."

Cull, for her part, felt no need to hide her sarcasm from an organization that wanted her head on a plate. "The one thing that puzzles me," she told reporters, "is, who is the employer in this case? I was under the impression that [doctors] were self-employed and independent." The Health minister had no objection to the BCMA declaring itself a union, but wondered if its executive could appreciate the class and economic differences that separate most doctors and health care workers. "I don't see a lot of unemployed doctors in this province, but I can tell you there are a lot of unemployed union members. If the doctors were interested in, for example, a 10 percent reduction in their numbers in return for a similar sort of social contract that we now have with the health care unions, I'd be very interested in talking to them about that."

Cull concluded her lesson in elementary labour philosophy by reminding the BCMA that unions had no power to negotiate provincial budgets. "I can only assume they realize that unions negotiate with governments about things like wages and benefits and the like. They do not negotiate over how much money we're going to spend in a budget, which is what the doctors want to do. The last time I looked, the teachers union isn't negotiating the education budget and the nurses aren't negotiating the hospital budget, so I'm not sure whether this will allow them to achieve their goal, which is to try to set the [medical] budget instead of the legislature."

BC Fed president Ken Georgetti, who had defended the BCMA's right to collective bargaining the previous year, had changed his tune considerably in recent months. First, he was offended by the decision of Nanaimo and Quesnel doctors to opt out of Medicare. But his good will toward the BCMA went out the window when a number of doctors slammed the Health Labour Accord. "They haven't demonstrated a keenness yet to act collectively," Georgetti told reporters. "As soon as the health care unions negotiated their agreement, it seems to me that doctors were quite critical of that. That doesn't lend itself well to the rest of the labour movement feeling sympathetic to the needs of doctors, when they don't reciprocate."

The BCMA union drive never got very far. Early in June, a forum at Harrison Hot Springs revealed deep divisions among the 300 doctors present. Many were concerned about the effect that union membership would have on doctor-patient relationships. If there was a strike and a patient was badly ill, how could a doctor justify a decision to refuse treatment? Why should a doctor be forced to choose between that option or strike-breaking, which could lead to disciplinary action by the union? Would "scab" doctors be shunned by their colleagues? Would they lose referrals? Other doctors were discouraged by public opinion polls that showed only 25 percent support for a doctor's union. Early in August, the question was settled for good when 64 percent of the membership voted against forming a union.

Meanwhile, unbeknownst to many of its members, discussions between the BCMA's negotiating team and the government resumed on August 9. Six days later, with Finance Minister Glen Clark out of town on holidays, a tentative agreement was reached. Clark, who had maintained a hardline approach throughout the dispute, was conspicuously absent from the August 23 press conference announcing the deal. Instead, a jubilant Premier Harcourt stood beside Elizabeth Cull and new BCMA president Arun Garg, celebrating an agreement that would last until the year 2000 and save the BC government $370 million over the first four years.

"Everyone has given, everyone has compromised and everyone wins," said Dr. Garg. But it appeared from the agreement that the government had done most of the giving and compromising. Although it did not alter the $1.27 billion global cap imposed the previous year on billings, the agreement did give the province's 6,000-plus doctors a greater say in how the money would be spent. And it also included a renegotiated cost-shared retirement savings plan, and allowed for the delisting of medical services like cosmetic surgery. As well, the Medical Services Commission, which was shelved several months earlier when the BCMA refused to join, would go ahead as planned. The

Commission would include three government representatives, three BCMA members, and three members of the public.

This was still not good enough for some doctors. In Nanaimo, a group of more than 30 dissenters led by "Nanaimo Seven" member Paul Mitenko, claimed that the agreement would force doctors to conspire with the government's cost-cutting agenda by limiting patients' access to health care services. In a September 9 communiqué signed by the "Nanaimo Medical Society," the group urged BCMA members to vote against the deal and accused the executive of clandestine tactics in reopening the negotiations without informing the membership at large. It also argued that the deal would jeopardize patient confidentiality by allowing the government to review patient records.

But most of their colleagues disagreed, and even some of the doctors who considered opting out were now willing to accept the new system. On September 21, BCMA members voted 87 percent in favour of the four-year working agreement, and on November 23 voted 93 percent in favour of the seven-year master agreement. Arun Garg's response to the Nanaimo communiqué revealed just how much doctors had gained. "If the profession lives up to its commitments," he said, "it is entirely possible to live within the available amounts which have been calculated based upon historical utilization rates, population growth, aging, and discounted for the responsibilities of the BCMA and government to deinsurance and practice guidelines and protocols." As for patient confidentiality, there was no risk at all because auditors of patient records would "no longer be handpicked by government"; instead, they would be chosen from a list of doctors proposed by the BCMA and the College of Physicians and Surgeons of BC.

To the three unions who had been accused of winning a sweetheart deal with the Health Labour Accord, the notion that the BCMA had somehow lost through this agreement seemed completely out to lunch. "The doctors got one of the biggest 'sweetheart deals' in Canada," said a Hospital Employees Union staffer. "The increase the average doctor will receive over the next three years is equivalent to the annual salary of the average HEU member. That's hardly consistent with the government's claim of freezing the top to help the bottom."

Elizabeth Cull, who had gained so much of her cabinet clout as a fiscal conservative, had compromised far more than expected. Glen Clark, who drove so much of the government's economic policy, was completely excluded from the final negotiations. And the premier? Harcourt had remained invisible for much of the dispute, but finally stepped in when he realized how formidable an opponent the government was dealing with. The premier simply decided that a fight with doctors just wasn't worth the trouble. "It was the wrong approach," Harcourt said in summing up the battle. "We used a sledgehammer with them."

Somewhere in the political wilderness, former Socred Health Minister Jim Nielsen snickered, "I told you so."

5

Strange Bedfellows

MIKE HARCOURT'S FIRST YEAR AS PREMIER, DIFFICULT THOUGH it was, was not without its blessings. Unlike Dave Barrett, whose 1972-75 NDP government faced a constant barrage of criticism from a depleted but competent group of veteran Socred MLAs, the Harcourt New Democrats had only a bumbling, inexperienced opposition to contend with. Most of the rookies in Gordon Wilson's Liberal caucus were too busy learning the basics of parliamentary procedure, or engaging in petty power struggles, to offer any sustained criticism of the government agenda.

The group of seventeen MLAs led by Wilson was, as *Province* columnist Brian Kieran put it, "a fresh crop ... most dedicated and well-meaning, some absolutely overwhelmed by their good fortune, and a handful who [needed] a road map to find the Parliament buildings."

Aside from Wilson, whose provincewide fame was the result of the CBC debate, only three members of the Liberal caucus had any reputation or experience in politics. David Mitchell (West Vancouver-Garibaldi) was best known as a political historian and author whose biography of W.A.C. Bennett was considered a definitive text on BC's first Socred premier. This was Mitchell's first venture into politics as an elected official. Art Cowie (Vancouver-Quilchena) was a former director of planning for Delta who spent three terms on the Vancouver parks board and served briefly on Vancouver city council. A right-wing crony of former Prime Minister John Turner and Vancouver mayor Gordon Campbell, Cowie was well connected in the business community. Finally there was bookstore owner Clive Tanner (Saanich North and the Islands), a longtime Liberal who had served as the Yukon's minister of Health in the early 1970s and had been involved in native land claims negotiations with the federal government.

The remaining members of the caucus, with one or two exceptions, were political neophytes. This ensured that the party's first year in Opposition was consumed by the formalities of orientation at the expense of any regular, focussed attack on government policy. Most caucus members had never met each other before the election. Critics had to be appointed for each portfolio and MLAs had to set up shop in their local constituencies before a single maiden speech could be made. Even then, the Liberals had barely begun their Opposition role of criticizing the government when the caucus became embroiled in a renewed attack on Gordon Wilson's leadership.

The rot set in at the beginning of the first session in the spring of 1992, when Linda Reid (Richmond East) was dumped as the caucus chair. With Art Cowie selected as her replacement, two of the three caucus officer positions were held by MLAs who had long been critical of Wilson. (During the 1991 campaign, Cowie had spoken out publicly against Wilson, saying that "the leadership issue" would be handled after the election.) The other was house leader David Mitchell, who had been touted as leadership material from the day he declared his intention to run in West Vancouver-Garibaldi.

Mitchell's motives for entering politics were never clear. Generally perceived as a Socred, his economic views embraced the right wing of the Liberal Party, although he was sufficiently concerned about the environment to be mistaken for a progressive. The party valued his political insight and knowledge, along with his ability to organize seminars and training sessions. But he was reluctant to discuss his personal philosophy of politics, and his relationship with Wilson had always been cool. There was a good reason for this: Mitchell's name was frequently associated with the federal Liberals and Vancouver business types who wanted Wilson gone. This put Mitchell in a difficult position when the legislature convened in March 1992. On one hand, the longtime student of politics could appreciate that caucus unity and loyalty to one's leader were crucial factors in the public's acceptance of the new Opposition. On the other hand, he understood that Howe Street wanted a free-enterprise coalition to replace Wilson – and Mitchell himself could well emerge as a leading candidate. Wilson's appointment of Mitchell as house leader was perceived as a shrewd attempt to stave off any coalition movement by showing that Socreds were welcome in his party. Ironically, Mitchell's appointment also put him in a better position to attack Wilson's leadership.

Although Gordon Wilson's downfall was ultimately his own doing, his claim of a conspiracy against him was by no means exaggerated. For the first four years of his leadership, he was often sidetracked by challenges from the federal party, most of them the result of arguments over his financial management. Now that he had returned his party to the legislature, Wilson had to contend with the more focussed attack of the Vancouver business lobby, which could smell an opening for Socred "retreads" and was anxious to move in for the kill. Liberals such as Pat McGeer, Allan Williams and Garde Gardom had all made the switch to Social Credit when the free-enterprise movement needed them so badly in the mid-1970s; now it was payback time. To the big business community, at least, enough time had elapsed (one year? eighteen months? who's counting?) that formerly disgraced Socreds could magically transform themselves into fresh new Liberals without raising suspicion.

Wilson's refusal to accept corporate donations with strings attached had not won him many friends in the business community. He realized this during a five-week fundraising blitz in the late summer of 1992, when he held a series of individual and group meetings with 200 of the top chief executive officers in Vancouver. Because he was leader of the dominant free-enterprise party in Opposition, there were a few smaller companies willing to support him. But when it came to Howe Street heavyweights like Jim Pattison, Michael Phelps and Edgar Kaiser, support was always conditional. Cooperate in a merger with Social Credit, they said, or step aside.

Wilson's contempt for big business was admirable but, in the context of this province, fatal for a Liberal leader. After one breakfast meeting during the referendum campaign, he returned to his office and took a phone call from the CEO of Cadillac-Fairview, who had been at the speech and was so impressed that he was willing to send Wilson a cheque for $5,000 — as long as Wilson agreed to change his vote from "No" to "Yes." Wilson made no commitment over the phone, but waited for the cheque to arrive in the mail before returning it with a note attached: "Thank you for your offer. My vote cannot be bought. Please feel free to support us at such a time as there are no conditions attached."

The final assault on Wilson's leadership began with his opposition to the Charlottetown Accord in the fall of 1992. Wilson's position on the "No" side was consistent with the anti-Québec stance of CKNW radio host Rafe Mair, as well as the anti-elitist argument of many leftist "No" supporters. But by opposing Charlottetown, Wilson was defying the federal party line once again, alienating himself from the big money people that funded it, and providing his enemies with yet another reason to challenge his leadership.

Wilson's decision to support the "No" forces was publicly condemned by Art Cowie and David Mitchell, whose "Yes" position was supported by fellow MLAs Val Anderson and Clive Tanner. Much of the name calling that occurred during this period was motivated by personal political agendas, but was amplified by a sudden financial crisis in the Liberal Party: since the corporate community had lined up in support of the referendum and Wilson continued to oppose it, business funding to the BC Liberal Party had dried up almost completely.

During a caucus retreat in Kamloops in late September, Cowie was dumped as caucus chair and replaced by Dan Jarvis. And Mitchell, who was out of the country for three weeks, was said to be on thin ice. Wilson, eager to convince reporters that he had achieved caucus solidarity on the accord, announced a compromise; as long as the "Yes" campaigners held back from public statements, he would refrain from wearing a "No" button or joining any public effort for the "No" cause.

For a few days, it appeared to be a solution everyone could live with. "The caucus is more important right now than our own personal opinions," offered a briefly conciliatory Cowie. But the compromise contradicted one of Wilson's most repeated promises throughout the 1991 election campaign: that the Liberal Party welcomed independent thinkers and would allow dissenting MLAs to express their opinions. On October 6, that promise came back to haunt Wilson.

First, in a letter to the Vancouver *Sun*, Cowie renounced his earlier promise not to rock the caucus boat, saying that Wilson's demand for silence from "Yes" supporters was nonsense and that he preferred to align himself with federal Liberals like John Turner, Jean Chrétien and former party president Iona Campagnolo. Then David Mitchell announced his resignation as house leader.

Mitchell's dramatic press conference was a direct attack on Wilson's leadership. His decision to sign on with the "Yes" campaign was hardly surprising, but Mitchell stunned the assembled media with a fifteen-page speech that heaped ridicule and scorn on Wilson's claim of caucus solidarity. He also accused the Liberal leader of Preston Manning-style fearmongering.

> To those who oppose this deal and encourage the people of this province to vote No, a word of caution: It is easy to play on the fears of people. It is easy to bring out the anxieties to stir up anger, it is easy to fuel the distrust and suspicion, whether it is about our aboriginal peoples or the place of Québec in Canada ... But it is cruel to make promises of a better day, a better constitutional package, when you know it is not achievable. It is the kind of politics which bring out the worst in all of us. It is not the kind of politics I am proud of.

Two months later, Mitchell completed his rejection of Wilson by quitting the caucus altogether to sit as an independent. This time, he made his announcement by standing up in the legislature. "If ever in the history of the province there was a crying need for a strong political Opposition committed to keeping a highly partisan government honest, it is now," said Mitchell, sounding a lot like an author delivering his final paragraph. The Liberal Party was missing an opportunity to provide that Opposition, he added, because of "the large amount of unproductive time spent dealing with internal party politics" (which, he implied, had nothing to do with him). Mitchell's departure from the House following his address was applauded by members of the Liberal caucus — a sure sign to the premier that the official Opposition was rapidly disintegrating. Socred house leader Cliff Serwa shook his head at the spectacle, calling the desk-thumping response to Mitchell's departure by Liberal MLAs "a childish and senseless act."

It had been a bad week for the Liberals. Just days earlier the party was embarrassed by the revelation that Saanich North MLA Clive Tanner had written a letter of reference for a convicted rapist. Tanner had used his legislature letterhead to write to a judge on behalf of a man who had raped a fourteen-year-old girl, masturbated in front of a seventeen-year-old girl and had a ten-year record of indecent assault, contributing to child delinquency and gross indecency. In the October 30 letter, Tanner asked for leniency, stressing that the 51-year-old Sidney restaurant owner had "worked hard to establish a successful business; in doing so, he has created something that is unique" and "an asset to the community." The man, who had been found guilty of two sexual assault charges, was sentenced to four years in prison. Tanner — who had previously written a character reference for a Yukon Liberal Party executive member and friend who had pleaded guilty to indecently assaulting boys — was temporarily stripped of the tourism critic's job and agreed to stay away from the legislature so as not to embarrass the Liberal caucus.

But these embarrassments — the caucus defections, the in-fighting over Charlottetown, the Tanner reference letter — were nothing compared to what was about to hit the party in early 1993. Within a few months, Gordon Wilson was to become an object of ridicule in a political soap opera that would have made even Bill Vander Zalm blush. By the time it was over, Wilson had resigned as Opposition leader, announced his engagement to his former house leader, Judi Tyabji, and called a leadership convention for October.

Liberals in Love

HE was the leader who brought his party out of the political wilderness. SHE was the ambitious young MLA who stood by him in his darkest moments. Together they were Liberals … Liberals in love.

DOES THIS SOUND LIKE THE HACKNEYED PLOTLINE OF A HARLE-quin romance? Maybe, but it was the plotline for the most bizarre Rchapter of BC politics since Bill Vander Zalm returned to his garden. And the story's ending had profound implications for three-party politics in BC

By her own admission, Judi Tyabji was an eccentric loner who floated through life until she met Gordon Wilson. She had studied political science at the University of Victoria and worked in radio journalism during the summers to pay the bills, but it wasn't until the year after her graduation in 1986 that she threw herself into party politics full time after meeting Wilson at the party convention that chose him as Liberal leader.

In the late fall of 1987, she agreed to be Wilson's regional representative for the Southern Interior. The following year, she ran unsuccessfully as the Liberal candidate for Boundary-Similkameen. That by-election, one of six that would signal the end of Social Credit, was the first real test of Liberal Party support under Wilson's leadership. Tyabji, at 23, was in tough against the NDP's Bill Barlee, a respected local businessman in his 50s. She did increase the popular vote for the Liberals, from 3 to 10 percent, but Tyabji was devastated by the loss to Barlee. She returned to Kelowna where she joined her husband, Kim Sandana, and their infant son. To pay off her campaign debt she worked as a stringer for a community newspaper, taught for a local tutoring service, and worked as a cocktail waitress at a Kelowna nightclub.

Disillusioned by her own loss and the federal party's continuing attempts to undermine Gordon Wilson's leadership, Tyabji drifted away from the Liberal Party for most of 1989-91. After the birth of her

second child, she took a six-month paid position with a local environmental group called Earth Care and even flirted briefly with the NDP
– a period she referred to in her autobiography as "an unsatisfying
few months."

Tyabji had given up on the Liberals partly because of her regret that
an idealist like Wilson, whose views she shared, was constantly under
attack. But she was reassured when he survived yet another challenge
in the spring of 1991 – after the advertising debt scandal – and the
federal party decided to separate from the provincial wing. On May
24, she wrote a letter to the Kelowna constituency office of the NDP,
advising the party of her decision to rejoin the Liberals. "Although
my husband Kim is a devout NDPer, and although I admire and
respect NDP policy and people, I have not felt comfortable with my
decision to become NDP," she wrote. "Part of my discomfort comes
from the reaction of many NDP members, who knew me in my public
Liberal incarnation, and no doubt viewed me with some suspicion,
and perhaps with some justification. Nevertheless, having been
brought up a Liberal, in a Liberal family, and given my own personal
history as a Liberal, I feel it is only fitting that I rejoin." By August,
Tyabji was prepared to run for the Liberals in Kelowna. This time, she
joined a flood of candidates who were swept into the legislature.

Tyabji's autobiography, *Political Affairs*, is a telling portrait of a
romantic idealist whose political world view was marked by naive
earnestness and lack of self-analysis. Aside from the unquestioning
support of her leader's theories – and her recognition that social injus-
tice is a bad thing – she never really explains why she went into politics or what she hoped to achieve. Clearly struck by Wilson's outsider
persona and professorial charm, she appears to have hung on his
every word since he first criticized the Meech Lake Accord in 1987.
Wilson, no doubt fatigued by all the challenges to his leadership,
must have found Tyabji's loyalty refreshing. After the election, he
appointed her as environment critic and put her on the land use committee.

As Tyabji's kiss-and-tell book reveals, the two crusading politicians
became lovebirds just before the referendum debate began, when
Tyabji revealed her feelings to Wilson in a series of coy confessions

over the summer of 1992. She reported that she was shocked he felt the same way, and both later claimed that their marriages were already on the rocks by this point — although their spouses offered completely different versions of the story. Almost everyone in the government, the Liberal caucus and the press gallery began to realize there were sparks between the 43-year-old leader and his 27-year-old protégée, but the relationship did not begin to have political implications until October 13, when Tyabji wrote a letter to Wilson confessing her undying love for him.

Three days after Tyabji's written confession, Wilson appointed her house leader in a move that enraged at least half of the caucus. (The position had been vacant since David Mitchell quit ten days earlier.) Clive Tanner and Fred Gingell disliked Tyabji because of her stubbornness and poor listening skills, but they and others in the caucus were also offended by her fawning, romantic devotion to her leader. Gary Farrell-Collins had also made it clear that he wanted the house leader's position. He, along with Cowie, Wilf Hurd and Alan Warnke, were willing to do battle with Wilson for alienating Mitchell in the first place.

By mid-December, some caucus members were ready to use Wilson and Tyabji's romance to undermine Wilson's leadership. Instead of going directly to the media, however, they began a whisper campaign that eventually exploded across the front pages. Near the end of the fall session, CBC-TV reporter Ian Gill approached Wilson to discuss an environmental proposal. In the course of the interview, Gill popped the question about Tyabji; Wilson refused to comment. Then Gill approached Tyabji who, without going into specifics, told him there was "no affair." (Moments earlier she had told CKNW radio reporter Kim Emerson that she was going through a separation — a confession that took her husband, Kim Sandana, completely by surprise.)

Over the next two months the rumours became more persistent, the denials more vehement and the revelations more pathetic. First there was the birthday ski trip in Kelowna (united by the stars, Wilson and Tyabji were both born on January 2), which was reported in the media as a getaway tryst. That prompted the January 14 press conference, demanded by the caucus, in which Wilson and Tyabji were to explain their relationship to the entire BC media. Instead, both denied having an affair and lashed out at the media, the Liberal caucus, and the Vancouver business establishment for invading their privacy.

Not since former NDP leader Bob Skelly's attack of the jitters at the start of the 1986 election campaign had a political career – in this case, two political careers – so completely unravelled before the cameras. "I am not going to have the media put a ring through my nose and drag me around Main Street as an exhibit on some kind of carnival show every time they want to dream up some kind of fictitious relationship," snarled Wilson, clearly flustered by the turn of events. "I am not in an affair with Judi Tyabji ... There is nothing untoward in our relationship." Then, in an astonishing display of bitterness, he dragged out the party's dirty laundry, pointing fingers at the "cadre of pernicious malcontents" who wanted to dump him as leader.

Tyabji dug their hole even deeper. First she said the attacks on her credibility were a form of gender harrassment (later offending victims of sexual assault by comparing the experience to being raped). Then she argued that no one in the media "would raise an eyebrow if Glen Clark had hosted Mike Harcourt and his family for a weekend" – an unfortunate comparison, since Clark was rumoured to be unhappy with Harcourt's leadership and almost certainly would have "raised eyebrows" with such a gesture. In any case, it would have been news if the two NDP bigshots were revealed to be having a romantic affair.

For a few days, it looked as though the story might disappear from the front pages. Even Wilson thought he had finally put the matter to rest when he called a meeting with caucus and senior staff to fully explain the relationship. But that only encouraged his enemies. On January 20, Gary Farrell-Collins delivered the final blow to Wilson's leadership when he went public with his resignation as party whip. "I'll walk to the edge of the cliff with you, but I won't jump," he reportedly told Wilson, adding that the Liberal leader's position would be in jeopardy if he refused to rule out any future relationship with Judi Tyabji. Since Wilson had refused to give that assurance, the party whip no longer wanted his job. Now only five of Wilson's sixteen fellow caucus members were on his side.

Farrell-Collins's political ambitions had always been transparent.

Shortly after the election, he had told Wilson that he intended to run for the leadership whenever Wilson was ready to step down, but few were aware just how shameless he could be in his manoeuvring for power within the caucus. Within a few weeks he had resigned publicly as whip (after promising to keep it quiet), voted to create two new caucus positions that would undermine Wilson's leadership, and then, on February 13, demanded to be appointed house leader. Furthermore, the articulate young opportunist had lobbied enough caucus members to threaten Wilson with a revolt if he didn't dump Tyabji. After a lengthy shouting match between the two men, followed by the open trashing of Tyabji by caucus members, Wilson worked out a compromise by removing Tyabji and replacing her with the more diplomatic Jeremy Dalton.

But the stories kept coming. On February 19, the *Province* published the words that would finally kill Wilson's leadership. "We cook meals together ... do laundry together," said Liz Wilson, claiming to know nothing of a separation from her husband. "We sleep in the same bed." Later that day, an emergency caucus meeting was called by chair Dan Jarvis at the request of Farrell-Collins, Cowie, Warnke and Lynn Stephens, all of whom demanded Wilson's resignation. Tyabji, Linda Reid and Bob Chisholm refused to attend, and Wilson himself was in Powell River. Fred Gingell delivered the decision to Wilson over the phone: at least six caucus members, possibly more, would leave the party and sit as independents if Wilson did not resign.

Wilson obliged with yet another compromise: he would appoint Gingell interim Opposition leader but retain the party leader's position until a successor could be named at a convention the following October. "If there are challengers who want my position, let them stop shooting from the shadows," he said, in a repeat of his 1988 challenge to Jack Poole. "If someone out there is interested, step into the light. I'm tired of shadow-boxing. Let's have a fair fight." He needn't have bothered with such bravado. Scores of federal Liberals, most of whom had only grudgingly supported him after the 1990 ad campaign fiasco, had been waiting ever since for the right opportunity to dump him. Now, with the financial support of prominent ex-Socreds and others in the Vancouver business community, backed up by the outrage of every cheated spouse in the province, they finally had their chance.

For an idealist like Wilson, who had predicted a rebellion at his very first caucus meeting in 1991, there was a sense of inevitability surrounding his purge. But it was still hard to accept. Wilson's first promise as Liberal leader was to elect a group of MLAs to the House within four years; he delivered on that promise, leading his party back onto the political map for the first time in sixteen years. And this was his reward?

In the first week of March, Wilson and Tyabji told the Vancouver *Sun* they were in love and planned to be married in the Catholic church after Tyabji received an annulment of her first marriage. The *Province* provided psychic readings of their relationship, and on March 12 the tabloid ran a photocopied image of Tyabji's October 13 love letter to Wilson – the letter that preceded her appointment as house leader by only three days. Wilson denied any wrongdoing, claiming that he did not receive the letter until after the appointment. By now, though, there was no point defending himself; both he and Tyabji had been effectively reduced to cartoon caricatures in yet another confirmation of British Columbia's wacky, sometimes infantile political culture. Interestingly, Wilson's disgrace was not reflected in Angus Reid polls; throughout the scandal he maintained a steady 35 percent approval rating – an enviable statistic for any politician, much less one who was being ridiculed and ripped apart on the evening news and front pages for days.

Furthermore, despite all the coverage, not a single connection was made by any of the major media outlets between the personal humiliation of Wilson and Tyabji and the carefully orchestrated plan by Howe Street CEOs and former Socreds to recapture the Liberal Party. Nor did the media seem interested when Art Cowie offered to give up his seat in Vancouver-Quilchena if Vancouver Mayor Gordon Campbell ever decided to run for the Liberal leadership. Perhaps this was because Campbell's intentions had long been a foregone conclusion.

A Tale of Three Gordons

"THIS IS A STORY ABOUT INDIVIDUALS, EGOS AND PRIVATE ambitions, a story of leadership and the most unmanageable challenge that can face any organization: leadership succession. And it's a true story." That's the cover blurb for *Succession*, David Mitchell's book on the transition of Social Credit leaders from Bill Bennett to Bill Vander Zalm. Mitchell could not have known it at the time, but this description would also be an apt description of the 1992-93 fight for control of the Liberal Party. While the Socred succession went from one Bill to another, the Liberals passed the torch from one Gordon to another.

Gordon Campbell's transition from civic politics to the messy arena of provincial affairs was not a smooth one. Campbell was an example of an "instant Liberal," one who joined the party after the 1991 election debacle that killed Social Credit. He had no links with the federal Liberals during his term as mayor – if anything, he was a Mulroney Conservative – and he didn't bother to take out a provincial Liberal membership until deciding to seek the leadership in 1993.

His first appearance on the provincial stage was no reflection of moderate Liberal philosophy, either. His stance against the NDP's 1993 reduction in the homeowners' tax was seen as hypocritical by those who recalled his own record on property taxes in Vancouver. In fact, his run for the Liberal leadership was contested by members of the Angry Taxpayers Action Committee, a group formed in 1989 to protest commercial property tax increases that were as high as 150 percent. The committee, whose twenty members represented most of the commercial districts in the city of Vancouver, attacked Campbell on the eve of the leadership vote for imposing property taxes that would force some proprietors to close down their businesses.

But that protest was like a fly on an elephant. Backed by a dozen corporations and law firms, 225 campaign workers handling the phones, and a team that one federal Grit described as the most efficient campaign organization he had ever worked with, Campbell captured 63 percent of the vote in an easy, first-ballot victory to become the new Liberal leader and leader-in-waiting of the Opposition just four months after taking out a Liberal membership card.

The leadership race, if one can call it that, began with Wilson's resignation in February. Aside from Campbell, who declared in May, the only other serious contender was former leader Gordon Gibson, who had tried to convince land developer Jack Poole to challenge Wilson in 1988. Other MLAs including Linda Reid, Wilf Hurd and Allan Warnke also ran, along with fringe candidate Charles McKinney, but the race quickly became A Tale of Three Gordons.

Given the format of the vote – most of the 6,500 delegates did not attend the convention but phoned in their votes after paying a $20 registration fee – the selection process lacked the tension or emotion that characterizes most leadership conventions. Cool, precise, and ruthlessly efficient, the televote was typical of Campbell's style. He finished with 4,141 votes, Gibson came second with 1,600 and Wilson finished badly in third with only 531. Campbell offered no specifics about his platform but only three vague promises: he would bring in laws to balance the budget, end the corporation capital tax, and make education an essential service – meaning, presumably, eliminating teachers' right to strike.

He also announced – to nobody's great surprise – that the BC Liberal Party would not support the federal Liberals in the upcoming October 25 election. Not only did Campbell reaffirm the provincial party's split from the federal party, he expressed a number of views on the economy that made him sound a lot more like his Progressive Conservative namesake, Prime Minister Kim Campbell. The two Campbells agreed, for example, that governments cannot create jobs. "We are going to have to challenge a lot of the conventional wisdom and I'm going to have to do it," Gordon told reporters after his victory. "I've been saying this stuff for years. The fact that it has filtered its way up to the federal level is great."

As for the man who had brought the Liberal Party back from the political wilderness, Gordon Wilson was inconsolable. He declined to make the traditional motion of support to make the vote unanimous, and he left the stage abruptly when Campbell began his victory speech. He and Tyabji quit the caucus to form their own party. "I

think there's still room in this province for a broad political movement
that espouses the liberal values and principles that many of the people
in this province believe in," said Wilson, determined to leave his
impact on BC politics. Unfortunately, someone forgot to tell Wilson
that this particular space on the political spectrum was currently
occupied ... by the governing New Democrats. What Wilson and
Tyabji may have lacked in self-awareness, they more than made up for
in sheer audacity. Within weeks of their humiliation, the two ex-Lib-
erals set up the Progressive Democratic Alliance (referred to by
Vaughn Palmer as the "Progressive Democratic Whatever") and were
pledging to field candidates in the next election. The lovestruck couple was already something of a house joke in the legislature when they
set up their office with facing desks and later appeared on the cover of
Saturday Night magazine, snogging for the cameras. In the spring of
1994, they were married in a civil ceremony attended by several sympathetic members of the Victoria press gallery, and the union was later
made official in a Catholic church. (Wilson, who had agreed to join the
church, acknowledged a conflict with his pro-choice views, but
added that he expected "some movement by the church on this
issue.")

Also in the spring of 1994, Tyabji published *Political Affairs*, the
tell-all account of her relationship with Wilson and a summary of her
young life and career in politics since 1987. The book was an embarrassing attempt at self-aggrandizement by an MLA whose sense of her
own historical importance was somewhat exaggerated. The writing is
cloying, and the author's account of events transparently self-serving.
But there are some comic moments. In one chapter she recounts an
incident in which Wilson, convinced they are being followed by the
media after their humiliating January 14 press conference, impresses
her by waiting for the car to pass before pursuing it on a wild chase
through Stanley Park, cussing loudly as he tries to ram it.

WITHIN MONTHS OF BECOMING LEADER, GORDON CAMPBELL
reestablished the cozy relationship the Liberals had once enjoyed with
Social Credit. The party's head office had already moved into the same

Richmond complex that housed the Social Credit nerve centre for so many years. Within a year of Campbell's taking over, so many familiar faces had shown up in key Liberal staff positions that one could easily assume the word "Liberal" was a euphemism for "Socred." Among the former Zalmoids and Bennett clones under Campbell's wing:

• Greg Lyle, an Angus Reid associate who worked on Kim Campbell's federal Tory leadership bid and organized for the Manitoba Tories and BC Socreds, including Rita Johnston's unsuccessful campaign in 1991. New job: director of campaign planning.

• Ian Jessop, former press aide to both Johnston and Bill Vander Zalm. New job: Gordon Campbell's communications director.

• Peter Jones, another ex-Johnston aide who helped run the Socreds' last election campaign and worked on Gordon Campbell's successful leadership bid. New job: informal communications advisor.

• Penelope Chandler, former political aide to, among other Socreds, Rita Johnston. New job: Gordon Campbell's executive secretary.

• Brian and Anne Baynham. Brian was a delegate to the 1986 Whistler convention; Anne managed the Social Credit office for many years. New jobs: Brian is chair of the election readiness committee; Anne is office manager for the Liberals.

• Anne Bellows, former Socred party official. New job: senior management position in Liberal head office.

At the party's fall 1994 convention, former Socred minister of Education Jack Heinrich, now a Liberal, waxed nostalgic. "Social Credit were the heavies and the provincial Liberals weren't going to go anywhere," said Heinrich, recalling the fateful defection of Liberals Pat McGeer, Garde Gardom and Allan Williams to the Socreds in 1975. "So the provincial Liberal Party became the farm team for the Socreds and now it's turned around, and many activists from Social Credit are coming back." Other Socreds seen schmoozing at the convention included party organizer Craig Aspinall, political aides Stephen Greenaway and David McPhee, and former candidates and activists like Christie Jung, Mike Pearce and Ken Tuininga.

For the Liberals' former party president Floyd Sully, this rightward shift was inevitable. "Coming into this convention there was some discomfort with [the conservative shift], but I think a lot of it has been laid to rest here," he said. But others were less optimistic. "These people are looking for a home somewhere," said Simon Fraser University student Kristian Arnason, commenting on all the ex-Socreds at the 1994 convention. "There are some real wingnuts out there. I'd hate to see them do to the BC Liberals what they did to their original parties."

Born-Again Socreds

MEANWHILE, THE REAL SOCIAL CREDIT WAS HAVING TROUBLES of its own. In the two years since the election, the party had not managed to shake off its association with Bill Vander Zalm, sleazy business deals and widespread corruption. The seven remaining Socred MLAs were relatively untainted by scandal (although as Health minister under Vander Zalm, Peter Dueck had to resign from cabinet over a technical breach of the conflict code), but it was clear to most observers that there was little chance of reviving Social Credit as a relevant player in BC politics.

The first MLA to abandon the sinking ship was Dueck, who gave up his seat in Matsqui. By the time Mike Harcourt called provincial by-elections for early 1994, Grace McCarthy — the grande dame of Social Credit who had lost the leadership to Vander Zalm in 1986 and to Rita Johnston in 1991 — decided to make yet another comeback. "Amazing Grace" was nothing if not optimistic. It was she, after all, who had revived Social Credit after its first election disaster in 1972. During a two-year term as Socred president, McCarthy canvassed the entire province, increasing party membership by over 50,000 to a record high of about 72,000 by the 1975 election. Perhaps she would pull off one more miracle before calling it quits.

Although Jack Weisgerber was acclaimed Socred leader on March 8, 1992, it was only on an interim basis. After calling a leadership convention for the first week of November 1993, Weisgerber dropped out of the race in August, saying he wanted the party to attract "new blood". But many observers suspected he was merely waiting for a chance to head a new free-enterprise party under the banner of Reform, a federal party that had much in common with Social Credit's right-wing agenda.

In any case, it was the "old blood" of Grace McCarthy that would end up assuming the Socred mantle. When McCarthy finally won the leadership on her third attempt on November 6, she quickly began to plot her return to the legislature. She could have made things interesting by running in Vancouver-Quilchena, where she would have faced Liberal leader Gordon Campbell. (Art Cowie had offered his seat to his friend and former civic NPA colleague.) Instead, she opted for the relatively safer Socred territory of Matsqui.

Like so many musical nostalgia acts that don't know when to quit, McCarthy soldiered on with her tired soapbox message of free enterprise for all, to the embarrassment of many reporters who genuinely felt sorry for her. Her campaign was plagued from the start by accusations that she was avoiding a showdown with Campbell by running in an easy riding, and by concerns from local residents that had she spent virtually no time in Matsqui before the by-election. She never recovered from this criticism, and her defeat to rookie Liberal candidate Mike de Jong on February 18, 1994 was a humiliating finish to her 30-year political career. Three months later she retired from politics altogether, allowing the Socred leadership to be decided the following November by a mail-in ballot that chose 41-year-old North Vancouver real estate appraiser Larry Gillanders.

McCarthy's loss in Matsqui was the final blow to Social Credit that allowed a provincial Reform movement to assume its logical place on the right side of BC's political spectrum. Reform had already proven to be a popular protest party in the federal election, and it clearly offered a comfortable home for Vander Zalm Socreds: it was rural, agrarian, populist, pro-small business, pro-traditional family values (Reform code for anti-gay and anti-choice on abortion), Christian fundamentalist, WASP to the core, and anti-immigration. Like its federal counterpart, BC Reform aimed to attract the disaffected voter, the free-enterprise supporter who had lost faith in government but didn't trust corporate business either. And, also like its federal cousin, provincial Reform was conspicuously lacking in people of colour, women, youth, gays and lesbians, or anyone professing a religion other than fundamentalist Protestant Christianity.

This kind of party was attractive to at least four of the remaining six Socreds in the house. In March 1994, Richard Neufeld (Peace River North), Jack Weisgerber (Peace River South), Len Fox (Prince George-Omineca) and Lyall Hanson (Okanagan-Vernon) all quit Social Credit to join Reform. With four sitting MLAs, Reform now had official status in the legislature while Social Credit, with only two, was officially irrelevant. When Harry De Jong stepped down in Abbotsford shortly afterward, Cliff Serwa of Okanagan-West took his place in history as the last Social Credit MLA in the province.

When Weisgerber and his three fellow Socreds joined the party, BC Reform was still led by its founder, Ron Gamble. Gamble was perceived as well meaning but naive, a political neophyte with few connections and even less clout. With no legislative experience, the small businessman-cum-politician was a longshot when he announced his intention to retain the leadership. But his chances were ruined for good on September 27, when he told a news conference that BC had an immigration problem because too many Asians hadn't learned to speak English. Racism had long been the Achilles' heel of Reform, and sure enough Gamble fell into the xenophobic trap.

"In the Richmond area there is a very heavy influx of Asians. It's a drain on our resources. A lot of the people coming in can't speak English," said Gamble, sounding very much like the average Reform Party MP. Gamble's comments were hardly surprising, given the federal party's clearly stated anti-immigration policy and lack of Asian members. But he had broken a cardinal rule of BC politics as defined by Social Credit: it's all right to be racist, classist, sexist or homophobic, but for goodness sake, don't say anything that makes it obvious! Gamble assumed that he was merely voicing the sentiment of most British Columbians when he offered his opinion. He was quickly ostracized by the caucus and was never considered a serious contender after that.

Weisgerber was the unanimous choice among the MLAs, and no other high-profile candidates emerged before the January 16, 1995, vote that elected him leader. He won with 58 percent of the 2,000-plus votes cast. Unless his quiet support of Bill Vander Zalm could be considered a crime, Weisgerber was untainted by Socred scandal, was genuinely respected for his work as a cabinet minister, and was supported by Neufeld, Fox and Hanson as the best choice for leader. Plus, with a seat in the House, he had an immediate advantage over any unknown candidates. But some party loyalists were upset by the opportunistic manner in which he distanced himself from Gamble's racist views, and by the thuggish behaviour of some of his supporters, who barred the other candidates from entering a Reform meeting in Abbotsford. One of the candidates, party executive member Terry Milne, was especially hostile to Weisgerber's Socred pedigree, describing the former Native Affairs minister and his colleagues as a "virus" that helped destroy the Socred government. "They aren't in because they're Reformers," he told the *Sun* in December. "It's a testament to the campaign they have waged that now there is a huge anti-Weisgerber feeling among many Reformers."

To party members such as Milne — and a good many other observers of BC politics — it seemed rather appropriate that when Weisgerber showed up for his first press conference as leader, the Reform Party banner behind him bore a striking resemblance to the red, white and blue of Social Credit.

6

The Premier in the Plexiglass Bubble

AS THE EVENTS OF 1993 DEMONSTRATED, NONE OF THE THREE official parties in BC politics were exempt from leadership uncertainties. In July, an Angus Reid poll showed that Mike Harcourt's personal approval rating had plummeted to 23 percent – a figure lower than any Bill Vander Zalm's had reached during his error-prone reign.

How had the unthinkable occurred? How could such a safe politician with presumably more political smarts than Vander Zalm have turned off the public in such dramatic numbers? How could the man who was once seen as the NDP's best asset have turned so quickly into its biggest liability? According to Angus Reid, it was all a matter of failed strategy. "Harcourt's inability to benefit from past Liberal leadership troubles," wrote the pollster, "seems to have had further negative repercussions now that the camera lens has been turned around more directly on the actions of his government."

It was true that Harcourt had not taken political advantage of the Liberals' abysmal performance in the House. But then the premier would have argued that it's not the government's job to focus its energy on the Opposition. As for the disembowelment of Gordon Wilson, Harcourt felt no need to benefit politically from his misfortune. What was the point of adding to Wilson's personal disgrace when so many backstabbing, opportunistic Liberal MLAs were willing to do it themselves?

Perhaps blaming the NDP itself for the premier's dismal standing in the polls would have made sense, if not for the fact that the party's approval rating was 4 percentage points higher than his own. Could it have been the anti-establishment cynicism that was currently sweeping North America, and which had ultimately killed the Charlottetown Accord the previous year? It couldn't have had much to do with the premier's handling of NDP scandals. For one thing, there were just too few of any substance during the NDP's first year and a half in power. Only on two occasions was Harcourt forced to discipline a minister.

In the first case, Harcourt expelled Forests Minister Dan Miller from cabinet for three months in September 1992 when conflict of interest commissioner Ted Hughes ruled that Miller should not have kept his seniority rights in a Prince Rupert pulp mill that was affected by one of his cabinet decisions. In July, Miller had approved the transfer of a timber licence to Repap Carnaby Inc. from Westshore Terminals in the Prince Rupert area. Because Repap was a subsidiary of Repap Enterprises Inc., which also owns Skeena Cellulose Inc. where Miller had worked as a millwright for eighteen years before entering provincial politics in 1986, media scrutiny of Miller's relationship with Skeena raised the question of a possible conflict.

Miller, acting on the advice of an aide, actually phoned Ted Hughes a few days before approving the timber license transfer and told the commissioner that he did not believe he was in a conflict, but Hughes said that he could not make a ruling based on what Miller told him over the phone. Instead, Hughes launched an investigation on July 31, when the premier's deputy minister, George Ford, asked him to make a formal judgment. Although Miller severed his ties with the mill on August 23, and while the premier agreed he did not profit personally from the transfer, Harcourt concluded that Miller had shown a "lack of judgment" by failing to step aside and decline participation in the decision. He expelled Miller from cabinet for three months, docking his salary by $10,000 before reinstating him.

The second incident was somewhat more embarrassing, given that it involved a popular, high-profile minister who had been so unforgiving of Socred foibles while in Opposition. Moe Sihota got into trouble in February 1993 when Robyn Allan, the woman he appointed the previous year as interim president of ICBC, was revealed to have run up 24 demerit points on her driving record after receiving seven speeding tickets in the four years before she joined the corporation. She had also been involved in five accidents and was currently on probation.

Sihota, questioned on his own driving record, claimed that he had six or nine penalty points. Two weeks later, however, the minister's guilty conscience caught up with him: on February 16, Sihota told the press gallery that he had collected seven speeding tickets in five years. With 21 demerit points, he was not exactly head and shoulders above Robyn Allan. The revelation was doubly embarrassing, given that Sihota had proudly trumpeted the government's December 1991 announcement of a 15 percent hike in penalties for law-breaking drivers.

At first he tried to deflect the criticism by comparing his lousy record to Allan's (he'd never had an accident, she'd had five; he wasn't on probation, she was), and Harcourt defended him. But Gary Farrell-Collins was having none of it. The Liberal house leader couldn't resist a well-timed poke at the spectacle of two lead-footed socialists telling other British Columbians to slow down. "With driving records like that," he told delighted reporters, "Moe Sihota and Robyn Allan should have raced in the Daytona 500 this past weekend."

But Farrell-Collins didn't stop there. For much of the next month, he dredged up whatever dirt he could find that would get Sihota dumped from cabinet. This included a two-year-old controversy about the shady business dealings of Sihota's late father, in which Sihota was alleged to have defaulted on seven mortgages. This issue, and his handling of a trust account for a woman while he was still a practising lawyer (in which a co-trustee absconded with the money, leaving the woman with nothing) were already the subjects of an investigation by the Law Society of BC that would come back to haunt Sihota in 1995.

Farrell-Collins reminded reporters of a previously discredited allegation that British Columbians had paid Sihota's legal bills resulting from a civil suit that arose from the 1990 Bud Smith tapes scandal. The Labour minister had also made the unfortunate choice of taking a government jet to an airport near his ski cabin on Mount Washington on Vancouver Island, and – even worse, for a New Democrat – used non-union labour in the construction of his new house.

Faced with such a mudslinging campaign from the Opposition, Sihota knew he had little choice but to show some humility. A veteran mudslinger himself, he knew it was payback time. "When I was in Opposition, I engaged in a lot of hardball politics, and I guess there are some who want to give a few body checks back now," he told reporters. "Sometimes I think there is a disproportionate amount of attention paid to me because of the style I had in Opposition. But that goes with the territory, I guess. Whether it's fair or unfair, I'm not going to say because it sounds like whining. And I'm not a whiner."

Harcourt wasn't surprised by the muckraking, either, commenting, "He was one of the pitbulls in Opposition. Glen Clark has people sharpening their knives for him, too. You'd expect a high-profile minister to have people firing at him." But even as he defended his two "pitbulls," Harcourt was compelled to diffuse some of the controversy surrounding them. In a minor shuffle of cabinet duties on March 10, he stripped Sihota of his ICBC duties and took BC Ferries off the shoulders of overworked Finance Minister Clark, handing both responsibilities to Transportation Minister Art Charbonneau.

There was some speculation that Clark lost the ferries because of a complaint the previous month that he had given preferential treatment to a union that had contributed to his campaign. The Independent Construction and Business Association, a group of non-union contractors, complained that Clark directed the ferry corporation to award contracts to members of the BC and Yukon Building and Construction Trades. Clark and ferry boss Frank Rhodes denied that such an order had taken place, but the controversy raised questions about Clark's partisanship that had potential to embarrass the premier.

Premier Pleasant and the Central Committee

BY MID-SUMMER OF 1993, THE PREMIER AND CABINET COULD take credit for a number of fulfilled NDP promises. Among the 336 new programs, legislative amendments, funding announcements and private sector partnerships listed in a 21-page summary of NDP initiatives (a government communications document typically packed with partisan claims and feelgood statistics), were an impressive number of developments bearing a distinctly NDP stamp.

There was, of course, the revised labour code, which reflected a broad consensus among business, labour and government – notwithstanding the predictable anti-NDP grousing of a vocal small-business minority based in Vancouver. The government also managed to introduce its health care reform program, New Directions, which shifted health care administration to the regions, at the same time juggling an employment security agreement with the province's unionized health care workers and a billing agreement with the medical profession.

In terms of the environment, the government had much to be proud of. First, the NDP introduced the toughest pulp mill pollution laws in the country, including CFC regulations to control ozone-depleting substances. It also established the Commission on Resources and the Environment (CORE), which created nine new coastal provincial park sites and earned international acclaim for protecting the million-hectare Tatshenshini-Alsek river system.

The government also appeared to be making good on its promises regarding aboriginal land claims and human rights issues. The establishment of the new BC Treaty Commission finally recognized the concept of aboriginal title on behalf of the province while formally launching the process of land claim negotiations. Amendments to the Human Rights Act prohibited discrimination on the basis of age, family status or sexual orientation, while protecting British Columbians from organized hate propaganda and activities. And the NDP managed to achieve more for women's equality in two years than the Socreds did in the previous fifteen, including: $40 million for pay equity for the public sector, guaranteed access to contraception and abortion services for women, 7,500 new childcare spaces in schools, training centres and work places, money for women's centres, transition houses and sexual assault centres, and legalized midwifery.

The NDP also increased spending in crucial areas. Education saw a 9.1 percent increase (almost $300 million) for 1992-93, plus a new $11.6 million school meals program which was estimated to help up to 50,000 children. Changes to the Assessment Act ensured tax benefits to working farmers in the Agricultural Land Reserve, and $9.5 million was allocated to the Buy BC program.

But despite these increases, the New Democrats were hardly the free-spending, shop-til-you-drop pigs-in-a-trough the media made them out to be. The government had cut the budget deficit by 35 percent in two years, from an inherited $2.4 billion to a projected $1.5 billion for 1993-94. Spending growth was cut in half, and BC maintained the second lowest direct tax and sales tax rate in Canada. Since November 1991, 91,000 new jobs were created – the largest increase rate in the country – and unemployment was down. In 1993, exports were up by more than 16 percent, housing starts were up by 10 percent, and retail sales were up by nearly 9 percent. In order to attract offshore investment and head office operations of international shipping companies, the government had also established a BC Investment Office and International Maritime Centre, plus a trade office in Osaka, Japan. In short, this was an NDP government that was open for business – not sitting in some smoke-filled study planning the revolution, as University of Victoria professor Terry Morley once put it.

There were also a number of measures designed to show that the NDP was not letting power go to its head – freedom of information legislation and tougher conflict of interest laws, for example, a freeze in salaries for MLAs and senior government officials, as well as a 5 percent cut in salaries for the premier and cabinet ministers.

Despite this flood of progressive change, the government failed to communicate any cohesive vision of its program to the general public. According to Harcourt, the NDP was caught in an impossible position: on one hand were the party's traditional supporters, who expected immediate change after sixteen years of Social Credit; on the other hand was the skeptical, apolitical or anti-NDP majority who thought the government was doing far too much. "It wasn't that we weren't carrying out what we said we were going to do," he said, "but it was so much that it became hard to comprehend all at once – like one simple theme that Ralph Klein has. His theme is 'We're going to get rid of the deficit.' Well, we were doing a hundred different things, all of which we said we were going to do. But there was a sense of, 'Is this being handled properly? Is this more of how people perceived '72 to '75 to be, trying to do too much too soon?'"

If anyone is ultimately responsible for communicating the government's vision, it's the premier. And during those first two years Harcourt was constantly accused of being little more than a puppet whose strings were being pulled by spinmeisters, hacks and political appointees. According to several government insiders and critics within the party, it was these people – along with cabinet heavyweights like Clark, Sihota, Cull and Miller – who were really calling the shots. And that was the reason for Harcourt's dive in popularity: he had become Premier Invisible.

One of the first things Harcourt told the party when he was selected leader in 1987 was that he didn't have a "Messiah complex." Unlike Bill Vander Zalm, who never hesitated to use his platform to air opinions about everything from premarital sex to the virtue of Christian worship, Harcourt believed that such grandstanding was beneath the dignity of the premier's office. "The public has never heard my opinion on abortion and a whole number of other private issues that, A, they're not entitled to and, B, they don't need to hear," Harcourt stated. "I look on my job as to run the province well, to give good government. I'm here to govern, not to lead. I'm not a church leader, I'm not involved as a business person for private enterprise – I'm here to foster a climate for private enterprise – but I believe there's a limit as to what I should impose on people."

Much of Harcourt's reluctance to play the charisma game was based on his discomfort with the politics of personality. Vander Zalm, he said, was a "Tom Campbell style of politician" who revelled in media attention for its own sake. "Tom Terrific's greatest moment in politics was when he hit the front page of the *Sun* and *Province* on the same day," said Harcourt, recalling the former Vancouver mayor. "My greatest moments in politics have been putting together the land use plan, starting the negotiating process for the aboriginal people, making sure that every young person, very shortly, is going to get the training and skills they need and don't have to be a brain surgeon to be successful. I get my personal satisfaction out of helping to bring about good changes."

Admirable as it was, Harcourt's disdain for the politics of ego often worked against him. Two years into his mandate, the premier was still an elusive public figure whose real leadership qualities – setting goals, delegating, chairing conferences, consulting and reconciling opponents – tended to play themselves out in the closed-door meetings of cabinet, constitutional negotiations and other political discussions. Not exactly conducive to ten-second soundbites on BCTV. This didn't mean that Harcourt was inaccessible to the average voter; after twenty years in politics he could press the flesh as well as anyone, and his self-confidence was especially evident in one-on-one encounters and main-streeting events. What he lacked, however, was the stage presence and oratorical skills that would allow him to appeal to the broadest section of the electorate – like, say, his hero, Tommy Douglas, or even Dave Barrett.

Because he was a bland public speaker with limited television skills, and because he was so reluctant to share his personal opinions about highly charged issues, the predominant image of Harcourt in the media was of a dull bureaucrat with no passion or wit, the "Premier Bonehead" character invented by the *Province*'s Brian Kieran and reinforced by other anti-NDP pundits. Harcourt's supporters argued that the "Premier Bonehead" label would never have stuck if he had been more willing to present himself as an evangelistic W.A.C. Bennett or Vander Zalm-style leader.

"People in BC, for whatever reason, like larger-than-life, big boss leaders," said Bill Tieleman, communications director for the BC Federation of Labour and a longtime NDP fundraiser." Perhaps the party misread that and said 'Look, we want someone who's out of the limelight. We don't want a guy who's doing policy out of the corner of his shirtsleeve every afternoon at the press gallery.' But people do want to see leadership from the premier of this province, no matter who that premier is or what the political stripe."

Harcourt's reluctance to lead stemmed, in part, from another of his early promises when he took on the NDP leadership: that he would not adopt the "one man government" method with which Bill Vander Zalm had brought the premier's office into disrepute. Harcourt promised a consensual approach in which cabinet ministers would work closely with deputies and career civil servants, and staff and bureaucrats would have more involvement in the daily workings of government. Under Harcourt there would be no policy announcements without the presiding minister's knowledge, and no personal crusades to set the agenda for the evening news. On the other hand, Harcourt's facilitator-style leadership did not afford much public visibility. It was a chairman-of-the-board approach which gave trusted lieutenants like Clark, Sihota, Cull and Miller centre stage while the premier came in for a few token appearances.

At first, this was a refreshing departure from the one-man government of Bill Vander Zalm, but soon it appeared that Harcourt was too much the opposite; instead of putting a distinctive stamp on the NDP program, he surrounded himself with a group of unelected hacks who were determined to set the government's agenda. In the course of the transition, he added so many layers of bureaucracy to his own office that he reduced his position to that of a figurehead. By 1993, senior staff were so much in control of his agenda that Harcourt was referred to around the legislature as "the premier in the plexiglass bubble." That is, he only knew what his advisors were telling him, they weren't telling him nearly enough about what was really going on, and their ventures into the world of policy were too often making the government look stupid.

Part of this problem may have been due to Harcourt's lengthy adjustment to provincial politics. When he became mayor of Vancouver in 1980, Harcourt was an independent candidate who could draw from years of experience as an alderman, and from his high profile in the city, to carry out a clear agenda for the public. He did not have to answer to any party executive; if anything, COPE was answerable to him because he was the only electable mayoral candidate who would carry out some of its progressive agenda. Harcourt was also able to maintain a hands-on approach to government because he had a relatively small staff as mayor.

As premier of BC, however, he faced an electorate which, outside of Vancouver, knew very little about him. He was accountable to an NDP executive hungry for power after sixteen years, and was in charge of a much larger bureaucracy than at Vancouver city hall. Harcourt's problem was that he had become too dependent on his staff, to the point of being insulated from what was going on. "There's always this fear that I have – and I'm not sure if Mike has it or not, and if he doesn't he should – that you have so much power or stature that your staff is going to tell you what you want to hear rather than what you have to hear," said Ken Georgetti, appraising Harcourt's performance. "As premier he always has to be cognizant of that fact that his reaction to bad news can change the way the news is delivered. But also, government is so large – caucus and cabinet are so large – that the premier has to rely on staff to synthesize information and data for him."

The NDP apparatchiks surrounding Harcourt were mostly out-of-province recruits with long records of party service in Ontario, Manitoba, Saskatchewan and the Yukon. Like most bureaucrats, these people were invisible to the general public for most of the first two years. But they took their role in the NDP government very seriously, even referring to themselves as "The Centre" – an unintentionally Orwellian nickname that said a lot more about the group than its members probably intended.

The Centre included three of the five party members who had worked on the transition planning committee before the 1991 election. George Ford, who had served for two decades in the public services of Manitoba and Saskatchewan before coming to BC in 1989, was named deputy minister to the premier and cabinet secretary – the most senior civil servant position in the province. Under the Harcourt regime, however, the deputy minister's influence was matched by that of the principal secretary, a political advisory position that went to Linda Baker, a veteran party strategist who had served as executive director to the NDP caucus since 1985.

Baker was weaned on NDP politics. The daughter of former NDP MLA Rae Eddie, who represented New Westminster from 1952 to 1969, she was a political protégée of Dennis and Yvonne Cocke, the husband-and-wife team whose NDP "Cocke Machine" in the seventies was one of the most powerful political operations in the province. In her new job she handled much of the premier's dirty work, including the government's negotiations with doctors and contract talks with the BC Government Employees Union.

The third member of the transition team who remained in The Centre was Chris Chilton, Harcourt's principal secretary while the NDP was in Opposition. A former city councillor from Ottawa who later spent five years as the federal NDP's policy coordinator, Chilton had also worked as executive assistant to Vancouver East MP Margaret Mitchell. His new position, chief strategist overseeing communications and policy, ensured that policymaking was centralized in the hands of a party loyalist.

Chilton worked closely with Linda Baker and Evan Lloyd, associate deputy minister for government communications and effectively the premier's number three political advisor. Lloyd had lived in BC longer than anyone on the premier's staff, having arrived in BC in 1982 after stints in Ottawa and Saskatchewan. The son of Woodrow Lloyd, NDP premier of Saskatchewan in the early 1960s, Lloyd was highly respected as Harcourt's press secretary before the election. His job proved to be far more difficult once in power.

For the first year and a half, Lloyd was left in the spotlight to defend the government while Chilton and Baker tinkered with policy in the background and made most of the strategic decisions. Before long, rumours began to surface about Chilton and Baker's curious advice to keep the premier as far away from decision making as possible. Clark and Sihota and, to a lesser extent, Cull and Miller, were deemed to be more genuine New Democrats than the premier, so they should be the ones in the spotlight, not Harcourt.

"Some of the more ideological staff people in the premier's office thought that Harcourt would be a loose cannon, too right of their own views, and that he had to be controlled," said one government insider, referring specifically to Baker and Chilton. "So, in effect, the premier's office 'captured' the premier. Delegations would leave meetings with the premier only to be told by staff, 'Never mind what he's saying. This is what's really happening.'" About the same time, a new joke began to filter through the halls of the legislature. "He might not be a good premier," it went, "but he makes a great lieutenant governor."

Baker and Chilton's influence extended well beyond the premier's office. Their insistence, for example, that Clark, Sihota, Cull and Miller make all major policy announcements was not well received by other cabinet ministers. On one occasion, Chilton caught wind of a major fisheries announcement. Rather than leaving it with Bill Barlee, the minister responsible for Agriculture, Fish and Food, Harcourt's chief strategist decided to refer it to Forests Minister Miller, apparently because Miller's North Coast riding encompassed a number of major fishing centres, including Prince Rupert.

That wasn't the only reason for Chilton's strategy. According to a member of Barlee's staff, there were concerns about Barlee's apparent lack of NDP credentials. Some members of the Centre casually dismissed the Agriculture minister as "a hick from the sticks," a right-wing small businessman who lacked an urban, academic or trade union pedigree and was therefore unsuitable for high-profile announcements. Chilton's plan was thwarted at the last minute when Barlee was tipped off by his staff. Reportedly appalled by such a crass display of power politics (not to mention the arrogance of an Ontario hack totally underestimating his value in the Okanagan), Barlee immediately issued a press release on the fisheries announcement.

This kind of power struggle was not unusual during the NDP's first two years. More often than not it happened behind Harcourt's back, which didn't encourage an image of the premier as a take-charge kind of guy. But there was at least one other reason for his poor showing in the summer 1993 polls, and it had to do with a single budget measure that the government never imagined would cause it any harm. By the time it was over, the premier was convinced it was time for a shuffle.

Class Warfare and the Oakridge Rebellion

MIKE HARCOURT'S BELIEF IN CUTTING DEFICITS SHOULD NOT have been a surprise to any of the NDP's socialist supporters. From the day he was chosen party leader, he repeated his economic creed:

deficit reduction was not in itself a right-wing concept. "We didn't do it [reduce the deficit] for right-wing reasons," he insisted. "We did it for the same reasons that Tommy Douglas never had a deficit; that if you let your finances get out of control, you've got to borrow. If you've got to borrow, you go to bankers. And if you go to bankers, they'll tell you to slash and crash services for ordinary working people ... health, medicare, social services, education. And I'd much rather have social democrats [deal with the deficit] than bankers. If you want to maintain some independence, then you can't put yourself in that position."

The problem was, though he may have convinced NDP supporters of this necessity, the premier's method of containing the deficit was bound to enrage the wealthier voters who didn't support the NDP in the first place. In the 1993 budget, for the second straight year, the government planned to raise personal income taxes to control the deficit.

The NDP's second budget experiment with higher taxes began with Harcourt's provincewide television address on January 21, 1993. In the upcoming budget, he said, grants for schools, hospitals, colleges and universities would increase by only 3 percent – less than half the increase they received the previous year, and barely enough to cover population growth. The big announcement, though, was that the wealthiest British Columbians would be targeted for much higher taxes, and sales taxes would also go up. Higher taxes were inevitable, said the premier, because of the 50 percent rise in the cost of health care over the last five years, and the need to increase education spending after years of Socred neglect.

"We must face the reality of higher taxes," said Harcourt, sitting beside a colourful display of charts and graphs. "I know they're unpopular, but I'm willing to take the heat to make sure our kids have good schools [and] our families have quality health care. While all of us must pay our share, we will look first to those who are most able to shoulder the heaviest burden. Even if it means risking my political career ... I'm going to do everything in my power to deal with these deficits."

The premier was already having to defend his tax policy against attacks from the Union of British Columbia Municipalities (UBCM). A week before his television address, Vancouver Mayor Gordon Campbell bashed the previous year's budget in an address to the UBCM that sounded very much like an election campaign speech. Glen Clark's elimination of the supplementary homeowners' grant, said Campbell, had "stunned the middle-income homeowner, frightened seniors ... appalled small business owners who were struggling to stay afloat" and this year threatened to "push the increase to the average homeowner's tax bill up over 16 percent."

With the government's second budget on March 30, 1993, the Finance minister announced a new homeowners' grant policy designed to hit the rich. The basic homeowners' grant would go up by $20, and the seniors grant by $25; however, the grant would be reduced by $10 for every $1,000 of a home's value above $400,000. Thus, any home with an assessed value of $447,000 or greater would not be eligible for the basic grant; nor would a senior's home assessed at $474,500. As well, homes valued at more than $500,000 would be subject to a new school surtax that would raise an estimated $37 million in the following fiscal year.

These measures, said Clark, would affect only the wealthiest 5 percent of BC homeowners – about 50,000 properties. Nothing unreasonable about that, he argued; the measure was entirely in keeping with the premier's desire for those most able to shoulder the heaviest burden – an argument for which Harcourt was willing to risk his political career. But Clark's decision to impose asset-based taxes ignored homeowners on fixed incomes, some of whom had bought their homes decades earlier at much lower values. It was these people, many of whom were seniors, who would suffer the most under the new system, and theirs were among the more vocal complaints heard by the government.

These people found allies in the media and Opposition parties. The media in particular saw the tax as a perfect example of socialist excess which, with the right spin, could turn the public against the government. In the following weeks, the homeowners' tax became a lightning rod for a provincewide "tax revolt" that seemed to address every imaginable grievance about NDP fiscal policy. Scores of upper-middle-class homeowners on Vancouver's west side became born-again

activists, erecting protest signs on well-manicured front lawns to pro-
claim the revolt that would bring the NDP to its knees.

For those who supported the government, the scene was amusingly
ironic. There was something incongruous about a large group of middle-class people taking to the streets and adopting tactics usually
employed by labour, the poor and the left to make their point with the
government. Many of these people had never raised a placard in their
lives, perhaps because their interests were well protected by Social
Credit. Now they were getting their activist feet wet by signing peti-
tions, writing letters to the premier and jamming their MLAs' phone
lines. They also attended rallies, joined tax reform groups and wrote
letters to Vancouver *Sun* tax columnist Barbara Yaffe, a former
lifestyles section editor who became an instant celebrity with her frequent attacks on the NDP and anything that hinted at a war on the
wealthy.

All this middle-class handwringing over taxes was perplexing to
members of Vancouver's anti-poverty movement. Frances Wasserlein,
for one, couldn't recall the last time any of the Oakridge protestors
had spoken out to help the poor achieve better housing choices. "I
didn't see the middle class of the city rising up to defend social programs against cuts by the Socreds in the '80s," said Wasserlein, a
member of the Vancouver eastside Grandview-Woodlands area council. Pam Fleming of End Legislated Poverty also found it difficult to
shed a tear over the issue. "They'll come out about a few extra dollars
out of their pockets," she told the *Sun*, "but have no problems with
the fact that there's people who literally can't afford to even pay their
rent."

The Liberals, meanwhile, were busy demonizing Glen Clark as a
vampire leeching off the good taxpayers of BC. "The fiscal life blood
of this province is being drained," said interim Opposition leader Fred
Gingell, in one of his more colourful metaphors. "The minister has
apparently embraced Count Dracula as his role model." The *Sun* story
quoting Gingell ran with the headline "Clark sucks life blood out of
BC, Liberals say," while another read "Business hits budget insanity,"
and a *Province* headline asked "What's so funny, Glen?" beside a picture of a grinning Clark pretending to hang himself by his necktie.

If the Finance minister was feeling the heat, he wasn't showing it. "I think the media tends to listen to powerful, vested interests like the business community and wealthy individuals, and that's not representative of the public," Clark told the *Sun*. "I mean, 28 percent of British Columbians actually see their taxes go down in this budget and I haven't seen that in any of the news columns."

Clark wondered why the media wasn't emphasizing that $220 million of the projected $800 million in new taxes would come directly from the richest people in the province in the form of new income tax. At the same time, he appeared to ignore criticism that an increase in the sales tax would affect lower-income wage earners disproportionately. Clark argued that the wealthy would bring in most of the sales tax increase, since they purchase more goods. The average British Columbian would pay $3 a week in sales tax as a result of the increase, or about $155 a year. Thanks to this approach, said Clark, the government would manage to reduce the deficit by almost 25 percent, to $1.5 billion from $2 billion.

But all this was of little concern to homeowners who felt they were being taxed out of the homes they had lived in for decades. Aside from Clark and Harcourt, no one took more heat for the homeowner's tax than the cabinet's westside MLAs, Darlene Marzari and Tom Perry. Both received a deluge of calls from NDP supporters, many of whom were middle-income earners and seniors who didn't think they should be included in the government's make-the-rich-pay scheme. Marzari in particular took a beating over this issue. Although she had represented the area since 1986, it was only a matter of time before class issues bubbled to the surface in Vancouver-Point Grey – an upscale residential district in which half the homes fell into the $550,000-plus range. When the surtax was announced, about 850 voters wrote to Marzari, and countless others picked up the phone. "Awful – that's how I felt," she told Barbara Yaffe. "It was the single biggest issue that I've dealt with in provincial politics in the six years. I was really caught in a terrible situation, I felt, where to stand up and speak for my constituents put me in a conflict with my cabinet colleagues."

As for the premier, he too could lose a grant for his $640,000 home, but he was still unwilling to overrule Clark. Asked by a reporter whether his wife had complained to him about the "tax grab" on their home, Harcourt quipped, "No, but when I came home last night she'd changed the locks."

While Clark showed no sign of bending to the protest, the mounting pressure did cause the government to reconsider some of its tax measures. The weekend following the budget announcement, cabinet wrestled with a central question that put the NDP's entire fiscal philosophy up for review: does owning a high-priced home make someone wealthy, or should wealth be based on income? On Monday, April 5, Clark answered that question by scrapping the school surcharge on property tax – saying goodbye to a potential $37 million in revenue.

But the government still faced the wrath of at least 6,000 seniors in the Lower Mainland, who faced big property tax bills in the coming year thanks to the loss of their homeowner grant. The evening after Clark's announcement, 4,000 people jammed the parking lot of Vancouver's Oakridge Mall in an anti-tax rally organized by the civic Non Partisan Association (NPA) and led by NPA Mayor Gordon Campbell. In addition to that event, hundreds of angry taxpayers jammed church halls in Kitsilano, West Vancouver, West Point Grey, Surrey, Coquitlam, Kelowna and Williams Lake. A second mass tax-revolt meeting at the Plaza of Nations on April 17 – also organized by Gordon Campbell – drew another 4,000 people.

Campbell, who was looking more and more like a candidate for Gordon Wilson's job, was roundly applauded at Oakridge when he likened the NDP's tax increases to *Indecent Proposal*, a movie playing in one of the mall's theatres. "You work hard, you sacrifice. You should be able to own a home," said Campbell, summing up his world view in a dozen or so words. The crowd was so large that people climbed onto the mall's rooftop to get a better view of the rally. The parking lot was full of cars, causing a traffic jam on 41st Avenue that was unusual for a weeknight. NPA supporters circulated a petition calling on people to "Protest the Provincial Property Tax Grab!" while others gave out bumper stickers saying "Tax! Tax!! Tax!!!/NDP – Not For Me!" Several speakers called for Glen Clark's resignation.

A Pender Retreat, a Shuffling of the Deck

AS HARCOURT'S POPULARITY DROPPED TO 23 PERCENT IN JULY, the government was in big trouble on a number of fronts. The Health Labour Accord was being blasted by the media as a sweetheart deal, the nasty, public fight with BC doctors was continuing, the tax revolt was fresh in voters' minds, and the government was taking a beating from environmentalists for its April decision to allow selected logging in some areas of Clayoquot Sound.

There were also problems in cabinet, where a number of promising ministers had turned out to be big disappointments. Deputy premier and Education Minister Anita Hagen was expected to play a major role in government policy after serving on the transition planning committee, but she never developed a strong voice around the cabinet table. Although she had an excellent record as Opposition education critic, as minister she was considered a bland and ineffective advocate of government reforms. Teachers and others in the system said they were left alone to defend NDP education initiatives from critics; Hagen was nowhere to be found as the controversial Year 2000 program was torn apart and a move toward charter schools and creationism in the classroom picked up steam.

Social Services Minister Joan Smallwood had the opposite problem. She was seen by some bureaucrats as too much of an advocate, pandering only to the NDP's traditional constituency. Smallwood's dedication to anti-poverty groups, in particular, put her in direct opposition to Finance Ministry officials concerned about welfare fraud. Confronted by reporters demanding an explanation for the increase in welfare spending, Smallwood angrily replied that welfare fraud was not a problem. Although the numbers of confirmed fraud cases were nowhere near what the Opposition was charging, Smallwood's remark set her apart from the hardline stance on welfare that her government was beginning to adopt.

Advanced Education Minister Tom Perry, another cabinet disappointment, still hadn't recovered from the previous year's controversy during the Langara College strike. He was perceived to have lost control of events when Glen Clark rejected a one-year faculty agreement that Perry had pledged to take to cabinet. Perry chided Langara faculty instructors, saying they were well paid and that many people would love to have their jobs. All this was after his well-publicized spat with UBC president David Strangway over a matching fund-raising program for universities. At one point, Perry wondered aloud how Strangway could have earned his PhD. Perry, an articulate and principled man, appeared to suffer from a terminal case of foot-in-mouth disease. The Langara controversy and the events surrounding it took their toll on the minister, and he soon began taping his interviews with the media to avoid being quoted out of context.

With so many problems facing his government, Harcourt was more than happy to go into self-imposed exile at his summer retreat on Pender Island. While most MLAs and bureaucrats enjoyed the seasonal recess from the House, the premier quietly drew up his plans for the largest cabinet shuffle in BC history. "My biggest concern was that we were losing public confidence in the government," Harcourt recalled later. "And the tremendous changes we were making were being lost in the anger that people were feeling about us – all those things were colouring far too much public life in the province for us politically ... So I wanted to not put the brakes on but get some focus, and I wanted to get some new people on certain problems that needed our attention."

He was also concerned about reasserting his own authority. When he finally unveiled the new cabinet on September 15, Harcourt raised eyebrows with a display of contrition unusual for a BC premier. "We've made our share of mistakes," he said. "At times we have been more interested in making changes than making sure people understood why, or moving ahead too fast before making sure we were listening to legitimate public concerns." First, he said, the government's effort to improve forest practices was poorly communicated to the public. Second, the Education Ministry dragged its heels in replacing some "clearly flawed elements" of the Year 2000 program. "And," he added, with a chastened Glen Clark smirking in the background, "our mistaken assumption that everyone who lives in high-priced homes also have high incomes should never have led to the surcharge on property taxes."

For all these problems, he said, the premier should take full responsibility. "These cabinet changes are more about me changing my attitude than the performance of individuals ... And the biggest change I intend to make involves me. When this government first took office I put a good team in cabinet and gave them a great deal of responsibility and independence. But what I have learned is that I must provide more direct, focussed leadership. I must set the priorities, establish a plan and demand accountability. I have made it clear to this new cabinet, and I pledge to the people of British Columbia, that I will provide that leadership from now on."

Harcourt's speech was significant in that he made several concessions to right-wing criticism. He cited, for example, the need to be "responsible to all the people of British Columbia, not to special interests, the bureaucracy, or partisan politics." This was a direct response to media criticism of Hagen, Perry and Government Services Minister Lois Boone, all of whom had been accused of being captured by their bureaucrats or pandering to lobbyists (although teachers would argue with that assessment of Hagen), and all of whom were dumped from cabinet. Harcourt's pledge to "keep our schools open" was his way of acknowledging criticism that the government didn't respond quickly enough to school strikes the previous spring.

Post-secondary education got a complete overhaul with the scrapping of the Advanced Education Ministry. In one of his most radical policy moves, Harcourt created a new Ministry of Skills and Training, and twinned it with the existing Ministry of Labour under a new minister, Dan Miller. Although the change had been in the works for years, the new ministry was the final result of the June Premier's Summit on Skills Development and Training, the second of six major thinktank sessions organized by the premier to solicit ideas on the economy from business, labour, local government, aboriginal and academic representatives.

The new ministry's flagship was a program called Skills Now, which would encourage welfare recipients to take training programs, link high schools to the work place through apprenticeships, reduce the cost of student placements in universities, develop advanced technology and applied education programs and expand retraining programs through partnerships with small business and industry. The Skills and Training Ministry would apply a more practical, job-oriented view of post-secondary education, a philosophy that had some university representatives crying "anti-intellectualism."

But the premier wasn't buying it. If anything, Skills Now was anti-elitist, not anti-intellectual. According to Harcourt, it was an attack on a philosophy of education that made most BC school children feel inadequate because they were fated to become carpenters, waiters or retail sales clerks – positions deemed less significant than being an academic or going to a university. "I don't accept that. I've never accepted writing off 70 percent of our kids, which is what that kind of thinking has led to," Harcourt recalled later. "It's been very destructive because a lot of people have gone to universities that shouldn't be there, and a lot have dropped out of school because they saw they weren't going to be a brain surgeon – it's just led to a whole terrible waste of human lives."

On the other hand, Skills Now would be tempered by a new standard of performance expectations. "It's a cruel hoax on young people to have them come out of Grade 12 passing and not be literate in a broad, modern sense," the premier explained. By Grade 10, he said, students would be expected to be literate in basic reading, communications and technology, with training in work place and interpersonal skills.

Even outgoing Advanced Education Minister Tom Perry, who was dropped from cabinet altogether, praised the new system. The premier's conference, he said, was a significant turning point in the NDP's approach to education. Clearly, Harcourt's consultation with community leaders had paid off. "I remember telling him, 'You're actually radical. You're much more radical than the system expects'," recalled Perry. "He was talking about how we need to involve the church basements, the community centres, volunteer efforts, the native elders – everyone we can possibly find – in education. It reminded me a lot of the Cuban literacy campaign in the late 1950s, where they enrolled high school students to teach elderly people how to read. And I think that's what philosophically is behind Skills Now, which I think is a brilliant idea." Perry's only reservation about Skills Now was whether the government was being naive by trying to expand apprenticeships by fiat. While both federal and provincial governments have provided useful technical training for apprentices, he explained, governments could not force employers to take on apprentices. "The question was, 'Should we directly subsidize companies to take on apprentices, and if so, are we then undermining an existing worker?' Are we simply giving them free money for something they ought to pay for themselves?"

Big changes were also in store for Social Services. Harcourt's promise to "do even more in social services to make sure money is going to the people who need it most and is not being wasted on welfare fraud or bureaucratic waste" was a rebuke to Joan Smallwood. Her demotion to the Ministry of Housing, Recreation and Consumer Services was seen by NDP insiders as punishment for bucking the right-wing trend in Social Services. Although she remained on Treasury Board, Smallwood's influence was greatly reduced in her new position. Cynics responded to her demotion by referring to her as "the minister of Small Kitchen Appliances."

Smallwood's replacement in Social Services was an ambitious newcomer to cabinet, Vancouver-Hastings MLA Joy MacPhail. A former assistant to BC Federation of Labour president Ken Georgetti, MacPhail had studied at the London School of Economics under the sponsorship of her father's union. In the early 1980s she coordinated bargaining for the BC Government Employees Union before taking on policy development, communications and liaison with union affiliates for the BC Fed. She had enough talent that she could have handled any number of ministries on her first try – although Labour would have posed a big problem. The NDP had long been accused of being "in bed with labour," but the metaphor took on literal significance in the case of MacPhail and her former boss, Georgetti. The new Social Services minister was annoyed by reporters' questions about her romantic relationship with the BC Fed president, but Georgetti didn't mind addressing the issue. According to the conflict of interest commissioner, he said, there was not even a potential for conflict of interest. "First of all, we don't live together – we go out together," Georgetti.

"The other thing is that our relationship is open and it's in the public ... Conflicts only exist if you let yourself stay in a conflict. Gordon Wilson and Judi Tyabji weren't in a conflict, they were in a lie."

MacPhail's relationship with Georgetti never became an issue, perhaps because there were too many important things going on in her ministry. Before long, the new Social Services minister was under attack by anti-poverty groups as the ministry made a complete about-face. In Opposition, MacPhail had been a passionate defender of affordable and secure housing for the homeless, and more education programs on child poverty. Two years into the NDP's mandate, however, her tune had changed considerably. With welfare rolls climbing faster than either population growth or unemployment, MacPhail was careful in her choice of words. "Spending smart," she said, would be her motto in handling the province's huge welfare rolls.

Glen Clark did not go unpunished in the cabinet shuffle. Thanks to his Darth-Vader-of-the-Left image in the business community – which the homeowners' surtax only reinforced – Clark was taken out of Finance and off Treasury Board, while his hand-picked deputy minister, Tom Gunton, was shuffled from Finance to Environment. Harcourt had no intention of marginalizing Clark; he only wanted to take him out of the spotlight, where he was bound to cause controversy. To make a place for his popular NDP pitbull, Harcourt created the brand new Ministry of Employment and Investment, which quickly became known among media pundits as "the ministry responsible for giving away money." It was a less glamorous portfolio than Finance to be sure, but Clark won a few favours as well. While he was taken off Treasury Board he was placed on Planning Board and retained, or regained, control of crown corporations (including BC Ferries, BC Hydro and BC Transit). Clark's marching orders for Employment and Investment were to emphasize jobs and growth in the hope that business would support the government's efforts to manage the economy.

Clark was also responsible for the new BC21 program, a series of investment initiatives in new infrastructure projects around the province. Designed to strengthen regional economies for the 21st century, BC21 added $350 million to the $1 billion already targeted for the construction of schools, universities and hospitals across BC. BC21 money was also earmarked for highway construction and expansion, two new superferries for the BC Ferries fleet, and expansion of research programs at various universities. To help Clark with this massive undertaking, Harcourt convinced BC Ferries president Frank Rhodes, a former Social Credit deputy minister, to leave his post and become Clark's new deputy.

The big winners in the cabinet shuffle reflected an unmistakable shift to the right on fiscal policy. Elizabeth Cull was promoted from Health to Finance and also became Harcourt's new deputy premier. Art Charbonneau's conservative pragmatism was rewarded with a move from Transportation and Highways to Education, while small businessman Bill Barlee moved from Agriculture, Fish and Food to the revamped Small Business, Tourism and Culture. (Barlee's new job included one third of David Zirnhelt's former Ministry of Economic Development, Small Business and Trade while Zirnhelt took Barlee's place in Agriculture.) Dan Miller went from Forests to Labour Skills and Training (taking one third of Perry's duties in Advanced Education, which was eliminated), Robin Blencoe took Lois Boone's place in Government Services, while Darlene Marzari took Blencoe's place in Municipal Affairs. Only Attorney General Colin Gabelmann, Energy Minister Anne Edwards, Women's Equality Minister Penny Priddy and the premier himself kept their original jobs. And Glen Clark was the only one to keep his old suite of offices.

Newcomers included MacPhail in Social Services, Paul Ramsey in Health and Jackie Pement in Transportation and Highways. Ramsey, the MLA for Prince George North, was president of the College Institute Educator's Association of BC before the election. In the months leading up to the shuffle he had taken an active role in the doctor's fee dispute, leading a crusade against physicians who opted out of the Medical Services Plan. Pement, who won the Bulkley Valley-Stikine riding by only 265 votes in 1991, was a 47-year-old community activist, college instructor and former school board chairperson from Burns Lake, who had served as chair of the legislature's environment and tourism committee and of a task force on post-secondary education in the North.

Most observers saw the cabinet shuffle as a clear sign that Harcourt was taking his government in a rightward direction. He had, after all, introduced a new get-tough stance on welfare, promoted conservatives like Cull, Charbonneau and Barlee, and demoted NDP lefties like Hagen, Perry and Smallwood. But the right-wing theory was hardly supported by the premier's approach to the three ministries most responsible for land use issues. Giving Environment to Moe Sihota may have reassured the IWA, but the former Labour minister had a green streak that nobody knew about when Harcourt shuffled the cabinet.

As for Andrew Petter's appointment to Forests, there was no fooling anyone in the business community or editorial offices around the province. Petter, a bright academic and the most passionate environmentalist in the cabinet, was perceived to be hostile to the timber industry. Similarly, Harcourt's appointment of former Environment Minister John Cashore to Petter's former Ministry of Aboriginal Affairs could hardly be considered a right-wing appointment. Cashore, a United Church minister who had served in the predominantly native community of Port Simpson, had an adopted daughter of First Nations descent and had long expressed a compassionate interest in aboriginal issues. With Sihota, Petter and Cashore in these three crucial ministries, the province would go greener and move further toward land claim settlements than at any point in its history.

"I think Premier Harcourt took a real risk when he put Andrew Petter and myself together in those two portfolios, because the two of us have a real chemistry," Sihota commented. "We think alike, we have very similar value systems, we are not at all territorial. And there was a very quick meeting of the minds between myself and Andrew, and it was kind of funny, because Andrew had a very green reputation."

Harcourt's deckshuffling extended into the public service. Aside from hiring Frank Rhodes for Employment and Investment, and moving Glen Clark's deputy minister Tom Gunton from Finance to Environment, he also transferred longtime NDP advisor John Walsh from Tourism to Aboriginal Affairs, promoted five women to deputy minister positions, named seven new deputies and fired four. He appeared to be more forgiving in his own office: principal secretary Linda Baker got a soft landing.

Baker had come under intense criticism for hiring a party loyalist to investigate patronage appointments. It was Baker who advised hiring Judith Korbin for the government's $1 million commission on public service costs and practices. Korbin, a 25-year member of the NDP whose husband helped the BCGEU fight Socred privatization plans for highways maintenance, was to preside over a politically sensitive task: her commission would study issues like contracting out, public sector bargaining, and salaries for senior public sector managers. By putting someone like Korbin in this position, Baker was contributing to the perception that the NDP was no less guilty of awarding friends and insiders than the Socreds were.

Baker's political influence around the premier's office had increased dramatically during a brief period when chief strategist Chris Chilton was ill. She raised eyebrows by showing up at the table for talks with the doctors, and at the BCGEU wage talks she played a more dominant role than the government's negotiator, Gary Moser. Before long she was raising comparisons to a principal secretary from the not-so-distant past, David Poole, who was drummed out of government after he was accused of political interference on behalf of his boss, Premier Bill Vander Zalm. Wary of such analogies, Harcourt sent Baker to the Ministry of Finance, where she became the new CEO of the public sector employer's council and secretary to the cabinet.

Harcourt's deputy minister George Ford, suffering from burnout, was granted an extended leave of absence before resurfacing in Municipal Affairs. His position was taken over by Douglas McArthur, who had come into the premier's office the previous year to handle the cabinet planning secretariat. Chris Chilton was promoted to the new position of chief of staff, which replaced Baker's old position of principal secretary. John Heaney, one of Chilton's troubleshooters in the premier's office, was moved into Chilton's old position, which then became the public issues and consultation office. And Sheila Fruman, yet another Chilton staffer, became Harcourt's director of communications.

Fruman would prove to be one of Harcourt's more controversial appointments. As a union strategist for the BCGEU in 1989, she had incurred the wrath of many when she advised BCGEU president John

Shields to modify his stance against privatization. During the same campaign, Fruman pulled Shields out of a press conference with the IWA's Jack Munro and Jim Sinclair of the Fisherman's Union, apparently out of concern that Munro would get all the coverage. During the Health Labour Accord negotiations, she butted heads with union leaders over the number of health care workers to be displaced under the new agreement. Now she was responsible for improving the premier's image.

Overall, the makeover was a typical Harcourt compromise: a rightward shift in some departments (Education, Social Services, Finance) tempered by a progressive approach in others (a "green" Forests minister, increased spending on infrastructure). Harcourt satisfied conservative critics by promoting a tough-as-nails union official to crack down on welfare abuse; vindicated Elizabeth Cull's record as Health minister by making her his deputy premier and Finance minister; showed the environmental movement that he was serious about protecting the forests for future generations; and, finally, proved to the media that he wasn't afraid to fire anyone who didn't follow the agenda that he, himself, had established. At last, it seemed as though the premier had shown real leadership. No more "chairman of the board." It was a welcome change, but only the first of many occasions that Harcourt's leadership mettle would be tested over the next two years.

PART II

Walking the Tightrope

A significant proportion of the business community simply would prefer to have a Socred-type government. However, I think we can get their grudging respect ... They might work against us, but I think it is going to be increasingly hard for opponents of this government, the business community, the media or our political opposition to be shrill about this government. If you look at the actual performance ... and at the economics, you can't argue with the facts.

> Harcourt the politician in a late 1993 feature
> interview for the private consulting firm
> Government Policy Consultants, for its report
> *The NDP at Two: The Harcourt Government
> at Mid-Term.*

When I saw that over a million dollars in personal loans had gone out to Dave Stupich and people around him, the amount of money that had been taken to pay back the bondholders – all the money that was owed to charities – I was so angry. I'm still angry. But I also know that, fair as it is – the Parks Report totally exonnerated me and my government – there was no way I could get out from under it.

> Harcourt to the author, November 23, 1995,
> explaining his decision to resign as premier.

7

Brazil of
the North

IF THERE WAS ONE AREA OF PUBLIC POLICY THAT BRITISH
Columbians associated with the NDP in the late 1980s, it was the environment. The governing Socreds were unequipped, strategically and
ideologically, to deal with the consequences of the changing ecosystem. As a business-first, pro-development party, Social Credit had
continued on its free-enterprise mission, only introducing an environmental task force in the final year of its mandate when public opinion,
an increasingly powerful green lobby, and a detailed blueprint by the
Opposition New Democrats demanded it.

How could Socred strategists have failed to recognize that the environment was fast becoming a major election issue? Likely many of
them still held on to a nostalgic vision of the past, the boom period of
the 1960s when the great Socred patriarch, W.A.C. Bennett, was able
to indulge in a spree of development and forest harvesting without
worrying about the consequences. Because the party had won successive elections without having to commit itself to biodiversity, the governments of Bills Bennett and Vander Zalm only had to pay lip service
to the environment while maintaining their collegial relationship with
corporate polluters and profit-rich forest multinationals.

Caught between the powerful lumber lobby and the increasingly

sophisticated green movement, the Socreds surprised no one by siding with their traditional allies. There was a cynical assumption on the
part of the government that the interests of loggers and conservationists would always be incompatible. The Socreds also believed they
could cut into the NDP's share of the union vote by spreading fear
among forestry workers that the changes proposed by NDP environment policy would threaten their jobs. (They weren't interested in
courting the green vote because they regarded environmentalists, for
the most part, as treehugging pinkos who wouldn't vote Socred if
their lives depended on it.) Consequently, the Ministry of Forests
spent the first three years of Vander Zalm's government trying to convince an increasingly skeptical public to embrace the concept of
"assured access" to trees – whatever that meant.

In one of the government's greatest miscalculations of the public
mood, Forests Minister Dave Parker pushed for a greatly expanded
system of 25-year renewable tree farm licences that would have
granted companies exclusive cutting rights to BC forests. When that
campaign failed, the ministry appointed a thirteen-member Forest
Resources Commission. The commission's final report called for a new
crown corporation to oversee the expanding log market and tree-
planting programs, produce up-to-date inventories of forests, and
develop an overall land use plan for the province. But every decision
the Socreds made regarding environmental protection was driven by
outside forces, not party policy, and was carried through with the
reluctance of a child forced to eat his spinach before moving on to
dessert.

The Opposition New Democrats, on the other hand, appeared to be
in tune with the changing times. According to Mike Harcourt, the
answer to BC's land use dilemmas lay in a 1987 United Nations report
by Norwegian Prime Minister Gro Harlem Brundtland, titled *Our
Common Future*. Brundtland, who chaired the UN World Commission
on Environment and Development, was credited with coining the
phrase "sustainable development," which was fast becoming the
environmental buzzword for the nineties. The basic assumption of
sustainable development was that economic growth and environmental sustainability could no longer be discussed as separate issues, and
the workings of the marketplace could not be relied upon to protect

the environment; governments, in fact, were morally obliged to provide intervene to ensure the right outcome. "The market needs political direction," the Norwegian prime minister said. "And governments
are dependent on public opinion. If the argument for the future of
humanity is convincing enough, governments are bound to listen to
it."

Harcourt had nothing but praise for the Brundtland report and was
fond of quoting *Our Common Future*. By February 1989, the NDP
leader was ready to translate some of Brundtland's ideas into a work-
able election platform. Just before the spring session of the legislature,
he issued a policy paper announcing sustainable development as a
party goal. Among the twenty private members' bills on the environment introduced by the NDP while in opposition were proposals to
impose a moratorium on tree farm licences until an inventory of forest
resources was done and a royal commission was established; start a
reforestation program that would increase jobs in the industry;
impose a ban on the export of raw logs; and establish a requirement
that company access to forest resources depend on a commitment to
value-added jobs. (In 1991, Oregon and Washington generated 1.8
jobs for every thousand cubic metres cut – about twice as much as BC.
Sweden generated 2.7 jobs from the same amount of timber.)

"We recognized that what distinguished us from the other parties
was our belief that environmental protection and economic development could go hand in hand," recalled Moe Sihota, who assumed the
Environment Ministry after the 1993 cabinet shuffle. "We also realized that we could not continue to harvest wood at a rate and in a fash-
ion that we had always done. We were witness to the pitting of
environmentalists against loggers, and the conscious decision of the
previous administration to take advantage of that division. And yet
we also realized that many of those people were part of our political
family: natives, environmentalists, IWA workers. And that if anybody could bring them together, we could. And if anybody could
bring together a change in the way we managed our forests, we could.
And if anybody could begin to say, 'Look, we cannot continue to log,
mine and fish the way that we have; we have a responsibility to future
generations to ensure that they inherit an environment that is as rich
and as bountiful, productive and as clean as the one we inherited,' we

could."

But some NDP supporters and longtime party members were not so enthusiastic about the shifting eco-paradigm. The first sign the party would face divided ranks came in 1989 during a major environmentalist campaign to save the Carmanah Valley, a 6,700-hectare temperate rainforest on the southwest coast of Vancouver Island. IWA president Jack Munro led a protest of 1,000 angry loggers at the legislature, bemoaning the loss of jobs that would occur if logging was prohibited in the Carmanah. Green New Democrats looked on in horror as traditional partners from the IWA cozied up to sympathetic Socred ministers.

Meanwhile at the legislature, former Barrett cabinet minister Bob Williams rose in the House to deliver a passionate speech on sustainable development. Shortly after Williams's speech, the party's political strategy committee held a meeting chaired by Linda Baker. "Colin Gabelmann made the suggestion that we should try to bring together these diverse groups and see if we can reconcile these differences," Sihota recalled.

The result was an NDP environmental study group that would have been unthinkable in the 1970s. Through the help of his special assistant John Walsh, Harcourt was able to bring together IWA chief Jack Munro, environmentalist Colleen McCrory of the Valhalla Society, and native representative George Watts to work out a land use charter for the province. The group submitted its recommendations to the party convention, but the NDP's plan to bring the policy to the electorate would not quite be the easy ride Harcourt was expecting.

On March 10, 1989, the NDP leader delivered his now-infamous "creation of wealth" speech to a business audience at the Pan Pacific Hotel in Vancouver. His comments may have reassured the business community, but Harcourt only raised suspicions among his party's green caucus when he said, "Don't forget, I'm the son of an insurance salesman. I know the importance of finding new business and closing deals. In the face of an enormous deficit, I know that we have to create more wealth, without harming the environment."

Colin Gabelmann compounded the suspicion among the greens. "There are people in the province, and some are in the NDP, who would argue for a limited growth strategy," he said. "But you should know that none of these people are in caucus or in influential positions in the party." That argument didn't sit too well with activist MP Svend Robinson, who rebutted Gabelmann in the May 1989 issue of the party's newspaper, the *Democrat*. "Of course there are, and must be, limits to economic growth in Canada and globally," said the maverick New Democrat. Robinson's remark was seconded by former provincial party president Cliff Stainsby, who described the NDP's sustainable development platform as "deficient in many ways" and "fundamentally flawed because it does not acknowledge the limits to growth."

The debate continued through 1989, but the party was ultimately willing to listen to its critics. During a fall meeting of the green caucus attended by 70 party members including six MLAs and assorted IWA workers, the government-in-waiting was challenged on the vagueness of its environment policy. "One thing this caucus has done is cause us to say what we mean by 'growth'," conceded NDP environment critic John Cashore. "If it's growth that ruins the world's capital and it's not sustainable, then that's not acceptable, but if it's growth that enhances the environment, then it is appropriate." Defining those two conditions of growth, however, would be easier said than done.

Meanwhile, the conflicts that continued to plague the Socreds provided election fodder for the NDP. In the mid-summer of 1989, the NDP's provincial council held a closed-door meeting on the Carmannah conflict. Afterward, Harcourt announced that his government would double parks and wilderness areas in the province and would strike an accord between environmental groups, the forest industry and native people. It was an ambitious proposal given that the three major components of the campaign platform – stability for forest workers, wilderness preservation and aboriginal rights – were bound to collide at some point.

With no plan of their own, the Socreds said little about the environment until January 1990, when Vander Zalm established a 31-member BC Round Table on the Environment and Economy chaired by industrial labour relations consultant Chuck Connaghan. The group's mandate was grand in scope, and the involvement of some key environmentalists was encouraging. But the round table was a product of political pressure resulting, in part, from the NDP's being far ahead on conservation policy, rather than a product of political will. In fact, Vander Zalm vetoed its very first decision because he was afraid of offending big business. The committee's goal to set pulp mill emission standards was achieved before year's end and was announced by Environment Minister John Reynolds, but Vander Zalm cancelled it after a last-minute lobby from the pulp industry. Shortly afterward, Reynolds quit as minister.

AS THE NEW DEMOCRATS DISCOVERED ONCE IN POWER, THE interests of forest workers, environmentalists and First Nations people were not so easy to reconcile. Less than three months after taking office, the NDP had kept just one of its eighteen election promises on the environment: passing the pulp mill emission standards law that was scrapped by Vander Zalm in 1990.

According to Syd Haskell, who formed his own group, the Carmanah Forestry Society, the Harcourt government's failure to impose logging moratoriums while developing its provincial land use strategy exposed the NDP as a spineless bunch of fairweather greens. "Environmentalists were betrayed, as the NDP did not honour their promise, and logging continued to the environmentalists' disbelief," said Haskell, threatening an international boycott. Added Sierra Club conservation coordinator Sharon Chow, "In a nutshell, the economic aspects far outride the environmental elements. As far as we're concerned, it's business as usual."

But just as its critics were crying "sell-out," the new government launched a plan that would eventually achieve many of the environmental movement's land use goals. In January 1992, Harcourt announced the Commission on Resources and the Environment (CORE), led by former ombudsman Stephen Owen. CORE was an amalgamation of government, forestry, environmental and aboriginal interests, very much a product of the NDP's reconciliation approach while in Opposition. By creating a regional land use plan for every pocket of the province, the government hoped to end valley-by-valley conflicts while striking a balance between increasing park lands and maintaining jobs in the forestry sector.

For the first year of its mandate, CORE stayed out of the headlines as its members set up preliminary meetings and prepared interim reports. The government was engaged in a prolonged scrap with the small business lobby over its new labour code, dealing with criticism of its first budget, negotiating with hospital employees and launching a failing campaign to support the Charlottetown constitutional accord. Only in 1993 was the Harcourt cabinet finally ready to put its land use policy to the test.

War in the Woods

TOFINO, FEBRUARY 13, 1993

USUALLY THE ARRIVAL OF A FAMOUS AMERICAN VISITOR IS cause for excitement, not resentment, in this tiny Vancouver Island fishing village. The media exposure that celebrities bring to a small community is good for tourism, especially in the off season. But then, most famous American visitors don't threaten the locals with politics. Robert F. Kennedy Jr., son of the late US attorney general, had arrived in BC for a three-day visit to Clayoquot Sound, a 350,000-hectare oasis of virgin forest.

Kennedy, a senior attorney with the New York-based Natural Resources Defense Council, had compiled an impressive track record as an environmental watchdog. The NRDC had lobbied for 40 federal environmental statutes, led successful fights to control acid rain and changed forestry practices in the Pacific Northwest. Kennedy himself had personally brought over 50 successful lawsuits against US polluters including industry, cities and governments.

The NRDC had recently turned its attention to forestry practices in BC, where deforestation rates rivalled those in tropical rainforests. According to environmental reports, the BC forest industry's unregulated clearcut logging was threatening to wipe out North America's last accessible coastal rainforests, along with their associated watersheds and ecosystems. "Since almost half of British Columbia's timber products are exported to the United States, a flow accelerated by successful environmental lawsuits against US foresters, it is natural that NRDC members and United States consumers take interest in where and how the timber is harvested," wrote Kennedy, for a Vancouver *Sun* guest column. "After all, it would be wrong for us to export our environmental problems to Canada."

Clayoquot Sound was of particular interest to Kennedy because it contained the largest remaining, low-elevation coastal temperate rainforest in North America, if not the world. Clayoquot Sound also drained three of the five remaining undisturbed watersheds of at least 5,000 hectares on Vancouver Island. Kennedy, accompanied by colleagues from the NRDC and Conservation International, was so moved by his experience at Clayoquot that he gushed about it at length in the *Sun* essay.

> Snowcapped mountains crowd the estuaries they feed with fresh water and nutrients. I hiked on snowshoes across the wide mudflats that form the second finest migratory staging ground in western Canada, providing vital sustenance for 70 waterfowl species. I gathered oysters and caught coho salmon and cooked them on the shore and followed wolf tracks through narrow mountain gorges beneath hemlock, giant cedar, sitka spruce, and thundering waterfalls.
>
> I saw great rookeries of sea lions and bald eagles congregate for the herring run and I watched fishermen harvest geoducks. If we ever had a country like the Clayoquot in the United States, we've long since destroyed it with failed forestry practices.

Tourism BC couldn't have written better promotional copy for Clayoquot Sound, but the Harcourt administration would soon pay a price for the famous American's enthusiasm. Kennedy's visit was a carefully orchestrated public awareness campaign designed to pressure the government to stop logging in the Clayoquot. It was an annoying distraction for Harcourt, given that Clayoquot just happened to be one of the only watersheds in the province excluded from the CORE decision-making process.

CORE was designed so that each region of the province had its own land use committee to decide the best course of development combining environmental, employment and other community interests. But Clayoquot Sound was not part of this regional review process. During a three-year period overlapping the Social Credit and NDP governments, thirteen interest groups including industry, aboriginal groups and environmentalists had tried to reach a consensus on the future of Clayoquot. This process had continued through the creation of CORE in January 1992. By the following September, however, talks broke down when ten of the groups recommended that the government approve a majority plan to double the park lands and restrict logging to one third of the region. The government was still dragging its heels on a final decision when Robert Kennedy made his first visit to BC.

Kennedy saw that the Clayoquot Sound decision would set a precedent for all other land use decisions in BC. "Any logging that begins in these watersheds before the plan is released may destroy CORE's effectiveness on Vancouver Island and will undermine the government's capacity to apply the CORE process elsewhere," he wrote, casting the issue in its most practical, political terms. "It will also call into question the government's ability to resist logging industry power and to manage BC's transition to sustainable silviculture." Finally, Kennedy aimed his pen at the company that stood to profit most from the Clayoquot's rich resources: "British Columbia will lose its investment and CORE its credibility if MacMillan Bloedel's and its allies' intimidation tactics enable the company to supersede CORE['s] mandate to recommend a comprehensive land-use plan for Vancouver Island."

Not surprisingly, Kennedy's presence on the Canadian political scene was not well received by the workers whose jobs were at stake. Dave Haggard, president of the Port Alberni local of the IWA, dismissed the 38-year-old lawyer as an "economic imperialist," adding that "only a multimillionaire would dare to come here, paddle a goddamned canoe up Clayoquot Sound, then start to put on heavy pressure and lobby this province when we're doing major things before there's any damage. He should spend more time looking after his own country."

THE "WAR IN THE WOODS" BEGAN IN JANUARY, WHEN THE
Western Canada Wilderness Committee (WCWC) threatened to drop
out of the CORE review for Vancouver Island. Unless the trees stopped
falling in the Clayoquot, said WCWC founder Paul George, there was
no point discussing anything. "I don't care what Harcourt says,"
George told reporters. "If they have logging as usual in Clayoquot
Sound and pretend the CORE process is coming to land use decisions
for Vancouver Island ... the hell with 'em. There's been too much take
and no give so far. We've lived through decades of Socred mismanagement. We can live through one short term of NDP mismanagement." Harcourt brushed off the threat with a brief, prepared
statement. "Our government will not be blackmailed by anyone
demanding their way or no way."

But pressure by the green movement escalated in the following
weeks. During an anti-logging demonstration to mark the opening of
the 1993 session of the legislature on March 18, 200 protestors
stormed into the building, injuring a 62-year-old security guard and
smashing a stained glass window. Viewers of that evening's six
o'clock news – many of whom still knew nothing about Clayoquot
Sound – were treated to the spectacle of a presumably pacifist movement resorting to aggression and mob rule to get its point across. The
commotion, which reached its climax as Lieutenant Governor David
Lam was reading the Speech from the Throne, began as a peaceful session of drumming, speeches and chanting on the front steps. Gradually the protestors moved inside, first filling the rotunda beneath the
central dome of the building. Moments after the session began, the
chanting grew louder and the crowd broke through the security
gates, pushing through the lobby and bursting open the doors of the
chamber to come face to face with the legislators of British Columbia.
The doors were quickly slammed shut by a sergeant-at-arms, but the
shock of the demonstration lingered for days. Three teenagers were
later convicted of forcible entry and mischief causing damage in
excess of $1,000 and causing bodily harm to security guard Gary
Miller, who spent a month in hospital with a broken hip. Harcourt
was visibly shaken by the incident, and joined the two Opposition

leaders in condemning the protest. "We don't base our decisions on who can shout the loudest and drum the loudest," he said.

In March the government incurred further wrath from the green movement when it was revealed that the province had purchased $50 million in shares of MacMillan Bloedel the previous month. Critics argued that the purchase of the shares, held by the Ministry of Finance's investment branch for the BC Endowment Fund, was a blatant conflict of interest which would influence the government's upcoming decision on Clayoquot Sound. "Imagine that Bill Vander Zalm and a Socred government had purchased millions of dollars worth of MacMillan Bloedel stock," mused Gabriola Island resident Bob Bossin, an activist and former member of the folk music group Stringband. "Then they sat down at the cabinet table to decide how much of Clayoquot Sound to give the company in which they had just invested. What would Mike Harcourt have said? ... True, the Mac Blo shares were not purchased for personal portfolios, so cabinet ministers are not deciding the future of Clayoquot Sound with one eye on their own purses. But surely they are aware of the effect their decision will have on what is in the public purse, which now includes three percent of MacMillan Bloedel. It strikes me that the conflict is still there."

The premier also had his hands full trying to reconcile his badly divided cabinet. At first, the issue drove a wedge between green ministers like John Cashore, Andrew Petter and Moe Sihota — all from urban ridings — who argued passionately for forest preservation, and Forests Minister Dan Miller, who stood alone in supporting a limited logging plan for the Clayoquot. By February, however, Miller had lined up urban support from Joan Smallwood and Elizabeth Cull, and by March the cabinet reached a consensus. On the eve of its announcement, Joe Foy of the Western Canada Wilderness Committee repeated the WCWC's threat to pull out of CORE if the commission was bypassed in the decision. "If it's out of CORE, so are we," said Foy. "If the [forest companies] can pull the largest wilderness area on Vancouver Island off the table, we're gone."

On April 13, Harcourt announced that one third of the Clayoquot Sound region would be preserved as wilderness, while the rest would be a working forest area subject to limited logging under the strictest controls in provincial history. Logging would be permitted each year in up to 1,000 hectares of the 260,000-hectare region, with an emphasis on harvesting methods such as aerial logging that would minimize the building of logging roads. No major clearcuts would be allowed, and forest companies would lose access to the timber if their logging practices were deemed unacceptable. Harcourt, accompanied by CORE commissioner Stephen Owen, several aides and a group of reporters, made the announcement on the windswept summit of Radar Hill in Pacific Rim National Park, overlooking Clayoquot Sound, after a helicopter tour of the region.

The environmental community responded with unanimous outrage. "The gloves are off," announced Colleen McCrory of the Valhalla Society. "The NDP has betrayed the environmental movement of this province and they're going to pay for it. I think the time may have come for an international boycott of MacMillan Bloedel." Paul Watson, the headline-grabbing leader of the Sea Shepherd Society, was more militant: "We will spike trees and we will attack logging equipment and we will defend the natural integrity of Clayoquot Sound." And from Washington, D.C., Robert Kennedy, who had implored the government during his February visit to prevent logging in the Clayoquot, said, "Today the timber industry won. But once those trees are cut down and an irreplaceable ecosystem is destroyed, we have all lost."

The premier's decision to stage a mass media event from a helicopter site was almost as badly received as the decision itself. "A mountain top?" sputtered Vancouver *Sun* columnist Stephen Hume. "What is this? Government by Monty Python? Can't the leader make a simple announcement without platoons of courtiers nodding and saying yes? All that was missing was the singing chorus line of jolly lumberjacks in crimson plaid." Hume, like many others in the green movement, was deeply offended by the sight of CORE commissioner Stephen Owen, being "dragged in like a stage prop for the premier's Zeus-like declaration from a mountain top."

Owen, whose career in the public service had been marked by a seemingly flawless record of good timing and diplomatic aplomb, appeared to be rattled by his sudden role as Harcourt's flunkie. Later he told reporters that he had been set up by the premier and did not approve of the final decision on Clayoquot. But that admission didn't help his cause or the premier's; Owen's criticism of the government plan was so strongly supported by environmentalists that some members of the forest industry began to question his objectivity.

If that wasn't enough to threaten CORE's integrity, the premier received more bad news when three environmental groups decided to withdraw from the commission. As threatened, the WCWC dropped out of CORE because of the government's failure to include Clayoquot in the regional plan. They were joined in the protest by Friends of Clayoquot Sound and, in the Kootenays, the Valhalla Society. The Sierra Club, on the other hand, decided to stay in CORE until the government responded to Owen's nine recommendations on Clayoquot.

One of those recommendations was that the government agree to a conflict of interest investigation concerning the MacMillan Bloedel share purchase. BC Appeal Court Justice Peter Seaton, who had headed the Royal Commission on Health Care and Costs, conducted the inquiry. Aside from looking for a conflict of interest in the share purchase, Justice Seaton would determine whether the government complied with the Financial Administration Act when it bought the shares, and make recommendations to protect the public interest arising from such a purchase. The investigation was now all the more intriguing, given the government's decision to open at least 45 percent of the Clayoquot to logging interests, of which MacMillan Bloedel was a major beneficiary. Another 17 percent was reserved for selective logging. (Seaton's report, delivered in July, cleared the government of any conflict, real or apparent.)

In June, the government followed five more of Owen's recommendations, including the appointment of an independent scientific panel to help develop "world class" harvesting standards. It also agreed to appoint an independent watchdog committee, including members from the local community, aboriginal leaders and experts in land use management, to monitor logging practices in the area, and designated Clayoquot Sound a UNESCO biosphere reserve. The government banned large clearcuts and imposed a requirement for compulsory logging permits from both Environment and Forest ministries, while ensuring stronger enforcement of regulations and tougher penalties for logging infractions.

But cabinet rejected two of Owen's recommendations: first, that CORE itself be responsible for much of the monitoring and enforcement of forestry practices, and second, that the government provide specific details of the new logging practices and standards before issuing new or revised logging permits for the area. This latter would have been, in effect, a moratorium on logging. In the first case, the government argued that CORE had enough work to do around the province already without the added responsibility of overseeing environmental management in Clayoquot Sound. In the second case, the premier recalled later, "We have said no moratorium or veto to anybody. We've said it to the aboriginal community, we've said the same thing to the environmental community, we've said the same thing to industry. I said 'Life goes on, you can't just freeze activity in a big huge province like BC.' So I've got to be consistent."

Owen could be forgiven for feeling undermined by the cabinet's approach to Clayoquot Sound – both in its decision to exclude CORE from the process, then with its rejection of two of his recommendations. But none of this seemed to bother the former ombudsman. "Generally, they seem to be addressing the concerns I outlined," he said. In the meantime, Owen released CORE's annual report in which he discouraged the government from making ad hoc decisions outside formal planning procedures in response to pressure groups and media campaigns. That approach "creates inconsistency and enhances public distrust and alienation," he wrote.

The Whole World is Watching

EARLY IN JUNE, THE WESTERN CANADA WILDERNESS COMMITtee built a fifteen-kilometre "witness trail" which began at Kennedy River and wound through a region in which MacMillan Bloedel had approval to construct a logging road. Providing public access to the watershed was the same tactic the WCWC had successfully employed in the Carmanah Valley four years earlier. The group had also used it in at least half a dozen other locations throughout BC since a 1984 protest on Meares Island, which was also part of Clayoquot Sound. The WCWC believed that, once people were able to witness the pristine forest, they would be more determined than ever to prevent its being logged. In the case of Carmanah, public pressure was so great that the Socreds were eventually forced to protect half of it from logging.

According to Paul George, the WCWC had no intention of seeking confrontation or intervening in logging operations in the Clayoquot. Mac Blo rep Dennis Fitzgerald concurred, adding that the company would not pursue a court injunction to stop the trail. The corporate thinking now was, Come one, come all, we've got nothing to hide. "If people are going to protest in Clayoquot Sound I would rather see them building trails than burning bridges," he said, referring to fires that were set at two logging bridges in the region. But Fitzgerald rep never did say what he thought about blocking bridges.

The other factor the Mac Blo rep never considered was just how sophisticated the environmental movement had become in the last four years. Since Carmanah, fax machines and poster campaigns had given way to computer modems and the Internet. Clayoquot Sound was one hot issue circulating on a worldwide computer network called Environmental Net. By early June, word was out that a major campaign was about to occur. Vancouver Greenpeace campaigner Karen Mahon sent out the first dispatch, calling for an international day of protest on Canada Day, July 1. The idea was to picket at least eight Canadian embassies and consulates, demanding the protection of Clayoquot. Responses began flowing back to Mahon's computer from Germany, the US, even India and Sierra Leone. Japan and Europe were slow to catch on to the issue, but in the US at least one organization, the Rainforest Action Network, was organizing demonstrations in 30 cities and was prepared, if asked, to launch a tourism boycott of Canada.

Boycotts had already achieved some impressive results when used against the pulp and paper industry. For example, a British publisher cancelled a newsprint order with Fletcher Challenge after viewing a BC clearcut. A German publisher which had previously done business with MacMillan Bloedel shied away from subsequent business citing, among other things, BC forest practices. In Japan, the Nippon Telephone Company was under pressure to cancel a 60,000-tonne pulp contract with Mac Blo because the Port Alberni pulp could contain wood fibre from Clayoquot Sound trees. In Europe, Greenpeace International was urging European Community forest ministers to adopt trade embargoes against wood or paper products originating in Clayoquot Sound. Greenpeace had singled out the area as one of two case studies where trade embargoes should be considered; the other was Brazil.

Meanwhile, the green movement was gaining political clout with increased consumer demand for eco-friendly wood products. Home Depot, a US national building suplies chain based in Phoenix, Arizona, was testing wood products in response to requests for material cut by companies practising selective logging outside of old-growth forests. And Wal-Mart, the largest retailer in the US, was opening an eco-store in Kansas to showcase environmentally friendly products including, ironically, beams made by Trus Joist MacMillan, a Mac Blo joint venture. The Trus Joist beams used less wood than laminated beams.

Valerie Langer, director of Friends of Clayoquot Sound, was also prepared to go international with the war in the woods. "We are going to raise temperate rainforests to the level of concern that tropical rainforests have," said Langer, a 30-year-old bed and breakfast operator who had moved to Tofino from Ontario. "[We will] focus the attention on Canada in the way that attention has been focussed on Brazil and Sarawak. And we are going to make sure that Canada has the reputation it deserves regarding environmental practices."

On the homefront, activists were bracing for a long, hot summer of civil disobedience, arrests and court injunctions. While WCWC stayed out of the confrontation, a broad coalition of about 30 groups, including Friends of Clayoquot Sound and Greenpeace, were more than willing to take part in what was fast becoming the direct action of choice for environmentalists and aboriginal peoples: the road blockade.

In previous summers there were usually no more than 60 or 70 arrests over the course of a single protest. Environmental groups would organize locally, contact mainstream and alternative media, distribute flyers at strategic locations, and face the police in actions that never lasted more than a few days. But those actions were nothing compared to what Valerie Langer was planning this year. "We're aiming for 1,000 [protestors]," said Langer. "With that number of people, [the issue] will be impossible to ignore." At last count, she said, 300 people had taken courses in non-violent civil disobedience. Now the coalition of groups was hoping for as many headline-grabbing mass arrests as possible. The assumption was that the glare of bad publicity in Canada and abroad would force the NDP to return to the drawing board and increase the protected area in the Clayoquot.

The Friends of Clayoquot Sound were aided by a wealthy landowner named Susan Bloom, owner of Clayoquot Island near Tofino. Bloom's undisclosed financial contribution provided the group with a house in Tofino, ten staff positions at $1,000 per month, daily bus service from Nanaimo's Departure Bay ferry terminal, and enough resources to set up a peace camp and information booth near the blockades. This contribution provided the Friends with much greater momentum, as the protests began, than they would have had otherwise.

Although the NDP cabinet still showed no signs of backing down, many believed that it was morally incumbent on the NDP to answer to its green faction. "Surely the government is somewhat receptive to public opinion, if nothing else," said Karen Mahon of Greenpeace. "Politically, it would be inappropriate for them not to respond."

JULY 5, 1993

THE FISHING VILLAGE OF TOFINO WAS NO STRANGER TO BLOCK-ades. Logging protests had taken place in the region since 1984, when native Indians and environmentalists blocked logging roads on Meares Island, north of Tofino, in an aboriginal rights protest. That action led to a BC Supreme Court decision to halt logging, an injunction that remained in effect in 1993. But those protests did not attract nearly as many people, or as much media attention, as the ones for Clayoquot Sound. On this day, about 80 protestors showed up at the

Kennedy River bridge – a logging road entry point that had been blockaded the previous summer and burned by arsonists in 1991. Police were staying put until Mac Blo filed a complaint. In the meantime, Richard Bourne, a private process server hired by the logging company, showed up to hand-deliver copies of a BC Supreme Court injunction issued the previous year, that prohibited members of the public from obstructing legal logging operations in nearby watersheds.

The scene that first day resembled a reunion of old rivals as Bourne and other Mac Blo employees confronted some of the people they recognized from previous blockades. One of the familiar faces was Svend Robinson, the Burnaby-Kingsway NDP Member of Parliament who had joined Haida Indians on Lyell Island in 1986 to demand an end to logging at the southern end of the Queen Charlottes. Robinson and his fellow protestors had won that round; South Moresby was now a national park. "We've seen this movie before, haven't we?" Bourne remarked to the MP. Robinson, standing with his arms linked with other protestors, stared straight ahead as the injunction notice was read aloud. "I'm standing here this morning to show my support for people who are here to join the voices of British Columbians and Canadians who are saying we can't allow this magnificent old-growth forest to be logged," he said. Like most of his fellow protesters, Robinson allowed the injunction sheet to fall to the ground. The next day, he was back at his Burnaby-Kingsway office on constituency business when the first twelve protestors were arrested.

Robinson's presence at the blockade, however brief, was enough to remind the public of the provincial NDP's dilemma regarding land use issues. Former provincial leader Bob Skelly, now the MP for Comox-Alberni, argued that Robinson's action had little, if any, impact on the Harcourt government's position. "People are going to say 'Oh well, it's just Svend there and we expect that kind of thing from him'," said Skelly. "We'd like to save all the rain forest and safeguard all the jobs, but even King Solomon couldn't do that." Forests Minister Dan Miller repeated the government's line that nothing would change. "Is there any chance of revisiting this? Absolutely not," Miller told reporters. "I don't know what people have in mind, but it appears there is some diminishment of the number of people who are willing to blockade the road."

If Miller truly believed what was he was saying, he was in for a big surprise. In fact, the number of people showing up at Clayoquot was rising every day. By the end of the summer, more than 10,000 people had visited the peace camp, and nearly 800 people had been arrested, charged and either jailed or fined for blocking the bridge.

While most of the protestors in the early stages were in their twenties and thirties, a large number of seniors began to show up at the blockades, and children were arrested along with their parents. Harcourt was alarmed at the sight of it. "I think it's really unfortunate, and I am disturbed children are being used that way," said the premier, adding that his eleven-year-old son, Justen, had accompanied him on peace walks and protest marches but never on an illegal blockade. At the protest site, a group of pro-logging mothers was heard shouting abuse at the anti-logging adults. "You're pathetic as parents!" yelled one. "If you're a parent, you need help. You ought to be ashamed of yourself."

In their concern for good parenting, however, these women and the premier appeared to have missed the symbolic significance of child protest: the children had a greater right than their parents to bear witness to and prevent unsustainable forestry practices. Come the next century, they would be the ones – along with their own children – who would have to live with the consequences of clearcut logging. To argue that they were too young to understand, completely missed the point, and in some cases, it just wasn't true. Asked why he and his eleven-year-old brother had talked their father into joining the protest, twelve-year-old Adam Harris of Galiano Island told the Vancouver *Sun*, "To help save Clayoquot and because of what MacMillan Bloedel did to Galiano Island. They bought half of Galiano and clearcut it. It looks pretty ugly, some parts."

Much of this argument about children was a reflection of the wide gulf between the lifestyles and politics of the two loudest parties in the dispute. The villages of Tofino and Ucluelet were witness that summer to a cultural clash between Vancouver Island environmentalists – and their cappucino-swilling, condo-dwelling supporters from the city — and the scores of bewildered loggers and families of forest industry workers who resented the intrusion of green radicals they believed had no compassion for people at risk of losing their jobs.

It was true that some environmentalists had little or no respect for families who had survived for generations by working in the forest industry. Many appeared not to care that people were losing their jobs as a result of the Clayoquot protests. But it was equally true that most of the loggers had done nothing to protect their own jobs when MacMillan Bloedel and other companies began introducing technological changes that increased company profits by reducing labour-intensive harvesting methods. (The number of jobs generated per 1,000 cubic metres cut in BC forests had dwindled from more than 2.5 in the 1950s to less than 1 in the early 1990s.) Forestry workers in general had shown little or no interest in sustainable forest practices throughout the 1970s and 1980s. Despite repeated warnings from scientists and environmentalists that their industry was badly outdated, loggers and other foresters continued working as they always had, leaving it to their multinational employers to "think globally and act locally." Now that some of them were paying with their jobs, they expected the public to support them, even as they continued to play a passive role in the industry's gradual shift toward sustainable forestry.

Loggers took out their frustrations on protestors and their celebrity guests. When the Australian rock group Midnight Oil arrived on July 15 to play a benefit concert for Greenpeace, the band was greeted with messages like "Wipe yer ass with a spotted owl" and "Go back to your Burning Beds" (a reference to one of the group's hit songs). Band leader Peter Garrett was greeted on his arrival by more than a dozen loggers who pounded on his van and hurled obscenities and insults at him. They also cut down the Western Canada Wilderness Committee's $800 "Save Clayoquot Sound" banner, tied it to a logging truck and drove off, dragging it down the Port Alberni-Tofino highway, even though WCWC had no role in the blockade.

But these were minor indignities compared to those suffered by protestors at the hands of the justice system. In an excessive display of law and order that was never explained by police, three women —

including a 72-year-old and a 65-year-old – were brought to court wearing leg shackles. The sentences handed down raised a number of questions about the justice system, particularly when they were compared to sentences for other "criminal" activity. Two dozen Clayoquot Sound protestors were thrown in jail the day after a Victoria man was given a suspended sentence after admitting that he had wandered the city with a loaded shotgun, looking for attractive women to kill. Why, many wondered, did peaceful protestors deserve three weeks to 45 days in jail, while a man with a shotgun hoping to kill some women was slapped on the wrist? And what kind of justice system would force a teenager to perform 50 hours of community work, or fine an unemployed protest organizer $1,500, for trying to save the forest, when a corporate giant like Mac Blo paid as little as $100 for destroying a salmon stream with logging debris?

This inconsistency was a concern for the government, particularly since Harcourt and his cabinet were tied to almost everything that happened in Clayoquot Sound. On October 18, a group of five Vancouver Island MLAs signed a letter telling their constituents that "the decision to commence contempt proceedings against the Clayoquot protestors was a decision of the courts – not the government." Moe Sihota (Esquimalt-Metchosin), Andrew Petter (Saanich South), Elizabeth Cull (Oak Bay-Gordon Head), Robin Blencoe (Victoria-Hillside) and Gretchen Brewin (Victoria-Beacon Hill) signed the letter, which outlined their concerns about the previous week's sentencing of 44 protestors to jail terms of 45 to 60 days as well as fines.

Their gesture prompted BC Supreme Court Chief Justice William Esson to make a rare public statement. He blasted the MLAs for misleading the public about the court's role and for appearing to support the protestors, and strongly defended the conduct of the protest trials, comparing them to those resulting from anti-abortion protests at the Everywoman's Health Centre in Vancouver several years earlier. Those two cases were identical examples of contempt of court, said Esson, and the crown proceeded accordingly in each one.

Slogans, Lies and Damage Control

ON JULY 20, THE SAN FRANCISCO CHRONICLE RAN A FRONT-page article on Clayoquot Sound under the headline "Ancient Trees Disappearing in Brazil of the North." Mike Harcourt and Environment Minister John Cashore shook their heads in recognition. The phrase "Brazil of the North" was a catchy slogan dreamed up long ago by Colleen McCrory of the New Denver, BC-based Valhalla Society. McCrory had used it as the title of a 36-page tabloid newspaper that she began distributing internationally the previous February. Clearly, her strategy was working.

Harcourt was frustrated by the constant need to counter McCrory's publicity. During his February address to members of the European Parliament in Brussels, Harcourt told legislators that the clearcut photograph on the cover of "Brazil of the North" was five years old, that trees ten to twelve feet high were currently growing on that site, and that a clearcut of that size would not be allowed in BC under current regulations. But the message didn't seem to filter through, and the San Francisco paper was willing to report McCrory's claims as fact.

"It's an ignorant bum rap," said Harcourt, dismissing the article. Cashore, after outlining the new Environmental Assessment Act in a speech to the Vancouver Board of Trade, told reporters that BC had some of the toughest environmental laws in the world. The problem was, the government was still haunted by the ghosts of Socred past. "We are being judged by old forest practices, we are not being judged by what we are bringing into place," said the Environment minister. "There is cynicism out there and twenty months isn't enough to turn that cynicism around."

On Harcourt's next trip to Europe, in October, Greenpeace organizers dogged his every step and shouted abuse at him. This time he was accompanied by a delegation that included the IWA's Gerry Stoney and former Nuu-chah-nulth Tribal Council president George Watts, a longtime New Democrat. The reception they received, both in London and Berlin, was far worse than what Harcourt had encountered on the trip to Belgium in February.

Watts was impressed by the premier's ability to withstand the abuse. "I did a lot of personal observation, and at the end of the trip I felt like, 'Jesus Christ, this guy must bathe in baby oil every morning' because nothing stuck to him. He just let it all slip off him," said Watts. "If I was in his shoes, [with] some of the stuff that was being said to him, I would have punched somebody – I wouldn't have put up with that bullshit. And he was just cool the whole time, totally respectful of people even though they were totally disrespectful of him. He said 'Yeah, let's talk about it, I'm more than prepared to come back and talk more about this.'

"They were certainly making his job tougher, and his interests were the same as theirs. He wanted to see an end to poor logging practices in the province. But at the same time, as premier there's no way he can agree to no more clearcutting. He'd have to shut down the whole industry ... What premier is going to survive an election if he does something that's going to lay 50,000 people off?"

Watts, like Harcourt and Stoney, thought that Greenpeace had gone too far and destroyed its credibility with claims made in several of its "fact" sheets. "If they'd not lied about stuff I thought they had a great case," he said. "I still believe to this day that – not just them but other groups are the reason that there is change in this province – that you're not going to see five or six hundred hectare clearcuts anymore. [But] it was their position that there should be no more clearcuts period, and that forest practices hadn't changed, [that] was hard for me to accept. I do a lot of travelling and I had had the opportunity to see a helicopter slow logging. And nobody can convince me that that isn't a hell of a lot different than past logging practices. There's no logging roads, there's no slides – so it is happening. It may not be happening to the degree or the pace that's acceptable to them, but they shouldn't go around and say it's not happening."

For the premier, confronting the Greenpeace protestors in Europe was a confidence builder. "We were right; they were lying about BC and I was going to confront them on it," he said. "I'm used to doing direct action, I'm used to doing zen politics. Walking around the barricades and the police to confront those Greenpeace activists and others who were lying about our province for whatever their cause, was important for me to do as premier. I was making a statement on behalf of 3.7 million British Columbians."

But wasn't he worried about alienating large numbers of traditional NDP supporters, who may have agreed with Greenpeace? "No, because we were right. We were making some profoundly important changes, and that's the reason I was able to go to the European Parliament and get them to not have any boycott resolution. And to tell them, hey, listen, we've made mistakes in the past, but we're making huge changes and you guys aren't perfect either, and you can learn from us. And we can learn from you. And it was the changes that we were introducing – CORE, Forest Practices Code, Forest Renewal, the settling with the aboriginal people, the treaty process – that fuelled my sense of righteousness. That I'm not going to be attacked unfairly and unjustly for what we're doing. And I'm going to tell them personally, and I'm going to go right into the lion's den of Greenpeace Germany and Greenpeace United Kingdom, and the major environmental groups that were trying to diddle us at the European Parliament in Brussels. And the best way to do it is for me to do it."

Back at home, the premier backed up his tough talk with action on October 22, when he announced the establishment of an independent, nineteen-member scientific panel to recommend minimum harvesting and reforestation standards for Clayoquot Sound. The group, chaired by Dr. Fred Bunnell, consisted of scientists from BC and Washington State, four representatives of the Nuu-chah-nulth Tribal Council and an observer from CORE. The panel was to explore issues of biodiversity, fisheries and wildlife, forest harvest planning and scenic resources. The Nuu-chah-nulth members provided a First Nations perspective on the forests. The panel's first report the following January would detail forest management standards and make recommendations for forest harvesting, road construction and engineering, access, slope stability and hydrology. A second report in March would advise the government on silviculture systems, soil conservation and second growth management, among other issues.

Soon after the October 25 federal election, newly elected Victoria Liberal MP David Anderson, a former provincial Liberal leader, offered his own unique solution to the Clayoquot question. Not realizing he would be named Revenue minister in Jean Chrétien's first cabinet, Anderson proposed that he step in as a federal forestry "expert" and help those bumbling socialists in Victoria turn Clayoquot Sound into a national park — then hand them the bill to compensate forest companies for timber they wouldn't be able to log. "The fact of the matter is that they're bleeding to death on barbed wire on the Clayoquot issue. I think they'll greet this opportunity to extricate themselves from the hole they've dug," said Anderson, clearly convinced that the province would welcome his generous, though unsolicited, offer of help. "By the way, there's no federal money to be put into this ... We're offering them a political solution for a basic political problem."

On November 2, the Angus Reid polling group confirmed what Harcourt had already suspected. In the first independent public opinion poll about Clayoquot Sound and related forestry issues since the government's decision in April, nearly 60 percent of respondents supported the "Clayoquot compromise," with less than 30 percent "strongly opposed" and 10 percent "somewhat opposed." And while no one would dare admit it, government insiders drew some strength from the fact that more than 70 percent opposed blockades of logging roads and 80 percent opposed the presence of children at the blockades. The only encouraging news for environmentalists was that two thirds of the poll respondents believed that the forest industry should be monitored more closely to ensure it complied with logging regulations designed to protect the environment. And they called for tougher penalties for any company that breaks the law.

These poll results were just fine with the government, which was set to release its new Forest Practices Code in mid-November. The tough new guidelines were released shortly after a government investigation into logging practices in Clayoquot Sound was made public by environmental groups on November 5. In a twelve-page letter to Mac Blo, provincial officials criticized the forest company for its "low level of compliance" with coastal fish-forestry guidelines, suggesting that Mac Blo had done very little to protect salmon streams. It outlined a long list of poor engineering and forestry practices that led to such problems as culvert washouts, slope failures and eroded roads.

Mac Blo officials argued that, since all but five of the 26 clearcuts with problems had been cleaned up, the government's criticisms were out of date, but few were convinced. Karen Mahon of Greenpeace claimed that the company had lied at least twice when it classified a stream as not having any salmon, when in fact the company's own studies revealed a salmon habitat.

On November 5 – the government's second anniversary – Harcourt travelled to Washington, DC, where he shared head table at a dinner the following night with US Vice-President Al Gore. Harcourt and Gore were attending a banquet sponsored by American Rivers, an organization that helped lead the successful fight to preserve the Tatshenshini as a wilderness park. While environmentalists trashed his reputation at home and abroad for the Clayoquot compromise, Harcourt accepted an award, along with Gore, in recognition of their governments' efforts to preserve the Tat.

Labour added its complaints to the environmentalists' wrath and the logging company's self defence. On November 23, a group of unions representing 25,000 Vancouver Island forest workers walked away from the CORE process only hours before the panel was to end its year-long examination of land use issues. The unions – the International Woodworkers of America (Canada), the Communications, Energy and Paperworkers Union of Canada, the Pulp, Paper and Woodworkers of Canada, and the Longshoreman's Union – demanded that the government commit funds to a transition strategy for workers displaced by pending land use decisions. Gerry Stoney, president of the IWA, said that halting logging at Clayoquot could end up costing more than 2,400 direct and indirect jobs. The unions also rejected arguments that job losses were caused by technological change and past overcutting of forests.

The Nuu-chah-nulth Deal

MEANWHILE, QUIETLY OCCUPYING THE BACK OF THE NEWS sections in most daily papers, were the native perspectives on Clayoquot Sound. Aboriginal people were not necessarily opposed to logging but were concerned about who was doing it, who was claiming economic title to the resources, and how the logging would affect native livelihoods. When the Kennedy Road blockade was first announced on July 1, a number of local natives voiced their opposition to a blockade which was composed almost exclusively of white environmentalists. "We don't support any form of blockade," said Tla-o-qui-aht chief Francis Frank, speaking at the Friends of Clayoquot rally in Tofino. "We have access to our salmonid enhancement project on that road and our peoples are feeling some discomfort in having to deal with the people on that blockade every single morning."

But that didn't mean the 500-member Tla-o-qui-aht nation supported the government's decision, either. In fact, a number of native bands in the area had invited Robert Kennedy Jr. for a second visit on July 30 to help them establish aboriginal title over the 360,000 hectares of Clayoquot Sound. The Nuu-cha-nulth chiefs, representing five First Nations including about 2,500 natives in the Sound, presented a land claims strategy to gain control over at least a share of the timber resources in the area. Such a strategy, if successful, would create jobs in a community where native unemployment was 70 percent.

One option the tribal council was considering was a court injunction to prevent logging until the land claims issue was resolved. Another was boycotting the 1994 Commonwealth Games in Victoria. First Nations people on Vancouver Island had been enlisted as key participants in the colourful opening and closing ceremonies of the event. Natives would also be featured prominently in local and international advertising for the Games, and an artist from the Nuu-chah-nulth had been commissioned to design the silver medal. A boycott would attract worldwide attention to the Sound while embarrassing local organizers.

By September 8, talks with the government had not convinced the native community to abandon the idea of a court injunction. The following week, the Nuu-chah-nulth began using some of the tactics developed during Kennedy's second visit. First, a native representative from Tla-o-qui-aht left for a six-week tour of Europe to call for a boycott of BC lumber – counteracting Harcourt's publicity campaign.

Shortly afterward, a group of natives prepared to paddle a cedar dugout canoe down the west coast of the United States to raise opposition to the BC government's plan to log in their traditional territories. "Our voices have not been heard in British Columbia," said Francis Frank. "All summer, the First Nations perspective was either bypassed or ignored. So we have no choice but to reach out to the international community." The canoe voyage was a particularly effective form of protest; Crees from Québec and Haidas from the Queen Charlottes had both successfully used the tactic to put international pressure on governments.

Before the canoe trip, however, Frank and three other chiefs from the Clayoquot area left on September 20 for a week-long visit to New York and Washington, where they called for an international boycott of Clayoquot Sound timber. The trip, organized by Kennedy, was a productive one; the chiefs met with Kennedy's uncle, Senator Ted Kennedy, as well as with Audubon Society vice-president Brock Evans and Elsa Stamapoulou, chief of the UN Centre for Human Rights. Frank said he hoped the trip would pressure Mike Harcourt to honour a recommendation of the BC Land Claims Task Force, signed by the current government, that called for interim measures to protect lands that are subject to aboriginal claims. "We're not trying to blackmail them," said Frank. "All we're asking them to do is to live up to their commitments."

On December 10, the government signed a two-year agreement with the Nuu-chah-nulth that gave the Tla-o-qui-aht people 70,000 cubic metres of wood, and provided $1 million to train and employ aboriginal forestry inspectors and park wardens, and establishing a system in which bands would co-manage selective logging. The two parties also agreed on a joint management process to oversee logging and related activities in the Sound, without changing the government's original decision in April.

Under the agreement, a new board would oversee regional activities of current timber licence holders such as Mac Blo. The board would include First Nations, government, labour, industry, environmentalists and local community representation. Decisions would require a double majority – the support of a majority of First Nations representatives on the board, as well as a majority of board members, would be required for any decision to be reached. A central region resource council, made up of hereditary chiefs and provincial cabinet ministers, would rule on matters referred by the new board. Finally, the agreement included a provision allowing the government to act as the ultimate decision maker if the council could not arrive at a decision on its own.

While the agreement was hailed as a triumph by the government and tribal council, Opposition critics accused the Harcourt cabinet of using the deal to deliberately derail environmental protests over logging in Clayoquot Sound – since most environmental groups supported aboriginal rights. Even green media pundits like Stephen Hume were suspicious. "Could this deal have less to do with a voluntary commitment to native justice than a cynical ploy for marginalizing the pesky environmentalists?" wondered Hume, in his December 15 column. "Let's hope not. But I also take note that some pro-government pundits were vocal in proposing just such a strategy for undercutting environmentalists. And that was well before the ombudsman criticized the government for showing bad faith by excluding natives in Clayoquot Sound." Hume's column quoted an anonymous Harcourt advisor: "The environmentalists can argue that all of Clayoquot Sound should be preserved, but it makes it hard now for them to say that this is what the aboriginals want."

The NDP managed to avoid an international boycott of Mac Blo when it finally put an end to clearcut logging in the region. On July 6, 1995, Forests Minister Andrew Petter announced that the government had accepted all 127 recommendations of its own scientific panel on sustainable forest practices.

The cabinet's approval of these findings meant that there would be no clearcuts larger than four hectares in Clayoquot Sound. Companies would be forced to adopt the "variable retention" logging system, where 15 percent of the trees in any one cutting area have to remain standing; roadbuilding would be restricted to 5 percent of any watershed's harvestable area; and there would be no logging in undeveloped watersheds until studies and inventories of species had been conducted.

While the IWA's Gerry Stoney found it "hard to feel any sense of relief or optimism" from this decision, it was clear the NDP had won over its environmental contingent. "This is a major achievement for the environmental cause," said Sierra Club conservation chair Vicky Husband, who was at the forefront of Clayoquot Sound protests two years earlier. "It's a recognition that clearcutting does not belong in the coastal temperate rainforest. We have moved a long way today in having science start to rule how we are going to manage our forests. We have never had that. We have had a total timber bias. [But] this is turning forestry on its head and saying we are going to manage for ecosystem integrity first and only after will we look at what fibre can be taken out."

There remained the question of how many jobs were affected by this decision, but for the time being the NDP could bask in the glory of having fulfilled one of its major campaign promises in the Clayoquot. "When people go back and look at the Clayoquot decision, it's very close to what we said we were going to do with the Environment and Jobs Accord," Harcourt explained. "People thought I didn't mean what I said [in 1993] and that I was going to protect all of Clayoquot. I never said I was going to protect all of Clayoquot, and we didn't. And they went nuts. They thought we'd back down, but we didn't."

In fact, the government did back down by appointing the scientific panel and conducting a battery of tests that would justify the final compromise on Clayoquot Sound. A more realistic assessment was offered by a former member of CORE, who said the government had misjudged the public mood in 1993 by accepting nearly all the recommendations of the IWA. The NDP's original Clayoquot decision, said the source, was a carbon copy of the proposal the IWA task force submitted for Clayoquot. "People were quite surprised that the [original] decision was that brown. They thought it would be a [compromise] between the greens and the IWA."

It took two years, but in the end the government was able to come up with just such a compromise. Clayoquot Sound may have been the most controversial land use issue the NDP faced in its first term, but its outcome went a long way to dispel the perception of BC as a "Brazil of the North."

8

Sustainable Province

FOR ALL OF COLLEEN MCCRORY'S CRITICISM OF BC FOREST POL-
icy, and the continuing skepticism of environmentalists like Vicky
Husband and Paul George, the NDP's track record on land use by
1995 was impressive enough that BC was awarded an A-minus rating
in the World Wildlife Fund's Endangered Spaces Report Card for
1994-95 – the best in Canada.

To be fair, McCrory's "Brazil of the North" slogan was not so much
an earnest argument as a calculated attempt to embarrass the NDP into
upholding its conservationist principles. Along with the focused,
aggressive campaign by eco-activists to prevent clearcut logging in
Clayoquot Sound, it may well have been a factor in the government's
decision to limit clearcut logging in BC. The "Brazil of the North"
label, however, would soon be rendered obsolete by the NDP's conservation record following the Clayoquot decision. In less than two
years, the government had moved to protect millions of hectares of
wilderness, was on schedule to double the proportion of park lands in
BC before the turn of the century, and had passed various pollution
laws to protect the provincial ecosystem. Indeed, BC's World Wildlife
Fund rating had risen steadily from the B-minus of Harcourt's first
year in power.

The WWF report for 1994-95 cited a number of recent achievements that earned BC the A-minus rating. In the previous year alone, the government had completed a land use plan for Vancouver Island, protected a vast tract of land in the Lower Fraser Valley for the government's Commonwealth Nature Legacy program, and made a commitment to protect 57 new areas totalling 928,242 hectares in the Cariboo-Chilcotin and the Kootenays.

Other achievements since 1993 included: World Heritage Status for the Tatshenshini-Alsek region in northwest BC; preservation of the Kitlope Valley, the largest intact temperate rainforest watershed in the world; establishment of the South Okanagan Wildlife Management Area; creation of Ts'yl-os Provincial Park; and the declaration of the Khutzeymateen Valley as Canada's first grizzly bear sanctuary. BC was also the first provincial or territorial government in Canada to establish a system for protecting marine areas.

"What British Columbia is successfully demonstrating to all Canadians is that a balance can be achieved between jobs and the environment," said Ric Careless, BC director for the Endangered Species Campaign, in a press release. "By focussing on employment strategies for resource communities ... while also placing a priority on preserving its endangered species, BC is showing that it is possible both to meet the economic needs of today's British Columbians and the environmental needs of those yet to come."

But such compromise didn't come easily. According to Moe Sihota, who assumed the Environment portfolio in the 1993 cabinet shuffle, the balancing act that created jobs while preserving wilderness was a far more difficult task than the NDP ever imagined while in Opposition. "Remember, these are uncharted waters," Sihota said. The NDP set out to double the park lands in the province.

Sihota, like most of his NDP colleagues, knew there was political risk in pursuing an agenda of wilderness preservation. All four of the NDP's reelection priorities – forests, jobs, the economy and the environment – were deeply intertwined, with often conflicting interests. It may have been easy to adopt the moral high ground in Opposition, but the act of preserving large tracts of forest while providing new jobs for the current generation, was quite a different story once the party came to power. Add the politics of native land claims to the mix, and the job was even tougher.

"When you're in government," Sihota explained, "you have to deal with the reality of jobs, the reality of wood running out, the reality of communities that have always voted for you up in arms, the reality of people that have looked to you – environmentalists, natives – up in arms. And I think that after Clayoquot, there was a realization that, inasmuch as we had the contours of what we had to do, it hadn't been fine tuned in a way that gave British Columbians a sense that there was a plan here."

That was evident when the government's proposed land use plan for Vancouver Island was announced in the spring of 1994. Under the plan, the province would protect 13 percent of the Island's forest base – 1 percent more than the average projected for the rest of BC – and establish more than twenty new provincial parks. The plan was immediately condemned by Island loggers, who predicted substantial job losses. One of the loudest critics was Port McNeill Mayor Gerry Furney, a failed Socred candidate who had opposed every stage of the CORE process.

Furney knew a thing or two about pressing hot political buttons with the right amount of rhetoric. He'd had plenty of practice since 1989, when he founded a group known as the BC Environmental Information Institute. The BCEII claimed to be a non-aligned organization carrying out purely scientific research, with a mandate to provide the most current and accurate information on land use in BC. In fact, Furney's organization was an advocacy group promoting "multiple use", the belief that logging and preservation could be achieved in the same place. The group was funded by forestry corporations including Mac Blo and Western Forest Products, and embraced by such business luminaries as Peter Bentley, the chairman and CEO of Canfor Corporation. Its directors included Graham Lea, Highways minister under Dave Barrett, who gave up politics after finishing last in the 1984 leadership race and failing to generate support for his centrist United Party (he was currently secretary treasurer of the Truck Loggers' Association); the managing director of the BC Yukon Chamber of Mines; and, a Vancouver Island business agent for the IWA. Needless to say, there weren't too many environmental groups on the BCEII's membership list.

By 1994, Gerry Furney's non-aligned and non-partisan approach to land use issues had him into a high-profile spokesmodel for the anti-CORE movement on Vancouver Island. "I've had my belly full of people listening to a very tiny, noisy minority who are trying to tell the government and ourselves how we should live," Furney told an angry crowd of 20,000 forestry workers on the legislature lawn on March 21, 1994. "We've got a report in front of us that was written by academics and backroom boys who have never had rain in their lunch buckets and who don't have to live with the consequences of their theory."

Furney's histrionics may have played well before a group of angry loggers, but his argument ignored the fact that this report by "academics and backroom boys" was supported by far more than a "very tiny, noisy minority" of Vancouver Islanders. And there was little possibility of winning a public relations war with an NDP government under increasing pressure to fulfil its green agenda. While Forests Minister Andrew Petter and Mike Harcourt's deputy minister Doug McArthur met with industry to sell the Vancouver Island Land Use Plan, Sihota took advantage of his union contacts from the Labour Ministry and travelled to towns like Duncan and Port Alberni to sell the plan to IWA members.

Recalled Sihota, "We were able to go to community after community, in the private meetings that we were having with the IWA, to persuade them, 'Look, we're gonna change the whole idea of what a logger is. You don't just go in there and cut the timber and haul it out. You're pruning, you're thinning, and you're doing road reclamation work. Yes, you do some stream cleaning, and yes, you cut the wood but [you] also make sure [you] get more value out of that wood.'"

In June, the government finally announced the completed Vancouver Island Land Use Plan. As promised, the plan increased protected areas to 13 percent of the Island (from 10.3 percent), while creating 23 new provincial parks including the Upper Carmanah, Walbran and Tahsish-Kwois. The plan also secured 81 percent of the land base for resource use and established a new Vancouver Island Jobs Strategy. This program was to create new opportunities for jobs in the Island forest industry.

The Vancouver Island Land Use Plan was, in many ways, the proto-type for two key pieces of NDP legislation: Forest Renewal and the new Forest Practices Code. The first component was designed to soften the impact of environmental change on the forest industry. While green chain jobs were on the decline, Forest Renewal encour-aged new jobs in value-added manufacturing and environmentally sound employment such as reforestation, restoring hillsides to pre-vent erosion, and repairing damaged rivers, streams and watersheds.

"We realized that we had to first of all make a commitment to work-ers that we were going to provide for some economic stability in those communities, hence Forest Renewal," said Sihota. "And going to industry and saying 'Look, we will take a royalty from you, in terms of increasing the stumpage, but we'll put it in this fund that you can have a say over.' Which persuaded them to come on board, because in the past they had seen governments that took this money, put into sil-viculture or whatever, and then depleted it close to an election. So that was the first pillar that we had to have in place."

The second pillar was the Forest Practices Code, which in effect would become the policing mechanism for the forest industry. Under the new code, the government reduced the number and limited the size of clearcuts, monitored logging operations, increased the maxi-mum for court-ordered fines to $1 million a day – $2 million a day for repeat offenders – from the previous $2,000 per day, and based approval of future logging permits on the company's adherence to the new standards and regulations.

The new code was sobering news for the forest industry, for it served notice that even the IWA workers who supported the NDP would have to play a role in saving the environment.

BC, Green Envy of the World

NOT EVERY LAND USE DECISION MEANT INSTANT JOBS. IN THE case of the Tatshenshini-Alsek region in the northwest of the province – an extremely rugged wilderness twice the size of the Grand Canyon – the government was willing to abandon 500 direct jobs and 1,500 indirect jobs when it cancelled the Windy Craggy copper mine proposal and declared the 1 million-hectare space a Class A provincial wilderness park in June 1993.

The Tatshenshini is part of the Haines triangle, wedged between the Yukon's Kluane National Park to the north and three US national parks on the Alaska Panhandle to the west and south. At 8.5 million hectares together, this region forms the largest international protected area in the world. Many who visit the region have described the Tat as an earthly paradise. Surrounded by some of the highest coastal mountains on the planet, including BC's highest peak, Mount Fairweather, the region is the epitome of biodiversity. Rich in unique and endangered wildlife species, such as the glacier bear and the King eider, the Tat is one of the last strongholds of the North American grizzly bear and home to half of BC's Dall sheep population. It is also the site of the largest non-polar ice cap in the world, with more than 350 valley glaciers, and three of the major salmon-bearing rivers on the northern Pacific coast.

But the Tat is more than just wildlife. Humans have been a major presence at least since the mid-1970s, when commercial river rafting began in the area. By the early 1990s, the area was a popular destination for hiking, mountaineering, cross-country skiing, fishing and camping. According to various scientific studies, all of these activities — apart from guided hunting, of course — could be accommodated without disturbing the wilderness of the region.

The same could not be said about mining. Since 1958, significant deposits of copper, cobalt, gold and silver had been identified at Tats Creek, a subsidiary of the Tatshenshini River, but it was only recently that a highly mineralized belt of rocks, covering at least 40 square kilometres and containing major copper deposits, had been discovered in the area. Geddes Resources, a Toronto-based company 40 percent owned by Vancouver's Royal Oak Mines Ltd., wanted to construct both an open pit and an underground mine 30 to 40 kilometres up Tats Creek, to tap a reserve of 327 million tons of rock. With only 1.4 percent copper and other metal content, the bulk of that rock would remain on site in waste dumps. The company, which had moved its operations to Vancouver in 1992 in anticipation of the project, was looking at an initial investment of $555 million for development, with a mine life of 20 to 40 years. Annual expenditures were estimated at $150 million, resulting in 500 direct jobs and 1,500 indirect jobs for contractors, suppliers and other support. Combined direct taxes for the first two decades were estimated at $720 million for BC and $545 million for Ottawa. By 1993, Geddes had already invested $50 million in the project.

One factor that didn't make it into the Geddes promotional material was the impact of acid mine drainage. This commonly occurs in a mineralized zone with high levels of sulphide; when ore sulphides are exposed to the air, they oxidize, turning into sulphuric acid which leaches heavy metals from the rocks and filters into streams and groundwater, destroying aquatic life. In the US, an estimated 20,000 kilometres of rivers have been contaminated by acid mine drainage. On Vancouver Island, the problem had already killed the salmon in the Tsolum River watershed. "This is not a temporary problem," said one former member of CORE. "There are mines in Sweden that have been leaching acid mine drainage for 200 years."

Geddes Resources did have one solution. They would dam the valley, dump the waste rock behind the dam and cover it with water so it wouldn't be exposed to oxygen. But there was one problem with that idea. The dam, like the mine, would be located on a fault that had already registered some of the biggest earthquakes in history, including the 1964 Alaska earthquake. "Will this work? Who knows?" mused the *Sun*'s Stephen Hume. "The *Titanic* wasn't supposed to sink, Chernobyl wasn't supposed to melt down, Bhopal wasn't supposed to leak and the *Exxon Valdez* was foolproof." According to Hume, the Harcourt cabinet had a chance to "set an enduring example of ethical stewardship for the rest of the world ... that seldom presents itself to presidents or prime ministers. ... How does the Harcourt administration wish to be remembered in 100 years? As leaders with vision who saved a corner of Eden for unborn generations? Or as another crew of fools who said 'business as usual' and sold off the last bit of paradise for a few jobs and 30 pieces of silver?"

In the end, the decision to save the Tat was not a difficult one. Although an interim report by CORE in January had recommended another six months of study followed by a final report, that delay was rudely interrupted by a series of protests surrounding the government's April decision to allow clearcut logging in Clayoquot Sound. The Clayoquot compromise was seen by many environmentalists as a concession to the NDP's union allies in the IWA. But given that mining unions had nowhere near as much clout with the NDP as the IWA did, and given that "there wasn't a marketable tree in the Tatshenshini" (as one former member of CORE put it), the government would not lose support for saving a major chunk of wilderness – especially so soon after Clayoquot.

To make matters even easier for the NDP, the US government had already announced that it was officially opposed to mining in the Haines triangle, and Vice-President Al Gore was encouraging Harcourt to ban mining in the Tat. The US had an interest in the project because Geddes Resources needed to run materials through Alaska to get them to market.

Thus it was no surprise when, on June 22, 1993, the premier declared the Tatshenshini a Class A provincial park and nominated the region for World Heritage Site status. "This is one of the most spectacular wilderness areas in the world, and today BC is living up to its global responsibility to keep it that way," said a beaming Harcourt. "With this global reserve, the Tatshenshini River will now be protected on both sides of the US border." The government recognized there would be economic costs from the decision, he added, but the environmental benefits of preserving the region would be unmatched.

Harcourt's announcement made the front page of the Washington Post and prompted congratulatory letters from Al Gore and Prince Philip (Queen Elizabeth's husband was president of the World Wildlife Fund), as well as full-page ads from a coalition of 21 environmental groups thanking the premier for an "outstanding environmental achievement" that showed "leadership and global vision."

Later, in his introduction to CORE's annual report, Stephen Owen criticized the government's decision to preempt the six-month waiting period on Windy Craggy, saying that such decision-making "creates inconsistency and enhances public distrust and alienation." Owen shouldn't have been surprised by Harcourt's action, given that CORE's interim report had determined that mining activity would be incompatible with full preservation of the wilderness, and that a final decision was unlikely to be reached through consensus. The Liberals took advantage of Owen's comment, arguing that Harcourt was interfering with due process. And BC Business Council president Jerry Lampert wrote the premier to complain about the NDP's "anti-business" attitude.

Ultimately, this criticism went nowhere, as Harcourt was supported by some high-profile industrialists. "As one who has spent much of my life in the mining and resource industries, I understand this [economic] concern," Maurice Strong wrote, from his chairman's desk at Ontario Hydro. "But ... my environmental friends in BC assure me that there is no other major prospective mining site for which this would be a precedent." Strong was a multimillionaire businessman and Pearson Liberal who created the Canadian International Development Agency in the late sixties, chaired Petro Canada in the seventies and helped organize various international conferences on the environment after that. A well-connected political animal, Strong's career was marked by an ability to ally himself to the right causes at the right time. He wrote that saving the Tat provided "a basis for a new spirit of cooperation between environmentalists and the resource industry which should greatly facilitate future mining developments in British Columbia."

Indeed, Harcourt's pledge to work with industry in developing other mine projects in the province was no empty promise. Cabinet had already approved thirteen mine development certificates, and was launching the first provincial Mine Strategy that spring. And just over two years later, the government worked out a compensation package for Windy Craggy shareholders. In a deal that Employment and Investment Minister Glen Clark called BC's largest mining development in twenty years, the government agreed to give Royal Oak Mines $104 million compensation in 1995 dollars, and assist in developing two new mines in northern BC. The government would also invest $50 million in one of the mines, in exchange for a royalty of 4.8 percent on copper extracted. The agreement would bring 550 jobs and $500 million in investment to BC's depressed mining industry.

To many New Democrats and environmentalists, there was a certain irony in the August 18, 1995, announcement as Glen Clark stood beside Royal Oak CEO Margaret Witte. The previous year, Witte had presided over a bitter labour dispute at Royal Oak's Yellowknife mine that resulted in nine miners dying in a bomb blast, and was later vilified by feminists after she was named *Chatelaine* magazine's Woman of the Year for 1994. "I'll bet you didn't expect to see me here walking down the road with the BC government," she told the press conference. For his part, Clark admitted that the decision would not look good to some of the NDP's loyal supporters. "You have your personal views, but you have to put them aside, and we have done that here," Clark said. "I don't make any apologies for that but not everybody, I am sure, will be pleased with that."

The year and a half that followed the 1993 Tatshenshini decision saw a flurry of park designations, as the government moved to catch up on its commitment to protect 12 percent of BC's land base. Harcourt and Sihota began 1994 by announcing Class A park status for the Chilco Lake region, a 233,240-hectare area in the Chilcotin Mountains that was nearly half the size of Prince Edward Island and comparable to Alberta's Lake Louise for its scenic beauty. Like the Tatshenshini and Khutzeymateen, Chilco Lake was rich in vulnerable wildlife, such as the grizzly bear and California bighorn sheep. It also was home to the third largest salmon run in the province.

The Chilco Lake decision was important because it gave the local Nemiah Valley Indian Band control over development in its valley and a co-management role in the new park. Two years in the planning, the decision was a triumph of local decision-making: native people, loggers, environmentalists, tourism operators, miners and ranchers were all part of the 37-member Chilco Lake Study Team that managed to arrive at a consensus. The decision established the new Ts'yl-os Park, co-managed by the province and the Nemiah First Nation, and the 45,000-hectare Taseko Management Zone, to be reserved for forestry, mining and other resource uses.

"It is beginning to look like this government is serious about its commitment to protect the biodiversity of our province," said George Smith, conservation director for the Canadian Parks and Wilderness Society. "Since coming to power they have protected the Tatshenshini, the Kutzeymateen, the Nisga'a Memorial Lava Beds, and now Chilco Lake. These are all critical and unique parts of the tremendous ecological puzzle which is British Columbia."

Harcourt scored several eco-victories in early 1994, including the preservation of the Kitlope Valley – the world's largest intact temperate rainforest watershed – but there were still battles ahead.

Hang 'Em High

100 MILE HOUSE, JULY 15, 1994

MILD-MANNERED CORE COMMISSIONER STEPHEN OWEN HAD never been the kind of guy to inspire partisan outrage. But as one of the major decision-makers in BC's emerging land use policy, he could not have been too surprised by the sight that greeted him outside the local meeting hall: someone had hung a noose over the front doorway just before his appearance to defend CORE's land use plan for the Cariboo region. Days later, Owen was hanged in effigy during a community parade in nearby Quesnel.

"I can't condemn people who have a real fear," said Williams Lake Mayor Walt Cobb, defending the anti-Owen sentiment. Cobb, leader of the Cariboo anti-CORE movement, added that some actions were "not acceptable or what I would like to see happen. But I can't condemn a person for being scared and trying to get his message across." What Cobb was reluctant to condemn was a series of actions, including property damage, verbal threats and physical harassment of local residents supporting CORE.

Tempers had been running high since CORE released its recommendation for the Cariboo: to reserve 20 percent of the forest base for a sensitive management zone and double park land from 6 to 12 percent. According to Owen's report, the forest industry accounted for 32 percent of the income and 39 percent of employment in the region. The Cariboo Forest Region, with an annual harvest of 8.4 million cubic metres of wood, provided direct employment for 7,200 people. The proposal would cost 600 to 850 jobs – a result which Cobb and Quesnel Mayor Steve Wallace said would wipe out 30 percent of the Cariboo economy. Wallace said the report's recommendations would lead to a timber harvest drop of 1 million cubic metres, taking $100 million out of the local economy; Cobb accused the environmental movement of "breaking up our families" and "holding us hostage for no specific reason."

The environmental movement's reasons for wanting the Cariboo park lands doubled were no less "specific" than those which governed every other land use recommendation by CORE: sustainability, biodiversity, long-term economic stability. The public outrage was so pronounced, however, that the government was compelled to review the CORE report. For the next two months, forestry consultant Grant Scott met with all interested parties, then reported back to cabinet. After a series of September meetings brokered by the premier's deputy minister, Doug McArthur, the forest workers, ranchers and conservationists of the Cariboo put an end to the two years of squabbling. On October 24, Harcourt triumphantly announced a new plan at a press conference broadcast on local radio in Williams Lake.

Under the plan, 80 percent of the land base was set aside in three separate zones for resource development; 12 percent, or one million hectares, was reserved for seventeen new parks. The remaining 8 percent was private. Ranchers were happy because they would retain the right to graze their herds in the new parks. Logging companies were happy because they were given a land base sufficient to keep log harvests at their present level (the zone area for intensive forestry was set at 40 percent of the land base, twice what CORE recommended), and forestry workers were happy because their jobs were protected. Finally, conservationists were happy because the new protected areas effectively linked a number of existing park lands.

For once, most parties agreed that the deal was a success. "It's a real groundbreaker, there's no question about it," said conservationist Dave Neads, one of a handful of eco-activists in the region. "This isn't a case of an urban treehugger going out to the Carmanah Valley. It's a case of people who have been making a living off the land for generations trying to maintain their livelihoods when change is coming. And change is coming fast." Even industry had to admit that there was no other way to break the deadlock. "What we have done today is to establish some ground rules," said Jake Kerr, chair of logging company Lignum Ltd.

The government had good reason to be proud of its land use achievements by the fall of 1994. But even as the Harcourt cabinet worked out the final details of the Cariboo compromise, the Opposition was quietly preparing to steal the limelight on another explosive issue.

Granola Gordon

OCTOBER 10, 1994

IT WAS A DRAMATIC ANNOUNCEMENT, COMING FROM GORDON Campbell. The Liberal leader was calling for the cancellation of Alcan's half-built, $1.3 billion Kemano II Completion Project (KCP), the long-awaited second component of a huge hydroelectric power project near Kitimat. "Times have changed and public values have changed over the last 30 years," said Campbell. "Society is now far more concerned about the impact of such development on the environment. The days of diverting significant amounts of water from BC's rivers are over." In his news release from Prince George, the Liberal leader repeated what scientists had long since established: a second diversion of the Nechako River water would lower water levels in the Fraser, the world's largest natural salmon river. Given the recent problems with reduced fish stocks in that river, plus the negative impact the first phase of Kemano had on the Nechako, the potential environmental and economic damage from KCP could no longer be ignored.

Gordon Campbell's embrace of the anti-Kemano cause was a sure sign that times had indeed changed since 1950. In that year, the last Liberal-Conservative coalition government signed an agreement with Alcan that gave the aluminum company unlimited access to the Tahtsa-Eutsuk basin, a string of intersecting lakes and rivers about 80 kilometres southeast of Kitimat, 575 kilometres northwest of Vancouver. In phase one of the project, Alcan dammed the Nechako River, reversing its flow through a sixteen-kilometre mountain tunnel to an

896-megawatt power plant which provided power for Alcan's aluminum smelter in Kitimat.

Before the project got the green light, however, the federal government forced the relocation of its residents. The Tahtsa-Eutsuk basin was the traditional homeland for twelve families of the Cheslatta Carrier Indian Band. To make way for Kemano I, the Cheslatta had to leave their homes and move 25 kilometres north to inferior land at Grassy Plains. Back in the basin, their homes were burned down and the area was flooded, creating a 92,000-hectare reservoir.

By 1979, Alcan wanted to exercise its option, offered in the original agreement, to improve its access to the Nechako water. The plan for KCP was to build a second mountain tunnel in order to turn four additional generators; excess energy would be sold to BC-Hydro. This plan was dismissed by the federal Department of Fisheries and Oceans (DFO), mostly out of fear that such a project would destroy the Nechako's salmon spawning grounds by lowering water levels to 12 percent of the Nechako's natural flow. Alcan went to the Supreme Court, claiming that its 1950 agreement took precedence over the Fisheries Act. The DFO preempted a court decision, however, by announcing a deal with Alcan in September 1987; KCP could go ahead, but Alcan would have to pay for modifications to protect the salmon stock. Immediately after this announcement, the company began construction of its second sixteen-kilometre tunnel.

KCP was similar to other water diversion projects throughout the country in that the corporations that stood to profit pulled whatever strings were necessary to circumvent federal environmental review guidelines. In Saskatchewan, the Conservative government of Grant Devine got into trouble when it began construction on the Rafferty-Alameda water diversion project in early spring 1988 before receiving the required federal licence. (The project was subject to a licence because the Souris River that would feed the Rafferty reservoir was part of an international waterway that flowed in and out of North Dakota.) Shortly after the licence was granted, the Canadian Wildlife Federation (CWF) took the federal government to court, claiming that it had not followed its own Environmental Assessment and Review Process (EARP) guidelines. The following year, in April 1989, the court ruled in favour of CWF and quashed the licence to build the dams.

As a result of this decision, any hydroelectric power project which could affect surrounding wilderness and wildlife was subject to an EARP review, including KCP. Fortunately for Alcan, however, it had a friend in Prime Minister Brian Mulroney, former president of Iron Ore of Canada, who was only too familiar with the nuisance of bureaucrats trying to impede the inevitable flow of industrial progress. In a gesture typical of his approach to natural resources, Mulroney signed a 1990 order-in-cabinet that forever exempted KCP from any environmental assessment review. Construction on the project continued.

Throughout all these events, KCP was vigorously opposed by environmentalists, the fisher's union and aboriginal bands throughout the province. In July 1992, Mike Harcourt appointed Victoria lawyer Murray Rankin to advise the government on the environmental, economic and social impact of KCP and make recommendations on the form, scope and timing of a public review. In January 1993, Harcourt announced that a full-scale public review would be conducted by the BC Utilities Commission. The final report would be ready in two years.

That summer, after reading an article about the KCP in *Harrowsmith* magazine, CKNW broadcaster and former Socred cabinet minister Rafe Mair became convinced that the project was an environmental disaster waiting to happen. Mair, a sport fishing advocate, was concerned about KCP's effects on salmon spawning grounds lower down the Fraser River. He researched the issue, and soon began a crusade on his radio show, speaking out against KCP at every opportunity and providing a strong, unifying voice for the broad coalition of interests opposed to KCP. Mair's coverage was significant because, to that point, no other mass media outlet was providing the same level of analysis of the issue. By the summer of 1994, an Angus Reid poll found that 64 percent of British Columbians polled were opposed to KCP. The NDP was convinced that Rafe Mair's anti-Kemano crusade had a lot to do with the shifting public mood.

With the Angus Reid poll and Mair's continual trashing of KCP – both on his CKNW show and in his column for the Vancouver weekly *Georgia Straight* – the government seemed less inclined than ever to save KCP. The NDP had often been accused of caving in to big business demands at the first sign of trouble, but now it appeared, for the first time, that the NDP would be able to scrap an industrial megaproject for environmental reasons without being labelled anti-business.

So it was hardly risky for Gordon Campbell to come out against KCP two months after the Angus Reid poll, on the eve of his appearance on Rafe Mair's radio show. Campbell was practically guaranteed a love-in from the former Bennett cabinet minister, and aside from a few temporarily disheartened CEOs on Howe Street, it wasn't as if the Liberal leader was going to make a lot of enemies by opposing the project. Strategically, the Liberals hoped that Campbell's anti-Kemano stance would soften his corporate, right-wing image. A year into his leadership, Campbell remained an elusive figure whose position on most issues was unknown to the public, but who was perceived as a front man for developers and big business. When it came to soundbites attacking the government, he knew how to spin all the right clichés – the Health Labour Accord was a "sweetheart deal"; the government's use of an NDP-friendly ad firm was a case of patronage for "friends and insiders" – but he hadn't spelled out what the Liberals would do instead, so it was hard for voters to see if his righteousness was genuine.

Campbell's stand on KCP smacked of opportunism. He claimed, for example, that his policy on KCP was prepared months in advance, but if that were the case, why hadn't he announced it at the Liberal convention three weeks earlier? Media pundits concluded that Campbell, afraid of prompting a messy internal battle at the convention, opted for the safer territory of Rafe Mair's show. He had yet to announce his party's platform on the environment, so it was not clear how, or if, the KCP policy fit into the Liberals' big picture – or if there was an environmental platform at all. Also, by opposing KCP before the BC Utilities Commission hearing was complete, Campbell was doing exactly what he accused the government of doing when the NDP preempted a CORE recommendation with its decision to preserve the Tatshenshini. Given his enthusiasm for the Windy Craggy mining proposal, it seemed rather cynical to use KCP to score points with the green movement.

Even Campbell's colleagues in the business community were puzzled by his October 10 announcement. "It's a confusing message," said Iain Harris of the Vancouver Board of Trade. "Maybe [the Liberals] thought the time to get the most attention is when it is quiet, but it isn't at all appropriate to make statements and conclusions prior to the BC Utilities Commission report." Harris and BC Business Council chief Jerry Lampert both agreed that the Liberal position represented a double standard, in contrast to the party's response to the Tatshenshini announcement.

The government was more disturbed by Campbell's suggestion for a compensation package. The Liberal leader was proposing that BC pay out $500 million for costs Alcan estimated it had already incurred, and promise to reimburse the company for potential lost revenue. According to the New Democrats, this amounted to giving Alcan a blank cheque.

In any case, the government's ultimate decision to kill KCP was backed by the BC Utilities Commission report, made public by Harcourt when he announced the cancellation of the project on January 25, 1995. The report confirmed fears about the effects of reduced water flows on the surrounding ecosystem, while giving Alcan a failing grade for the remedies it proposed for these problems.

"KCP was a dog of a project – financially, economically, environmentally," the premier later summed up. "The evidence was pretty conclusive ... Environmentally, there wasn't much doubt from the BC Utilities Commission that it was going to bring the water down to a trickle and have adverse effects right throughout the Nechako River system, and great potential for serious harm to the Fraser River fishery."

In scrapping the project, the premier transferred all financial responsibility to the federal government. It was Ottawa, not BC, said Harcourt, that agreed to exempt Alcan from environmental studies when it signed the 1987 settlement. The Social Credit government of the day did not have enough information about reduced water flows when it signed the agreement. "It was just phoney," Harcourt explained. "The project, to be completed, would have to involve another $800 million. So the original price of $600 million was becoming $1.4 billion. If we did that, we'd lose two or three hundred million dollars on it. Why would you go ahead with a project that you'd lose [that much] on? It doesn't make any sense to me. And to prove the point, why did Alcan come to me in 1993 and say they wanted $350 million from the provincial government to make the project viable?"

In passing the buck to the feds, Harcourt continued the traditional waltz of political brinkmanship between Victoria and Ottawa that takes place whenever big money is at stake. Federal Fisheries Minister Brian Tobin – who later received international acclaim for his tough-guy response to Spanish turbot trawlers off the east coast and Alaskan salmon fishers off the west – accused the BC premier of rewriting history to avoid accountability for a project long championed by BC governments.

The political jockeying continued until July, when Harcourt struck a deal with Alcan to settle the dispute out of court. The final agreement, expected by March 1996, would require the province, through BC Hydro, to supply Alcan with the power it needs. BC would be required to deliver 285 megawatts per year to Alcan for a period of 60 to 80 years, for which Alcan would pay the province a total of about $900 million in 1995 dollars. Alcan agreed not to take the province to court while the two parties were in talks; the government agreed not to impose a settlement through legislation.

But this solution was cold comfort for the workers who had stood to gain from KCP. Hours after Harcourt announced he was scrapping the project, the premier boarded a plane for Prince George to begin a series of meetings in the northern communities affected by the decision. Harcourt was praised in Prince George, but received a stern lecture about job creation in Smithers and was greeted with disappointment in Terrace. He knew he'd be in for a much tougher ride in Kitimat, the centre of the dispute.

By the early 1990s, Alcan claimed to employ 1,800 people in the community, with annual exports of $500 million. Kitimat was "the town Alcan built," and it remained dependent on the company's continued development. According to the local chamber of commerce, KCP would have increased incomes by $27 million and created 475 worker years of employment over a three-year construction period.

Thanks to the premier's decision, a chamber news release direly predicted, "the province has just shut the door on future investment in the north" and thrown away 1,000 jobs.

It was a hostile crowd of 600 local residents and Alcan workers that greeted the premier when he arrived at the Riverlodge Recreation Centre. "Is that Rafe Mair, David Suzuki or Gordon Campbell I smell on your breath?" shouted one worker, interrupting Harcourt. "How are you going to explain to people that you can rip up a legal contract?" shouted another. "Does that mean I can rip up my contract with you to pay income tax?"

The reception was so bitter that Harcourt was unable to finish his speech. Instead, he waited in silence as more than 30 people shouted abuse at him and vowed never to vote NDP again. Police officers stood outside the door, ready to jump in if the premier was threatened physically. But he didn't need a bodyguard; the residents of Kitimat simply wanted to vent their frustration with a government they believed was increasingly out of touch with the north. In a classic showdown between the rural, resource-based working class of the interior and the urban, white-collar culture of the coast, Harcourt took his lumps as Kitimat residents showed their contempt for Victoria.

"The people that were most angry, in Kitimat, had been sold a bill of goods. And it was up to me to go in there and say that," Harcourt recalled. "Now they weren't going to hear me at first, but I was going to at least hear them out, face the music, stick up for my MLA [Skeena New Democrat Helmut Giesbrecht], and let them know that the decision was made because it was a dog ... So I thought it was important that I go in and get beat up but stare 'em in the eyeballs."

Harcourt knew it would be tough to promote sustainable development to people whose jobs were at stake. Was it possible for an urban politician to walk into a rural community whose residents have worked in the same industry all their lives, and convince them that the future is arriving so quickly they will soon be forced to find other kinds of work? Should they be expected to believe that this decision, painful though it may be in the short term, is the best possible solution for the future?

"Well," Harcourt shrugged, "sometimes you can't [convince people]. Sometimes people are going to be locked into 'This is the job I wanted, this is the job I didn't get, and you're to blame for it and I'm never going to support you.' You just let the chips fall where they may in politics."

In the end, it may have been Harcourt's determination to maintain the moderate approach that allowed the NDP to keep a reasonable level of support within both the green and unionized forestry constituencies; by the fall of 1995, several environmental groups and the IWA were committed, however grudgingly, to reelecting the NDP. CORE was maligned by critics as just another layer of bureaucracy, yet it set standards for sustainable growth while ensuring that previously irreconcilable interests were able to meet at the same table and work together on a land use plan that considered parks, biodiversity, industry, economic interests, and even socio-economic factors such as education levels in each region. Such consultation and compromise were inconceivable during the polarizing reign of Social Credit.

While the government's forest and land use policies dominated the headlines, there were other environmental accomplishments worth noting. The NDP set new air emission standards, introducing legislation to force polluters to pay for costs and cleanup; began publishing a list of violators in bi-annual reports; introduced BC's first Environmental Assessment Act, which provides for open public review of major projects; and resurrected the pulp mill emission standards law cancelled by Bill Vander Zalm in 1990.

But managing the forests was by far the government's biggest environmental achievement. Cabinet had to learn the hard way with Clayoquot Sound, when its IWA loyalties clashed with the desire to be green. For obvious reasons, Harcourt had no desire to create a rift between the party and the union. The NDP would never have survived without the money, memberships, volunteers and candidates supplied by the IWA – and the union knew it. But the IWA also knew that times were changing, and the union ultimately went along with the new policy, swallowing "sustainable development" like a mouthful of cod liver oil, and was still committed to the NDP by the fall of 1995 – with reservations.

"CORE was not the IWA's favourite vehicle for solving anything,"

said IWA president Gerry Stoney. "CORE didn't have a process of resolution. There was no end, there was no point in time when somebody
came in and said, 'Okay, you can't reach consensus and I am the arbitrator and I will decide, or this judge from Geneva is the arbitrator and
that judge will decide, somebody will decide.' There was no end to
the process. CORE just rambled until politically it looked like maybe
the best way to go was this way, or the best way to go was that way …
My mind says now that if we would have known the far-reaching
impact of the path we were heading on, I'm not sure that the reaction
wouldn't have been somewhat different, a much tougher response."

While the IWA chief said the union would support the NDP in the
upcoming election, Stoney still wanted the government to listen to
people like John Cuthbert, former chief forester of BC, who before he
retired in 1994 told Stoney that there was no reason BC couldn't establish an annual allowable cut of 90 million cubic metres a year, as
opposed to the current allowable cut of 53.5 million.

Despite these differences, the NDP was confident that the IWA preferred its approach to land use over any other party's. "Intuitively,
they knew that we were right," recalled Moe Sihota. "They knew that
in as much as they had jobs today – $20 to $25 an hour jobs – they
could see that their children may not have those jobs. Everyone realized that in the long term things had to change. So we were always
able to say 'Yes, we know your concerns, we know your fears, but
you have to understand that these are changes that you have advocated, you have given us the political mandate to bring about. So
work with us.' Because one thing that Gerry Stoney has is access. For
Gerry Stoney to pick up the phone and get access to Andrew Petter or
Moe Sihota wasn't a difficult thing. Whereas previously, to get access
to Claude Richmond or Bruce Strachan, you'd have to go through layers of bureaucracy."

But the government's record on land use was by no means the only
area of NDP policy that would divide its supporters, as well as the
general public. After four years in power, the Harcourt New Democrats were still struggling to arrive at a just and reasonable settlement
in their negotiations with aboriginal peoples.

9

Giving a Hundred and Eleven Per Cent

APRIL 1, 1995

ONE HUNDRED AND ELEVEN PER CENT. YOU COULD ALMOST FEEL the backlash coming as you read that number on page one of the Vancouver *Sun*'s weekend edition. The feature on aboriginal land claims – complete with colour-coded map showing the province carved up in pieces larger than Ireland – seemed calculated to provoke outrage. According to a cartographer hired by the newspaper to calculate the native "wish list" on the treaty negotiating table, aboriginal groups were calling for 111 percent of British Columbia's total land mass.

This was no April Fool's joke, the *Sun* assured its readers. With overlapping claims by 43 aboriginal groups representing 86,978 people, the BC Treaty Commission established by the provincial government appeared to be negotiating away more than one million square kilometres of land – several thousand kilometres more than is even contained within BC's borders. "An area 2½ times the size of Vancouver Island will be transferred to Native ownership if the BC government follows the same approach as in the Nisga'a talks, the only publicly known land claims settlement offer to date," the *Sun* story said.

There were other startling figures as well. Although the average claim was 24,000 square kilometres (or 12 square kilometres per band member), the largest claim filed with the BC Treaty Commission was 285,000 square kilometres, "an area the size of the United Kingdom and the Netherlands combined." The Lheit-Lit'en Nation claimed 332 square kilometres for each of its 210 band members. Even more alarming to the average reader was the fact that the figures quoted in the article and factored into the provincial total did not include the lands claimed by seven groups which refused to release maps of their territories. Nor did it include the 82 Indian bands that had yet to join the treaty process.

Mike Harcourt wasted no time responding to the *Sun*'s alarmist coverage. "I thought it was a dreadful article," he told reporters the following Monday in Victoria. "It didn't, for example, lay out the fact that traditional territories are territories that, say, the Musqueam, or the Carrier-Sekani, have used and occupied for 5,000 to 10,000 years, to hunt and fish, and the concept of aboriginal title is quite different than the non-aboriginal view of title ... We look on ownership as fee simple, as something you can register in the land registry office, or that you can get a hold of as a tree farm licence, or a long-term lease for mining, which is a different concept of ownership than the aboriginal people. I think that's a very important distinction. The aboriginal people are saying they want to use and occupy these territories and economically sustain themselves and to share the bounty of British Columbia ... I prefer the process of negotiation of fair and just treaties. I prefer that to the Okas that have happened in the rest of Canada."

Unfortunately, many readers may have missed the final and most important point of the article, made by Barbara Fisher, acting chief of the BC Treaty Commission. Just because native groups were submitting maps that reflected the lands they believed their ancestors occupied, said Fisher, didn't mean they were claiming the entire area. The actual area dimensions would only emerge as the treaty talks progressed. "It's too soon to say," she said. "A description of a traditional territory is one thing, and what they end up putting on the table is another."

Reform Party leader Jack Weisgerber was having none of it. "The government's actions seem to give lie to the premier's words," said Weisgerber. The actions he was referring to included Victoria's offer of a 1,900-square-kilometre settlement, including control of forests and mineral resources except oil and gas, to the Nisga'a Indians in northwestern BC. (The Nisga'a settlement was being negotiated separately from the BC Treaty Commission process.) According to Weisgerber, the fact that some lands were offered to the Nisga'a in fee simple title clearly contradicted the premier's words about the differences between aboriginal and white concepts of ownership. Furthermore, he said, a series of interim measures agreements signed by the province had already given aboriginal groups significant power over resources in lands they claimed as traditional territories. Weisgerber felt these developments, along with what he called the "secrecy" of the negotiations, were enough to put the entire treaty process into question. "The premier talks one story," said an indignant Weisgerber, "but it appears [the government] would be prepared to surrender ownership and control to a far greater extent."

Weisgerber was by no means a lone voice in the wilderness, and his complaint was far more ominous in its political implications than most of the anti-NDP rhetoric that made up the bulk of his daily soundbites as Reform Party leader. Suspicion of native people in general, and hostility toward the aboriginal rights agenda in particular, had become the stock in trade of media pundits like CKNW hotline host Rafe Mair, Vancouver *Sun* columnists Gordon Gibson and Trevor Lautens, and a number of right-wing academics hoping to cash in on the politics of hysteria.

But these pundits were only reflecting the bigotry and prejudice that had long characterized race relations in BC. As former *Sun* native issues reporter Terry Glavin put it, "In the 124 summers that have passed since British Columbia entered Confederation, the people of this province have not once demonstrated that they have the backbone for the difficult work of negotiation and reconciliation with native people."

The most recent example had occurred during the Constitutional referendum debate of 1992, when opponents of aboriginal rights added fuel to the "No" side by dismissing native self-government as a third order of government, like a municipal government. This claim was somewhat hyperbolic since, as one former provincial negotiator put it, "few Indian communities have either the population or the economic wherewithal to finance, say, a weed control district, let alone the grander institutions of sovereign government."

Ironically, the NDP's efforts to reverse the trend of anti-native hysteria were based partly on a model developed by Socred Premier Bill Vander Zalm in the dying days of his government. In fact, the treaty process itself was initiated provincially by Vander Zalm's presiding Native Affairs minister, a fellow by the name of Jack Weisgerber. With all his rhetoric four years later, it seemed that the Reform Party leader was suffering from a severe case of selective amnesia.

A History of Denial

THE BC TREATY COMMISSION PROCESS, LAUNCHED ON DECEMber 15, 1993, would have been inconceivable fifteen years earlier. In 1978, then-Premier Bill Bennett restated the policy the province had held since the 19th century. "The provincial government does not recognize the existence of an unextinguished aboriginal title to lands in the province," said Bennett. "Nor does it recognize claims relating to aboriginal title which give rise to other interests in lands based on the traditional use and occupancy of land. The position of the province is that if any aboriginal title or interest may once have existed, that title or interest was extinguished prior to the union of British Columbia with Canada in 1871."

Bennett's statement was entirely in keeping with the colonial mentality that had governed aboriginal land policy in BC for the previous century. In fact, the province's early settlers never formally acquired the land from its inhabitants, as was required by British colonial law and Canadian tradition. The lone exception to this rule was Hudson's Bay Company factor James Douglas, who began a lengthy negotiation process with Vancouver Island native communities after he was named governor of the colony of Vancouver Island in 1851. He signed fourteen treaties over six years, but the treaties were declared invalid after his retirement in 1864. His successor, the future lieutenant governor Joseph Trutch, referred to natives as "uncivilized savages" who were more "bestial" than human.

After assuming control of BC Indian policy, Trutch denied the existence of aboriginal land rights, declaring that the crown owned all the land. And when BC formally entered Confederation in 1871, its founding settlers ignored the 1763 Royal Proclamation that clearly recognized the concept of aboriginal title.

In 1872, the provincial government prohibited Indians from voting. Two years later, BC ignored a protest by Salish chiefs and refused to observe federal requirements to expand reserves to 32 hectares per family. And in 1887, the Nisga'a — in the tribe's first attempt to regain aboriginal title from the province — travelled to Victoria with Tsimshian chiefs to demand recognition of Indian land title. They were dismissed by Premier William Smithe, who informed them with language typical of the times: "When the whites first came among you, you were little better than the wild beasts of the field."

Attitudes hadn't progressed much 40 years later, when the federal government passed a bill stating that lawyers could be disbarred for accepting fees to represent native people in land disputes. Haida chief Peter Kelly, in his address to a joint committee of the Senate and House of Commons, expressed the growing frustration that was all too familiar in native communities for the next seven decades. "We are sure that the government and a considerable number of white men have for many years had in their minds a quite wrong idea of the claims which we make, and the settlement which we desire," he said. "We do not want anything extravagant ... anything hurtful to the real interests of the white people. We want that our actual rights be determined and recognized; we want a settlement based on justice. We want a full opportunity of making a future for ourselves." Kelly's request, contained in a resolution put before the joint committee, was denied — as was every other request by aboriginal groups in the first 120 years of Confederation in BC.

BC natives did not regain the right to vote in provincial elections until 1949. Nor did they regain the right to hire lawyers to pursue land claims until 1951, the same year the federal government repealed the ban on potlatches — the main social, cultural and political institution of coastal native peoples. Federally, natives did not regain the vote until 1960, and only then did residential schools finally begin to shut down. It was another three decades before the full extent of their devastation of native culture – through psychological, physical and sexual abuse – was revealed to the Canadian public.

In 1969, the Trudeau cabinet introduced its controversial White Paper on Indian Affairs. The policy, drafted by Indian Affairs Minister Jean Chrétien, would have phased out existing treaties, abolished all references to native people in law, and absolved Canada of any legislative responsibility for native people. The purpose of this system, motivated by the Liberal program of multiculturalism, was to foster "self-reliance" among Canada's aboriginal peoples. It was essentially an assimilationist document.

But the Trudeau cabinet's approach to native affairs was very much governed by events in the Supreme Court. The same year the White Paper was released, the Nisga'a Tribal Council began litigation to establish aboriginal title to their traditional territory. The Nisga'a claimed that aboriginal title to the Nass Valley had never been extinguished and that their land was illegally taken away by the crown without their consent. This litigation became known as the Calder case, named after Frank Calder, the first native elected to a Canadian legislature when he became a BC MLA for the Cooperative Commonwealth Federation in 1949.

While the court judges were evenly divided over whether the Nisga'a title had ever been extinguished, the judges ruled that the tribe did own their land before BC was created. Trudeau, realizing that natives now had a strong case for land claims, went back to the drawing board and began a process to open talks with the Nisga'a. Dropping the 1969 White Paper, the Liberals introduced a new land claims policy which affirmed the federal government's willingness to deal with traditional native interest in land and accepted in principle "that the loss and relinquishment of that interest ought to be compensated."

In 1973, when the Calder case decision was coming down, Frank Calder was a minister without portfolio in Dave Barrett's NDP government, with special responsibility for Indian Affairs. Ottawa anticipated that BC would be a willing partner in the new land claims policy, but Barrett was unwilling to enter negotiations unless Ottawa first acknowledged its responsibility for settling claims and bearing the total cost – something the Trudeau government was unwilling to do.

BC did not show up at the negotiating table for another fifteen years. With Bill Bennett's unequivocal rejection of land claims in 1978, anxious whites concerned about the impact of land claims on resource industries and private property were able to rest easy for another decade. Amazingly, it was Bennett's successor, Bill Vander Zalm, regressive on so many other human rights issues, who accelerated the process that eventually created the BC Treaty Commission.

Vander Zalm was not merely speaking rhetorically when he said the province had a "strong moral obligation to set the historical record right" in its dealings with native communities. A federal precedent had already been established in 1982, for example, when Canada's Constitution was patriated and proclaimed as the Constitution Act, with a Charter of Rights. Section 35 of the Constitution Act states: "The existing aboriginal and treaty rights of the aboriginal peoples of Canada are hereby recognized and affirmed." Section 35 defines "aboriginal" as Indian, Inuit, and Métis, and the definition of "treaty" includes future treaties as well. Vander Zalm may also have known of a 1984 decision of the Supreme Court, in which the Musqueam Band of Vancouver was told that its aboriginal interest in the land was a "pre-existing legal right."

The Socred premier would certainly recall the incident in 1985 when the Nuu-chah-nulth people on Vancouver Island won a court injunction to block MacMillan Bloedel from logging Meares Island near Tofino. With four other injunctions slapped on companies around BC, it didn't take a rocket scientist to figure out that resource extraction could well be threatened if land claims were not settled. Vander Zalm at least had the political savvy to recognize that treaty negotiations were in everyone's best interests.

Thus it was no surprise when he established a Native Affairs Secretariat in March 1987. The following year he added a new Ministry of Native Affairs to his cabinet, naming Jack Weisgerber as its first minister, and in 1989 established the Premier's Advisory Council on Native Affairs. One month after the council presented its report to cabinet in July 1990, the government accepted its recommendations to join in federal negotiations with aboriginal groups.

Despite this gesture, however, the province was still passing the buck to the feds. In its official response to the Advisory Council, cabinet agreed "to assist the Government of Canada in its responsibilities to negotiate and settle outstanding land claims in British Columbia." Ultimate responsibility still rested with Ottawa, and the federal government would be expected to compensate both native people and the province for any settlements reached.

While most of BC's native leaders and the media hailed BC's arrival at the negotiating table as an historic breakthrough, others, like Saul Terry of the Union of BC Indian Chiefs (which did not recognize provincial governments and wanted only to deal with the feds), Don Ryan of the Gitksan and Wet'suwet'en hereditary chiefs and Ernie Crey of the United Native Nations, were unimpressed. Another skeptic was former Socred Attorney General Brian Smith. Smith, concerned about the number of native demands at the table, compared BC's involvement to "going the Neville Chamberlain route." Smith later said his comment was unfairly misconstrued to suggest he was comparing the native cause to that of Adolf Hitler. In fact, he said, he was only likening the federal government's approach to native issues to the British prime minister's policy of appeasement: "Never saying no, raising expectations. When I was dealing with federal aboriginal affairs ministers in the late 1980s, they wanted to put everything on the table. Nothing was ruled out, everything was up for grabs. I told [federal Native Affairs Minister David] Crombie, 'You've got to deal with one band at a time.'"

Whatever the case, it was clear that the legal landscape for aboriginal rights in BC was changing. It was also true that increased awareness of native culture, along with the growing self-confidence of natives around the country, was rendering the old policies obsolete. When a group of Mohawks began a three-month standoff with provincial and federal authorities at Oka, Québec, in the summer of 1990, BC natives showed their solidarity by setting up roadblocks and rail blockades all around the province.

In January 1991, Native Affairs Minister Weisgerber announced the principles that would guide the province in future land claims negotiations. Settlements would be fair, consistent, affordable, final, and binding, and would respect private property interests. They would also include a framework for natural resource conservation and management, and would provide all British Columbians with comparable levels of government services on the basis of comparable levels of taxation. Weisgerber also announced a Third Party Advisory Committee to advise the government on land claim negotiations. This would include representatives from the major resource sectors, unions, business, local governments, outdoor recreation and tourist groups, and environmental organizations. Finally, the province joined the federal government and First Nations Congress on a task force to define the scope of land claim negotiations, including time frames, the parameters for interim measures agreements, and public education.

On March 8, 1991, Chief Justice Allan McEachern delivered his long-awaited decision on the Gitksan-Wet'suwet'en land claims suit, otherwise known as *Delgamuukw vs. The Queen*. In his decision, McEachern ruled that present-day aboriginal title did not exist, and rejected the right to self-government, because there had been a "blanket" extinguishment of aboriginal rights in BC prior to Confederation. (This particular ruling was overturned by the BC Appeal Court two years later in a unanimous decision.) McEachern also ruled that both federal and provincial governments were bound by a legally enforceable "fiduciary duty" – that is, they owed it to the public confidence – to behave in a non-adversarial manner toward native peoples.

McEachern also granted natives a "right of consultation" in land use decisions that encouraged native consent and agreement. And the fiduciary duty effectively forced Victoria to consult and negotiate with natives over every provincially sanctioned activity that might interfere with aboriginal activities. Since these areas included hunting, fishing and mineral extraction among other things, it made more sense than ever to solve these issues through treaties.

Three days after McEachern's decision, the Socreds renewed their commitment to the treaty process. "Let's not consider this a win-lose situation, but an opportunity," Attorney General Russ Fraser said in the legislature, prompting a rare show of applause by both government and Opposition benches. "The government is committed to working with natives throughout the province to resolve their legitimate differences." On March 29, only four days before his resignation as premier, Bill Vander Zalm added his signature to the framework agreement that finally brought the province into negotiations with the Nisga'a and the federal government.

Politically speaking, the Nisga'a decision was to the treaty process what Clayoquot Sound would be for the Commission on Resources and the Environment. If an agreement was ever reached, it would mark the first modern-day treaty in BC and many believed it would set a precedent for whatever followed under the Treaty Commission. Under the framework agreement signed by the Socred government, all parties promised to make every effort to settle the Nisga'a claim within two years, in other words, by the end of 1993.

The framework agreement also stipulated that a wide variety of issues would be on the bargaining table. These included: lands, renewable and non-renewable resources, environmental issues, cultural artifacts and heritage, economic development, Nisga'a government, compensation, as well as direct and indirect taxation. It was left up to federal and provincial governments to work out the costs of settlement before signing an agreement in principle. (This would become an issue in the summer of 1995, when BC left the negotiating table after a disagreement with Ottawa over the value of the land and its potential resource revenue.) Finally, all parties agreed that the public should be informed "in a general way" of the nature and progress of negotiations, but that details of positions and documents exchanged or developed during negotiations were to remain confidential unless otherwise agreed to by the parties. This stipulation would come back to haunt the NDP government when media and Opposition critics, including Weisgerber, used it to attack the NDP government for conducting "secret" negotiations.

At the end of June 1991, the first report of the BC Claims Task Force recommended the establishment of an independent BC Treaty Commission to oversee a six-stage process for negotiating treaties. The task force's report was a revolutionary document for aboriginal affairs; it called for a new relationship with government in which "recognition and respect for first nations as self-determining and distinct nations with their own spiritual values, histories, languages, territories, political institutions and ways of life must be the hallmark."

Premier Rita Johnston received the Task Force report on July 3, 1991. Eight days later, the cabinet accepted its recommendation to establish the BC Treaty Commission. By that time, however, Social Credit was already in free fall; when the NDP swept to power three months later, it was up to Mike Harcourt's government to put the treaty process in motion, at long last.

The New Social Order

WHEN THE NEW DEMOCRATS TOOK OFFICE IN NOVEMBER 1991, First Nations people in BC had good reason to feel optimistic about the new Treaty Commission. Social Credit deserved full marks for getting the process started, but this positive stand on aboriginal rights was a relatively recent phenomenon. The NDP, on the other hand, had long been identified with the kind of human rights issues of which native land claims were an obvious component.

But the NDP was far from perfect. As former Nuu-chah-nulth Tribal Council president George Watts recalled, the Barrett government said all the right things but took to the hills when it came to serious work on native land claims. Thus, there was a lot of disillusionment following the NDP's victory in 1972. "I think a lot of Indian people who had been involved in the party thought that we were going to have a different reception for our concerns, but we didn't," Watts said. "It was no different than the Socreds when it came to Indian issues, except for that old bleeding heart liberal shit. And there are still some bleeding hearts in there. You can always tell who they are, because [the good will] is so surface that it quickly disappears."

It remained to be seen how far the NDP's consciousness of aboriginal rights had developed since 1975, but one significant difference between the two NDP governments was that the Harcourt cabinet was full of pragmatists who saw the long-term socio-economic benefits of settling land claims. Harcourt's first Aboriginal Affairs minister,

Andrew Petter, was an articulate, 37-year-old University of Victoria law professor with a strong interest in native issues.

As far as land claims were concerned, Petter's ministerial agenda was straightforward. Since the NDP in Opposition had committed itself to recognition of aboriginal title and the right to self-government, and since the Socreds had virtually gift-wrapped the treaty negotiation process just in time for the transition, Petter wasted no time announcing the new government's acceptance of the BC Claims Task Force report.

"One hundred years of policies aimed at denying aboriginal peoples their historic rights are at an end," Petter said at the December 10 press conference. "It is my hope that through this process we can establish a new social order, one in which aboriginal peoples and non-aboriginal peoples can live side by side with mutual respect, each pursuing their own social and economic aspirations." Squamish chief Joe Mathias, who sat on the Task Force, was especially pleased with the announcement. "What comes clear to us is that there's renewed energy from the cabinet of the province of British Columbia to address this issue squarely, and honourably, to reach conclusions on what we consider treaty negotiations," he said. While Union of BC Indian Chiefs president Saul Terry continued his role as skeptic (he was concerned that provincial government lawyers were still arguing in court that aboriginal rights had been extinguished in a legal sense), the majority of tribal groups in BC supported the First Nations Summit task group that informed the treaty process.

On September 21, 1992, the British Columbia Treaty Commission Agreement was announced with a traditional ceremony at the Squamish Indian reserve in North Vancouver. Prime Minister Brian Mulroney and Mike Harcourt joined native leaders in signing a deal that committed Ottawa and Victoria to settling all land claims in BC by the year 2000. In March 1993, the province signed a memorandum of understanding with the Union of BC Municipalities, recognizing that the land claims negotiation and settlement process "must be fair, open, principled and community based, and the process must be democratic, efficient, inclusive and acceptable to all parties." To this end, municipalities would be represented as advisors in treaty negotiations and, in some cases, would actually sit at the table. The BC Treaty Commission would also hear from the Treaty Negotiation Advisory Committee (TNAC), which represented forestry, mining, fishing, ranching, small business and wildlife interests.

The first commissioners, appointed on April 15, 1993, spent the rest of the year establishing the policies, initial procedures and priorities that would guide the treaty process. The chief commissioner was Chuck Connaghan, a labour consultant who had sat on Bill Vander Zalm's BC Round Table on the Environment and the Economy in 1990. Connaghan, who retired a year into the job, was succeeded by lawyer Alec Robertson, a former president of the BC branch of the Canadian Bar Association. Robertson had also served as chairman of the Law Foundation of BC and as a member of the CBA's Gender Equality Task Force.

In the words of its annual report, the Treaty Commission was to be "Keeper of the Process" uniting the First Nations, Canada and British Columbia at the table. The Commission would have three basic functions: to identify the aboriginal groups in the treaty process; determine the current method of governance for each (band council, etc.); and provide a map outlining the areas inhabited by each group. The Commission would not negotiate treaties but bring the parties together while ensuring a table was set for negotiations once the parties were ready. Once that happened, the Commission would be responsible for allocating funds provided by Canada and BC, through loans and contributions, to enable First Nations to participate. Then it would monitor the progress of each set of negotiations, "assisting the parties to obtain dispute resolution services where requested." Finally, it would report to the principle parties and the public.

There were six stages to settlement in the treaty process.

Statement of intent: Native group submits a statement to the BC Treaty Commission indicating its willingness to negotiate a treaty.

Preparation for negotiations: Native and government negotiators conduct research, prepare for talks, and identify the issues they want included in the treaties. Initial meetings are held.

Negotiation of framework agreement: the three parties negotiate framework agreements, which identify the issues to be addressed in the treaties, consult the public, and establish a timetable for talks.

Agreement in principle: negotiating teams reach a tentative agreement on the substance of the treaties. Public consultation continues and parties decide how the changes brought about by the treaties will be carried out.

Finalizing a treaty: treaties are finalized and signed. Each treaty must be approved by natives in a referendum. Legislation is drafted to implement each treaty, making it law.

Implementation of treaty: treaties come into effect. Costs are carried by federal and provincial governments, with Ottawa providing most of the cash and Victoria most of the land.

Once treaties were signed, reserves would be replaced by "settlement areas" – in some cases, expanded reserves – where natives would have some form of ownership of the land. Those settlement areas would be surrounded by larger "treaty areas" where local natives would exercise resource rights as defined in the treaty. In total, the treaties would result in about 2,000 pockets of aboriginal settlement areas throughout the province, some of them just extensions of the current 1,600 reserves. Despite this extension, the actual amount of land base governed by aboriginal groups would not total more than 5 percent of the entire province. (The 111 percent figure used by the Vancouver *Sun* includes traditional territories, many of them overlapping, that native groups claim historically.)

Even after the geographical revisions, however, these lands would not become sovereign states within Canada. "The provincial vision is we're not negotiating sovereignty," said Angus Robertson, BC's assistant deputy minister for Aboriginal Affairs. "We're not in this to create mini-states. We're in this to create a new working relationship."

To an extent, this new working relationship was already developing in the private sector. Forest companies, for example, had been forming joint ventures with native bands for the last twenty years. More recently, groups like the Nisga'a were going international. The Nisga'a had established a joint venture with the US-based Rayonier Inc. to harvest BC timber and, with a special BC forestry permit, were exporting raw logs to Japan. Even banks, formerly reluctant to enter relationships with native bands, were coming on board. Major banks now had vice-presidents of aboriginal banking, and native-run trust companies were being established. "There is a very strong corporate will to try and pursue business relationships with aboriginal groups," said TNAC member Marlie Beets, a vice-president of aboriginal affairs for the BC Council of Forest Industries.

According to former Musqueam chief Wendy Grant, this new spirit of cooperation may have been partly the result of the Canadian business community's recent experience with Asian investors. "Canadian business has always been based on a five-year make-a-quick-buck-and-get-out [model]," Grant told the *Sun*. "The people in the Asian countries have a different concept that's more secure, and they are looking at twenty years and not being so worried about the kind of revenue you are going to get in the first five years. It's the same way with First Nations communities and as business people start to make relationships with First Nations, they see the same kind of things happening in our communities and the way we want to do business."

Grant found an unlikely ally in former Attorney General Brian Smith, who had left provincial politics in 1988 to become chair of CN Rail. Smith had apparently come a long way since his 1990 criticism of the Native Affairs Ministry for "going the Neville Chamberlain route." He had begun organizing informal dinner and breakfast meetings with native band chiefs and white chief executive officers to promote working relationships between corporations and native bands – relationships separate from CN Rail's corporate strategy but "parallel", according to Smith, to the treaty process. "I want to see the treaty-making process and the non-native relationships work," said Smith. "This process can't work if other people don't help to make it work. And the treaty-making process can't work if it's left to lawyers, negotiators and officials to do it."

Despite all this good will, there were still fears about the consequences of economic prosperity for native people. "We will be as equal as Orwell's pigs," said contract logger Tim Menning of Williams Lake. "Some of us are going to pay more." Menning was not alone in his concern that new joint ventures with native bands would mean a loss of jobs for whites. This was especially a concern in the Interior, where contractors are not unionized to the same extent as on the coast.

In Menning's view, the push toward land claim settlements was being done "off the backs of the working people." Curiously, this was the same argument being used by Reform Party critics who wanted to scrap the federal Indian Act. Releasing natives from the chains of paternalism and bureaucracy was one thing, but offering them the same economic opportunities as white people – and in the same work-force – was quite another.

AS THE TREATY COMMISSION WAS BEING ESTABLISHED IN 1993, the BC Appeal Court overturned a key section from Chief Justice McEachern's 1991 decision in the Gitksan-Wet'suwet'en case. Contrary to McEachern's judgment, the court ruled that there had been no "blanket extinguishment" of aboriginal rights in BC prior to Confederation. The new decision confirmed the aboriginal right to self-government while acknowledging that a limited form of aboriginal title continued to exist. Because Canadian law had already designated areas of jurisdiction to Ottawa and the provinces, however, it was up to both those levels of government to ensure that non-native governments were able to co-exist with proposed native governments, whatever form those might take.

"The establishment of some form of Indian self-government beyond the regulatory powers delegated by the Indian Act is ripe for negotiation and reconciliation," wrote the judge, Alan Macfarlane. That statement marked the first time in Canada that a court fully acknowledged that aboriginal title still existed. Now the ball was in the governments' court, instead of in the Supreme Court.

By September 1994, 41 aboriginal groups in BC had applied to negotiate treaties. That number represented 60 percent of the Indian bands in the province and 65 percent of the native population. (BC is home to about 172,000 people of aboriginal ancestry, or 5.3 percent of the provincial population, including 87,400 registered status Indians.) Negotiators had met with 30 mayors, 100 city councillors, and had held seventeen meetings with various lobby groups. A public forum was held in Prince George in June, and advisory committees were set up in a number of communities affected by the negotiations. Despite these events, designed to demonstrate the openness and accountability of the treaty process, the effort to promote native land claims in the media was plagued by misinformation, fear and paranoia as critics blasted the BC Treaty Commission in particular and land claim negotiations in general.

If the Reform Party was to be believed, First Nations people were laying claim to private property and were planning to kick white people out of their homes. The truth was that private property was not subject to land claim negotiations without owner consent. Another myth was that land claims would shut down resource industries. In fact, many native groups planned to continue logging and mining their own traditional lands. The problem was, they currently had no right to do so. Another complaint of Reform and other critics was that the negotiations were shrouded in secrecy and that the NDP was attempting, through the Treaty Commission, to turn BC into a giant reserve while an unsuspecting public was kept in the dark. For native people, this kind of fearmongering had become amusingly ironic. "We kind of get a kick out of it, in the Indian community, about how people from the Reform Party are saying the NDP government is giving away the store to us," George Watts commented. "I mean, somebody better come to our community and show us, because we certainly don't see it."

Similarly, complaints about secrecy were misguided, given the range of interests involved in the treaty process. Industry was well served with the 31-member Treaty Negotiation Advisory Committee, and municipalities had a place at the table. Local treaty advisory committees and regional advisory committees were being established, and negotiating sessions were open to local cable television stations. The secrecy complaint smacked of a double standard, given that many critics in the business community had benefited from secret backroom negotiations on Socred megaprojects.

"The treaty talks are no more secretive than the resource-management meetings between government and industry that take place every day," said former Vancouver *Sun* native issues reporter Terry Glavin, who had done research for the Treaty Commission. "In fact, the most secrecy-shrouded player in BC aboriginal affairs is TNAC, many of whose members were intervenors in the Gitksan case. They're the ones making all the noise, demanding a referendum for white people in BC While the entire media was going on about secrecy, there were no negotiations going on, so I don't know what there was to be so secret about."

As for Weisgerber's complaints, the Reform leader's posturing about secrecy was another example of his selective amnesia on the issue. As Bill Vander Zalm's Native Affairs Minister, Weisgerber had insisted on confidentiality. "We got this confidentiality agreement that I didn't want to sign," said BC Federation of Labour president Ken Georgetti, recalling the Fed's involvement with a Socred-appointed aboriginal affairs committee. "We checked with our lawyers, and the only way we could participate on the committee was to sign this confidentiality agreement. And it was insisted upon by Jack Weisgerber."

How the former Socred managed to evolve from Closed Door Jack to Open Door Jack in less than four years was anybody's guess. In any case, Weisgerber's record as Native Affairs minister was hardly of the macho, chest-thumping variety he was now promoting as Reform leader. Harcourt recalled how, late in the Vander Zalm government's term, Weisgerber had allowed a blockade by the Mount Currie Indian Band to go on for two months before doing anything about it. As the premier later explained in the legislature – much to the delight of NDP backbenchers and Opposition Liberals – Weisgerber had "sat there and squirmed and wiggled, and wondered what the heck to do, and then he went up to the blockade and asked, 'Would you please take the blockade down?' They said, 'No,' and blew him away, and he turned around and walked back to the car with a dejected look and his shoulders bowed like this ... "

In September 1994, TNAC sent a four-page letter to both federal and provincial governments, complaining about the effect of confidentiality requirements on TNAC members' ability "to communicate with and obtain input from those they are supposed to represent." TNAC also claimed that the Harcourt government was using interim measures agreements to make unilateral concessions to aboriginal bands, and wanted the government to consult TNAC members before approving any more of them. (Interim measures agreements occur before formal treaty talks begin. They cover revenue sharing, resource use and controls on development. Such agreements are not subject to approval by the legislature, but are authorized by cabinet and form the basis for resource management until treaties are signed.)

Harcourt appeared to anticipate these concerns. Even before TNAC released its letter, he cancelled a Socred-approved interim measures agreement in the Queen Charlotte Islands that would have allowed the Haida to control the growth of the recreational fishery in the Charlottes. This followed a protest by seventeen organizations representing anglers, resort operators and conservation groups concerned about their access to the fishery. On September 20, the premier held a press conference in Victoria where he laid out five principles the government intended to follow in opening up the treaty process.

Most of these conditions were already well-established, and the information was available at the BC Treaty Commission office for any curious member of the public. But Harcourt, pushed into a corner by an increasingly hostile media, decided he had no choice but to play Mr. Rogers and spell it out for the TV news audience. Open negotiations, he said, would be "the rule, not the exception," and all British Columbians would have an opportunity to provide "meaningful input." BC's negotiating mandate would be made public, and the province would share as much information as possible about the negotiating sessions. Finally, all treaty settlements would have to go through the legislature before completion.

By now it should have been clear that the NDP's motivations for settling land claims were as pragmatic as they were altruistic. Faced with court decisions favouring native rights, an estimated $1 billion in lost investment because of roadblocks, and consumer uncertainty over land use and resource ownership, the Harcourt cabinet knew there were good economic reasons to negotiate claims. BC's treaty process would also allow the federal government to eventually opt out of aboriginal affairs, primarily by scrapping the Indian Act. The federal government had its own reasons for participating in the treaty process. For one thing, Ottawa could reduce the number of natives on welfare by negotiating self-government and creating self-sustaining

First Nations communities. According to a November 1994 report by the federal auditor general, 43 percent of on-reserve Indians were on welfare, costing Canada about $1 billion a year. The potential of other savings in social service costs and health treatment were inestimable.

AS 1994 CAME TO AN END, THE HARCOURT GOVERNMENT FACED a number of challenges on the native affairs front. On Vancouver Island, the Nanoose First Nation Band went to court October 31 to block a condominium development on private property just south of Parksville. For some years it was known that the property lay on an ancient burial ground with remains dating back from 2,000 to 4,000 years, but the 50-hectare project was given the go-ahead after band chief Wayne Edwards signed a detailed agreement with Intrawest, the company that owned the Craig Bay Estates condo development.

The agreement called for an on-site archeologist to ensure that remains were properly documented, stored and reinterred at another location. But problems began when the number of remains turned out to be higher than expected. One estimate was that up to 400 people were buried there. After consulting with his band, Chief Edwards went back to the developer and demanded that no further excavation take place. Instead, the band wanted the development cancelled under the Cemetery Act, which prohibits the disturbance of burial grounds. Intrawest modified its development plans in order to meet the band's request, but the band responded by claiming the entire site and threatening a blockade. The situation was serious, given that some of the condos had already been sold, and families were waiting to move in.

For several months the government watched with growing concern as the band's lawyer went to court to have the excavation permits quashed on a legal technicality. The dispute dragged on into the spring of 1995, at which point Bill Barlee entered the picture. (The dispute fell under his jurisdiction, since the permits were granted under the archeological department, a branch of the Small Business, Tourism and Culture Ministry.) The government eventually bought fourteen acres of land, including the area where remains had been found, with the intention of creating a green space that would be accessible to the entire community.

At a cost of $7.8 million (a figure based on an independent assessment of the land value), cabinet saw this as the simplest available solution. According to ministry estimates, if the project had collapsed and the company and residents had sued, potential liability to the taxpayer could have been as high as $100 million, based on full compensation for the project including foregone profit. By buying the property for public use, however, the government managed to avoid further liability while preventing the Nanoose band from using native burials as leverage to lay claim to private property. "Contrary to the usual media spin on how this government makes decisions," said Barlee's ministerial assistant, Mike Geoghegan, "we didn't 'cave in' to the Indians. We bailed out the developer."

Another controversy was brewing in the Okanagan during the fall of 1994. On November 2, the Penticton Indian Band, along with the Upper and Lower Similkameen bands, erected blockades on three access roads leading to Apex Ski Resort near Penticton. Band leaders, concerned about the environmental effects that the $20 million expansion of the ski hill would have on their traditional lands, initially set up blockades that kept out all construction workers and some resort staff, although skiers and owners of recreational property were allowed to pass through.

Three weeks later, Apex estimated it was losing $1 million a week in business. The government responded by providing a $500,000 loan to Apex to help the resort complete a 90-room hotel and further renovations in its expansion project. The blockade was eventually scaled down to an information picket on one of the highway routes, and no violence resulted from the action, but questions remained about the government's role in mediating local disputes with Indian bands. Moe Sihota, responding to demands for the government to call in the RCMP, offered the party line that soon became familiar when blockades went up. "It's up to the courts to determine whether it's legal or illegal," Sihota told the *Sun*. "We as a government have made it very clear if there are further discussions [with the bands] the blockade has to come down. Now if they don't, I am not going to go there and physically remove it."

Hysteria Reigns

SIHOTA'S STAND ON NATIVE ROADBLOCKS WAS AN EASY ONE for an NDP politician to take in the fall of 1994. By the following spring, however, the government was under increasing pressure as a series of roadblocks went up around the province and critics tried to connect the events to the treaty process. With the Vancouver *Sun*'s April 1 announcement that land claims totalled 111 percent of the land base in BC, the debate surrounding aboriginal title reached new levels of hysteria.

Much of the fearmongering was served up by federal and provincial Reform Party members, who were more than willing to exploit the self-interest of the least informed British Columbians. Skeena MP Mike Scott, for example, was particularly fond of using the Indian-as-bogeyman argument, predicting that full-scale Armageddon would result if the Nisga'a treaty went through. "I'm not a scaremonger, but I hear it every day. It's frightening," said Scott, adding that there would be "social unrest like never before ... Yes, by non-native people. We are so close to violence in rural BC that it's not funny."

Scott's views were shared in the media by columnist and former Liberal Party leader Gordon Gibson and radio talk show host Rafe Mair. Gibson used all the stock phrases of the anti-native movement: "selling the farm," "third order of government," "compromising the future" and so on. He even offered the bizarre suggestion that the NDP no longer had a moral right to negotiate treaties because the government was below 25 percent in the polls and had therefore lost its mandate to do anything controversial.

Mair described the aboriginal rights agenda as "a frightening journey through the looking glass where everything is backwards." Confident that most British Columbians shared his assumptions about the stakeholders, he complained that "victories" in court were being treated as "losses" by governments, that native communities were being "given" land while the majority of Canadians were "kept in the dark," and that the Canadian Constitution was being "ignored" by land claims negotiations.

Mair wrote these words in the foreword to *Our Home or Native*

Land? What Governments' Aboriginal Policy is Doing to Canada, a book that spells out the anti-native agenda in its broadest context. The book's author, Melvin H. Smith, was a constitutional affairs specialist who spent three decades in the BC public service and was an influential voice in the "No" campaign during the Charlottetown referendum debate. Smith was also an evangelical Christian who wrote a regular column for *BC Report* magazine. The basic premise of his book can be summed up as follows: there has never been a preexisting right to aboriginal title, Canadian politicians are breaking the law by negotiating land claims, and the BC Treaty Commission should be dismantled immediately. Smith also argued that native people had no right to call themselves "First Nations" because, in his view, the term was historically inaccurate. But these arguments weren't of much concern to the native leaders he attacked throughout his book. "I note that he's been acknowledged as the 'foremost constitutional lawyer in British Columbia.' I don't know who gave him that distinction," Nisga'a Tribal Council president Joe Gosnell said of Smith. "He was an advisor to the BC government, and how many of his ideas were actually put into policy? Very little, I think. I don't know how the devil he got awarded being the 'foremost constitutional lawyer in British Columbia.'"

Nevertheless, Smith's book became something of a Bible for the Reform Party's aboriginal policymakers. It also provided fodder for government critics who thought the NDP was taking too passive an approach to native roadblocks. On May 3, the Upper Nicola Band in the Interior put up a blockade on Douglas Lake Road after several of its members were charged with illegally gillnetting trout in a lake that was stocked by the local Douglas Lake ranch. At first the band said the issue was about fishing rights. Before long, though, it was clear that the dispute was largely the result of deteriorating relations between band members and the ranch. In the 1970s, many band members had worked as cowboys and sold feed and grazing rights to the ranch, while native children played freely on the property. In recent times, however, the ranch employed fewer natives and no longer bought hay from the band. While the band lost money, the ranch continued to prosper, and the Upper Nicola community watched with growing resentment as truck traffic to the ranch increased. The fact that Douglas Lake Road ran through the heart of the reserve – but was cut out of the reserve property by a federal order – only compounded the insult.

By the end of May, this local dispute in a hidden pocket of the province made front page headlines and topped the six o'clock news broadcasts. This was partly because of the blockade's ominous resemblance to the Oka dispute: for many white television viewers, the sight of a native Indian wearing a mask and standing defiantly in front of a roadblock was a frightening reminder of the showdown between Mohawk warriors and Canadian armed forces at Kanesetake five years earlier. Unlike previous native roadblocks in BC, where getting arrested was merely a strategy to gain attention for a native cause, this dispute carried the threat of real violence.

On June 5, however, an agreement was reached and band members took down the blockade only hours before the RCMP planned to take it down by force. Attorney General Colin Gabelmann, responding to weeks of abuse from Opposition and media critics, angrily dismissed accusations that the NDP was a "weak-kneed negotiator." Aboriginal groups attempting to use blockades as a bargaining tactic, he said, were wasting their time. "Let me say this to those who would choose the path of lawlessness as a means to achieving their ends: that path will not succeed," Gabelmann told the legislature. "Roadblocks will not achieve justice for aboriginal people. There will be no negotiation on substantive issues concerning aboriginal people while the roadblock is in place."

Given the timing of the blockade, it was hardly surprising that Opposition parties tied the dispute to the treaty negotiations. In a pre-election period, the Douglas Lake roadblock gave Liberals and Reformers a perfect opportunity to attack the government, implying that the integrity of the treaty talks was in jeopardy. Gabelmann's failure to prosecute in the Douglas Lake dispute, said Jack Weisgerber, "sends a message to all native people that they can break the law with impunity and then bring the government to its knees at a blockade."

Conveniently missing from this critique, however, was any

acknowledgement that the Douglas Lake dispute had nothing to do with the treaty process. The Upper Nicola Band was a sovereigntist group and a member of the Union of BC Indian Chiefs, which did not recognize BC's role in treaty making and wanted to negotiate strictly with Ottawa. "The difficulty with this approach," wrote Aboriginal Affairs Minister John Cashore, in a letter to the *Sun*, "is that land claims ultimately involve lands and resources, which are the jurisdiction of the province. The First Nations that have filed statements of intent with the BC Treaty Commission have accepted a tripartite process [and] ... accept the province's role and our responsibility for governing lands and resources."

Although the NDP remained fully committed to the treaty process, there were signs that the constant bashing from Opposition critics was beginning to have an effect. The government's rightward shift on aboriginal rights could be seen, for example, in its treatment of the gaming issue. While the government's prohibition of large-scale, destination resort gambling by native bands was consistent with other decisions on gambling – particularly its cancellation of the union-supported Seaport Centre the previous fall – native negotiators were shocked in May when the premier abruptly cancelled talks on aboriginal gaming altogether, thus dismissing any chance of approval for eighteen proposed native casinos.

Also in May, a leak of the government's land claims negotiating position revealed that Victoria had capped its planned settlements with native groups at 5 percent of BC's total land base. In other news, Aboriginal Affairs Minister John Cashore described First Nations governments as "subordinate" within the context of the Canadian constitution, and the premier refused to accept the Nisga'a demand for $2 billion in cash and 10,660 square kilometres of land to settle the claim of the 6,000-member band. By mid-July, talks with the Nisga'a collapsed when the federal and provincial participants began arguing over the increased value of stumpage fees. The federal government was prepared to match BC's payment of $175 million, but stated that the increase in resource revenue for the province was unfair and that BC should boost its cash contribution. BC refused.

As the end of summer 1995 approached, another confrontation was underway at a ranch on Gustafsen Lake, near 100 Mile House. The standoff between police and natives began like many others across the country: a group of natives which had gathered annually in June for a sundance festival fell out of favour with the ranch owner when they rebuilt an old fence around the area. Told they were in breach of a 1988 agreement, the sundancers were told to leave the property and were later confronted by a posse of ranchers who threatened the group, saying that an RCMP invasion was imminent. This only fuelled paranoia among the sundancers. The group refused to leave, eventually attracting several other native and non-native supporters who referred to themselves as Defenders of the Shuswap Nation. Many of the people in the camp by August did not live in the area and were later discredited by representatives of the local Shuswap Nation.

What separated this dispute from most other native protests was the presence of guns. Big guns: AK-47 assault rifles, semi-automatic pistols and an arsenal of other firearms. When the standoff began in the third week of August, the group's leaders demanded a meeting with the Queen and vowed that they would only leave the scene in body bags.

For the next 30 days there were several exchanges of gunfire with the police as the area surrounding the encampment turned into a military post, complete with armoured personnel carriers and a field hospital. By the end of the occupation, 400 police officers had taken part in the largest and costliest RCMP operation in Canadian history – $5.5 million, or $240,000 a day. Meanwhile, a constant stream of negotiators, lawyers and spiritual leaders passed through the encampment in a series of failed attempts to end the occupation peacefully. Assembly of First Nations chief Ovide Mercredi failed to broker an agreement, and the lawyer representing the natives, Bruce Clark, was later wrestled to the floor of a courtroom after threatening the judge and accusing the entire legal system of complicity in treason and genocide.

It was beginning to look like another Oka – a situation Harcourt had promised would never happen in BC – but the standoff ended peacefully on September 17, when the final twelve occupants of the camp were flown out by helicopter and taken into police custody. Although no one was seriously injured during the siege, there were questions in the wake of the dispute. The police, for example, came under attack for using the criminal records of some of the camp occupants in a media propaganda campaign. Many believed the RCMP released the records to garner public support for the use of force in the event of an invasion.

There were also questions about the NDP government's role in all this. The New Democrats had faced a difficult balancing act as they tried to maintain public support for the treaty process while convincing voters that an NDP government would not simply roll over and play dead in the event of an armed insurrection.

Much of the credit for the ultimately peaceful resolution and the NDP's refusal to negotiate with the armed camp went to BC's new attorney general. Harcourt had appointed Ujjal Dosanjh to the position after a minor cabinet shuffle on August 16. Dosanjh, who had been elevated to cabinet only four months earlier, replaced the much-maligned Colin Gabelmann (who was admittedly relieved to swap portfolios with the Government Services minister). As a practising lawyer, Dosanjh was a popular choice for the AG's job, and he was unequivocal in his stance on law and order. In his first statement as attorney general, Dosanjh promised a crackdown on crime. "I have some definite ideas, and stay tuned," he told reporters. "Within the next three or four weeks, you'll hear more."

He didn't need to wait that long. Only four days after his promotion, the new attorney general had the Gustafsen Lake dispute fall in his lap. When police confiscated the first cache of weapons found at the site, Dosanjh responded, "Gustafsen Lake has nothing to do with aboriginal land claim issues. It's purely to do with the weapons found there and the shots that have been fired. The criminal law of Canada applies to every inch of British Columbia. The legitimate First Nations leaders in the area have distanced themselves very clearly from these individuals."

Dosanjh maintained this stance throughout the dispute, while encouraging the RCMP to take as long as necessary to end the standoff peacefully. His handling of the affair was praised in the media. Many reporters recalled Dosanjh's own brush with death ten years earlier. In 1985, the young lawyer was brutally beaten because of his outspoken opposition to Sikh nationalism, which he expressed often in columns he wrote for a Vancouver East Indian community newspaper.

Harcourt's appointment of Dosanjh as attorney general was one of the high points for a government that was already in pre-election mode by the end of summer 1995. But the Gustafsen Lake standoff raised more serious questions about its overall performance. How, for example, would the NDP's record on aboriginal issues stack up against its promises of 1991? Could the government have moved along the treaty process, or the Nisga'a negotiations, any faster than it did? These were issues, after all, that the premier claimed he would be willing to take to voters.

"Harcourt wanted to face [land claims] head on, but I don't think he appreciated just how complex an issue it is," said Terry Glavin. "I think the New Democrats have come to realize this."

Racism, he added, continues to be the biggest roadblock in this process. "I'd no more trust British Columbians to address these issues today than I'd trust the good citizens of Alabama to deal with race issues in 1962. The real question, from the NDP point of view is, where's the social justice in all this? How have we allowed this to develop so that workers are on one side and bureaucrats and natives are on the other? ... What I've seen is a real demonization of native people on every front. A strange, populist barbarism is sweeping the small towns of this province, and it's not grounded in reality ... There's this overwhelming public sentiment that native people are getting a free ride from the provincial government and it's the exact opposite. They've done everything they've had to in law."

The Nisga'a, in particular, have done everything they've had to in law since 1887, the first time they attempted to settle their land claim with a provincial government. In those days, there was no such thing as liberal guilt. Instead of negotiating with the Nisga'a, BC Premier William Smithe told the Tribal Council to consider itself lucky to be living on reserves. "When the whites first came among you," he had said, "you were little better than the wild beasts of the field."

One hundred and eight years later, the Nisga'a Tribal Council president and chief negotiator, Joe Gosnell, couldn't help chuckling at that remark. "Put that in bold letters in your book," he told the author.

"Underline it or something." Gosnell, like so many other native leaders over the decades, has waited patiently while governments jockeyed for position over cost-sharing agreements, using public opinion to guide them while native lives continue to hang in the balance. After all these years of stonewalling and posturing by white governments, you'd think Gosnell would be fed up by now. But with so few items separating Ottawa and Victoria, the Nisga'a leader was sounding very much like someone who could see destiny on the horizon. After 108 years, what's a few more weeks of haggling over the small print?

"If we can come to terms it would paint a very positive picture of our aboriginal people," Gosnell said. "It would clearly indicate to the general population that, yes, we can do the job without violence being involved or civil disobedience being imposed by the aboriginal people on the general population."

The suspension of talks in July made the Nisga'a leader feel like he was "sitting on a powder keg with a very short lit fuse," he added. But with increased native militancy arising from the Gustafsen Lake standoff, and the NDP's determination to fulfil one of its major campaign promises, there was a growing sense of inevitability by the end of September. "We view the settlement of outstanding claims in British Columbia as a justice issue that needs to be addressed, irregardless of what political party comes into power," said Gosnell. "If the Liberal Party comes into power, or – God forbid – the Reform Party comes into power, are we going to receive less justice with these parties? My question is, why should justice be gauged by the political party in power?"

It was a good question. The answer had a lot to do with conflicting attitudes about race, community living and above all, money.

IO

Beancounters
of the Left

FOR MANY OF THE NDP'S TRADITIONAL SUPPORTERS, ONE OF
the more distressing developments since the party came to power was
its gradual shift toward fiscally conservative economics. Like their
colleagues in Ontario (and, to a lesser extent, Saskatchewan) concerned about the changing priorities, many New Democrats believe
that the party has no reason to exist if it is not going to defend the
social programs and basic human services that established its reputation as a social democratic party in the first place. By the time they
came to power, however, the NDP governments of Mike Harcourt,
Bob Rae and Roy Romanow all decided that sacrifices had to be made
in order to survive social program funding cutbacks on a federal level,
and the changing economy on a global level.

The federal government's neo-conservative fiscal policy reached
alarming proportions with the 1990 budget, in which the Conservatives introduced an Expenditure Control Plan that froze the per capita
transfer of health and post-secondary education spending for the five-
year period from 1990-91 to 1994-95 (a period that included, ironically, most of the Bob Rae government's term in Ontario and Mike
Harcourt's first term in BC). By 1991, when the Socreds were in disar-
ray over ethical scandals and Bill Vander Zalm's leadership, BC was

just completing a boom cycle that allowed the government to generate budget surpluses from 1988 to 1990.

The Socreds tried in vain to campaign on the achievement of being the only province in Canada to generate a surplus. Their problem was that, due to declining revenues and increased expenditures, both the projected deficit and the debt were much larger than their own numbers indicated. Once the auditors got hold of the books, they discovered that the $700 million deficit projected by the Socreds was closer to $2 billion. According to the associate deputy minister of Finance, Ian McKinnon, the per capita debt for all government spending had gone from $250 in 1975, when the last NDP government cleared its desks, to $2,200 in 1991.

How the new government dealt with this reality would say a lot about the NDP's current philosophical makeup. The shift in the party's economic thinking was evident before the 1991 election, when the NDP was preparing its 48-point platform titled "A Better Way for British Columbia." During this process, the party's economic subcommittee was repeatedly thwarted in its efforts to influence the document. Chaired by retired UBC economics professor Gideon Rosenbluth, the subcommittee was regarded among the party executive as hopelessly out of touch with the 1990s reality of global capitalism. Instead of soliciting input from the subcommittee, the party sent its members a draft of the final document which stated that the new government would balance the budget immediately. This set off a major debate between leftists and moderate capitalists within the party.

"We sent urgent messages over to Victoria," Rosenbluth recalled. "We said 'Look, we may not know much, but one thing we can tell you for absolutely sure is that nobody can balance the budget in British Columbia in 1991.' The cycle had just turned, you could see we were going into a recession, and what essentially drives the deficit is the business cycle. The most you could expect to do was balance the budget over the business cycle."

Shortly afterward, the draft was changed so that the final version of the NDP's campaign platform read, "We'll balance the budget over the business cycle." That one qualification, said Rosenbluth, may well have made a world of difference to the NDP's future electoral prospects. "We saved them from a disaster, because if you look at 1991, the deficit was substantial." But that advice was about the only influence the party's economic subcommittee would have on the new government. Not long after the new government took office, Rosenbluth was dumped as chair, and the committee's role in policy formation became increasingly irrelevant.

Meanwhile, two weeks into office, the new government was already forced to back away from its promise to balance the budget within a five-year business cycle. "I guess at this point, all that's fair to say is that it will be much more difficult to accomplish, given the numbers we were operating under were not real numbers," Glen Clark told reporters on November 13, 1991, after a media briefing by Finance Ministry officials. Faced with projected deficits of about $2 billion for the current fiscal year and $2.5 billion for the next, Clark responded by calling for a spending reduction of 15 percent in all ministries.

The move delighted Howe Street businessmen and media pundits like the *Sun*'s Vaughn Palmer, whose tongue was planted firmly in cheek when he referred to Clark as "the most right-wing Finance minister in Canada." Having inherited the mess left behind by Social Credit, Palmer mused, "the rookie New Democrat ... is responding with the traditional Socred solutions: spending restraint, program cuts and higher taxes."

Although this characterization was decidedly ironic, for once Palmer was saying something that socialists could agree with: the NDP, under Clark's Finance Ministry, had indeed embarked on a fiscal agenda far right of anything one would recognize as socialist. It was a path that the recently discarded Gideon Rosenbluth and other left-wing economists described as "deficitphobic," inspired by the fear that the government would lose its credit rating during a deficit-spending period if it didn't impose high interest rates and fight inflation. Deficitphobes typically compare the fiscal role of government to the budget realities that households and businesses must face every day – forgetting that households and businesses only have to look after themselves, while governments have to look after everyone else as well.

The problem with deficitphobia was that, when gross domestic

product (GDP) and ten-year population growth estimates were factored into a government's economy, it was "highly unlikely that
increases in government deficits to help fight the current recession
would impair the credit rating. On the contrary," argues Rosenbluth;
"the credit rating is more likely to be impaired by persistent levels of
low output and employment."

The NDP had bought into the assumption of business that the government would not be able to borrow if its credit rating dropped significantly. But this concern ignored the fact that most Canadian
governments have very high ratings, and BC's had consistently
remained the highest. Besides, as Rosenbluth also points out, the
financial institutions of the world don't think twice about lending
money to Olympia and York "and every Third World dictator they
could find, whose credit ratings cannot be anywhere near those of
Canada and its provinces." The notion that BC would not be able to
raise the capital it needed on international money markets was absurd.

The premier was aware of this criticism but maintained that the
NDP approach to deficit reduction would be kinder and gentler than
the slash-and-burn approach of Social Credit. For the right-wing free-
enterprise party, said Harcourt, deficit cutting was "almost a game.
Like, who can be the toughest son of a gun on the block [with] the
toughest scorched-earth policy on government services? Who can cut
the most in the way of government expenditure and get the greatest
tax increases? For most of the wealthy and big business, it's an end in
itself." The NDP, on the other hand, would attack the deficit for
purely social democratic reasons. "It allows us to have the fiscal flexi-
bility to maintain basic services, to maintain a positive role for government in a mixed economy. To be able to invest in a pay-as-you-go
[scheme] for borrowing for basic infrastructures that people need. It's
a means to an end."

Indeed, Clark managed to recover from the "right-wing Finance
minister" label very quickly with his first budget. In addition to a
wealth tax on everyone making $60,000 a year or more, Clark
increased business taxes by $300 million, scrapped the fully subsi-
dized doctors' pension plan, imposed a sales tax on legal services, and
reduced supplemental benefits for wealthy homeowners. Although he

froze welfare rates, Clark did recognize the increase in migration rates that was causing the welfare rolls to swell, so he added $231 million for temporary assistance in the coming year.

But Clark's days as Finance minister were numbered. By the spring of 1993, Harcourt was under increasing pressure from the business community to replace his Finance minister because of the corporate capital tax, the surcharge on high income earners and the controversial homeowners' grant reduction that prompted a tax revolt following the NDP's second budget. Clark, one of the NDP's brightest cabinet ministers, also exuded a smug, Trudeau-esque, "just watch me" self-confidence that many in the business community felt was not servile enough. These critics accused him of waging an arrogant form of class warfare by soaking the rich. In the 1993 cabinet shuffle, Clark was encouraged to tone down the rhetoric in his new capacity as Employment and Investment minister. Meanwhile, the premier served notice that the two-year NDP experiment in tax increases was about to end. Under new Finance Minister Elizabeth Cull, the government would revert to the deficitphobic policy that some of its economic advisors on the left had warned it against two years earlier.

Cheats, Deadbeats and Varmints

THE MOST GLARING EVIDENCE OF THE NDP'S SHIFT TO THE right was found in the Social Services Ministry, where a compassionate approach to welfare spending had long been considered a sacred trust of NDP social policy. During Joan Smallwood's two-year reign as minister, the welfare budget saw annual double-digit increases even as the unemployment rate dropped and the government boasted of job creation projects. Most democratic socialists responded to this news by pointing to recent structural changes in the economy that made it harder for many working people to survive without help.

As Michael Goldberg, research director for the BC Social Planning and Research Council pointed out, welfare premiums had gone up partly because there were more single parents and more people working part-time and in low-paying jobs. Despite the levelling off of unemployment numbers, in other words, there simply were not enough jobs. According to Goldberg, a "tremendous erosion in the lower end of the pay scale" had led to an increase in welfare premiums among the working poor "because at minimum wage if you have kids, you just don't earn enough."

The NDP may well have considered these factors before adopting its new policy, but by 1993 the government was clearly spooked by the numbers. With 323,000 British Columbians now on welfare, Joan Smallwood's marching orders were fairly simple: get the numbers down, or someone else will. Unfortunately, playing the heavy was not a role suited to the former community worker and social activist. And Smallwood, a faithful member of the NDP left, was becoming increasingly uncomfortable with her party's willingness to buckle under the media pressure, particularly in adopting the assumption that a Social Services minister's job was to bash the poor. By resisting her government's inevitable move toward a welfare crackdown, however, she had begun to lose her grip on the portfolio. Rumoured to be "soft" on welfare abuse, Smallwood was gradually undermined by bureaucrats determined to introduce tougher regulations.

The first sign of a welfare shakedown was the ministry's release of a new income assistance form in January 1993, that included a separate box asking recipients to claim the incomes of dependent children. Single mothers were stunned by the new policy. Was the government saying it would deduct earnings from their teenager's babysitting, paper route, or part-time job at McDonald's? Given the ministry's vague response to media inquiries about the new policy, it was hard not to conclude that the NDP was walking away from its traditional policy of compassion for the poor, instead adopting a cold, bean-counter's approach to welfare – a position its members would have railed against before the 1991 election.

Harcourt only compounded the suspicion the following September, when he replaced Smallwood with the tough-as-nails former unionist Joy MacPhail. On September 21, a week after shuffling his cabinet and pledging a crackdown on welfare abuse, Harcourt stepped out of a meeting to face a throng of reporters. What did he mean by a "crackdown", they wanted to know. Was he saying that he would hand out shovels to anyone physically capable of working, like Bill Vander Zalm once did?

Harcourt was startled by the question. "Where there is work and where there are training programs," he began, "people who are able to work who won't take those training programs, who are taking advantage of the good will of British Columbians, who refuse to get back into the workforce – those people will be cut off of welfare … We want to clear the cheats and deadbeats off the welfare rolls … We want to catch those varmints."

Harcourt's choice of words was indeed reminiscent of the shovel-clutching bravado of Bill Vander Zalm. Political pundits assumed the premier's get-tough stance was partly motivated by the polls, partly by a desire to reassert his leadership, and partly by a need to convince skeptical voters that the government had its spending under control. To anti-poverty activists, however, it was nothing more than an insult to the poor that would fuel hysteria among the general public.

"We wish Harcourt wouldn't be talking like this," said Jean Swanson, of End Legislated Poverty (ELP). "It's like pressing an angry button. It brings out the worst in people." Swanson, who had been a COPE aldermanic candidate supporting Harcourt when he was mayor of Vancouver, tried to get an apology out of the premier when she confronted him in his Mount Pleasant riding two days later, but Harcourt merely smiled and walked past her.

In an ironic twist, the premier found himself defending hurtful remarks about welfare recipients in the same low-income neighbour-hood where he began his career as a storefront lawyer and social activist 25 years earlier. Like many a welfare client in 1993, the Harcourt of the late sixties, with his "long, flowing hair and Fu Manchu moustache," could easily have been mistaken for a hippie deadbeat by the older generation. Now the politician in pinstripes was being forced to account for an insensitive remark about the same people whose cause he once championed.

"If anybody is trying to associate my remarks with poor-bashing, they can go elsewhere," Harcourt told a group of social workers at the Powell and Main welfare office. The point was not to lay a guilt trip on ordinary welfare recipients, he said. He was just trying to identify those few, sophisticated computer fraud artists who duplicate welfare cheques, hotel landlords who evict tenants after collecting their cheques, and individuals who use multiple sets of identification to claim cheques from different locations.

But his reasoning still seemed rather alarmist, given that only 107 (or .03 percent) of the province's 323,000 welfare cases were convicted of fraud in 1992-93. And as ELP activists pointed out, the general public can't always appreciate the distinction between sophisticated criminals and a single mother who doesn't declare her teenaged daughter's babysitting income. Another welfare advocate and long-time NDP member, Reg Clarkson, was angry enough about Harcourt's comment that he said he would call for a leadership review at the next party convention. "He's way out of line," said Clarkson, a card-carrying NDP member for 40 years. "The NDP are sending single mothers to food banks."

Looking back on the incident two years later, Harcourt was willing to concede that he blew it. "That was unfortunate. I shouldn't use those [words] and I apologize for doing that. But I was gooned by the media. They threw this question at me and I got provoked and angry and said something dumb and had to suffer sixty days of getting beat up in caucus and cabinet and [by] welfare activists."

While he may have been embarrassed by the political fallout of his "welfare cheats" comment, that didn't mean the deficit-slashing premier had any lasting regrets about the policy behind it. Two months later, the NDP took another hardline stance with Clayoquot Sound protestors collecting welfare cheques after serving prison time for contempt of court. Thanks to daily television coverage of the jailed activists, it wasn't long before Opposition MLAs had new ammunition to throw at the government. Critics turned up the "welfare bums" rhetoric when three young protestors were filmed by BCTV collecting welfare cheques immediately after their release in Nanaimo.

"These people seem willing to openly defy society's rules and then turn around and willingly receive society's handouts," said Jeremy Dalton, the Liberal attorney general critic. Dalton wanted Harcourt to investigate whether fraud had occurred, but corrections branch officials said the whole matter was being blown out of proportion; prisoners, as a rule, are not released from jail with no money in their pockets. Nonetheless, the new Social Services minister was willing to support the Liberal critic's argument.

"The taxpayers of British Columbia are not obligated to pay Clayoquot Sound protestors who have the ability to work," said MacPhail, establishing her own get-tough stance. "They can continue to protest, but it is not their God-given right to be on social assistance while they're doing that if they're also capable of working. We don't pay people to protest." MacPhail promised to investigate how many of the 800-odd people charged with defying the court injunction in Clayoquot Sound had recently received welfare. She subsequently learned that such an inquiry would violate confidentiality rules, so she dropped it.

According to Mervin Harrower, director of Social Services' fraud division, "detected fraud" – that is, confirmed cases of double dipping, false identification, multiple claims or falsely declared lost cash – amounted to 3 percent of the government's annual $1.8 billion expenditure on social assistance – or $54 million in 1994-95. Harrower was unable to estimate the percentage of undetected fraud in BC.

The Fraser Institute, on the other hand, was only too happy to hazard a guess. In a March 1995 report, the neo-conservative thinktank managed to factor in "client error" as a frequent source of fraud, implying that when a welfare claimant made a mistake, it was intentional. Including these figures pushed BC's welfare abuse rate into the 9 to 15 percent range. Estimated losses were now between $162 and $270 million in 1994-95. Few economists were fooled by such a manipulative equation of "client error" with fraud. Some saw the assumption that mistakes were intentional as an overly cynical reading of human nature; others called it an attack on the poor, who clearly comprised the vast majority of welfare recipients. But according to one uncritical reading by a Vancouver *Province* columnist, the Fraser Institute figures were merely the tip of the iceberg.

"We're talking your tax dollars," harrumphed Kathy Tait, a love advice columnist who was inexplicably trumpeting right-wing economics in her "Matters of the Heart" column, giving the *Sun*'s Barbara Yaffe a run for her money. Tait's column of June 18, 1995, was filled with hyperbolic gems like "we've been ripped off for billions by welfare scammers," and unsubstantiated claims that "loose eligibility rules" had fattened the welfare rolls. She did not acknowledge the fact of chronic unemployment or the increase in low-income earners who were forced to rely on welfare to make ends meet. Instead, she offered nightmare examples from other right-wing studies, turning welfare into a kind of fiscal virus. "The worst scenario," she wrote, citing a California study, was that "100 percent of a sample of 25 welfare cases studied in depth had unreported income." Well, stop the presses. One might ask Ms. Tait how many "single employables" – never mind single-parent families – she knew who could afford to live exclusively on today's welfare rates.

Harcourt was happy to boast about saving $46 million in welfare "fraud" over the previous year. But his figure was misleading; most of the savings came from reducing benefits given to claimants, not from stopping fraud. According to figures supplied by ELP and the Ecumenical Coalition for Economic Justice (ECEJ), $35.4 million was saved by loaning rather than giving money to people waiting for UI benefits. Another $3.85 million was saved through increased recovery of rental security deposits.

Even with 350,000 British Columbians on social assistance (nearly 10 percent of the population), the number of confirmed fraud cases remained minimal in 1994. And for all the media's focus on welfare's high cost to the taxpayer, there was seldom any discussion of how corporations deprive the tax base. Company shareholders and CEOs frequently channel profits into offshore tax havens and secret bank accounts, but they're never held accountable. Also, they don't always pay taxes on profits they declare, but that's not called "fraud." It's called "deferment." Deferred corporate taxes are a huge drain on the economy (according to ELP and ECEJ, 77 corporations made $5.2 billion in profits in 1994 without paying income tax), but for reasons known only to the mainstream media, such corporate welfare doesn't tend to make headlines.

In any case, Harcourt remained confident about his welfare philosophy as the NDP approached the next election. "Why should we continue to defend what is essentially a right-wing concept – a welfare system?" he asked. Welfare was conceived in the 1930s as a stop gap for the unemployed during the Depression, but since then the system had become paternalistic and punitive, making welfare an endless cycle of impoverishment from which it was impossible to escape. Harcourt – a social liberal to the end – had a plan to free British Columbians from welfare's chains.

If the NDP was elected to a second term, he said, the government would eventually shift welfare recipients classified as "single employables" over to the Ministry of Skills and Training, where they would be placed in subsidized job training programs that would presumably lead to more permanent work. Those considered "unemployable," such as those with disabilities, would continue to receive benefits through a pension plan in the Ministry of Finance. The remainder of Social Services' clients at that point would be people who could just as easily be served by the Ministry of Health.

This would include those "who have crashed into the safety net instead of hitting the ground," said Harcourt. "Their personal lives have fallen apart, their family's dysfunctional, they've lost their job, [they have problems with] alcohol … What you're left with are people that are basically using mental health, alcohol & drug, facilities for battered and abused women and children, and counselling for low self-esteem and self-worth. Basically health facilities that community health boards can deal with. So you really don't need a Social Services Ministry at the end of that process. You transform it into what social democrats believe in, which is full employment and more pensions."

It was an ambitious plan, particularly given the difficulties that ministry social workers were bound to face during the classification process. How would they determine the line between "employable" and "unemployable" where mental issues are involved? But by the end of 1995, Harcourt appeared determined to put some kind of NDP stamp on a system that had become dominated by deficitphobia. Releasing the details of that plan would be one of his final acts before resigning as premier.

Of Debt Monsters and Silent Killers

FEBRUARY 22, 1995

IT WAS SUPPOSED TO BE AN EXERCISE IN TELE-DEMOCRACY. Instead, the premier's live "town hall meeting" on the economy was a public relations nightmare that would spark 90 days of scandal-mongering in the media. Aside from a combative audience and a series of technical glitches including shaky camera work and a toll-free phone line with the wrong number, there was also that day's leak by the Opposition Liberals of a Treasury Board report calling for immediate action on the provincial debt.

According to Treasury Board chief Chris Trumpy, the province's total debt was $27 billion and would continue to rise unless the NDP responded with firm action. "The Achilles' heel of the government's sound fiscal record is the rapid and unsustainable growth in non-operating, tax-supported debt resulting from capital spending," wrote Trumpy. "Even if the government is prepared to run small operating surpluses over the next ten years," he added, "the government's existing plans and commitments" would make it impossible to reduce the debt.

Gordon Campbell, who released the report seven hours before the premier's televised town hall meeting (which was also attended by Finance Minister Elizabeth Cull and two UBC economists), accused Harcourt and the NDP of "deliberately misleading the people of BC." With predictable hyperbole, Campbell declared that "the debt monster created by the NDP is the silent killer of our core health and education services and future economic opportunity."

Trumpy's report revealed that the Harcourt government had added $7 billion to the debt since coming to power in 1991. Of that figure, $2.4 billion came from operating deficits; the rest came from capital projects. Campbell promised that a Liberal government would slash spending without raising taxes in order to reduce the debt. Harcourt wasn't impressed. "Where Gordon Campbell sees debt, I see new schools for our kids," said the premier. "What we've been doing these past two years is catching up on ten years of Social Credit cutbacks, ten years when schools weren't built, hospitals weren't built, the transportation system was allowed to decay." There was no point attacking the debt, he explained, until the province completed its capital projects.

What amazed Harcourt and Cull was that the Opposition and media – and, for that matter, the Treasury Board chief – neglected to take population growth into account before pronouncing that the sky was falling. It wasn't just a matter of blaming the Socreds for the debt; it was a matter of spending now to avoid a much worse debt crisis in the future. Population in the Lower Mainland alone was doubling every 30 years. This meant that by the year 2021 there would be as many people in Greater Vancouver – 3.7 million – as there were in the entire province in 1995. This meant a million more cars. It also meant gridlock, smog and a push for expansion to the suburbs that would strain provincial highways and the ferry system. "In 1994, we had a record in-migration to British Columbia," said Cull. "We can't simply say 'Sorry, we're not building any new schools, sorry we're not expanding our health-care facilities.'"

In any case, BC was going to follow Saskatchewan's example and balance its budget a year ahead of schedule. "We've cut the deficit by 80 percent, we're well on our way to balancing [the budget], we've got a three-year tax freeze and we have the lowest debt in the country, and we have the highest credit rating as a result of having the lowest debt," said Cull.

The Finance minister had faced her share of battles in recent months. In October, the Opposition and business community railed against Cull when she failed to include crown corporation spending in her summary of the government's deficit-cutting record. Cull's first quarterly report for the 1994-95 fiscal year showed that employment was up 4.6 percent, revenue was up by 8.9 percent, and the deficit was down to $92 million in the first three months – compared with $367 million in the same period the previous year. Thus, the government was on target for the $900 million deficit projection for 1994-95. But Cull wasn't including the $379.2 million in crown corporation and agency spending that added to the long-term debt.

According to Suromitra Sanatani of the Canadian Federation of

Independent Business, Cull's report was "an excellent job of creative writing" because it attempted to hide both tax increases and expenditures. In response to the criticism, Cull accepted a recommendation by Auditor General George Morfitt to "streamline" reporting of the debt so that crown corporations would no longer be listed as assets if they could only be repaid through future government grants.

If it wasn't Sanatani and the small business lobby crowing at the NDP, it was Michael Walker and the Fraser Institute. In December, the right-wing thinktank published a new book called *Tax Facts 9*, which claimed that BC was the worst place to live in Canada based on its rate of taxation. According to the Fraser Institute's estimates, an average family earning $86,330 in 1994 was taxed $35,396 – or 41 percent of its total earnings. The ratio was higher than any other province in the country – although only marginally greater than that of Ontario (40 percent), Québec (39.8 percent) and Alberta (38.1 percent).

Cull was mildly amused, but not overly surprised by the Fraser Institute's findings. "Their calculation is fictitious [and] misleading," said the Finance minister. "They have inflated the family income as if the government doesn't exist and added on payments by corporations on payroll taxes and all the rest." The Fraser Institute, said Cull, was ignoring Statistics Canada estimates which put the average family income in BC at $60,809.

None of these critiques mattered at the end of March 1995, when the NDP announced its fourth budget. As predicted, the government eliminated the deficit a year ahead of schedule, making this the first balanced budget since 1990. Now the province was ready to set limits on the provincial debt which, excluding crown corporations, accounted for 20 percent of the GDP. "We've listened to people's concerns and are taking an aggressive approach to controlling BC's debt," said Cull. "We're starting immediately by directing $414 million – including this year's surplus – to paying back direct debt." However, the province vowed to continue carrying the debt for building infrastructure – as long as the debt remained below 15 percent of the GDP and interest payments remained below 9 percent of revenues (they were currently at 7.5 percent).

The budget stole some of the Opposition's thunder, given that the

Liberals and Reform were calling for balanced budget legislation. In addition to the $114 million operating surplus, the 1995-96 budget extended the previous year's tax freeze for another two years.

Despite what the Fraser Institute's Michael Walker was telling reporters, Cull appeared to have done her math homework. "With inflation and the 100,000 new British Columbians projected for next year," said the minister, "the 2.9 percent spending increase in this budget works out to a real cut in spending per person of 2.3 percent." In addition, spending controls and "better than expected" revenues allowed the government to borrow $1 billion less than projected in 1994-95. This meant the province could now afford the $730 million required to build new schools, health care facilities and major infrastructure and transportation projects.

Several areas of essential public services would also receive increased funding in the following year. Among the beneficiaries: health ($252 million, a 4 percent increase); post-secondary education ($1.32 billion, a 3.8 percent increase); apprenticeships, technical education, retraining and upgrading programs ($106 million); elementary and secondary school systems ($3.4 billion, a 4.4 percent increase).

Cutbacks – amounting to $100 million – would occur mostly in areas of government administration. Among the casualties: supervisory positions in the bureaucracy (450 jobs); consulting budgets ($26.5 million); Pharmacare ($37 million); Ministry of Health ($19 million); transportation and highways ($12 million); school districts and education ($7 million). There would also be cutbacks in government advertising and travel costs, as well as a continuing freeze on salaries for MLAs and senior public servants, and a review of the MLAs' pension plan.

If the business community required further proof that the government was still committed to the deficit-cutting agenda, Cull also announced the appointment of a "blue-ribbon team of outside experts" (including Vancouver Board of Trade chair Jill Bodkin and BC Business Council past chair Michael Phelps) to help cabinet come up with new ways to "make government more efficient and less costly."

Cull's olive branch to the business community appeared to pay off, as most reviews of her budget from Howe Street were supportive. "This budget will not change the market's perception that BC and Alberta remain the top tier provincial credits," said a press release from the brokerage firm of CIBC Wood Gundy. Similarly, BC Business Council president Jerry Lampert, formerly a foe in the Socred camp and now a Liberal, had nothing but praise. "We welcome both the elimination of the deficit in 1995-96 and the clear emphasis on debt reduction in the new budget. Minister Cull deserves good marks for leading an open and constructive pre-budget consultation. It is apparent that she has listened to the advice she received, from business and others, who have been urging the government to scale back its borrowing in order to get the province's debt under control."

So much for Gordon Campbell's "silent killer." BC's "debt monster" appeared to have no more basis in reality than Ogopogo, that mythical dragon creature rumoured to be living on the bottom of Okanagan Lake.

On May 10, 1995, Moody's Investors Services – the major North American bond rating agency – confirmed BC's "Aa" credit rating, saying the province had the lowest ratio of tax-supported debt of any Canadian province. "I have the best credit rating in the country," boasted Cull. "What Moody's is telling us through confirming the rating is that our budget is a good plan and that the debt-management program has been well-received." The New York-based bond rating agency praised the NDP government for, among other things, combining spending restraint with strong revenue growth for a sound deficit-reduction program. Moody's also cited the province's "strategic location ... export orientation [and] large and increasingly diversified economic base" as major factors in the Harcourt government's ability to manage its financial operations and debt servicing requirements.

Elizabeth Cull and Mike Harcourt's boasts about the high rating from Moody's struck many left-wing New Democrats as mildly obscene, but the premier and Finance minister both knew that a good rating from Moody's – the preeminent credit rating superpower – was an easy way to silence criticism from the business community. They agreed with New York Times foreign editor Thomas L. Friedman, who argued that, while "the US can destroy a country by levelling it with bombs, Moody's can destroy a country by downgrading its bonds." According to Friedman, Moody's message was that "either you vote the economic pain on yourself – in the form of deep cuts in government spending and higher domestic interest rates to suppress inflation – or the bond market will force you to do it by withholding capital."

In accepting the importance of the bond rating agencies, however, Harcourt and Cull also bound themselves to deficit reduction at all costs. In May 1995, the same month that Moody's conferred BC's sterling credit rating, the government suddenly found itself short of its $114 million budget surplus projection when Bonneville Power Administration, a US power utility, backed out of an agreement in principle to pay BC $5 billion over 30 years for the rights to surplus power from Columbia River dams. The first payment of $250 million was due later in 1995, and the government had already budgeted for the money. Now the NDP was left with egg on its face as it tried to answer criticism that it had been naive in its revenue projections.

Despite a tough-talking visit to Washington, D.C., by Energy Minister Anne Edwards and Employment and Investment Minister Glen Clark, who attempted to salvage the deal, Bonneville did not budge. On September 1, Cull announced that BC would cut spending by $300 million in the 1995-96 fiscal year, to compensate for revenue lost when the Bonneville deal collapsed. Reductions included a 1 percent budget cut by all ministries, amounting to about $200 million; tighter eligibility requirements for welfare, which would save the Social Services Ministry an estimated $50 million; health care cuts totalling $30 million; and a range of other cuts which could lead to layoffs of up to 100 full-time employees (this in addition to 450 middle-management positions already on the chopping block). These changes, said Cull, would restore the balanced budget she had announced in the spring, with the promised surplus of $114 million.

While Howe Street may have been reassured by this news, the NDP's left-wing critics saw Cull's September 1995 budget cuts as nothing more than political window dressing, designed to appease the right before a rumoured election call. Despite the fact that the $250 million Bonneville payment was well within the typical range for forecasting errors typically made by governments, the NDP reacted as if its entire fiscal agenda was put in jeopardy. "If you compared, year by year, the budgeted deficit with the actual deficit that appears two years later when the public accounts come out, it's always out by hundreds of millions of dollars," said Gideon Rosenbluth, the party's former economic subcommittee chair. "You can't blame anybody for that, because a budget is partly a forecast. And you can't forecast accurately, it's ludicrous."

Rosenbluth was by no means alone in his critique. Many of the party's traditional supporters thought the Harcourt government could have taken more risks and experimented with the budget, without jeopardizing its credit rating. By the mid-1990s, however, it was not NDP governments that were taking the lead on progressive economic ideas. It was grassroots organizations like the Canadian Centre for Policy Alternatives which, along with Winnipeg's Choices, introduced an Alternative Budget ten days before Paul Martin released the Liberal government's 1995 federal budget.

The Alternative Budget, endorsed by 50 economists across the country, proposed a number of pragmatic solutions to deficit reduction. Not all of the ideas were new (the NDP had already introduced higher taxes for corporations and people earning over $60,000 – a salary cap $15,000 lower than the Alternative Budget proposal), but some of them posed a direct challenge to the Harcourt government's way of dealing with the business community. Imagine the NDP imposing, for example, a tax on speculative currency trading, or taxing estates worth over $1 million.

The government had shown some creativity with the introduction of BC Savings Bonds, which encouraged capital generation within the province. But the Alternative Budget took this one step further by proposing a tax on Canadian residents receiving interest payments from foreign sources. This would discourage people from purchasing mutual funds that invested in foreign bonds. "When you first propose this to people they say 'Oh my God, we can't do that, it's a violation of the Free Trade Agreement,'" says Rosenbluth. "That's nonsense. This kind of discrimination against income from a foreign source is something we already have in place [with] dividends." (Dividends from domestic sources are eligible for a tax credit, but not those from foreign sources.) And Americans were hardly qualified to object, given that they already have tax-free bonds, issued from within each state, which are not subject to income tax.

Although the Alternative Budget was essentially a left-wing document, it shared two of the right's key assumptions. As one Winnipeg columnist put it, "It acknowledges the gravity of the ... deficit/debt problem. And it agrees that there should be no new taxes on the middle class." Otherwise, it was a fundamental challenge to the neo-conservative political culture spreading across Canada. It chose the option of confronting the entrenched financial power of the wealthiest citizens, rather than accepting a reduced standard of living for the less well-off as proposed by the business community and deficitphobic governments. The Harcourt government had to consider the ideas behind the Alternative Budget if it was serious about regaining the backing of traditional supporters before the next election.

Back to the Future

WHILE ECONOMISTS WERE ARGUING ABOUT HOW TO DEAL WITH the deficit, Mike Harcourt continued to hold summits and economic forums in the hope of gaining a consensus on BC's future. Harcourt – who came of age during the heyday of encounter groups in the 1960s – enjoyed sitting down with large and diverse groups of people, and reconciling opposing points of view. At his first such gathering, the Summit on Trade and Economic Opportunities in June 1992, he met with representatives from big and small business, labour, local governments, First Nations and universities to develop ideas for a long-range, sustainable development plan for BC. That session was followed by the Summit on Skills Development and Training (June 1993), two forums on jobs and investment (July and November 1994), a summit on the economy (January 1995) and a forum on working and living (March 1995). In all these meetings, working groups made recommendations to help guide government policy.

The result of all this consultation was *Investing in Our Future: A Plan for BC*, a blueprint for 21st-century development that encompassed four priorities established by Harcourt: long-term job creation and economic growth, skill development, forest sector renewal, and taxation and fiscal management.

The tone of *Investing in Our Future* is one of pragmatism. The NDP recognizes the global trend toward deregulation and free trade, as well as the shift toward production based on export potential rather than domestic sales. "Like all governments," the pamphlet says, "the BC government is faced with two opposing visions of how it should improve our ability to compete in the changing global market."

One view was the more deficitphobic one, which argued that costs and services must be reduced in order to compete with less developed economies, "whose comparative advantage is often cheap labour and an absence of regulations which properly protect the environment." That view discouraged environmental and labour laws, capital investment and universal medicare – things which maintain the high quality of life people enjoyed in BC.

The second view encouraged the government to invest in skills training programs, quality infrastructures and the strength of BC's natural resource base. "Rather than engage in a 'race to the bottom' with less developed economies, the BC government's approach is to ensure we keep pace with the advanced economies of Japan, the US and the European Community ... This strategy will lead us to a high-skill, high-value economy ... " This approach was the one chosen by the Harcourt government.

Although the plan could hardly be described as earth-shattering, *Investing in Our Future* was significant in one respect: it marked the first time a BC government had developed an economic strategy since the Post War Rehabilitation Plan, produced in 1944 by a Coalition government MLA named W.A.C. Bennett. Completed just before the end of World War II (a full eight years before Bennett became the first Social Credit premier), that scheme anticipated the boom period of BC's economy and several years of rapid technological development around the world. Apparently, it was also the only plan BC needed for the next half century. Aside from Bennett's pre-Socred model, no BC government bothered to develop a long-range plan for the economy until Mike Harcourt took office.

According to Harcourt, that idea simply wouldn't have occurred to the Socreds – nor, for that matter, the Gordon Campbell Liberals or

Jack Weisgerber Reformers. "They don't, by definition, believe in planning," chuckled the premier. "It's alright for businesses to have strategic plans, to look ahead ten to twenty years, but governments shouldn't do that – it's socialism. 'Plan' is a four-letter word." But Harcourt was quick to add that long-range planning will be crucial to the financial health of BC if the economy takes a sudden downturn: "If you don't have a really accurate analysis of what's happening in the world and have a good game plan, you're going to get buggered around by somebody else."

It will take years before history can judge the effect of Harcourt's "game plan". But the NDP seemed confident that it's a much better strategy than the ultra-right agenda currently being pursued by Alberta Premier Ralph Klein and Ontario's Mike Harris. "We've had a number of businesses coming in from Alberta because they can't make it [there]," said Tourism, Small Business and Culture Minister Bill Barlee. "I think [Klein's] short term agenda of slash and burn is not working. That's very obvious from the economic indicators coming out of Alberta right now ... Alberta has the fattest bureaucracy in the country by 24 percent, and the thinnest by a wide margin is British Columbia, at 12 percent below the average. So Ralph Klein is given a lot of credit where credit is not due, and I think we'll find that it will not work for Mike Harris, whom I do not consider a Rhodes scholar. Nor do I consider Ralph Klein a Mensa IQ, for that matter."

Barlee argued that Klein's spending cuts had destroyed consumer confidence in Alberta, thus prompting increased out-migration. "You have to have disposable income in every province to make the economy work," he said. "That's what we've done here, and it's working." The numbers seemed to bear him out. BC had led the country in retail sales for four years (1992-95) in a row. In 1994-95 the increase was 10.2 percent; Alberta's was .4 percent. According to the Conference Board of Canada, BC had the largest increase in tourist revenue from 1993 to 1994, going from $5.8 to $6.3 billion, and would likely lead the country once again in 1995. BC also led North America in hotel occupancy in 1994 and 1995.

Anti-socialists like to argue that governments can't take any credit for these developments. But the numbers were too overwhelming to suggest a coincidence. In 1990-91, the year before the NDP was elected, retail sales declined by 2.7 percent. "That meant that under the business party, $663 million less money was being spent in retail shops," wrote the *Sun*'s Stephen Hume in a rare op-ed page endorsement of NDP fiscal policy. "After Mike Harcourt and the NDP took office, retail sales took off like a rocket. They haven't stopped yet. British Columbians pumped an extra billion dollars through retail outlets in the year after Harcourt came to power [1992]. In the second year, we spent another $1.9 billion; in the third, another $2.5 billion ... This is not evidence of people who believe their personal economic situation is grim or whose confidence in an NDP government's ability to manage the economy is waning."

Barlee, the NDP's small business lieutenant, was prepared to take that message to voters in the coming election campaign. "I'm saying to the average business person, who probably is not inclined to vote social democrat, that you have a choice," Barlee explained. "You can vote in another direction if you so wish, but if you're really concerned about your future, about your investment, about your assets, you ought to take a hard look at what we've done in the last three years, because they're in good hands and no one in the country can touch us. Perhaps in North America."

By 1995, no amount of right-wing criticism could dismiss the fact that BC had the most vibrant economy in Canada, the lowest unemployment rate (9.1 percent), the highest growth rate (4.6 percent), the highest number of jobs created (50,000 new jobs in 1994), and the strongest credit rating. "Whatever its method of accounting," the *Globe and Mail* conceded, "the provincial deficit relative to gross domestic product is around 0.5 percent, the second lowest in Canada. The resource sector is thriving. Vancouver is booming. Investment pours in. With all this good news, why is Mr. Harcourt behind in the polls?"

For the NDP's traditional supporters, the answer had a lot to do with the government's obsession with budget balancing and deficit slashing. For its opponents, however, the answer had everything to do with the government's treatment of its natural allies – those ubiquitous "friends and insiders".

II

Friends and Insiders

AS A SOCIAL DEMOCRATIC PARTY THAT CONSTANTLY CLAIMED the moral high ground in Opposition, the NDP was taking a calculated risk in 1991 by promising a standard of ethics well beyond anything experienced in recent BC politicical history. The Harcourt New Democrats, said Promise Number One of the NDP's 48-point platform, were committed to open and balanced government that would deal fairly with ordinary men and women instead of playing favourites with political friends and insiders.

Most NDP supporters knew who the party was referring to when it talked about "friends and insiders." Harcourt was saying that business executives, used-car salesmen and other Socred cronies could not expect to profit personally under an NDP government. But that went without saying. What the media and business community wanted to hear – but what Harcourt never actually promised – was that the new NDP government would not reward its own friends and insiders in the labour movement and other left-wing organizations considered anathema to business. But that was too much to ask, given that BC had just been through sixteen years of Social Credit government in which big business "friends and insiders" were rewarded with perks and patronage at every turn. In a polarized province like BC, was it not

conceivable that a social democratic party would hire people sympathetic to its world view?

BC government, like its federal and provincial counterparts, has a
lengthy tradition of patronage when it comes to bureaucracy appointments and advertising contracts. Governments have always preferred
dealing with advisers and employees whose ideas are ideologically
consistent with their own. Such a relationship allows for a better climate of trust and a more efficient working environment. As the *Globe
and Mail*'s Jeffrey Simpson put it in his book *Spoils of Power*, "Patronage is endemic to organized human society because everyone natu-
rally prefers and trusts the company of friends to that of adversaries."
If the Socreds did it, and the federal Liberals, the Mulroney Tories and
even the Saskatchewan NDP did it, why should BC New Democrats be
any different?

You Scratch My Back, I Won't Stab Yours

BESIDES, HARCOURT'S DEFINITION OF "SPECIAL DEALS" WAS
also bound to differ from that of the Liberal Opposition and media.
When the NDP leader said these words, he was referring to government favours in which individuals benefited financially from their
party affiliation. When the Liberals and the media said them, however, "special deals" could even include progressive legislation. Even
though it is standard practice for governments to reform laws drafted
by their opponents, the Harcourt government's efforts to replace legislation imposed by Social Credit was treated in the media as shameless
pandering to "special interest groups," not the logical response of a
party elected to enact such policy. The new labour code, for example,
was presented in the media as a "special deal" because it was
applauded by the unions; the Employment Standards Act was a "special deal" because powerless employees who don't earn $60,000 a year
were also considered NDP "friends and insiders," too. One slogan fits
all — even if it's inaccurate.

When the new government announced its intention to replace the
labour code imposed by Bill Vander Zalm, the news didn't come as a

surprise to the general public. Replacing the pro-employer Industrial Relations Act was one of the NDP's major campaign promises. The new code represented 98 percent agreement among the business and labour representatives that drafted it, and was the result of extensive consultation. Despite the unprecedented degree of discussion and consensus surrounding the new code that most parties agreed was fair (at least, compared to Bill 19, for which Vander Zalm excluded even labour ministry input), a small but vocal minority in Vancouver tried to derail the bill because it allowed secondary boycotts and banned replacement workers. Chief among the agitators was the Coalition of BC Business, headed by Kathy Sanderson. When she stepped down, her replacement, Suromitra Sanatani who also chaired the Canadian Federation of Independent Business, was active in the protests and returned to media prominence less than three years later when the NDP tabled the Employment Standards Act (ESA) on May 24, 1995.

With the ESA, the government was again accused of making a sweetheart deal with labour. Sanatani, who by this time had become the NDP's most frequently cited critic, dismissed the ESA as a "real job-killer." She was miffed that "the business community" (meaning, presumably, her Coalition) wasn't given an opportunity to pore over the 61 pages and 142 sections of the bill, removing whatever clauses it found offensive. "Bill 29 is ... a rat's nest of new rules and paperwork that will drive good employers crazy and drive the rule-breakers underground," charged Sanatani, in a letter to Harcourt.

Labour Minister Dan Miller, offended by Sanatani's arch tone of self-righteousness, responded by releasing a pile of documents describing several meetings between his ministry and her Coalition from July, 1994 to March, 1995. Letters showed Sanatani expressing apparently genuine gratitude for her meetings with the government. But apparently no degree of access, or input to the ESA, was good enough for the Coalition, if the bill was going to favour employees. Among the provisions Sanatani's group opposed: a $7.00 minimum wage, bearing the cost of family responsibility and bereavement leave, and the posting of shift times and meal breaks in work settings where "customer service is essential".

Another sign that the NDP was hopelessly in bed with labour, according to the media, was its apparent indifference to occasionally violent behaviour by its union supporters. In November 1994, a group of workers blocked the entrance to a construction site at MacMillan Bloedel's new Nexgen pulp mill in Port Alberni. The workers were protesting Mac Blo's decision to hire an open shop company, TNL Construction, after the unionized Souther Construction offered the lowest bid on the initial phase of the $205 million project. (Souther lost the contract because its construction unions refused to work alongside open shop, non-union workers.) On November 24, a crowd of about 300 people had been picketing quietly for several hours when an altercation broke out. One TNL worker suffered a broken cheekbone, while a police officer was injured and a BCTV camera operator was punched.

The incident got a lot of coverage in the *Sun*, which seemed to relish the appearance of hypocrisy in the labour movement's government comrades. Despite Mike Harcourt's righteous pronouncements against violence at abortion clinics, and the attorney general's willingness to arrest 800 peaceful protestors at Clayoquot Sound, "the New Democrats have shown great reluctance to take action – or even to speak out – against violence and intimidation when it arises in connection to protests mounted by the labour movement," wrote Vaughn Palmer. "While labour tried to blame the violence on the victims ... the response from the New Democrats was mainly the silence that implies consent."

Harcourt's failure to either condemn the violence or discourage a consumer boycott of Mac Blo products was characterized as yet another indication that the NDP's strings were being pulled by labour. At the very least, it represented a double standard.

But the media were not as quick to point out examples in which the party compromised its long-held principles with regards to the labour movement. At its spring convention in 1995, for example, the party was facing a revolt by public sector unions over its proposed restrictions on annual wage increases. The proposed 1.2 percent increases were introduced by the government's Public Sector Employers' Council, a regulating body headed by Mike Harcourt's former principal secretary, Linda Baker. (The council included representation from cabinet and employers' groups in sectors such as health and education.) Heading into the March 31-April 2 convention, the unions had prepared several resolutions attacking the Council's guidelines as a dressed-up version of the old Socred wage controls. A labour revolt against the government – especially at the party's annual convention – would be disastrous given the NDP's low standing in the polls and the ongoing investigation into the NOW Communications/town hall meeting fiasco.

At a last-minute meeting on Saturday morning, only hours before the issue was due to explode among the general delegates, Finance Minister Elizabeth Cull and the heads of 28 public sector unions reached an agreement. Despite the usual accusations of "sweetheart deal" from the media, there weren't a lot of trade unionists jumping for joy at the final result. In their biggest concession, the unions agreed to respect current budget constraints and direct whatever surplus money was available for wage increases to the lowest paid workers. In return, the wage guidelines would likely evaporate following a review by Judi Korbin, who headed the NDP's commission on the public sector in 1992-93. The unions also agreed to the government's wish to have certain employee groups – such as the public health sector – negotiate contracts together. "I don't think it's a victory for any one party," said the BC Government Employees Union's John Shields, who had learned a few things about media relations since his disastrous compliment to Bill Vander Zalm before the 1986 election. "It's a mutually satisfactory agreement. What we have acknowledged to the minister is that public sector unions accept the reality that there is a finite pot, there is just so much money to go around. We want to participate more actively in how that pot is divided."

In discussing the government's "backroom concessions" with unions, media pundits frequently painted New Democrats as weak-kneed pushovers who would cave in at the slightest union demand. But that image doesn't square with what the three major health care unions saw when they faced Sheila Fruman in talks preceding the Health Labour Accord in 1993. At one meeting with union presidents, the premier's communications chief declared that there would be massive displacement of hospital workers under the Employment Security

Agreement. "She wanted us to go along with it, without any protection for our members," recalled one union official. When Debra MacPherson of the BC Nurses Union voiced her objection, Fruman reportedly leaned across the table and said, "We'll either do it with you, or we'll do it to you." So much for solidarity.

The other common criticism about the Harcourt government was that labour had the government's ear more than business did, and that the BC Federation of Labour's Ken Georgetti was "the nineteenth cabinet minister." The premier, not surprisingly, scoffed at this notion. "The business community has never had the access to government that they've had with our government," he said. "You talk to people in the forest industry. They've never had an opportunity to sit down with [the previous] deputy and [premier] and put together a four-sector strategy committee [a land use group combining government, industry, conservation and aboriginal interests]. Peter Bentley said it, this is the first government in 40 years to take a long-term view on forestry. They say the same thing in mining, the same thing in tourism. So the fact is, we've had an open-door policy for the business community, for everybody, because I believe in it."

Ken Georgetti wasn't about to argue with that comment. In fact, the BC Federation of Labour president challenged the media to file a freedom of information request on the number of meetings Jerry Lampert and Suromitra Sanatani have had with the government. The ratio compared to labour, he guessed, would probably be eight to one. As for his own status with the NDP? Georgetti had long been considered the most powerful extra-parliamentary New Democrat in BC, so he was used to media criticism about his direct line to the premier's office. But when Vaughn Palmer called him "the nineteenth cabinet minister," that was taking the idea a little too far.

"If that were to come from my officers and our affiliates, I would take it as a compliment," he responded. "But where it usually comes from is the other side, trying to paint this picture out there in the public of someone not elected [having] too much influence in Victoria." Georgetti figured his access to the government table was long overdue after sixteen years of Social Credit government in which labour had no input whatsoever. Nor were unions ever invited to participate in premier's summits or forums as they are today.

"With Vander Zalm, it was quite easy," Georgetti recalled, with some irony. "All I needed was 30 seconds. I could criticize him, I could be accurate and I could be in and out ... We were more of an extra-parliamentary opposition. Basically, what our research amounted to – beyond [what] we did for our affiliates on bargaining and other issues – was research on how to accurately and adequately criticize the government. To be opposition. With this government, you have to do more thinking. It's a harder job, because you have to be responsible for being at the table ... Our research is proactive, and although we don't have our way all the time – despite what most of the mainstream media say – we do know that when the government makes a decision, our views were considered. And that is a significant breakthrough."

On the Waterfront

GEORGETTI AND OTHER LABOUR LEADERS, PARTICULARLY THOSE in the building trades, were still smarting over two NDP decisions in which labour did not get its way. One was the Bamberton residential project on the Saanich peninsula north of Victoria. The other was the Seaport Centre waterfront project in Vancouver. Both of these projects drew from union pension funds for capital financing, and together would have created thousands of union jobs.

In 1989, the BC Fed president helped create VLC Properties Ltd., a Vancouver-based development company headed by one-time BC Liberal leadership hopeful Jack Poole and endorsed by Vancouver mayor Gordon Campbell. Although its main purpose was to provide modest rental apartments, some union critics were wary of putting their pension funds into a real estate venture headed by a well-known Liberal. Others had more economic reasons to worry about sinking money into building projects: Nanaimo's Coast Bastion Hotel, for example, built partly with union pension funds, began to lose money in 1985 when interest rates shot up.

Notwithstanding these concerns, the BC Federation thought it had a winner in the Bamberton housing project in 1992. The property – 650 hectares on the west slope of Saanich Inlet, about 30 kilometres north of Victoria – was bought for $13 million with the pension funds of unionized carpentry, telecommunications and woodworkers. The plan was to build a self-contained, environmentally sound collection of small neighbourhoods, plus a golf course, including 50 percent green space. People would live and work in their own community, reducing the need for cars, and there would be no strip malls or clearcutting. It was an environmentalist's utopia.

The union-owned South Island Development Corporation was to build 4,900 housing units over twenty years, for a total of 12,000 residents. By 1992, South Island had already invested $3 million on hearings, zoning preparations and environmental impact studies. But the project never did get the green light. Although Bamberton promised to inject $40 million a year into the local economy, with $1.1 billion in construction spending, Premier Harcourt found several reasons to delay the project.

First, there was the conflict of interest ruling on Robin Blencoe in August 1993. The Municipal Affairs minister had made three key decisions on Bamberton that were bound to create an advantage for his former campaign fundraiser, who was one of the principals in the project. When Harcourt removed Blencoe from Municipal Affairs and replaced him with Darlene Marzari in a cabinet shuffle the following month, the new minister ordered another study of the project. That was followed in July 1994 by three more reviews on whether the Saanich Inlet could tolerate the project's waste water. "In retrospect the South Island Development Corp., backed by union pension funds which so far have sunk $20 million into the plan ... must be wondering if it pays to be on good terms with the NDP," mused the *Sun*'s July 14 editorial.

"We got slowed down basically because we were going to put a sewage outfall into this bay that they don't think has enough turnover, and it would be completely treated effluent," Ken Georgetti recalled. With a series of reviews that would take years to complete, it was becoming ever more likely that Bamberton would never go ahead. "That concerns us," said Georgetti. "We're trying to repatriate pension money, to stimulate our economy. We own the largest construction company in Western Canada [VLC Properties Ltd.], and have the largest venture capital fund in the province now. We're trying to be agents of change and those two projects – the casino and Bamberton – represent $2.3 billion in infrastructure construction."

The casino project was officially called Seaport Centre. In February 1994, the federally owned Vancouver Port Corporation chose Seaport Centre over three other finalists in a bidding process to develop 38 hectares of waterfront property just east of Canada Place in downtown Vancouver. Seaport Centre was to be a $750 million to $1 billion complex which would contain a convention centre, hotel, cruise-ship terminal and casino. The project was a partnership between VLC Properties and Mirage Resorts of Las Vegas. Among the unions behind the VLC's bid were the Telecommunication Workers Union, the Communications, Energy and Paperworkers Union, the International Woodworkers of America (Canada), and the United Food and Commercial Workers. The project was also supported by Local 40 of the Hotel, Restaurant and Culinary Employees and Bartenders Union, thanks to the promise of up to 12,000 jobs in hospitality, construction and other services, all of them unionized.

But while the city stood to gain new cruise ship facilities, a convention centre and entertainment complex at no cost to the taxpayer, there was a catch: the entire deal hinged on the casino, which would attract up to 10,000 people a day for its slot machines and gaming tables. This posed a problem, since for-profit gambling was still illegal in BC. The Harcourt government raised suspicion among casino opponents in Vancouver when it announced a review of provincial gaming laws at the same time the Seaport Centre proposal was announced.

To make matters worse, the province owned $15 million worth of VLC shares, or 16.5 percent of the company, when the Port Corporation made its announcement. The government had bought the shares in 1993 through its BC Endowment Fund because VLC was a union pension fund-backed company that was building housing. But now, because Seaport Centre required provincial approval, the government quickly moved to divest itself of its interest, immediately prompting some observers to wonder whether the government was, in fact, in a conflict situation.

Even beyond these legal problems, the project was facing opposition within the NDP caucus, and from NDP supporters. Three Vancouver backbenchers – Tom Perry, Ujjal Dosanjh and Bernie Simpson – opposed the project, saying that any form of Las Vegas-style casino on the city's waterfront would be offensive and unwanted. "This massive project would desecrate the natural beauty of the waterfront," said Simpson.

There was also division within the labour movement. Cliff Andstein, director of negotiations for the BC Government Employees Union, urged the government to kill the project, even though it had won the endorsement of the BC Federation of Labour executive council, of which he was a member. "I question the advisability of a social democratic government teaming up with a Las Vegas casino developer. I question whether that is a socially progressive thing for Canada," said Andstein, describing the development as "a huge urinal blocking off the community."

For the Harcourt cabinet, Seaport Centre was in some ways like the Charlottetown Accord revisited. The bizarre alliance that supported the project – including labour leaders, federal Liberals like Port Corporation chair Ron Longstaffe, and Las Vegas gambling wizard Stephen Wynn – sent a confusing message to the public: whose interests were truly at stake here? Even the opposition was a strange mix. A small minority of the business community opposed it, along with segments of the labour movement and a broad coalition of community groups. Seaport Centre was an especially divisive issue for the civic left. "I haven't spoken to one party person who supports it besides David Levi," Alayne Keough told *Pacific Current* magazine. (Keough was president of the Point Grey NDP constituency association and a COPE candidate in the 1993 civic election.) On the other hand, Peter Norris, president of the civic NDP and a member of the Vancouver local of the Carpenters' Union, said, "It has been weeks since I've bumped into anybody against it. In the construction industry gambling is a non-issue, but it's not hard to get excited about a bunch of jobs, especially when those jobs would be union."

Indeed, Georgetti was perplexed by the degree of hostility he encountered in Vancouver's downtown eastside, given the potential employment bonanza involved. He later recalled his failed attempts to sell the project to the Downtown Eastside Residents Association, an advocacy group representing low-income residents. "`Look," Georgetti recalled saying. "All things being equal, the biggest enemy of the people you represent is unemployment and poverty. And we've got 2,000 jobs here. I mean, they're entry level jobs. You don't need rocket science degrees to do [them]. You can walk in, and in eight hours train 2,000 people to do these jobs. Those jobs are committed to people in the downtown eastside.' And yet [you] reject it out of hand because of gambling."

The labour leader was doubly disappointed because he believed that Seaport Centre would prevent luxury housing developments from encroaching on the downtown eastside. Without a casino, the area could face a massive housing development if Gordon Campbell's Liberals were elected, he said.

One day, Georgetti and his fellow VLC board members arrived for a downtown meeting where they were confronted by a group of casino opponents. "There were five representatives from Carnegie [Centre] leafletting us," he recalled. "We went in, and when the meeting was over we had representatives from Mirage up. They wanted to see what a charity casino looked like, so we went to the Renaissance downtown – a charity casino – and you'll never guess who was in the change cage, giving us change." Yes, it was the Carnegie Centre people, working their own casino.

It was a bitter irony for a so-called "insider" who was supposedly used to getting his way with the NDP. The winners in the waterfront casino fight were not the thousands of potential employees led by the BC Federation of Labour, but the non-unionized inner city poor who wanted to preserve their own neighbourhood. The Carnegie volunteers were probably NDP supporters too, and would no doubt do their part, like the Fed, to reelect the government. But for now, they were earning casino money to fund community projects. Their community projects.

Faced with mounting opposition from grassroots local organizations like Concerned Citizens Against the Casino (which included former civic councillor Harry Rankin) and the downtown eastside's Carnegie

Community Action project, the government was already prepared to scrap the project in late June. But Harcourt changed his mind after intense lobbying by Georgetti, and advice that such a decision would jeopardize a review of the province's gaming policy. By mid-July, however, Mirage Resorts Inc. was having second thoughts about the project.

The company had already spent $750,000 on architect's fees, polling, public information brochures and site planning. But poll after poll showed that Vancouver residents didn't want a resort casino in their back yard. In one Angus Reid poll, 56 percent of respondents opposed Seaport Centre. On July 26, the government put the Seaport Centre project on hold, announcing that it would finish its gaming review before any gambling project would be approved. "The people of Vancouver don't want this thing, no matter how many jobs and dollars it might bring into the city," a *Sun* editorial said two days later. "Full marks go to the provincial government for standing its ground and refusing to be stampeded into rushing its gaming review to accommodate the casino proposal, even though some of its close union friends are among those with a stake in it."

The final blow for Seaport Centre came on August 8, when a City of Vancouver impact study was released to the media. The study, coordinated by the planning department, determined that a major casino would likely have a negative impact on affordable housing stock, especially rooming hotels. The pressure to redevelop the downtown area would probably increase in order to meet the demand for tourist accommodation and housing for casino employees. The report also cited a lack of government programs to help gambling addicts, a negative impact on charity casinos, a drain on other parts of the local economy, increased pressure on traffic patterns, erosion of neighbourhood character, and insufficient policing resources.

Not surprisingly, Seaport Centre was officially scrapped on October 4. In announcing the decision, Harcourt struck a socially conscious note. British Columbians, he said, had rejected big gambling casinos in the same way they once rejected uranium mining and nuclear power development. "As long as I'm the premier there will not be Las Vegas-style casinos," he said.

However, there would be Las Vegas-style video lottery terminals (VLTs) under the province's new gaming policy. Harcourt set a compromise in which 5,000 legal VLTs would knock out 10,000 illegal ones currently in use, while raking in $120 million annually for the province. This decision appeared to contradict the social consciousness that was reflected in the casino verdict. Under the new rules, up to 500 restaurants and bars in Vancouver would be allowed to introduce electronic gambling, VLTs, and electronic bingo. Where Seaport Centre would attract high-rolling tourists with expendable incomes, many believed that the "VLT syndrome" would bankrupt the people who could least afford it. "If I had to choose between a casino at Seaport Centre and this, Steve Wynn, come on back," said councillor Gordon Price. "This goes far beyond what was ever planned for the casino." The Vancouver council unanimously opposed any expansion of gaming activities, but it wasn't until the spring of 1995 that the province decided to scrap VLTs. In the meantime, a major development proposal had been defeated, and BC's most powerful labour leader was left shaking his head.

"You can't blame the government, because there wasn't enough support from any quarter for them to [approve] the casino," Georgetti recalled. "I think that if it were done in the model of Ontario, where the government themselves owned a [crown] corporation that ran as a large-scale, destination tourism resort as we proposed, it would have been very lucrative for this government. The casino operated by the Ontario government in Windsor is the most profitable company in the world. I think BC missed the mark."

Whatever the case, the failures of Bamberton and the waterfront casino provided at least two examples of pro-union development the NDP had no intention of forcing on the public. But if these decisions quelled fears that the NDP was overly generous in its favours to friends and insiders, the same could not be said for a couple of patronage appointments that threatened to embarrass the government toward the end of 1994.

Scandal-By-Request: Paper Trails, To You

WHEN GORDON CAMPBELL AND JACK WEISGERBER USED THE pejorative "NDP hacks" to describe the government's hiring decisions, they conveniently ignored the long list of "Socred hacks" who had benefitted from government largesse for 37 of the 40 years prior to the 1991 election. After sixteen years in Opposition, the NDP had every moral right to hire as many of its own "hacks" as it saw fit. To suggest otherwise – as the media did throughout the NDP's first term – is to reflect a naive misunderstanding of parliamentary democracy since Confederation.

That being said, it is important for governments to make intelligent hiring decisions. Ironically, two of the NDP's more embarrassing appointments may not have been discovered, were it not for the party's decision to introduce freedom of information legislation in its first session. Could some of the NDP's difficulty in the fall of 1994 be blamed on its attempt to ensure open government? "A good chunk of it is," the premier agreed, in retrospect. "Essentially I tell Weisgerber and Campbell every day, 'You don't have to even wait for the brown paper bag with documents in them to be slid under the door – you just go Xerox them!'"

And Xerox they did. In the first year following proclamation of the Freedom of Information (FOI) Act in October 1993, the Opposition and media filed hundreds of requests on everything from ministers' expense accounts to the use of a phone sex line at a crown corporation. Occasionally, there were constructive inquiries about excessive spending or government neglect in a personnel matter. One early example was the Vancouver *Sun*'s investigation of Lynda Fletcher-Gordon in the fall of 1994. The government was already mired in the "bingogate" scandal (see next chapter) when Fletcher-Gordon – appointed as vice chair of the BC Gaming Commission two years earlier by Colin Gabelmann – was fired after the *Sun* filed an FOI request on her involvement with another NDP-connected, non-profit society.

Fletcher-Gordon was a founder, director and later executive director of the Lower Mainland Purpose Society for Youth and Families, a

New Westminster non-profit organization formed in 1983 to raise funds for troubled youth. The society had barely completed its first bingo before the Gaming Commission was threatening to revoke its licence because of questionable accounting practices. According to commission records, Fletcher-Gordon showed no interest in cooperating with regulators, and one branch audit showed that only $10,000 of $250,000 raised in bingo proceeds went to youth programs. In the first five years of its operations, most of the money went to staff, a hall and a money-losing restaurant and record store.

There were plenty of red faces in the government when these details were made public by the *Sun*. In another twist, Fletcher-Gordon neglected to tell Colin Gabelmann before her appointment as vice-chair of the Gaming Commission that the Purpose Society was under investigation by the RCMP. Given her previous show of contempt for the commission and her longtime involvement with the NDP, it was hardly appropriate that she represent the commission at hearings involving the NDP-affiliated Nanaimo Commonwealth Holding Society in Nanaimo. Faced with this ugly scenario, Harcourt had little choice but to fire her and confront the inevitable demands for Colin Gabelmann's head.

Score one for the Vancouver *Sun*.

Another NDP "friend and insider" exposed by an FOI request was the chief appeals commissioner for the Workers' Compensation Board (WCB). Connie Munro, aside from being the ex-wife of longtime IWA mouthpiece and Forest Alliance chief Jack Munro, was a loyal New Democrat and high-powered labour lawyer who once argued cases before the WCB. In 1990, she ran for the Vancouver-Fraserview NDP nomination, enlisting the support of trade union heavyweights like then-husband Jack, Ken Georgetti and Cliff Andstein. "BC is run by a small group of Social Credit insiders," she said at the time, not realizing the future irony of her statement. "We must throw them out and be sure that we have a strong team to stay in power for years."

Munro lost the nomination to party fundraiser Bernie Simpson, who later went on to win the seat in the election. But the consolation prize wasn't so bad. In 1991 she was appointed to the WCB as chief appeals commissioner. During her first term, she and WCB chair Jim Dorsey were credited with improving the method of adjudication for compensation awards, and placing the agency's money into higher yielding investments. "Because of the decisions of Jim Dorsey and Connie Munro, the WCB is slowly moving away from deciding cases on the basis of outmoded medical and scientific data and personal prejudices and predilections," said Judith Lee, co-chair of the Canadian Bar Association's workers' compensation division.

Not everyone was enamoured of the two. According to Lee, certain business leaders wanted Dorsey to resign from the WCB because they were threatened by his efforts to clean up the agency. And in December 1994, the Business Council of BC finally found a reason to have him removed when Connie Munro was reappointed after a bizarre contract renewal process. Most of Munro's first term had passed without controversy, until her $158,000-per-year contract, due to expire the following spring, was renewed early. Munro bypassed a proposal that she submit to a performance review, and managed to squeak through a close vote thanks to the unanimous support of labour representatives on the WCB's governing board.

Dorsey was already in trouble because of a number of concessions he had made to Munro. The previous April, Labour Minister Dan Miller had written Dorsey to complain about Munro's $900 monthly car allowance. (After Miller's complaint, it was lowered to $600.) Now, in an effort to preempt a Liberal Party FOI request by Gary Farrell-Collins, Miller wrote Dorsey in mid-December, demanding to know why Munro's 1991 contract contained an "appalling" provision for moving and auxiliary costs of more than $88,000 – despite the fact that Munro had lived in West Vancouver all that time. Munro explained that the money was actually reimbursement for costs incurred when she folded up her law practice and had to pay deferred taxes, but Dorsey ended up resigning.

As it turned out, the $88,000 in "moving expenses" was part of a clause in Munro's contract stipulating that her expenses match those of former WCB president Ken Dye. "Every time the WCB paid Dye's mortgage, every time they paid to fly him home and every time they paid for him to phone his wife, Connie Munro received the same amount in cold, hard cash," said Farrell-Collins on January 10, revealing the results of his FOI request.

The FOI also revealed that Munro spent two months negotiating the tax-free, $900-per-month car allowance so she could afford to buy a new car. The purchase was necessary, she said, because the Pontiac provided by WCB did not fit in the small garage of the new house she bought following her breakup with Jack Munro. Before she negotiated the new car allowance, she asked the board to buy her a 1995 Volvo GTLA 850. Dorsey refused, saying it was too expensive. Eventually she settled for a Lexus.

The Liberals released further documents showing that the WCB picked up a tab of more than $12,000 for the lawyer Munro hired to represent her in contract talks. This revelation prompted Dan Miller to reassure the public that it wasn't too late to renegotiate Munro's contract. But few were convinced. Munro, who apparently knew everything there was to know about contract law, was confident that her current position was locked in until May 1999. In late April 1995, the Connie Munro issue forced the WCB to acknowledge that it "should not have delegated complete responsibility for [Munro's] contract" to the chairman. The board struck a new committee to undertake an internal review of current salaries and benefits for senior executives.

In the meantime, the NDP was forced to squirm in embarrassment as the Liberals released even more damning revelations about the great socialist working for WCB. Munro returned her first expense cheque uncashed because she had "considerable concern" that it did not include the entire $25,000 she was expecting (deductions for pension, unemployment insurance and income tax had been taken off). She accepted a new cheque for $25,000, despite knowing that failure to deduct income tax might violate the law. Finally, after complaining to Jim Dorsey about being billed for her share of a Christmas lunch with WCB secretaries, Munro was reimbursed for $80.

Score one for the Liberals.

The freedom of information law was often a useful tool in exposing government mistakes and excess, particularly in the cases of Lynda Fletcher-Gordon and Connie Munro. But at some point, the Opposition's taxpayer-funded use of FOI requests was bound to become a form of politically motivated excess itself. Throughout 1994 and 1995, research officers for the Liberals and Reform filed countless FOI requests, digging through meal receipts and travel expense forms, hoping to find something that would embarrass the government. By the spring of 1995, FOI revelations were fast replacing government policy as the main focus of Question Period.

Jack Weisgerber in particular was enthusiastic in his use of the FOI Act. In the spring of 1995, the Reform leader released some FOI results on the use of a 1-900 phone sex line by employees of a crown corporation. Some argued that this was a cynical attempt to cash in on the NDP's embarrassment regarding an investigation into allegations of sexual harassment against Robin Blencoe, but Weisgerber managed to embarrass himself more than the government with his petty attack. After an earlier story about a lewd chain letter posted on government e-mail, the media wasn't about to fall for another one.

"It's very easy to do a funny story on 1-900 numbers," said Moe Sihota. "But there are far more important issues in the life of government than that. When we were Opposition, we used to have all sorts of this kind of drivel – we just never raised it. Obviously we had bigger and more important issues, and there was a lot of scandal in that administration. The big problem with [the Socreds] was that too many of them actually had their hand in the cookie jar. And that is the big difference between us and them; you haven't found anybody in our government with their hand in the cookie jar.

"We knew full well there was every risk that the Opposition would use [FOI legislation] to their advantage," Sihota concluded. "And they have. [But] I think we are now just starting to get to the point where the media and the public are about to start asking, 'Why is it that the Liberals and Reform are running up such tabs to the taxpayer for political gains?' We always knew the risk was there, but I think in the long run it will backfire on them."

Jack and Kim and Poli Sci 101

BY FAR THE MOST GLARING MISUSE OF FOI LEGISLATION WAS the spring, 1995 investigation of NOW Communications prompted by requests from Weisgerber and CKNW radio reporter Kim Emerson following the government's disastrous televised "town hall" meeting of February 22. Following the broadcast, questions arose about the roles played by Ron Johnson, manager of NOW Communications, and Karl Struble, the NDP's Washington, D.C.-based spin doctor.

As targets for a muckraking campaign, Johnson and Struble were irresistible. Johnson, 43, was the former federal campaign chair for the BC NDP and the party's communications director for the 1991 provincial election campaign. Demonized in the media as a six-time "failed NDP candidate," he was accused of using his longtime loyalty to the party to feed from the government trough. His wife, Johanna den Hertog, also an unsuccessful NDP candidate in Vancouver Centre, had been the national NDP president and was currently working as the premier's liaison with the BC Trade and Development Corporation.

Struble was portrayed as Johnson's shadowy American mentor. First hired by the NDP in early 1991 when the party was anticipating an election, he was introduced to prominent members of the media during the following summer's Socred leadership campaign. His firm, Struble-Totten, worked for several Democratic Party congressional and senatorial candidates; his main talent appeared to be retaliatory negative advertising. The NDP, convinced the Socreds were recruiting a top Republican advisor to orchestrate an aggressive attack campaign, decided Struble's talents would be crucial if the party was to maintain its huge lead in the polls.

The intrigue surrounding Johnson and Struble made for titillating headlines and pseudo-investigative coverage. But few political observers could have predicted that it would have led to a conflict of interest investigation into the premier himself. However, according to CKNW radio reporter Kim Emerson and Reform leader Jack Weisgerber, Mike Harcourt was slimed with the following evidence: $5 million in government contracts for NOW Communications since the election; a $556-per-day retainer fee for Karl Struble, plus a $70,000-per-year average earning in contracts for his Struble-Totten firm since the election; and 995 telephone calls from the premier's advisors to Struble and other partners in his firm.

Although there was nothing to suggest that Harcourt derived a personal benefit from any of this, Emerson and Weisgerber were convinced that a precedent already existed for their complaints to the conflict commissioner. In August 1993, commissioner Ted Hughes had ruled that Municipal Affairs Minister Robin Blencoe was in an apparent conflict because the Bamberton housing project, in which Blencoe was involved as a minister, was run by two of his campaign supporters. Hughes's decision set a precedent by making past political contributions a factor in conflict rulings: it stretched the definition of "private interest" beyond direct financial gain. Weisgerber and Emerson argued that the premier's relationship with NOW Communications was a "private interest," similar to Blencoe's in the Bamberton case, because Harcourt stood to gain politically from NOW's business.

Filing this complaint was a calculated risk, since no one had yet established whether Harcourt had any direct knowledge of the contracts with NOW. Once Hughes determined that he hadn't, Weisgerber and Emerson were left looking foolish. They had tied up the conflict of interest commissioner – at enormous expense to the taxpayer – with an inquiry about a routine transaction between a government and its only partisan ad agency.

"The distinction that I drew in the Blencoe decision between contributions to the candidate and contributions to the Party must be maintained," Hughes wrote. "To fail to make that distinction when the Premier is the Member concerned would not only be unfair to the Premier but could hamstring the operation of government." Ted Hughes's point was well-taken; in the 90 days between the town hall meeting and George Morfitt's final report, it often seemed as though the government had nothing else on its agenda but damage control surrounding the various media attacks related to NOW.

Furthermore, Hughes concluded, "The mere fact that decisions about awarding contracts were made by government officials accountable to the Premier does not mean that the Premier exercised an official power or performed an official duty or function in relation to those contracts ... In my view, the reasonably well-informed person would not perceive that the Premier would be involved in such bureaucratic minutiae or, in the words of one senior official, an issue of 'micromanagement.'"

As for NOW's decision to funnel a $556-per-day retainer to Karl

Struble, Hughes ruled, "It may well have been more cost effective for the government to retain Struble this way. According to what I heard, it could have cost the government more to retain him on a fee-for-service and project by project basis." There it was: the same conclusion reached by nearly every ad industry professional in the province. CKNW's Kim Emerson maintained that the inquiry was "the only way" he could have determined whether a conflict existed. Clearly, neither he nor his news director had any interest in consulting the ad industry for a second opinion.

Several ad company executives, whose industry had long been a welcome home for Socred loyalists, were willing to admit that the whole issue was blown out of proportion. Gordon Kallio of BBDO told the Vancouver *Sun* that the NDP had "bent over backwards to be fair" with the ad industry. "There are plenty of firms working for the government. They've thrown the net pretty wide in terms of dispersing business about on the advertising side," said Kallio, whose firm in its earlier incarnations had close ties with Social Credit dating back to the W.A.C. Bennett era. Although Kallio was not expecting a lot of work from the new NDP government in 1991 (his firm was virtually ignored during Dave Barrett's administration), BBDO earned $8 million worth of government contracts in 1994 — $3 million more in one year than NOW had earned through the government's first term.

"This left-of-centre group was supposed to have its pick of the NDP litter [such as Tourism BC and major crown corporations]," said communications consultant Michael Shandrick. "But all it got was the litter box ... The fact is, I don't think BC has spent enough. You can ask any agency in town and they'll tell you that the government has really cut to the bone ... What NOW has done is peanuts. It's not even a blip on the screen in relative terms to what state governments do in America. In California they spend millions of dollars on advertising campaigns. It wouldn't raise an eyebrow in San Francisco." Ad executives also said that Johnson's $550-a-day retainer fee and $3,500 charge for a letter were standard rates in the industry.

All this suggests one of two possibilities, neither of which make Jack Weisgerber or Kim Emerson look particularly adept. Either they were engaging in a wilful abuse of conflict laws to score quick political brownie points, or it was an honest mistake and they truly didn't appreciate the difference between conflict and patronage. In the first case, Weisgerber should have resigned as Reform leader and Emerson should have been demoted to the traffic beat or sent back to the studio as a producer. There is only one reasonable remedy in the second case: Weisgerber and Emerson should have voluntarily submitted to undergraduate studies in public administration and political science. They obviously weren't learning enough about these things through daily exposure to the workings of government.

"Anyone can describe something as conflict of interest and it tends to bring the whole political agenda of the government to a crashing halt," said John Langford, a professor of public administration at the University of Victoria. If Langford were to welcome a certain former Socred cabinet minister and a legislative radio reporter to his class, he would no doubt inform his two wayward students that "conflict of interest" is not a phrase to be used indiscriminately to describe any form of potentially inappropriate behaviour, patronage or otherwise.

Even former Socred cabinet minister Jim Nielsen agreed that the revised conflict legislation had become trivialized. "It's becoming abused, mainly because of accessibility to the system," he told the *Sun*. "It's just too easy." And Jess Ketchum, the former Socred campaign manager who had criticized the NDP's use of Karl Struble in the 1991 election campaign, was now willing to concede that conflict had become "a political football," and that the opposition had "gone overboard."

But that was only a warmup act for the main event. The Opposition – and its unofficial soulmate, the Vancouver *Sun* – had a much bigger scandal to exploit with a mysterious tale of theft and fraud by NDP "friends and insiders" in the sleepy, mid-Vancouver Island community of Nanaimo.

12

Trouble in Hub City

THE STORY OF THE NANAIMO COMMONWEALTH HOLDING SOCI-
ety (NCHS), or "Bingogate" as it came to be known in the
media, was a political scandal that Mike Harcourt managed to inherit
from a previous generation of New Democrats. Four decades in the
making, its history reveals a complex web of bizarre accounting practices, questionable ethics, and political gameplaying that not even six
investigations were able to unfold completely.

The NDP's relationship to NCHS and its member groups was never
much of a secret in the socialist stronghold of Nanaimo, a former mining town. From the day the society was founded in 1954, directors
continually referred to it as the "fundraising arm of the NDP." Its goal
was to promote socialism while raising money for local charities
through bingos; party works and charity works, it seemed, did not
have to be mutually exclusive. The stated objectives of NCHS were
"to purchase and hold property to provide hall facilities for the use of
the organization in the Nanaimo Regional District and to assist in the
pursuit of socialist education in this area."

While the NDP got money for community building projects and
party headquarters, NCHS funded dozens of charity groups, including organizations for seniors, the disabled, minor hockey clubs, boys

and girls clubs, arts organizations and immigrant communities.

"There's very few people we turned down," NCHS president Bill Duncan recalled. "The society was about helping people." In fact, the NCHS mandate of promoting socialism through charity bingo proceeds was not much different, ethically speaking, from the Catholic church's practice of promoting Christianity through bingo. The local St. Peter's diocese, like the NCHS, had been running bingos for decades, but no one ever questioned how it spent its money.

Problems with NCHS fundraising methods only became apparent after the BC Lottery Commission was revamped to become the BC Gaming Commission in the 1980s. Charity bingos were already subject to strict regulations, but now the NCHS was bound to pay its charities 25 percent of the take from games. With 60 percent going to prize money, that left only 15 percent to pay for operating costs and employees. The NCHS could have managed this new format over time, but for one small problem: the holding society had gone $2 million in debt after two of its building projects fell victim to rising interest rates in 1985. Part of the debt was $1 million in debentures owed to NDP loyalists who thought they were becoming shareholders in the projects, a hotel and an office tower.

The first project was the Coast Bastion Hotel, which was acquired by a group of union pension funds after NCHS had contributed almost $1 million to it. The Coast was built on the Bastion Street site of Dave Stupich's constituency office – a modest lowrise where the longtime MLA had held potluck dinners for party faithful. The second project was Dunsmuir Centre, a six-storey office tower that soon became known as "Red Square" because of its function as the local nerve centre for both NCHS and the NDP. Red Square was to be the new riding office for Stupich, who had also served as president of the provincial NDP. Located in the same building was Marwood Services, a financial administration company Stupich directed with his live-in companion, Betty Marlow. Marwood provided bookkeeping services for dozens of MLAs (and also did the books for former NDP premier Dave Barrett's 1989 bid for the federal NDP leadership). On the bottom floor of Red Square was the bingo hall, where all the NCHS-connected charities held their events. What few people knew at the time was that some of the money raised for charities was helping to pay off these two building projects.

In 1979, the RCMP investigated NCHS accounting practices, but no charges were laid. It wasn't until the spring of 1988 – about the same time local New Democrats were gearing up for a federal nomination meeting for Nanaimo Cowichan – that the story began to unravel.

In April, Frank Murphy, a director of NCHS Charities Society (a subsidiary of the holding society), was informed by the newly revamped Gaming Commission that the NCHS bingo licence was being revoked. Charities were not receiving all the money allotted to them, he was told, and the society had accumulated a debt of $628,000. Murphy claimed not to have known anything about this debt, nor of an alleged $88,000 payout for management services. (Between 1983 and 1988, $1.9 million in expense cheques went to Marwood Services.) Knowing that much of the accounting for NCHS was being handled by Marwood's director, Dave Stupich, Murphy decided to confront his fellow New Democrat.

"I asked Dave Stupich for an explanation and he wouldn't give me one," Murphy told the author, recalling a phone conversation with Stupich he had shortly afterward. "He said, 'You were at that meeting where [the $88,000] was approved,' and I said, 'No I wasn't.' So I asked him for a copy of the minutes and he promised to send it to me. He never did." Murphy said he was later told by another director that the transaction was never approved by the board, so he reported the missing money to the RCMP and Revenue Canada, before responding to the Gaming Commission.

Meanwhile, Murphy and Stupich were headed for a much nastier confrontation. On May 1, the newly created federal riding of Nanaimo-Cowichan held its nomination meeting in advance of the election expected sometime before year's end. May Day, the traditional socialist holiday around the world, was supposed to be a time for working people everywhere – including their party affiliates – to join in communal resistance to global capitalism. But there wasn't a trace of brotherly love or solidarity at this meeting. One of the candidates was Stupich, Nanaimo's long-serving MLA who had decided, after three decades in provincial politics, that he wanted to finish his career in

Ottawa. Stupich's main opponent was Ted Miller, who had served as MP for the riding (Nanaimo-Alberni) from 1979 until 1984, when he was defeated by Conservative candidate Ted Schellenberg in the first majority election win by the Brian Mulroney Tories. Since the defeat, Miller – a director of NCHS Charities Society from 1973 to 1985 – had retreated from public life, only declaring his intention to run at the last minute. His campaign manager was his father-in-law, Frank Murphy.

"I remember the day Dave called a few trusted people aside to announce that he was going to seek the nomination," recalled his campaign manager, NCHS president Bill Duncan. "I had second thoughts about it, and said to Dave that Ted should have the opportunity to run." But Miller kept everyone guessing about his intentions, added Duncan, waiting until just before the deadline to file his papers for the Nanaimo-Cowichan riding. On May 1, Stupich defeated Miller for the seat the former MP believed was rightfully his. "I think [Miller] was upset with Dave that he was going to jump into the nomination," recalled Duncan. "I guess he figured, if you're an [MP] and you're defeated you have the ultimate right to [assume the nomination is yours]. I don't think so. You have the ultimate right if you're a sitting member, but if you're a defeated member and you want to come back, there's a difference."

Miller's devastation following the defeat was matched only by that of his father-in-law. Frank Murphy, a longtime member of the Nanaimo NDP executive, decided that his next executive meeting, at the end of May, would be his last. "He said he would not be working for me as the NDP candidate, would not be voting for me – might very well be voting for the Tory candidate," Stupich later recalled. "He said that at an NDP executive meeting."

But that wasn't all Murphy said. At the end of the meeting, Murphy approached Stupich and confronted him about the missing charity money from NCHS they had discussed in their earlier phone call. "What's going to happen," he recalled asking, "when the Socreds release information showing that an NDP-connected society was ripping off charities with bingo funds?"

"Frank," Stupich reportedly replied, shaking his head and chuckling at the naivete of the question. "What makes you think they'd do that?"

Later, Murphy was called onto the carpet by the Nanaimo NDP and told to "back off." What was he trying to do, the local executive asked him – have Stupich go to jail? Get him to resign? Several party members accused Murphy of being a sore loser; that he was only trying to make life difficult for Stupich because Ted Miller had lost the nomination. "That's not the case at all," Murphy told the author. "They (NCHS directors) should have acted in '88, and that would have been the end of it. (But) they took Dave Stupich's word, that this all happened because he beat my son-in-law for a nomination."

MURPHY HAD KNOWN SINCE AT LEAST 1973 HOW SOME OF THE bingo money was being spent. According to a subsequent forensic audit on NCHS, Stupich had written a lengthy letter to Murphy that year, explaining "that NCHS was purposely circumventing government bingo regulations with respect to charitable donation requirements so it could keep more of the money raised through its bingos." Stupich's letter explained how the Nanaimo Handicapped Workshop Society, funded by the BC Tomorrow bingo on Friday nights at CCF Hall, was giving some of the donations it received back to NCHS:

> From time to time, a cheque is turned over to me for donation to the Handicapped Workshop Society. I collect "rent" back from that society, on delivering this cheque, record as hall rent an agreed portion of it, and show any surplus between rent paid by the Handicapped Workshop Society and reasonable hall rent as a loan from the BC Tomorrow Committee.

In 1983, a report by Gaming Branch inspector Carl Bolton showed that only $91,483 of the approximately $300,000 raised from five bingo licensees by the NCHS Charities Society in its first three years had gone to local charities. Five years later, Frank Murphy wrote Bolton to clear himself of any knowledge of the affair. "I was not aware that charity money was being used to pay off a bank loan incurred by the Nanaimo Commonwealth Holding Society," Murphy wrote in May, after quitting the party. "To the best of my knowledge, the directors of NCHS Charities did not vote to have this done." He also wondered aloud whether the money had gone to Nacom Holdings, Executive Mortgage Investment Ltd. or the NCHS – all of which included Stupich as a director.

Murphy wasn't the only person asking questions about NCHS. Tony Hennig, a former local NDP president, had tried to blow the whistle in 1983 when he noticed that $60,000 in party money had been transferred to pay off debentures. "When I tried to find out more, I was told to keep out of it," Hennig told the *Sun*. He later quit the party to join the Liberals. It was the same for Jack Little, a Nanaimo city councillor and NDP supporter who served as president of the Harewood Community Centre, one of several NCHS satellite groups. Little quit after two years of "feeling like a puppet" when he found he was constantly excluded from crucial meetings in which financial decisions were made. And Cliff Shoop, another longtime NDP loyalist, had offered to chair a special audit committee to examine NCHS business practices – only to be "stonewalled at every turn."

Shortly after the three-person committee was formed on June 23, 1985, Stupich was asked to supply all financial documents used to prepare NCHS's annual financial statements. The committee also requested that the Society's books be audited by an independent professional company or person, as NCHS had never been audited to this point. But Stupich refused to cooperate, instead beginning a series of written correspondences with the committee in which the committee questioned Stupich's independence and Stupich replied that his methods were supported by NCHS board members. Shoop indeed got no cooperation from the board, as he explained in a letter to the committee dated April 20, 1986. "It was clear that the board was content to accept (Mr.) Stupich's statements as the last word," wrote Shoop. "Other than claiming each had spent countless hours of soul searching deliberations, the Directors refused to accept any suggestion that there was a lack of proper business control and judgement exercised by them."

The audit committee disbanded shortly afterward and was never revived. According to NCHS records, the committee was the last open challenge to Dave Stupich's control over the Society's finances.

Even the RCMP investigation was clouded in mystery. Shortly after Murphy's written complaint, a commercial crime officer spent three weeks digging through NCHS files at the BC Gaming Branch. According to an anonymous government official who spoke to the Vancouver *Sun*, the officer was about to go to crown counsel and recommend that charges be laid when he was "warned by a Gaming Branch official that the Nanaimo file was politically loaded and he'd better check it out at higher levels before laying charges ... Those instructions had filtered down 'right from the west wing [of the legislature, where cabinet sits].'" Despite the lack of any written memo or direct order from anyone in cabinet, the investigation quietly died. Interestingly, although NCHS bingo licences were routinely reviewed from 1984-88, government regulators did not probe the society's operations in any depth. "We felt there was some political or bureaucratic power that was sort of preventing us from doing that," said Carl Bolton. "Whether it was real or not, is another question."

"It is ironic," one Vancouver *Sun* article concluded, "that both investigations (1979 and 1988) stalled under Social Credit governments. Why would the Socreds do anything to protect the NDP? One theory is the Socreds didn't want to make an issue out of Nanaimo because it might lead to troublesome inquiries elsewhere."

Indeed, someone in the Social Credit government may well have had access to information at the Gaming Branch about the party's accounting practices on raffles, ticket lotteries and bingos. Of the seven Socred files later released by the Gaming Branch, three events failed to file financial statements and one suffered a loss. In one file, there were insufficient receipts from charities, in another there were deficient charitable donations. "We concluded from this review that to some degree, all of the political parties who operated gaming events were deficient in some way in either their applications, their returns, their receipts or in their overall operation of gaming events," wrote Ronald Parks in his 1995 report.

In the spring of 1988, only the NDP was being investigated for dubious gaming practices. Stupich, concerned about the increasing pressures on NCHS, paid a visit to the Socred attorney general during this period, Brisn Smith. "He contacted me about problems he was having with the Gaming Commission, and I indicated that it wasn't my role to be a referee with the Gaming Commission," said Smith, recalling the private meeting. "He'd have to go and deal directly with the Gaming Commission, which I gathered he did."

Asked about his own role in the 1988 RCMP investigation of NCHS, Smith would only say that he inquired about its outcome and was told that "no wrongdoing had taken place." He would not discuss the matter further on the record.

But the former attorney general was quick to dismiss any theory that the Socreds called off the investigation because of bingo skeletons in their own closet. "We didn't stop investigations because they were going to lead somewhere, because the investigations weren't done by political people," he explained. "They were done by non-political people. They were done by police and prosecutors, so it wasn't a case of 'getting' anyone. Nobody told me to get anyone or not get anyone."

Besides: "The Gaming Commission was just getting started. They weren't about to launch a big huge investigation of bingo charities run by the Official Opposition. People who suggest they should have are looking at history selectively through rose-tinted glasses."

Years later, Stupich recalled bumping into Smith at a retirement party for Jim Hume, political columnist for the Victoria *Times-Colonist*. "Brian was there, and I asked him if he remembered a certain incident in the legislature when he was getting raked over the coals by Lyle MacWilliam (North Okanagan New Democrat) about bingos in his area," Stupich recalled. "And [Smith] said something to the effect that there were bingos all over the province that were having problems. 'For example, there's one on the island that's having a great deal of difficulty right now, we know exactly what their problem is, and we know how they're trying to work it out and we have no intention of interfering.' He was looking straight at me as he said it. I asked him if he remembered that, and he said 'I don't remember saying it, but I might very well have. And we didn't [interfere], did we?' And I said, 'No, you didn't'."

IT WASN'T UNTIL MAY 1992, WHEN A COALITION OF 58 LOCAL charities pulled out of "Red Square" – headquarters for both NCHS and the local NDP – that the NCHS story finally broke in the provincial media. (The Nanaimo *Times* covered it briefly in 1987, but the story sank without a trace.) According to Jacques Carpentier, president of the Nanaimo Community Bingo Association, charity groups were losing $250,000 a year to NCHS and its subsidiary, NCHS Charities. NCHS president Bill Duncan said the organization had spent most of its money in the last decade paying off the $2 million in debentures incurred from the Coast Bastion and Dunsmuir Centre projects. Suddenly the Vancouver *Sun* realized it had stumbled upon a scandal: the New Democratic Party, notorious in Opposition for its pious self-righteousness, was revealed to have made a bad investment while tainting the "good works" it had promised to charity groups. Anti-NDP columnists and editors could barely contain their delight.

On May 25, 1992, Attorney General Colin Gabelmann referred the matter to the BC Gaming Commission, which promptly announced an audit of NCHS finances. Gabelmann, realizing that the NDP-related issue could put him in a conflict of interest, deferred to his deputy attorney general Bill Stewart, and asked him to appoint a special crown prosecutor. Stewart chose Ace Henderson, who had gained a high profile as prosecutor for the insider trading case involving former premier Bill Bennett and lumber baron Herb Doman.

Meanwhile, conflict of interest commissioner Ted Hughes launched his own investigation, examining past and present use of MLA constituency allowances by the premier (Vancouver-Mount Pleasant), finance minister Glen Clark (Vancouver-Kingsway), Dale Lovick (Nanaimo), Emery Barnes (Vancouver-Burrard) and Gabelmann (North Island). All MLAs were eventually cleared of any wrongdoing.

By October 1993, investigators had compiled 32 counts of alleged fraud and charity fund skimming. They also determined that NCHS had made at least one unexplained payment of $100,000 to Dave Stupich. With this discovery, it was announced that the investigation would continue until the following February 1. As Ace Henderson was preparing to announce the charges, Stupich called a board meeting of NCHS directors.

"Dave relayed to us that the report was coming down, and there would be three people charged," recalled Bill Duncan. "There were three names mentioned – mine wasn't one, fortunately. And the preference was that if we plead guilty, the societies would be charged but no individuals would be charged. My statement at that time was, 'What's going on here? Are we guilty? No, we're not. How are you going to define guilt?' ... There was no damned way I would sit there and say 'I'm going to plead guilty,' even [if] they charged the society, because I wasn't guilty of anything. And nobody else was ... Nobody made any personal gain, but it was political and you kind of raise your eyebrows. When I first got involved with it, I thought it was more ethical than that."

Henderson's May 4, 1994, decision implicated the NCHS and three related societies. There were fourteen criminal charges for misappropriation of funds of up to $200,000 that had been raised for charity over two and a half years. On June 7, the NCHS and its three related societies pleaded guilty to misdirecting charity funds and were fined a total of $155,000. Stupich, in a rare statement to the media, blamed the scandal on over-zealous workers. Some office employees, determined that NCHS should keep as much money as it was legally entitled to, had "unfortunately ... crossed the line," Stupich told reporters.

By the end of September, three of the four societies charged – the NCHS Charities Society, the Harewood Community Hall Association and the Harewood Social Centre Society – had not paid their $30,000 fines. Stupich said they had no assets and never intended to make good on the fines. When Henderson replied that it was their "moral obligation" to pay up, Stupich wryly responded, "I thought he was a lawyer, not a preacher."

Stupich's apparent lack of contrition, along with the embarrassment of daily media coverage, was beginning to wear on Mike Harcourt's patience. "I want to reinforce that I find the actions of the Nanaimo Commonwealth Holding Society disturbing and unacceptable to me and my party," said the premier. At a closed-door caucus meeting in Prince George on September 30, Harcourt told NDP colleagues that he was fed up with NCHS and would no longer take the heat for Stupich and the Nanaimo party. Stupich was now entirely at the mercy of the courts and the media.

On October 5, Harcourt announced that the registrar of societies would begin a forensic audit covering all transactions from 1988 until 1991 – a period that included recent court proceedings as well as Harcourt's leadership of the NDP before the election. But some Opposition members pointed out that this period still exempted the party from some scrutiny: it conveniently excluded, for example, the period before the 1986 election, in which charity money could well have been used for campaigns by any one of the eighteen New Democrats who were elected then and were still sitting in the House. Independent MLA David Mitchell was curious about one NCHS statement of accounts from 1982 showing that the NDP put up more than $20,000 to help the society when it was experiencing financial difficulty with real estate debts. Aside from owing the Dave Stupich campaign fund nearly $3,300, NCHS also owed the NDP caucus $10,800 and party headquarters more than $6,700. What was this money for? Mitchell wanted to know. And how much of it came from bingo proceeds?

On October 12, the audit was expanded. Vancouver forensic auditor Ronald Parks was appointed by Finance Minister Elizabeth Cull to investigate NCHS activities dating back to the early 1970s, well before the 1988 to 1991 period involving the current crop of NDP MLAs. He would also have the power to subpoena any person associated with the society to give evidence under oath. As far as Harcourt was concerned, this expanded investigation was sufficient proof that the government was committed to blowing the lid off NCHS once and for all. "This is the last step as far as I'm concerned," he said. "Whatever mechanism you choose, what I want and what the public wants is to get at the truth of what happened to these funds and who did they go to, and who made the decisions about who should receive those funds. That's what is going to be found out."

But Stupich would have nothing to do with the investigation. In March 1995, Ron Parks issued a subpoena to obtain missing documents from Stupich and two other directors, but the scandal's main figure refused to comply. Instead, he petitioned the BC Supreme Court, stating that Parks had no legal authority to force him to produce material that included his personal bank accounts and documents held by his daughter, Marjorie Boggis, and partner, Betty Marlow. The judge agreed, but Stupich's failure to cooperate with the investigation clearly annoyed Harcourt. "Just say I rolled my eyes," he told reporters. "I can't request Mr. Stupich to do anything. That's up to him. But my goal is that of the people of British Columbia: to get to the bottom of what happened to these funds."

Finally, on June 5, Ronald Parks travelled to Victoria with eighteen copies of his completed report. Parks met with Elizabeth Cull, who was accompanied by the premier's chief of staff, John Walsh, and John Heaney, the main troubleshooter on the NCHS issue since the story broke in the media. Parks advised Cull to release the report as soon as possible, and the finance minister assured him that she would. First, however, the premier's staff had to review it, then print it for wide distribution and prepare briefing notes and question and answer materials for the media. In all likelihood, such a process would take about three days.

At least two of the report's findings made its release all the more sensitive, in terms of potential political damage to the current government. First, it was established that in 1993, the party had become aware of $60,000 in tainted NCHS funds that had gone to the *Democrat*, the NDP's membership newspaper, and had approved a transaction to repay the money in order to clear itself of NCHS debts. Second, it revealed that a current sitting NDP MLA, former NDP fundraiser Bernie Simpson, had included donations from large Canadian corporations as part of the NDP's $80,000 repayment of its debt to NCHS resulting from the Society's payment to a trust account for former Dave Barrett cabinet minister Bob Williams. (Williams had agreed to resign his Vancouver East seat after the December 11, 1975 election so that NDP leader Barrett could return to the legislature after losing his own seat in the election.) During the period in which the corporate donations were made, the Parks report noted, the NDP's stated policy forbid its members from accepting "directly or indirectly any corporate donations, except for those from small businesses who support the principles and policies of the NDP; all such business donations are to be approved by the Provincial Executive." Since the donations had been offered on condition of anonymity, it was impossible for the Executive to have known the identity of the donors. Therefore, wrote Parks: "The concealment of corporate donations at NCHS was a further example of the use of the Society to achieve political ends without full disclosure to either the party or the membership of the Society."

As if to add insult to injury, Parks reported that "on May 26, 1983, $12,500 in fifty dollar bills was deposited into the NCHS bank account" and credited to the NDP Headquarters account. The source of the deposit, Parks noted, was identified in Stupich's 1983 working papers as "D.B." Parks was unable to identify who "D.B." was, but it wasn't hard to guess that it may very well be Dave Barrett. It certainly made sense, given that the deposit was made on the day after Barrett resigned as NDP leader following the party's third consecutive election defeat on May 5. With Barrett's resignation, Stupich immediately declared his intention to run for the leadership. Eighteen months after the money was deposited, Stupich used it to pay off some of the $39,000 shortfall in his losing campaign for the NDP leadership. One entry in his journal noted: "funds raised by D.B. committed to pay off L/ship campaign deficit."

Given the media's treatment of the NCHS scandal to that point, it wouldn't have taken a rocket scientist to conclude that the report's impact on the party would be explosive. While Parks revealed no wrongdoing by the current cabinet or any questionable activity by NDP MLAs while in office, it was clear that the current party executive had pulled off an exercise in damage control with the $60,000 repayment to the *Democrat*. It was also clear that, at the very least, some of its members were willing to turn their heads while the party's chief fundraiser, Bernie Simpson, was allegedly stretching the limits of acceptable donations. While this information would not be known by the general public for another four months, what happened next in the provincial capitol would be a subject of much debate even after the report was released.

On Tuesday June 6, the morning after Elizabeth Cull received the report, Parks telephoned Cull to discuss whether he should contact the Attorney General's ministry about his report. Cull gave him the phone number of Ernie Quantz, the assistant deputy attorney general for criminal justice. Then she met with the political priorities committee of cabinet, also attended by NDP provincial secretary Brian Gardiner and government communications staffer Gerry Scott, to share a briefing of the report. Satisfied that the report would be ready for release Thursday morning, Cull went home Tuesday night to prepare herself for the inevitable media onslaught. Parks, meanwhile, went to see Ernie Quantz at the attorney general's ministry.

The premier, interviewed after the Parks report was released, offered this version of what happened next: "Eight o'clock Wednesday morning, prior to cabinet, Ernie phoned Elizabeth and said: 'Do not proceed any further. I have read the Parks report. There is a criminal investigation under way. I want all copies of the Parks report, I want to make sure there's no Xeroxes of it. You can not discuss this with anybody. Walsh and Heaney cannot discuss this with anybody, or you will be interfering with a criminal investigation, which is breaking criminal law.' Now that's a pretty intimidating thing for a lay person to hear. She did all those things and she then went to cabinet and said 'Here's what's happening' and she told them 'We cannot proceed. The matter now rests with the RCMP and Mr. Quantz.' And that was it."

Or so they thought at the time. Once the media caught wind of the meeting between Cull, Walsh and Heaney – and the next day's briefing with Gardiner present – the government was once again on the defensive. Cull was a minister of finance with a high position of trust in the province, wrote Vaughn Palmer. Now she had placed that trust in jeopardy by engaging in an exercise of damage control.

The inference in Palmer's critique, which he repeated for several months afterward, was that Cull had breached some sort of parliamentary protocol by sharing the Parks report with NDP hacks; that it was ethically inappropriate for a minister of the crown – and the deputy premier, at that – to mix partisan politics with a sensitive matter of the state.

The premier didn't mince words responding to this argument. "It's a bullshit issue, as far as I'm concerned," Harcourt said several months after the incident. "It's where Palmer has gone way over the mark of presuming the worst of motives. This is where Elizabeth Cull has been shafted in my opinion. Why would Parks come in on Monday morning, demand an undertaking from Elizabeth that she was going to release this report as quickly as possible, and why wouldn't she give that assurance when I wanted it released as soon as possible? And then proceed with my staff and make sure that (a) it was printed for wide distribution, (b) there were briefing notes, (c) there were question and answer materials. Otherwise, what would you guys in the media say if we just dumped the report out? You would have given us hell if we hadn't done all that. So of course my principal secretary and fellow who's heading up public issues were going to be involved in doing all those things ... So what, that Brian Gardiner was there? He's at these meetings on occasion. It's a government priorities committee, it's a political committee where Brian and Patrice [Pratt, NDP president] and other people come in from time to time. What was he going to do with that information? The report was going to be out within 48 hours."

But Allan Blakeney, chair of the NDP renewal committee struck in the midst of the Parks report fallout, suggested that Cull could have avoided criticism by convincing the attorney general's office that the report should be released because it had already been shown to party officials and the premier's staff and could therefore not be kept secret for long. "I think I would have just said to the deputy attorney general, 'You're a little late in the game here. Parks knew this stuff for months and he had a lawyer. His lawyer didn't get in touch with you and this creates a real problem for me. We have got these people in the loop here. The chances of us keeping this under wraps for long is remote and you can tell the police they've got seven days, ten days, to get their search warrants or whatever they want, but that's all I can do because otherwise we're in an impossible situation."

Former Socred attorney general Brian Smith, an acquaintance of Cull since she began her political career in Oak Bay, Smith's old riding, said Cull was caught in a difficult position. "I had sympathized with her position," he said. "I would have had an independent crown counsel look at it right away to determine whether charges would be laid, and I wouldn't release it or discuss it until a decision had been made on that, because it would prejudice the investigation. That's what I would have done. And what happened with her was, she got into a committee before she realized what was [involved], and that's why I sympathize with her."

Months after the incident, Harcourt was still frustrated by the outcome of those crucial few days in June. "I don't know why [Parks']

$300-an-hour lawyer at Farris & Company didn't think about maybe getting in touch with the RCMP and the Attorney General's ministry prior to coming in to see us – that's an interesting question," he said. The premier couldn't help noting that another of the three Farris lawyers involved with NCHS was acting on behalf of the Vancouver *Sun* in its efforts to have the Parks report released. In his final interview for this book, Harcourt displayed a degree of emotion and focussed anger rarely, if ever, captured on the six o'clock news. When asked why he never responded to the media's frequent calls for a public inquiry into Nanaimo Commonwealth, Harcourt responded with a lengthy tirade many of his supporters would argue was long overdue:

> I've said it over and over again to the *Sun* and other people: the Westray mines inquiry was tossed out because of a criminal investigation and court proceedings. The Susan Nelles inquiry was tossed out.
>
> So it's very clear that when a provincial government brings forward a matter that clearly infringes on the federal government's jurisdiction under criminal law, it's *ultra vires*. You can't. You have to let the criminal investigation conclude, because you're affecting people's rights by forcing them to come and testify when they don't have to, they're under criminal investigation. You've got presumption of innocence, you've got due process, you've got all these things that are built into our criminal law that you can't have a provincial government come along using a provincial jurisdiction, i.e. gaming or the Societies Act, or the Public Inquiries Act, and infringe on it. You know, goddamn it, the media has high-powered, $300-an-hour lawyers who should understand that. Reporters should understand that. ...
>
> If after all those investigations – police, and the special prosecutor, and the lottery branch and all that, had not been able to – as the police themselves said – "untie the gordian knot of the monster account" of the Nanaimo Commonwealth Holding Society – how the hell would a public

inquiry do that? The only way you could have got at the truth was the way I went, which was the best forensic accountant around. That's the only way you could have got that truth. What the hell would a public inquiry unfold? It would just have been a political media circus – there would be accusations made but still no evidence or proof. The only reason this is happening is because I had Ron Parks appointed under Section 85 of the Societies Act by Elizabeth Cull, and because I had the records seized that Dave Stupich was driving to pick up. They asked him what he was going to do with the records, and he said, "Well I don't think we're going to store em, I'll shred 'em." And I was up in Prince George then, and I went nuts. I said "Oh no. Seize those records," and appointed Mr. Parks, who had done some background work on this file and done some previous work with the RCMP. So it's ironic that the reason we have the truth is because I got it.

Sadly for Harcourt, the "truth" wouldn't arrive before an early morning raid of NDP headquarters on October 12 by four anonymous, plainsuited RCMP officers armed with search warrants and a couple of briefcases. Gordon Campbell's strategists couldn't have planned it better. The completed Parks report that was supposed to have been released to the public in June was still under lock and key, but with the RCMP's raid of NDP headquarters, Dave Stupich's Gabriola Island home and five other locations, its imminent release was inevitable. And, if that weren't enough for the cheap detective novel scenario, Stupich just happened to be vacationing in the Caribbean on the day of the raid. (His $800,000 home, it was said, was up for sale.)

The RCMP search warrants cited an astonishing list of allegations against Stupich. According to police, the former Dave Barrett cabinet minister, along with common-law wife Betty Marlow and daughter Marjorie Boggis, the NCHS and an affiliated society had committed up to 25 criminal violations involving theft, fraud and illegal transfer of more than $1 million in charity bingo funds. If the allegations were substantiated, Stupich would face up to eighteen criminal charges involving amounts totalling $936,758.

Five hours after their arrival at NDP headquarters, the RCMP officers walked away with two briefcases packed with party documents. The Vancouver *Sun* and other media, tipped off about the raid, quickly prepared court applications to have the Parks report released immediately. This was Thursday, October 12 – a year to the day after Harcourt appointed Ron Parks to conduct a forensic audit of the NCHS.

It was, appropriately enough for the government, on Friday the 13th that BC Supreme Court justice John Hall ordered the release of Ronald Parks' long-awaited report. Although many of its details had already been reported in the media, the cumulative impact of the 136-page document – along with fresh revelations about the $60,000 payment for the *Democrat* and the use of corporate donations – was devastating. "Mr. Stupich's accounting records show that he used NCHS money as if it was his own," wrote Parks. "Accounting records, created by Mr. Stupich, show he regularly borrowed money from NCHS to fund private real estate purchases and to buy shares in Canadian public companies for his personal account."

THE NEXT FEW WEEKS WOULD BE A PERIOD OF SOUL-SEARCHING for the NDP, as rank and file party members and their executives struggled to come to terms with the Parks report's findings. Few in the party would argue that the revelations about Nanaimo Commonwealth did not constitute a scandal, or that the current party was not at least partly accountable for the lack of ethics in Nanaimo. Indeed, many New Democrats were offended by the government's apparent double standard in defining who the real "cheats and deadbeats" were. Some cabinet ministers, for example, were willing on one hand to adopt a vengeful and untrusting attitude toward poor welfare recipients accused of fraud; on the other hand, they were willing to dismiss the fraud of party operatives in Nanaimo as nothing more than an "unfortunate occurrence" created by a "sour real estate market."

But anger toward the party's handling of the NCHS affair was eclipsed by another belief among NDP supporters: that the media's reporting of the scandal – particularly that of the Vancouver *Sun* and

BCTV — was no altruistic attempt to learn the whereabouts of stolen charity funds, but a deliberate strategy to destroy the Harcourt government by exaggerating the extent of its responsibility for wrongdoing in Nanaimo.

It had been more than three years since the *Sun* had launched a series of articles exploring the questionable ethics of Nanaimo Commonwealth and its grand patriarch, Dave Stupich. Many of the facts disclosed by Mark Hume, Vaughn Palmer and other *Sun* staffers would indeed be verified by the Parks report. But it was the impression that the *Sun* was engaging in a vendetta that many readers found so disturbing. NCHS was, however, only the most extreme example of the mainstream media's failure to serve its audience during the Harcourt years. As several other examples would show, there was plenty of evidence that the media not only didn't want the NDP in power but would stop at nothing to discredit, trivialize or dismiss a party that had basically done a good job.

13

Digging
for Bones

BY THE TIME THE FANTASY GARDENS FIASCO CAUGHT UP WITH
Bill Vander Zalm in April 1991, few members of the media were willing to defend the hapless premier in public. Some reporters took a per-
verse delight in his predicament: there was something satisfying
about witnessing the humiliation of a premier who once considered
the media his courtiers, who charmed and seduced them until they
started reporting things he didn't like, at which point he turned on
them and blamed them for his woes. Thus, there was a hint of overkill
when the cameras descended on Vander Zalm for his final performance.

There was one person, however, who was willing to defend Vander
Zalm in the week following his disgrace. Always the devil's advocate,
media critic Stan Persky questioned the ethics of pack journalism in
his "Mixed Media" column for the *Sun*. "What struck at least some
people," wrote Persky, "was an image of the journalistic corps as a
bloodhound pack, relentlessly pursuing its harried quarry, snapping
at him with questions that increasingly revealed their contempt for
his vapid, evasive answers ... The moral of this modern Aesop's fable?
Simply this: Good dogs not only hound, they also dig for bones."

Four years later, Mike Harcourt could appreciate that analogy. Since

1991, the NDP premier had survived what many believed to be an impossible highwire act: pursuing a program of debt management that kept the hounds of Howe Street from snapping at his heels, while enacting bold, socially progressive legislation that should have satisfied the NDP's traditional supporters on the left. But what did Harcourt have to show for it in public relations terms? "Premier Bonehead" for a nickname, a bingo scandal in Nanaimo, and constant accusations that his government had no program. Harcourt was not given to complaining about media coverage, but by 1995 he couldn't help wondering: where was the media when things were good?

In realistic terms, the mainstream media are not in business to promote the ideals of democratic socialism. But then, there were many who would argue that the Harcourt New Democrats were anything but socialist. With the government's crackdown on welfare, its attempt to woo the business community and its willingness to embrace the rhetoric of deficitphobia, was this NDP not more of a traditional liberal government than a socialist one? And if that were the case, couldn't the Vancouver *Sun*, BCTV and others have afforded to be a bit more generous in their coverage of NDP accomplishments?

Apparently not. While the media tended to be positive in its coverage of one-time funding announcements for feelgood projects like daycare centres, drug rehab programs and artistic events, the same could not be said when it came to the more substantial and controversial issues facing the government. Notwithstanding its professional role as government watchdog, the mainstream media's approach to the NDP during its first term in office was characterized by three kinds of negative reporting: trivial emphasis on, or kneejerk response to, the government's toeing what appeared to be a politically correct line; a downplaying of genuine achievements, or under-reporting of news that reinforced government policy; and construction of "scandals" in which circumstances were exaggerated so that guilt could be ascribed to the government by the mere fact of NDP association.

Trivial Pursuit

THE FIRST KIND OF REPORTING WAS RELATIVELY HARMLESS. Stereotypes are, to a certain extent, unavoidable for reporters facing daily or hourly deadlines. And in a politically polarized province like BC, they're hard to resist. How many political scientists, never mind tabloid reporters, haven't made at least one reference to Social Credit as a party of used car salesmen?

Occasionally, the government fell into the media's trap by failing to anticipate the potentially loaded, "politically correct" significance of a story. Who can forget Mike Harcourt's embarrassing gaffe in 1994, when the party rejected its candidate for the Matsqui by-election? Sam Wagar did not inform the party of his pagan beliefs before he was approved as the NDP candidate. When party headquarters discovered he was a practising warlock in the Wiccan religion, there were two courses of action it could have taken.

The smartest move would have been to leave it alone, since the NDP didn't have a chance of winning the traditionally Socred seat in the predominantly fundamentalist Christian riding. They could have stood behind their candidate and practised the tolerance they preached. Instead, the party chose to withdraw his candidacy, ensuring maximum media publicity that made the NDP look ridiculous. Meanwhile, Harcourt offended the NDP's new-age left – and played into right-wing intolerance – by displaying his ignorance of the Wiccan religion. "Some people would say it's a cult," a befuddled premier told reporters, who were more than willing to exploit an NDP, er, witch hunt.

Later that year, Government Services Minister Robin Blencoe upset Victoria's sizable Christian community by ordering a choir performing Christmas carols at the legislature not to sing songs about Jesus Christ. Blencoe insisted the whole incident was a misunderstanding; he was only asking for an "inclusive" performance celebrating the religions and cultures of all the nations that attended the previous summer's Commonwealth Games. But the press gallery jumped on the issue, and Blencoe's NDP colleagues didn't go out of their way to defend his gesture. "Lord help us," chuckled Health Minister Paul Ramsey. "This ranks right up there with putting bras on the maidens in the rotunda." (In an earlier incident, the government had considered touching up murals of bare-chested aboriginal women.)

More often than not, the media's discussion of NDP political correctness took on a form of sneering. In November 1994, the *Sun's* Jamie Lamb took exception to the government's failure – for the third consecutive year – to attend the Douglas Day celebration in Fort Langley. An annual tribute to the founding of the British Columbia colony and to its first governor, James Douglas, Douglas Day was basically a politician's photo op in which the provincial cabinet ate lunch with local dignitaries before marching to the fort to hold a meeting at the site of the first formal gathering of the BC government.

"The real reason why the New Democrats won't attend is because they don't feel it is politically correct to honor anything connected with the idea of a 'colonial' government," wrote Lamb, barely concealing his contempt. "Colonial governments weren't sensitive, weren't about caring'n'sharing, weren't imbued with the delicate sensibility the NDP feels it, and only it, possesses. Besides, showing up at a ceremony to mark James Douglas and Matthew Begbie and the beginning of government and law might offend aboriginal groups, who feel they were not treated well by the coming of the colonials." The premier's press secretary, Andy Orr, couldn't have put it better himself.

For all its clever mockery of NDP "political correctness", however, the media was capable of trivializing a genuinely disturbing issue. In the spring of 1995, Robin Blencoe was forced to resign as Municipal Affairs minister when three women from his office filed sexual harrassment complaints against him. Because Blencoe was the first minister to be dumped from cabinet for reasons of alleged misconduct, and because of the serious nature of the allegations, the issue received ongoing media coverage throughout the province. For a few reporters, Blencoe's disgrace became an opportunity to explore the larger issue of sexual harrassment in the work place.

In the midst of this coverage, stories began to surface about an obscene chain letter posted on the government's e-mail system. The letter promised, among other things, "great sex" for people who "need to get laid within 96 hours." Among the cyberspace culprits were John Heaney, head of the government's public issues and consultation department, Marnie Caron, the premier's executive secretary, and two support staff members in the premier's office. The incident was nothing more than an office prank requiring a slap on the wrist. However, the overwhelming impression left by media coverage was that the government was full of leering perverts with dysfunctional sex lives who were amusing each other with sophomoric jokes at the taxpayer's expense. Reporters quoted Liberal MLA Gary Farrell-Collins's argument that the chain letter constituted a form of harassment (i.e. Robin Blencoe + lewd e-mail = rapist government). The media's eagerness to exploit a minor lapse by a few wayward bureaucrats trivialized the genuine harassment suffered by women throughout the public service. It added insult to injury for Fran Yanor, the first of two women to go public about Robin Blencoe's alleged harassment. "I hope nobody is going to make the comparison of an inappropriate joke with the seriousness of the allegations made against [Blencoe]," the premier's chief of staff, Chris Chilton, told the *Sun*. Unfortunately, several reporters already had made the comparison.

Another popular media target was any law that could be presented to make the NDP look like communist dictators out to curtail press liberties and freedom of speech in general. In 1993, the government introduced Bill 33, the Human Rights Amendment Act, which prohibited hate propaganda, including material advocating genocide or wilfully promoting hatred against any group based on colour, race, religion, ethnic origin or sexual orientation. Anita Hagen, the minister responsible for Human Rights, naively assumed – as did everyone else in cabinet – that no one would object to what was largely a symbolic measure, given that the revised law only reinforced a principle already entrenched in the Criminal Code of Canada. The law was specifically a response to recent incidents of racist and anti-Semitic vandalism in the Lower Mainland prompted by an increase in immigration in recent years. The NDP was only serving notice that racist intimidation was unacceptable in a multicultural society.

Judging from the response, however, one would think that BC had become a Stalinist gulag and that the Ministry of Truth would soon be raiding personal libraries to get rid of the filth. Bill 33, said one critic, would be used to "intimidate and silence not only those among us who do not subscribe to politically correct ideas, but also those who merely sell or display the politically unpopular expression of others … Bill 33 means that anyone, ranging from a radical Christian televangelist to a corner grocery store operator selling *Playgirl* magazine, can now be dragged into costly, time-consuming hearings … on the strength of a telephone complaint."

It was hard to believe such a response was serious. "We were criticized, I think quite savagely and unfairly," Harcourt said. "The press went nuts. I was quite shocked. I thought, this is absurd. This is not an infringement of freedom of speech. It's a classic definition of liberty: you're free to do what you want, as long as it doesn't harm somebody else. You don't stand up in a crowded theatre and yell 'Fire!' … Allowing somebody to preach racial hatred could lead to a pretty good likelihood of it occurring." And it was. In Surrey, there were burning crosses on the lawns of East Indian residents; throughout the Lower Mainland there were anti-Semitic slogans spraypainted on synagogues. But how silly of the premier to assume he'd be congratulated for attacking racism.

Progress! What Progress!

THE SECOND KIND OF NEGATIVE COVERAGE, IN WHICH THE media either downplayed NDP achievements or avoided comment on developments that reinforced government policy, was more subtle in its effect. The NDP's progress on environmental issues, in particular – generally considered the government's strongest policy area – garnered some of the lamest reporting from BC's mainstream media outlets. BCTV's coverage of the Cariboo land use decision focused more on critical reaction to the CORE process and Stephen Owen being hung in effigy than on the farsighted compromise reached by all the players. The Kitlope decision, which preserved the largest intact temperate rainforest watershed in the world, was practically ignored by the *Sun*, which never hesitated to hammer the NDP with front page coverage of the slightest blunder. And in May 1995, when the Bonneville Power Administration pulled out of a 1994 agreement to purchase surplus power from Columbia River dams, the *Sun* buried a poll suggesting that the public thought the government was doing a good job of handling the issue. According to an Angus Reid poll commissioned by the government after Bonneville reneged on the agreement, 44 percent of respondents in a poll of 600 thought the NDP was doing a "good or very good job" of handling the issue, as opposed to 38 percent who thought the government was doing a "poor or very poor job." This was the best news for the NDP since Moody's had awarded BC the top credit rating in the country the previous month. But the *Sun* relegated it to a few lines at the end of a four-column business story inside the Lower Mainland section.

Another example of this kind of under-reporting occurred in February. Throughout that month, business leaders and other critics condemning the secrecy of the government's land claim negotiations with the Nisga'a Tribal Council, and the *Sun* ran prominent articles calling for more openness in the negotiations. The stories tended to favour the opinions of industry representatives and local chambers of commerce skeptical of Nisga'a claims that non-native industry had stripped native lands of "billions" of dollars in fish and lumber.

On February 21, the Nisga'a Tribal Council delivered its proof with a press conference at the UBC First Nations House of Learning, an event that seemed as worthy of front page coverage as the anti-native arguments of the previous week. At the conference, tribal council president Joe Gosnell released an audit by Price Waterhouse which determined that the band had lost between $2.1 and $4.3 billion in timber, fish and minerals since the lands were colonized in the 1800s. The low figure was based on the amount the Nisga'a would have received if they had only collected royalties from non-native resource companies, the high figure if they actually controlled and profited from the resources directly.

The results of a Price Waterhouse audit which directly answered the front page challenge of the previous week should have received the same degree of coverage by the *Sun*. The announcement was especially newsworthy, given that a Nisga'a land claims settlement would set a precedent for other treaty negotiations in the province. But you'd never know it by the *Sun*'s coverage on February 22. Instead of running the audit story on page one, the *Sun* opted for a feature about a 19th-century missionary whose family's ownership of valuable native artifacts was being contested by various parties. Other stories on the cover that day included the tale of a Chicago stockbroker whose hot air balloon crossed the Pacific and landed in Saskatchewan, and yet another article about alleged abuse of Canada's immigration system. The Nisga'a story was buried on page B7.

Grasping at Straw Men

THE THIRD KIND OF NEGATIVE REPORTAGE WAS THE CONSTRUCtion of "scandals" in which circumstances were exaggerated to produce maximum negative impact on the government.

On April 28, 1994, the *Sun* ran an editorial under the headline: "Socreds were saints compared to the NDP". The newspaper's argument went as follows: because the NDP had come to power in 1991 pledging "different" ethical standards than Social Credit, and because four NDP cabinet ministers had failed to offer their resignation after being accused of unethical or improper conduct, the party was morally bankrupt, its ethical standards "definitely lower" than Social Credit's, and Harcourt's support of his ministers an appalling display of "arrogance" and "sanctimonious hypocrisy".

The "criminals" in question were agriculture minister David Zirnhelt, forests minister Dan Miller, attorney general Colin Gabelmann, and municipal affairs minister Robin Blencoe.

Zirnhelt came under scrutiny after he was approached by a constituent seeking the government's help to improve the road access through a piece of property leading to her own lakefront residence. Zirnhelt told her that as it was a private road, the government could not interfere; he referred the woman to another MLA, but failed to tell her of his own interest in the land, which he and a partner later purchased. The woman, Linda Brady, took her case to the Liberal Party, which tried to accuse Zirnhelt of using his position to profit from the land purchase. But Zirnhelt was correct that the access route through the property had long been considered a private road, and while his judgement was called into question, he was ruled not to have broken the law in his purchase. The only question that remained was whether he had misled a constituent.

As for Miller and Blencoe, neither of their 'conflicts' were damning enough to force a resignation. Ironically, Miller's involvement with a decision on a mill with which he maintained seniority rights was not deemed to be a conflict, but he was suspended from cabinet for three months nevertheless. Blencoe's involvement with the Bamberton housing project, on the other hand, was deemed to be an "apparent" conflict, because one of the principal players was a longtime friend and campaign contributor. Instead of being dropped from cabinet, he switched portfolios in the first cabinet shuffle.

Gabelmann had long been a favourite target of NDP opponents because he was viewed as an ideologue who had "politicized" the attorney general's ministry. Throughout the NDP's first term, the Opposition made several calls for his resignation. There was the alleged perjury, when he claimed not to recall having signed a memo regarding the surveillance of an anti-abortion protestor; then there was the ministry's e-mail tapping of senior corrections officials during a provincial inquiry into the escape of a teenaged killer; and finally, there was the BC Gaming Commission appointment of Lynda Fletcher-Gordon, who neglected to inform Gabelmann that a society in which she was involved was undergoing an RCMP investigation.

Gabelmann was never found guilty of any wrongdoing, but by the summer of 1995 his office was so constantly under attack from the Opposition and media that he was finding it difficult to do his job. When Harcourt decided to have Gabelmann switch positions with the relatively uncontroversial government services minister, Ujjal Dosanjh, the outgoing attorney general had no difficulty telling reporters he was relieved.

Of this particular group of ministers, the only one whose ethics remain in question is Robin Blencoe, who was fired from cabinet on

April 4, 1995 amid allegations of sexual harassment by three women who had worked for him. Blencoe's guilt was never confirmed by any official process, because his firing by Harcourt effectively terminated a cabinet-appointed investigation by labour lawyer Stephen Kelleher. But the premier was satisfied that his government services minister should be dropped from cabinet, because Blencoe had apparently told him the previous month that there was only one allegation of harassment, not three. Aside from his anger over being misled, Harcourt was horrified by the details. "These were not innocent, flirty types of come-ons," one official from the premier's office told the *Province*. "This was a very serious situation."

By the last year of its mandate, the NDP could claim only one cabinet casualty due to questionable ethics. The last Social Credit government had twelve. But the Socreds were "saints" compared to the NDP, according to the *Sun*.

ROBIN BLENCOE MAY HAVE BEEN THE ONLY MEMBER OF HARcourt's cabinet to be fired for ethical reasons, but he was by no means the only minister the Opposition — and some members of the media — wanted dumped. For years they had been gunning for Moe Sihota, the smart alec from Esquimalt who rose to prominence in Opposition by hammering the Socreds on every conceivable ethical fumble. There were signs, even before the NDP came to power, that Sihota's holier-than-thou, "gotcha"-style of investigation would come back to haunt him. Long touted as attorney general-in-waiting, the young lawyer blew any chance of getting the job during the Bud Smith tapes scandal of 1990.

Sihota had come into possession of taped cellular phone conversations between then-attorney general Smith and two other parties. Instead of turning them over to the RCMP, he tabled them in the legislature for maximum political effect, alleging a cover-up. Smith resigned, but Sihota didn't come off looking all that clean either. Lawyers who cross-examined him during a subsequent inquiry called him a liar and a political opportunist.

Once he was in cabinet, much would be made of Sihota's 21 demerit points for speeding, his use of non-union labour to build his house, and a number of other personal pecadilloes that would have had any lesser minister consigned to the backbenches. In the end though, it was his profession, not his actions in the political arena, that caught up with him. On May 5, 1995, Sihota voluntarily resigned from cabinet when the BC Law Society found him guilty of breaching ethical conduct rules seven years earlier as a practicing lawyer. He was banned from practicing law for eighteen months and fined $2,000.

A case similar to Sihota's normally takes a few weeks for the Law Society to complete, but this one took two years and one of the most extensive inquiries ever conducted – even though no complaint was brought forward. When the Law Society ruling was made public in 1995, Sihota admitted having "screwed up" in 1988 when he advised a client to enter into a real estate deal with his father, Bas Sihota, without telling the client that his father was in financial trouble. Under Law Society rules, a lawyer is required to recommend independent legal advice to the client in such a circumstance, but Sihota admitted that he failed to do so. Earlier he had borrowed $170,000 from his client's common-law wife to remove a foreclosure against BC property he held for his father. She got the money back but lost it when the California real estate deal with Bas Sihota went sour. Moe's father declared bankruptcy in December 1990 and died of a heart attack weeks later.

The woman involved in the case, Edith Antonio, maintained that Sihota had done nothing wrong and that the real estate venture was a simple case of caveat emptor. "The market was blazing hot," she told the *Sun*. "They were lining up to buy houses, sight unseen. I thought, 'How could they fail?'"

When the Law Society approached her, Antonio told investigators that Sihota had done nothing wrong but that her common-law husband, Harvey Williams, and Sihota's father, were at fault. "I told them Moe was always honest with me, but they didn't want to hear that," she said.

"They pressured me to change my story. I'm really angry at the Law Society because they did not want to hear the truth. And that is, Moe Sihota owes me nothing." Antonio added that an independent lawyer hired by the society to interview her became upset when she did not want to sue Sihota. "He yelled at me and I was in tears. He followed me [from his law office] to the street and continued to yell at me. It was one of the more horrible experiences of my life."

The Law Society repeatedly denied that its investigation of Sihota was politically motivated. The probe took an unusual length of time to complete, said a spokesperson, because of the "complexity" of the transactions and the difficulty of tracking down all the documents and parties involved, from BC to California. But there were doubts about this explanation. Sihota may have been a whiz kid among NDP types, but he was never a favourite among the legal establishment. By releasing its report this late in the NDP's mandate, it was hard to avoid the impression that the Society was trying to take maximum political advantage. "Why did it take them two years to nail Sihota?" mused Victoria columnist Hubert Beyer in the weekly *Saanich News*. "The reason couldn't be that there are a lot more right-wing lawyers than left-wing ones, and that the political damage inflicted on the NDP government is that much greater this close to an election? Naw, couldn't be."

The word "disgrace" was thrown around quite a lot in the days following Sihota's resignation, but there was an air of disbelief about it all. Sihota's transgression seemed no different, really, from David Zirnhelt's apparent dishonesty with a constituent, and yet the agriculture minister was not forced to step down. There was no public outcry about Sihota's "mistake", and most interviews with constituents, legislative reporters, environmental activists and even Sihota's political rivals suggested that his credibility had suffered very little as a result. There was talk that his resignation from cabinet was in fact a mutual agreement with the premier to take a breather – to sit in the "penalty box", much like then-forests minister Dan Miller did after his brush with conflict laws in 1992 – before eventually returning to the fold. And, sure enough, Sihota was back in cabinet before the summer was over. Finance minister Elizabeth Cull relieved him of his duties as environment minister for just over three months before Sihota was reinstated by Harcourt in the mini-shuffle of August 17. Not even the media's constant criticism was enough to permanently marginalize one of the NDP's strongest cabinet ministers. While the media and legal establishment groaned, Sihota's legion of admirers breathed a sigh of relief.

From May 1987 until May 1991 – a period that saw twelve cabinet resignations, various conflicts of interest and countless ethical breaches by the Socreds – the Vancouver Sun had run 286 stories combining the words "Socred" and "scandal". Four years into the NDP's first term, however, the *Sun* had published 341 stories combining the words "NDP" and "scandal". If those statistics seem disproportionate, given the NDP's tame track record of scandals compared to the Socreds, the *Sun* itself could take a great deal of the credit. For much of 1995, its news agenda was dominated by two issues with which the newspaper was determined to discredit the government.

Spin Doctors From Hell

FOR A GENUINE NDP HATER, THERE WAS NO BETTER WAY TO attack the party during the Harcourt regime than to point an accusing finger at the decision makers behind the scenes – those shadowy apparatchiks rumoured to be pulling the strings. Guilt by association was one of the most effective tools the media used to embarrass the NDP government and, more often than not, it worked. A prime example of this coverage began on February 22, 1995, when the premier and Elizabeth Cull appeared in the "town hall meeting," broadcast live on BCTV. The event was supposed to highlight the government's accomplishments in dealing with the economy; instead, the production was a total disaster.

From a public relations perspective, the town hall meeting was probably the worst mistake of Harcourt's first term. Cameras had never been kind to the premier. The 1991 election debate on CBC had lost him valuable points when he was clearly the frontrunner, and several media scrums since then had made Harcourt look defensive, wooden and uptight. Nevertheless, the premier's handlers were convinced that a town hall meeting was a perfect way for Harcourt to reassert his leadership before an increasingly cynical public. British Columbians needed only have direct contact with their premier – with no media filter – and all would be well. They couldn't have been more mistaken.

Whatever Harcourt's intentions, the experiment at Science World on February 22 was fated to become the NDP's "Black Wednesday." Conceived by Karl Struble, produced by Ron Johnson and arranged by Harcourt's communications director Sheila Fruman, the $233,000 taxpayer-funded experiment in direct democracy was a total disaster from the opening credit. For starters, the scheduling was bad. Whoever chose the time and date clearly didn't consider the number of viewers they would offend by preempting a Vancouver Canucks hockey game scheduled for the same night. Thousands of Canuck fans were looking forward to one of the first televised games of the season after a lengthy lockout by NHL owners, so the NDP managed to alienate working-class sports fans before the town hall meeting had even begun. "I can't believe they'd show this instead of a Canucks game," said one fan interviewed at a sports pub. "It's more boring than watching paint dry." To make it worse, BCTV, which is owned by a broadcasting company affiliated with the Canucks, made no secret of the fact that the air time was bought at the taxpayers' expense.

As it turned out, no time or station (except, perhaps, local cable at 3 a.m.) could have saved the NDP from major embarrassment. First, the toll-free telephone number displayed on the screen was wrong, and efforts to correct the problem prevented callers from getting through to the studio for half an hour. The camera work was shaky, giving the whole production an amateurish feel. Finally – despite earlier allegations that the live audience had been "stacked" with NDP supporters – Harcourt and Cull faced a constant barrage of hostile questions from the studio audience.

Suddenly an event that was supposed to make the government look good degenerated into a ritual humiliation. Harcourt, joined onstage by Elizabeth Cull and UBC economics professors Angela Redish and Jonathan Kesselman, said nothing as a woman in the audience delivered a lengthy tirade against the NDP. The image of Harcourt, shifting in his seat and attempting an awkward smile (which only caused his moustache to quiver), remained with viewers for days afterward. While Sheila Fruman rushed nervously about the studio, trying to reassure cynical reporters that everything was just peachy, other New Democrats tried to pretend they were someplace else.

"The format, in retrospect, was hopeless," the premier recalled, with considerable understatement. "I just showed up. The problem wasn't Elizabeth and I answering questions. The problem was all the other stuff that happened around us. We'd been doing these town hall forums – maybe not as elaborate as this – for the last five months ... so this was just the conclusion of that process before we put the budget to bed. In retrospect, they probably shouldn't have had me on there. They should have had her there and had me do a state-of-the-province address as I'd done the previous two years, which were received pretty well ... It was an incompetent, amateurish production from which a whole bunch of other things got manufactured around it to create a tough 90 days. I think a bunch of people wanted to go thermonuclear on me and us, whether or not there was any substance to it, and they did."

Harcourt was forced to retreat to Victoria for a hastily assembled caucus meeting. Heads would roll over this travesty, he promised the media. Reporters, casting about for a scapegoat, grew suspicious when they learned that the show was produced by longtime New Democrat Ron Johnson. Within days, the media was accusing Johnson of winning government contracts through his party affiliations, and Harcourt of showing preferential treatment in doling out contracts to an NDP-connected communications firm. Within a few weeks, the NDP dropped another ten points in the polls, and Harcourt became the second premier in five years to face a conflict of interest probe by Ted Hughes.

In the days that followed the town hall meeting, the media focus shifted to Ron Johnson's NOW Communications, an NDP-affiliated ad firm, and Karl Struble, the American spin doctor who advised the government on its contents. Struble did not appear to have been paid by the government for his work on the project, but when it was learned that his fee was funnelled through NOW, the media pricked up its antennae. Wasn't this the same guy who worked on the NDP's election campaign? What was he doing for the government now? And how many contracts was Ron Johnson getting for government work?

For the media, Ron Johnson was pay dirt: the quintessential "failed NDP candidate" who presumably reflected socialist incompetence for no other reason than that he had lost six elections in downtown Vancouver (never an easy NDP riding at the best of times). Taking Weisgerber and Gordon Campbell's cue, the *Sun* and *Province* implied that Johnson was being awarded a disproportionate number of government contracts, wondering aloud whether patronage was involved. BCTV tracked him down like a fugitive, asking him to explain his $556-a-day retainer and $3,500 fee to write a single letter for the government. On March 6, Harcourt responded to the pressure by cancelling the retainer and requiring NOW to bid on government work in an open tendering process.

But before the premier could get on with the business of governing, conflict of interest commissioner Ted Hughes announced on March 10 that, prompted by the FOI requests filed by CKNW's Kim Emerson and Reform leader Jack Weisgerber, he would launch the investigation of the government's dealings with NOW Communications. Emerson claimed that he was acting as a citizen, but his FOI request had set a precedent: a journalist had become actively involved in the proceedings of government by making an event happen, by generating a news story in which both premier and reporter would be central figures.

Despite this questionable manipulation of events, Gordon Campbell saw Emerson's gesture as an opportunity for political gain and immediately called for the premier's resignation during the course of the investigation. Confronted by reporters once again, the normally sunny Harcourt blew his stack. "I'm not going to let the Victoria bureau chief of CKNW, a major commercial radio station in this province, hijack my role as premier or hijack my government," he said. "These CKNW allegations are without foundation, they are unfair and highly political. CKNW has surrendered its role as journalists and moved from reporting on the political process to being political activists."

Several media analysts were willing to agree. The announcement of the Hughes inquiry on Friday coincided with the annual convention of the Canadian Association of Journalists, which was being held in

Vancouver that weekend. CKNW news director Gordon MacDonald's defense of Emerson — that he was just doing his job by asking questions on the public's behalf — was not well received by most journalists in attendance. Responses ranged from "bullshit" (Brian Mulroney biographer John Sawatsky), to "Some people have described it as nudging the line. As far as I'm concerned, it's a mammoth leap over the line" (Southam News reporter Stephen Bindman), and "It's a breach of the way journalism should operate" (Ottawa *Citizen* media writer Chris Cobb).

On April 18, the premier was officially cleared of conflict by Ted Hughes. Emerson, in a series of interviews with colleagues, maintained that he was right to call for the inquiry because it was the only way he could have established whether a conflict had occurred. Apparently the CKNW bureau chief didn't subscribe to the school of investigative reporting; few of his colleagues would have had the modesty to make that admission in public.

Meanwhile, Harcourt still faced the disclosure of financial details of the NOW contracts by Auditor General George Morfitt. The auditor general's report, released on May 18, revealed that NOW's contracts accounted for 23 percent of government payments to advertising and public relations in the last four years. Although he found irregularities in sixteen NOW contracts, he uncovered no pattern of favouritism toward the firm. The only blemish in his report was the finding that controversial subcontractors like Karl Struble had been "masked" in some contracts by having payment for their work funnelled through NOW Communications. "In these cases," wrote Morfitt, "the billings and sometimes the accounts do not reveal the identity of the true supplier."

Harcourt, on the defensive after three months of media attack, finally shuffled his office staff on May 18 after Morfitt released his report. Much to the Opposition's chagrin, heads didn't exactly roll, as Harcourt had promised three months earlier. Sheila Fruman, the communications chief widely believed to be responsible for the town hall fiasco, was offered a job in the Social Services Ministry, where she was reported to have an ally in Joy MacPhail. She declined the offer, accepting a $64,000 severance package instead.

The other casualty of the NOW saga was the premier's chief of staff, Chris Chilton. Morfitt's report blamed Chilton and Fruman for using NOW Communications to funnel contracts to Struble and Hans Brown, former NDP president. Instead of firing Chilton, Harcourt transferred him to a senior post in the Ministry of Health, where he would serve as a special assistant to the premier and retain his annual $125,000 salary. "I'm not happy to be leaving the position, but I accept full responsibility for what happened," said Chilton.

Harcourt was eager to paint the demotion as "a significant loss for Mr. Chilton," but the Opposition wasn't about to let the premier off so easily. "Harcourt continues to believe that the public service is just a playpen for NDP political hacks," said Gordon Campbell. "There is absolutely no penalty. I am shocked," added Jack Weisgerber. "The premier has in fact given taxpayers the finger, given [his advisors] a pat on the back, a nice fat paycheque and a soft landing."

This sentiment was certainly shared by the Vancouver *Sun*. Splashed across the top of page one on May 19, the lead story was headlined "Premier misled BC public on NOW work, critics say." Inside that day's edition, an editorial described Harcourt as "wilfully ignorant and determinedly opaque in his comments" on NOW, while Vaughn Palmer accused the premier of being a weak-kneed wimp who wasn't macho enough to amputate Chilton and Fruman at the knees. "When the long-promised trip to the woodshed finally materialized, it was more like a trip to the candy store, a milquetoast response from a leader who has never faced up to the seriousness of this scandal."

Nor would he "face up" to it in the months that followed. The premier, much to the outrage of his critics, did not accept the Vancouver *Sun*'s definition of a scandal. And until Kim Emerson's extraordinary debut in politics, he had never really complained about the media's treatment of him. But Harcourt could barely contain his rage about the *Sun* coverage of May 19. "It was a real consciously put together hatchet job on me. They were bloodthirsty, they wanted bodies. I had to throw people out in the street, destitute."

What bothered him most was that, despite having been cleared by Hughes and Morfitt — who both ruled that the premier had no prior knowledge of how contracts were awarded ("Nor should I," said the premier. "It's inappropriate to get that involved in micromanagement") – it seemed there was nothing he could do, short of resigning, that would satisfy the *Sun*.

"Seven or eight [of the contracts], the auditor general expressed some concerns about," Harcourt continued. "And, as a superfluous, peripheral comment, the conflicts commissioner – outside the area of his jurisdiction – made some comments [about] two of the contracts to Struble's firm that were masked. Well, I agree; I said they should have had the subcontractor's name on it, and the details. I accepted all of the auditor general's recommendations – when it should be put out to tender, when it should be reported, all those sorts of things. That was a minor set of concerns ... So what's the story? The story is, that I personally deceived the public when both Morfitt and Hughes made it very clear I had no knowledge of it, nor should I have. That's the kind of dishonest bullshit that occurs [in the media] sometimes."

At least one Vancouver *Sun* staffer was willing to agree. "We're not being journalists, we're advancing a political agenda," Elizabeth Aird had written much earlier in the controversy. "You tell me why voters should be the patsies in political plotting. Trumped-up 'scandals' are a waste of citizens' time, and divert us from real issues." But "trumped-up scandals," as everyone knows, sell newspapers. And even before the NDP had completed its first year in power, some of Aird's colleagues decided that the current government should pay for the mistakes and dishonesty of its NDP predecessors.

The Sun Shines on Bingogate

BY THE SPRING OF 1995, THE NANAIMO COMMONWEALTH Holding Society (NCHS) had been in the news for three years and had gone through six investigations, with Opposition and media repeatedly calling for a public inquiry. Harcourt was running scared, the pundits said. The mud was beginning to stick. BC voters were fed up. Or were they?

NCHS appeared in the news only intermittently in 1993, as various investigations were under way. But the *Sun* can take most of the credit for keeping the scandal near the top of the news agenda for the better part of 1994 and early 1995. Aside from veteran reporter Mark Hume's regular investigations, there was frequent commentary from legislative columnist Vaughn Palmer. Palmer had set the tone for the *Sun*'s coverage on June 1, 1992, when he compared the diversion of charity funds by NCHS to Socred Tourism Minister Bill Reid's diversion of $250,000 in Lotto BC funds to a company controlled by two of his friends. Palmer suggested that the two issues were comparable because both involved revenues from "publicly regulated gambling" and both involved helping out "political friends and insiders." This was a curious comparison, given that Reid was a minister of the crown who committed his sin while under the authority of Bill Vander Zalm; NCHS was an NDP-connected society whose actions were directed long before Mike Harcourt became NDP leader by an individual, Dave Stupich, who had no influence with the current government.

On October 15, 1994, the *Sun* published a sensationalistic front page article headlined "The Commonwealth Connection." Mark Hume's report was packaged with a rogue's gallery of mug shots featuring prominent NDP politicians and associates. In addition to Stupich and current NDP ministers Moe Sihota, Colin Gabelmann, Anne Edwards and Robin Blencoe, there was Nanaimo MLA Dale Lovick, former Premier Dave Barrett and party guru Bob Williams, former federal candidate Johanna den Hertog (wife of NOW Communications' Ron Johnson), former party president Hans Brown, past party executive Cliff Andstein, IWA Canada president Gerry Stoney, and of course, federal MP Svend Robinson — whose presence in any news story involving the NDP was never much of a surprise. (Some party members expressed mock envy that they hadn't been included; with a higher profile, they too could have appeared on page one.)

The only reason these particular NDP bigshots were included was that they had all been directors or members-at-large of the Vancouver Commonwealth Society — an organization with no connection to the NCHS other than its partisan loyalties. None of these people were interviewed for the story, but Jacques Carpentier was portrayed as a dragonslayer who took on big bad Dave Stupich and won, while special crown prosecutor Ace Henderson was seen as a weak-kneed political hack for having had the nerve to treat the NCHS case like any other commercial crime prosecution.

"That is why the Commonwealth scandal has not died," wrote Hume. "It is not like any other commercial crime case – because at the heart of it lies the New Democratic Party and all the unanswered questions about who got the money. Those are questions that go outside the narrow confines of the Criminal Code and were not dealt with by the police, or by Henderson, because they are about ethical conduct and political integrity."

For all its platitudes about ethics and integrity, however, the *Sun* chose a curious method to make its case for NDP corruption. "There's absolutely no connection between the [Vancouver Commonwealth Society and NCHS]," said Bill Tieleman, communications director for the BC Federation of Labour. The longtime NDP activist explained that the Vancouver organization is basically a holding company which owns the building the NDP office is located in. "It has never run a bingo or anything else. But the Vancouver *Sun* is more than willing in a front page story [to print] photos of all the prominent individuals who are involved in the Vancouver Commonwealth Society, and the only link at all was Dave Stupich being on both of those societies and the fact that it was an NDP grouping.

"[They did] not even talk to anyone in the NDP for a response [or] interview any one of those people pictured. It was just a smear job, unequivocally so. And people privately in the newsroom at the *Sun* and in other media have all said it was an absolutely sleazy, shoddy story that should never have run. People in the newsroom thought it was particularly bad because it gave the paper no defense. It was an appalling and obvious effort by the Vancouver *Sun* at the highest levels to go after and make the most of that scandal and make it more than it was. And BCTV had a similar approach."

On November 23, the front of the *Sun*'s second section featured a tabloid-style headline and subhead surrounding a portrait of Harcourt draped in the BC flag: "Scandals stack up as an embattled premier tries to keep them ... UNDER WRAPS." It was becoming a self-fulfilling prophecy. The premier was certainly "embattled" by the Vancouver *Sun*; NCHS was indeed "the scandal that won't go away," because the

Sun kept repeating the same information week after week; the issue could certainly do "serious damage" to the NDP's reelection chances as long as the *Sun* kept up its coverage.

On December 17, the paper ran its second major exposé of NCHS by Mark Hume – "BINGO: The Charity Scandal: How corruption killed the NDP's 40-year dream." The two-page spread, with six photos of Stupich dating back to his early career in the 1950s, was far more baroque than Hume's earlier feature. Stupich, who he described as a "failed chicken farmer," was portrayed as a mysterious warlock whose accounting books "became almost mythical. They were like the sorcerer's volume of spells, tomes full of unknown power and meaning." The story began with a 500-word, cloak-and-dagger account of an unnamed bingo worker who enters the Red Square complex at midnight and encounters the obsessive Stupich, "bowed over a coffee table littered with accounting ledgers … making neat handwritten entries in the ledgers." Award-winning journalism? Maybe. But it would also make great *film noir*.

Hume's colleagues continued this approach well into 1995. On January 6, the *Sun*'s civic affairs reporter Jeff Lee uncovered a tidbit from Harcourt's 1984 reelection bid as Vancouver mayor. One of Harcourt's fundraisers was Bert Rougeau, who sold debentures and raised funds for NCHS. According to documents obtained by the *Sun*, Rougeau's work for Harcourt was financed by the Nanaimo NDP Association, a group closely associated with NCHS. Rougeau's ten-year-old invoices and statements of account regarding his employment were cast in the context of stolen and tainted monies. Although Harcourt was not likely to recall in 1995 how a non-profit society in Nanaimo was conducting its own finances eleven years earlier, Lee used Rougeau's involvement with the mayoralty campaign to suggest that Harcourt had intimate knowledge of NCHS and its operations. The day after the article appeared, the *Sun* ran an editorial predicting the demise of the government. On January 10, 1995, Vaughn Palmer – for whom, it was now apparent, no hair was too thin to split – offered a guilty-until-proven-innocent verdict on Harcourt's leadership. "With the premier unable to produce anything to back up his version of events," mused Palmer, reaching into his grab bag of blanket judgements, "Mr. Harcourt's own credibility and conduct are now at issue in this affair."

Cynics liked to joke that Palmer used this line for nearly every issue involving the premier – that he was so obsessed with discrediting Harcourt that he simply forgot how many times he had used it. But it remained to be seen whether Palmer and some of his media colleagues would show as much enthusiasm in their critiques of Gordon Campbell as they had with Harcourt.

14

Membership Has Its Privileges

LIBERAL LEADER GORDON CAMPBELL MANAGED TO ENJOY A honeymoon with the media for much of his time in Opposition, but not even he was able to avoid scrutiny. Of all the issues that haunted the former Vancouver mayor following his debut on the provincial stage, none was more delicate a topic than his relationship with Jim Moodie, a Vancouver land management consultant whose company's profits mushroomed while Campbell was mayor and who later managed Campbell's campaign for the Liberal leadership. The details of Moodie's business transactions with city hall were first revealed in a series of articles by Russ Francis, a former Vancouver *Sun* intern who later became the chief news reporter for the *WestEnder* and Kitsilano *News*.

The Francis articles focused on Jim Moodie's direct line to the mayor's office and the generous helping of city contracts he received once Campbell was elected in 1986. Francis raised a number of provocative questions about conflict of interest, and whether Campbell would appreciate the distinction between provincial and municipal standards were he ever to become premier.

Like any good newshound, Francis had a fine sense of timing. Just weeks before the 1993 convention that crowned Gordon Campbell the new Liberal leader, the reporter sold a major op-ed piece describing the mayor's relationship with Moodie to the *Sun*. The facts, as Francis revealed them, were compelling. Jim Moodie, a close personal friend of Campbell who was now a co-chair for the mayor's Liberal leadership bid, had earned $2.4 million in city contracts since early 1987, shortly after Campbell became mayor. Moodie had done city work for about five years before that, but the figures jumped drastically after Campbell was elected.

Francis also uncovered Campbell's financial interests in the Georgian Court Hotel, a money-losing venture designed to cash in on the Expo 86 world's fair, in which Campbell had a direct role as developer. While Campbell divested himself of shares in 1984, and later claimed not to have voted on issues involving the Georgian Court, his brother Michael – publisher of *Equity* magazine – and father-in-law Lawrence Chipperfield still held shares. The future mayor had also done some nifty stickhandling to avoid the appearance of conflict. After selling his shares, Campbell retained part ownership of the hotel through Baobab Enterprises – a company owned by Campbell and his wife, Nancy – while Citycore Development Corp., the company he initially formed to build the hotel, was handed over to other directors. Campbell retained 12,000 class A shares in the Citycore partnership. Francis noted that, according to the latest financial statement signed July 14, 1993, Baobab "continue[d] to pay the mayor for services he perform[ed]" for it.

While all these arrangements were being made, Mayor Campbell voted in favour of several projects that would directly benefit the hotel, rather than removing himself from city chambers. The projects included the $163 million General Motors Place complex, new home for the Vancouver Canucks hockey team, built practically across the street from the Georgian Court, and permits for the annual Molson Indy car race, which took place near the hotel. The Georgian Court's marketing director even referred to it as the "hotel of choice" for the Molson Indy.

Campbell's attitude toward the arena typified the relationship he enjoyed with land developers throughout his seven years as mayor. First, despite vigorous objection from the opposition COPE councillors, his NPA-dominated council fast-tracked a $40,000 subsidy to the GM Place developers, Northwest Sports Enterprises. Then, in an unprecedented move, the mayor granted Northwest Sports an exemption from obtaining a development permit before beginning excavation. Suddenly – faster than Russian Rocket Pavel Bure on a breakaway – the Canucks were on their way downtown.

Campbell had little to say about his involvement with the Georgian Court Hotel, but he was more than willing to defend his relationship with Moodie. He bristled at any suggestion of conflict and said he was being targeted by opponents of his leadership bid. "I have tried to act in the public interest at all times, and I have never tried to mislead the public," Campbell told the *Sun*'s city hall reporter, Jeff Lee. He said he was acting on staff recommendations when he voted to extend the Fraser Lands, a $22 million social housing development in southeast Vancouver. "I'm leaving the city and I'm simply endorsing the recommendations of staff as someone who has worked for the city for seventeen years. That's a reasonable thing to do."

A year later, however, Campbell completely revised his position, admitting he should not have approved city hall contracts for Moodie while he was mayor. Campbell's main regret about his dealings with Moodie appeared to be the political controversy their friendship engendered. "It might have been wiser for me to say, 'I won't vote on anything that he has to do' … Maybe it would have looked better," he told the *Sun* in December 1994.

The NDP, for its part, was relieved to see Campbell on the hot seat. In a provincewide poll commissioned by the NDP in November, 62 percent of respondents believed that Campbell "gave" contracts to his friend and campaign manager Jim Moodie. In the same poll, 54 percent of respondents agreed with the statement that Campbell was not a "real Liberal" but a Social Credit clone, and that he could accurately be described as a "slick opportunist."

In late November 1994, the NDP's caucus research department made a formal request for Gordon Campbell's city files on Jim Moodie under the freedom of information legislation passed into law the previous year. However, the NDP researchers were told by Vancouver city officials that the request would cost up to $23,000 to process. While the

NDP's haggling over costs was debated in the papers well into the new year (they eventually settled on $2,500), Gordon Campbell managed a preemptive strike on the issue on March 9, 1995, when his office released a series of documents outlining his relationship with Moodie. Since the records showed that Mike Harcourt had approved more contracts (nine) for Moodie than Campbell had (eight), the Liberal leader argued, how could he be seen to have given preferential treatment?

But Campbell overlooked some of the most damning evidence in those files. Certainly the chatty tone between Campbell and Moodie, revealed in city hall memos, was noteworthy. In January 1988, Moodie had written to Campbell with the news that some land might become available adjacent to a project he was working on; in his note, he asked the mayor to see if the owner would be interested in cooperating on development. Shortly afterward, Campbell complied with a gushing note to the landowner, "If Mr. Moodie is correct, it seems to me that we may be able to do something incredibly exciting!"

The documents also revealed that city manager Fritz Bowers had opposed the anticipated $220,000 per year payments to Moodie, and recommended the city do the work in-house, instead. This dispute presumably arose after an overly zealous Campbell, who had just arrived in the mayor's chair, told Bowers in late 1986 that he wanted to extend one of Moodie's contracts without further tendering. "I would like to initiate this work as a priority," Campbell wrote Bowers. "This is a logical extension of the work Moodie Consultants are currently doing for the city."

Glen Clark, who crashed Campbell's press conference, emphasized the personal aspect of the former Vancouver mayor's relationship with Moodie, but much of the debate was lost on the public. To the Liberals' great fortune, a far more sensational story broke in Victoria on the same day: Government Services Minister Robin Blencoe was forced to step aside amid allegations of sexual harassment from a woman (later, three women) who had worked in his office. The Blencoe affair overshadowed the Campbell/Moodie affair in the media, but the Liberal leader's questionable dealings with land developers and other political friends were not about to vanish.

Initially, the Moodie story was slow to catch on in the mainstream press. Far from providing the spark that would lead to further investigation, the Russ Francis revelations about Campbell and Moodie were casually dismissed by Vancouver's corporate media, particularly the *Sun*. Predictably, the *Sun*'s city hall reporter Jeff Lee moved quickly to defend his turf, quoting a UBC ethics professor to downplay the political significance of the Francis research. And Trevor Lautens, the *Sun*'s Edmund Burke wannabe, rushed to the Liberal leader's defense: "I think Campbell's okay. I'd trust him."

One of the few dissenting journalists was Sid Tafler, editor of Victoria's award-winning *Monday* magazine, a mainstream news and entertainment weekly that the *Sun* conspicuously referred to as an "alternative newspaper." Tafler, who supported the idea that Campbell's dealings with Moodie would have put him in a conflict of interest had he been a provincial cabinet minister, raised a more pertinent question about the media's lack of interest in the story. Comparing the *Sun*'s coverage of the Moodie issue to its focus on the Nanaimo Commonwealth Holding Society, the *Monday* editor came up with some interesting numbers: a dozen articles about Moodie in seventeen months, 25 stories about NCHS in only three months.

The *Sun* would no doubt defend its coverage of NCHS on the basis that the stories concerned the party currently holding power. The Campbell/Moodie connection, on the other hand, was a city hall story of limited interest. But Tafler had a different view. Unlike the Moodie issue, in which Gordon Campbell was intimately involved, "there is nothing in the NCHS story that connects any member of the NDP now in the legislature to the bingo disgrace," he wrote. "Certainly the NCHS story is deplorable, but it was the work of an unethical, shortsighted group of NDPers operating out of Nanaimo, not of Mike Harcourt and the people who make up his government. And unlike the Campbell/Moodie deal, the NCHS scandal has been investigated by the justice system and dealt with by the courts – the society found guilty and fined appropriately last year."

Even when the bingo issue appeared to have been resolved, the *Sun* gleefully followed the Opposition's calls for a public inquiry, continuing its own pursuit of NCHS with all the gusto of its Fantasy Gardens coverage of 1990 to 1991. Perhaps it was the paper's right and duty to get all the facts, Tafler concluded, "but these rights and duties are no different when it comes to Gordon Campbell voting to spend millions of taxpayer dollars for contracts for his friend and supporter." Surely the public deserved to know the extent of such favours to friends Campbell offered while he was mayor, before it decided whether to elect him as premier.

This issue would come up again a few months later on May 2, when the NDP caucus communications office released a pile of documents on Campbell's relationship with Atlas Travel, an agency run by Campbell's sometime business partner George Taylor. Coming so soon after coverage of his business relationship with Jim Moodie, the revelation was intriguing because it suggested that the Liberal leader's tendency to reward friends and insiders was potentially more serious than the premier's.

According to the documents obtained by the New Democrats, Atlas Travel and its owners made financial donations to Campbell's by-election campaign in Vancouver-Quilchena. Atlas also provided a Liberal phone bank for by-elections in Abbotsford and Matsqui. Campbell's former constituency assistant, Forman Howes (now a Liberal Party staff organizer) used Atlas's offices to prepare Liberal election readiness material – including riding profiles describing potential nomination candidates and local media biases, and voter identification software for Liberal campaigns.

It was impossible to determine the extent of Atlas's contribution to Campbell's Liberal leadership campaign, since Campbell refused to release his donation list. But given the former Vancouver mayor's longtime relationship with Atlas principals George Taylor and Helen Graham, it's a wonder the media never pursued it further.

Campbell and Taylor had worked together since 1976, when the young Campbell was TEAM Mayor Art Phillips's executive assistant, and Taylor was a TEAM candidate, TEAM president, and Vancouver planning board appointee. After Campbell left Phillips's office, he joined Taylor and Martin Zlotnick on several development projects. On July 24, 1986, four months before the civic election that brought Campbell to office, Helen Graham entered into a partnership with

Campbell's development company Citycore Development Corp. Together they borrowed more than $270,000 to purchase land in Burnaby. Graham's Graywest Enterprises was a major investor in the Georgian Court Hotel, built by Campbell and Martin Zlotnick. As of 1995, Graywest still owned $41,000 worth of shares in that hotel.

Meanwhile, Atlas was the agency of choice for the mayor's office throughout Campbell's term at city hall, and in April 1993 – three weeks before Campbell launched his bid for the Liberal leadership, and while he was still mayor of Vancouver – council voted to give Atlas an exclusive, three-year travel services contract for the city. Given his longtime association with Atlas principals, Campbell probably should have removed himself from the council chamber for the vote – or at least disclosed his personal, political and business relationship with Taylor. But he didn't. And Taylor was already on the organizing team for Campbell's campaign. Following Campbell's move to provincial politics and his ascension to the Liberal leadership, Taylor was hired as organization chair of the BC Liberal Party.

Despite all this, Campbell didn't hesitate to tell the *Sun* on May 1, 1995, that "Atlas, per se, has no involvement with the Liberals," and he didn't recall that Atlas had the city's contract until he was questioned about it by a reporter. Apart from the standard reportage of his denial the next morning, the media showed no interest in Atlas Travel or the "special deals" that Campbell offered his political and business ally, George Taylor, while in office. The few facts revealed in a routine government communications document were potentially more damning to Campbell's credibility than anything uncovered in the NOW Communications inquiry was to Harcourt's. "The abuse of office by Gordon Campbell is systemic," Harcourt said. "If you compare what he did with Moodie – the memos directed to staff to give him the contracts – and with George Taylor and Atlas Travel getting the monopoly, it's clear that if he was judged under our conflict law, he'd be gone."

A broader question still remained about Campbell, according to Harcourt. Namely, if he was willing to reward business partners like Moodie and Taylor while in the mayor's office, what would he be willing to do in the premier's office? Harcourt provided his own doomsday scenario with a litany of questions about Campbell's friends and insiders. What, for example, was he offering "those 2,800 people that paid almost $200 a plate to come to his fundraiser?" asked Harcourt. "What was he offering some of the people in the forest industry that want to strip mine the forests? What was he offering the mining community that want to mine the Tatshenshini? What was he offering the land speculators and housing speculators about blacktopping over farmland? What was he offering the gang on Howe Street in terms of getting rid of the clamps down on the VSE? If he was prepared to do what he did as mayor, what's he prepared to do as premier?"

Given the resources spent by the media to bash the NDP's treatment of "friends and insiders", the premier could be forgiven for venting his frustration at its overall indifference to Gordon Campbell's cronyism. But then, perhaps the media's laissez-faire approach to Campbell had something to do with their own relationship to the Golden Boy of Howe Street.

As he faced his first great challenge from the BC electorate, Campbell could expect an easy ride from BCTV and CKNW, both of which remained closely connected to the Vancouver business monthly *Equity* magazine, whose general manager until 1995 was Campbell's brother Michael. Before leaving *Equity*, Michael Campbell enjoyed a relationship with the private broadcasting company that saw the financial analyst provide regular business commentaries on both stations. Meanwhile, CKNW hotline host Rafe Mair began writing a column for *Equity*, and the radio station supported the magazine with regular advertising. In April 1995, for example, CKNW ran four full-page ads in *Equity* featuring Mair and several other 'NW heavyweights. "With regional magazine ad rates running at more than $2,000 per page," reported the *Georgia Straight*, "that adds up to more than $8,000 worth of advertising – unless, of course, the ads are contra for goods and services that *Equity* might be peddling on the CKNW airwaves."

Equity even tried unsuccessfully to woo the *Province*'s legislative columnist, Brian Kieran, to become *Equity*'s editor-in-chief. Securing Kieran would have been a coup for the Campbell fraternity, since the acid-pen columnist is a legendary NDP-hater, but Kieran remained with the *Province* after reportedly being refused a buy-out of his contract there. For much of the last decade, there were at least two other prominent media types that Gordon Campbell could have depended on for optimistic coverage. Among the high profile investors who lined up to cash in on Campbell's Georgian Court hotel in the early 1980s were Anthony Parsonage, otherwise known as BCTV news anchor Tony Parsons, and Moira Farrow, a veteran Vancouver *Sun* news reporter who retired in 1995. For those wondering why some Vancouver journalists were slow off the mark to criticize Campbell and his business exploits, perhaps a few of his media "friends and insiders" could provide the answer.

Campbell's marriage of convenience with the media did not go unnoticed, of course, among his left wing critics. "It seems that it's all the same people," said BC Federation of Labour president Ken Georgetti, himself a frequent target of media scrutiny for his apparent access to government. "I saw [BCTV news anchor] Tony Parsons for fifteen days non-stop, on the news, at exactly twenty after the hour, refer to 'tickets are still available for Michael Campbell's one-stop RRSP. Oh by the way, for $29.95 these last series of financial information that Michael had on our TV, you can get by writing to BCTV, blah-blah-blah, and now we'll go to a commercial.' Right on the air! I mean, this is just sickening politics." Some critics would describe Campbell's relationship with the media as somewhat incestuous. But industrial labour leaders and working class critics like Georgetti preferred a saltier, down-to-earth description: a "circle jerk."

A Scent of Power

WHILE HIS BUSINESS CONNECTIONS MAY NOT HAVE RAISED eyebrows among the mainstream media, there was at least one aspect of Gordon Campbell's career that was bound to receive further scrutiny as the election date approached. According to Libby Davies, a longtime civic opponent for the left-wing COPE slate who ran unsuccessfully to succeed him as mayor in 1993, Campbell's greatest weakness was an autocratic leadership style that could alienate even his political supporters. According to Davies, the NPA mayor's reign from 1986 to 1993 was marked by a contempt for public debate in which closed-door meetings became the norm and major decisions were made with little or no public input. "He tried to turn council into a legislative style of government, which is not what municipalities are meant to be," recalled Davies. "He went to great lengths to censor and manipulate the public in a way that was not superficially apparent. He did it very skillfully. He has the ability to substantially change things and make them look the same."

One example was Campbell's gradual phasing out of citizen delegations. Before he was mayor, it was possible for any citizen of Vancouver to apply directly to speak to council on any issue. But Campbell removed delegations from all meetings except for public hearings dealing with quasi-judicial decisions (such as zoning by-laws), or special council meetings on particularly explosive issues. Even then, the most contentious issues were often bumped off the Tuesday council agenda and sent to committee meetings for discussion on Thursdays. Following his reelection in 1988, Campbell reduced the number of committees by half (from four to two), and placed all councillors on each one, ensuring that issues would be resolved as quickly as possible with the least public input. "These subtle changes produced a dramatic difference in how delegations were heard," said Davies. "Often the media would show up on a Tuesday when nothing was happening and miss a lot of the real stuff on Thursday. [The NPA] just wanted to silence the criticism, to shut people up."

But Campbell wasn't entirely successful with this strategy. In 1989, council was under pressure to address a series of demolitions of heritage buildings. A number of community groups had written to city hall and asked to address council directly, but were told they would have to apply for a committee hearing. The number of bureaucratic hoops set up for the mayor's critics contrasted greatly with the NPA's treatment of developers, who appeared to have no problem getting an audience with the city. "Finally, the community groups came to city hall and pushed their way into the council chambers," Davies recalled. "They demanded to be heard, and they were, because council didn't have a choice at that point. This action was a direct result of people being denied due process."

Once people were granted the privilege of addressing council, they often found they had a choice between Campbell's way or the highway. On one occasion, the mayor refused to adjourn a public meeting on a community garden project, even though tempers were beginning to flare. "We begged him to adjourn because people had to work in the morning, and there were some who had babysitters at home, but he forced the debate to continue until 3:30 in the morning," Davies recalled. "I know a provincial government can use filibuster to continue a debate all night in the legislature, but [a neighbourhood meeting] is not the same situation at all."

Davies's description of Campbell's autocratic style at the civic level was consistent with his approach as Liberal leader. "Critics say he does not inspire loyalty because of a presidential style of top-down leadership that relies on the input of only a few close advisors," said a *Globe and Mail* report in July 1995. Some of this top-down leadership was evident during the Abbotsford by-election a few months earlier. During the campaign, the president of the Abbotsford Liberal riding association quit over the high-handed tactics of Campbell's hired "honchos" from Vancouver. Shirley MacGillivray said that Campbell's organizers took over the by-election campaign while all she was asked to do was "stuff envelopes or make coffee." Campbell claimed never to have heard of MacGillivray, but said he suspected she was acting out of spite to avenge her friend, Chilliwack MLA Bob Chisholm, whose failure to win renomination as the Liberal candidate was blamed on Campbell forces. "He comes into town and talks to people he regards as important," said MacGillivray, a longtime Liberal, adding that she was confused that Campbell did not consider the views of the riding president even worthy of a phone call. "It's as if he invented the party. Being high in the polls is one thing but it's too far right," she said. "We have to bring the Liberal Party back to the middle ground."

But those who presumed the Liberal Party still represented anything moderate, or that Campbell had any loyalty to the ideals of Liberal MLAs elected in 1991, would soon be in for a rude awakening. Art Cowie, for one, was especially disillusioned by Campbell's behav-

iour when the former Vancouver-Quilchena MLA made his attempt to
return to the legislature in November, 1995. Cowie, a longtime Campbell colleague during their days in the civic NPA, had happily stepped
aside and offered Campbell his seat in 1994, when the newly minted
Liberal leader was looking for a way into the legislature. Knowing that
Campbell planned to fight the provincial election from Vancouver-
Point Grey, Cowie figured he would easily win back Quilchena after
securing the nomination at some point before the election.

What he wasn't counting on was that Campbell's 1994 by-election
campaign manager, Colin Hansen, would waltz in and claim the nomination for himself. Hansen, a 42-year-old past president of the
Quilchena riding association and executive assistant to former Liberal
leader Gordon Gibson, was a well-connected Liberal and committed
free enterpriser. (His logo-producing company, The Image Group,
sold promotional items like coffee mugs and pens with company
logos.) His decision to compete for the nomination – announced in a
phone call to Cowie the night before his public declaration – stunned
the former MLA, who had assumed that Campbell would at least have
gently discouraged anyone he knew from running against him.
Instead, Hansen drew from an energetic team of 250 campaign workers in coasting to an easy, first-ballot victory (584 to 259) on November 26. Cowie supporters were left scratching their heads over the
whereabouts of Gordon Campbell – who, according to the official
story, had stayed away from the nomination meeting to attend his
son's sixteenth birthday party.

Cowie tried to put on a brave face, but there was no mistaking his
personal anger and disappointment when he quit politics the next
day. "I wanted some loyalty and I wanted some support," a bitter
Cowie told reporters. "I believe loyalty is the most important thing,
apart from honesty, in a party. If you don't have loyalty you don't
have a party."

But Campbell's failure to endorse Cowie was less likely a deliberate
personal slight than a calculated decision to avoid confrontation at all
costs. Even the *Globe and Mail*, the newspaper of record for Canada's
business community, has noted that Campbell has the "scent of
power" about him – that he appears to be motivated by the privilege

of office itself and spends a great deal of energy on the pursuit and maintenance of power. According to the *Globe*, Campbell's personal style "depends less on charisma than on making sure he holds all the right cards before he shows his hand."

Mike Harcourt had smelled that "scent of power" since the early 1970s, when Mayor Art Phillips first took the 24-year-old Campbell under his wing and Harcourt was a TEAM councillor. Since then, Campbell had confounded all efforts to identify what lurks beneath the photogenic exterior. "I think the people who have the most trouble in politics are like Robert Redford in that movie, *The Candidate*," says Harcourt. "Robert Redford ran and got a Senate seat, got all the way and won, and to his campaign manager said 'What do we do now?' That to me is Gordon Campbell. What are you there for? What's the reason you're there? Is it power? Is it just being there? Having the position? That's a pathetic reason for being in politics."

What do British Columbians know of his reasons so far? In terms of a political platform, Campbell appears to be motivated exclusively by an insatiable desire to reduce the size of government. Among his promises, Campbell has pledged to cut the cabinet by one third, from eighteen to twelve ministers, and reduce the number of MLAs from 75 to 60. He also intends to sell BC Rail and BC Systems, and will examine every crown corporation – including BC Hydro – to see if any can be sold to pay off the provincial debt. A Gordon Campbell government would remove school taxes from property tax bills and cut the number of school boards, eliminate the corporate capital tax, tear up the Health Labour Accord and the Fair Wage law, and bring in balanced budget legislation.

Campbell outlined his platform in a pre-election address at the Union of BC Municipalities convention in October 1995. In addition to the above measures, he promised to cut personal income taxes, give municipalities the right to choose whether they want photo radar (an anti-speeding scheme that government critics have dismissed as a tax grab), scrap any deal reached with the Nisga'a and undermine the Treaty Commission by recommencing negotiations with native bands so that aboriginal land claim settlements are more difficult to achieve (referenda and free votes in the legislature), and force employable welfare recipients to sign "job preparation contracts" before they receive their benefits.

"I think one of the things we're very lucky about in British Columbia and Vancouver is that we actually have huge opportunities if we're just willing to get beyond the polarization that takes place," a carefree Campbell once told the *Globe and Mail*. Like most classic liberals, Campbell is a promoter of individual rights and the concept of "positive liberty" that encourages the pursuit of unfettered self-interest. Unlike progressive liberals, however, Campbell appears to have nothing to say about collective rights, or the concept of "negative liberty" that encourages the protection of citizens from the exploitation of others.

Campbell's critics argued that his policy platform was a carbon copy of the Mike Harris agenda in Ontario. Harris, whose Conservatives defeated the Bob Rae New Democrats in June 1995, quickly moved to scrap the provincial labour law introduced by the NDP, cut personal income taxes and force the unemployed to work for welfare benefits, all in an attempt to reduce the provincial debt. Harris said he was inspired by Alberta Conservative Premier Ralph Klein, who proved that it was possible to get elected on such a platform. Campbell, accused of copying Harris, rejected the comparison. "I've been talking about [debt reduction] since 1993, before I even heard the name Mike Harris," Campbell told a reporter. "I think it's too bad we always have to think the ideas come from somewhere else. They come from British Columbia."

Indeed they do. In fact, the one politician pundits failed to compare Campbell to was a homegrown, BC right winger who had much more in common with Campbell than Klein or Harris did. Gordon Campbell's political trailblazer was none other than former Socred Premier Bill Bennett, whose restraint policies of the early 1980s provided the blueprint for cutbacks by both Klein and Harris. Like Bennett, Campbell is backed by the Howe Street big business community and is also fond of using the optimistic rhetoric of free enterprise to minimize the impact of debt reduction on social services. His promise to increase funding for municipalities while cutting the corporate capital tax and school property tax – letting go of $1.7 billion in revenues – without reducing health or education spending, seems unrealistic.

By the fall of 1995, many British Columbians had forgotten the devastating impact that Bennett's restraint program had on the province more than a decade earlier. But if Gordon Campbell were to become the next premier, their memories would no doubt be refreshed.

EPILOGUE

Picking Up the Pieces

BY THE FALL OF 1995, A CHARITY BINGO RIP-OFF THAT ONCE seemed nothing more than a media-generated nuisance had finally become a real crisis to the government. The manner in which the party had dealt with abuses by the Nanaimo Commonwealth Holding Society (NCHS), years after the fact, had badly damaged the NDP's credibility – and not only in terms of its longstanding commitment to high ethical standards. With its repayment of $60,000 to NCHS for funds paid to the *Democrat*, and with its obsessive dependence on spin doctors to deal with every aspect of its disclosure, the NDP had exposed itself as (a) overly cautious about everything, and (b) hopelessly inept at damage control.

Of more immediate concern, however, was how the $60,000 repayment, along with the party's acceptance of corporate donations, confirmed that the credibility problem was not limited to a few party operatives in Nanaimo. These discoveries sparked several battles among New Democrats, many of whom had conflicting visions of the party's purpose and of how it should raise money. By the time the dust settled on November 15, the party president had offered to quit, a cabinet minister had been fired, a former party fundraiser was suing a high-profile MP, and the premier had resigned, citing the "baggage" he had inherited from the NCHS fiasco. As traumatic as these events may have been, however, they also provided the NDP with a timely opportunity for renewal and a chance to delay an election that almost certainly would have been a disaster for the government.

The series of events leading to Harcourt's resignation took place in the month following the Parks report's release on October 13, a period in which the government was constantly on the defensive and the party seemed ready to implode. Typical of the NDP's chronically bad timing, the Parks report's release managed to coincide with a long-awaited federal NDP leadership convention in Ottawa. Party members had been waiting for more than a year to select a new leader,

But with only three major candidates (a fourth, author Herschel Hardin, provided the novelty of an intellectual candidacy), much of the campaign was uninspiring and poorly reported – a sad statement for a party trying to rebuild itself. With a traditional convention including delegates, placards and plenty of TV cameras, the party was hoping that a high-profile NDP love-in would bring disaffected members back into the fold.

The event certainly didn't lack for good drama. Shortly after the first ballot, which saw Svend Robinson leading Nova Scotia's Alexa McDonough by a few dozen votes, the maverick MP handed her the leadership when it became apparent that he could not win on a second ballot. (Former Saskatchewan MP Lorne Nystrom's supporters indicated their intention to support McDonough.)

BC New Democrats, on the other hand, could be forgiven for being a little distracted by events back at home. Only hours after the federal leadership vote in Ottawa on the afternoon of October 14, Mike Harcourt's return flight from Ottawa touched down at Vancouver International Airport and the premier's final nightmare began. Besieged by a throng of reporters demanding to know whether the Parks report's findings were serious enough to force his resignation, Harcourt – suffering from a flu – told the media he had only just been briefed on its contents. The next day, having finally read the entire report, Harcourt had only one reaction but decided to keep it to himself: Game Over.

"When I saw that over a million dollars in personal loans had gone out to Dave Stupich and people around him, the amount of money that had been taken to pay back the bondholders – all the money that was owed to charities, I was so angry. I'm still angry," Harcourt told the author, adding that he twice had to go out for a walk to let off steam before he read the whole report. "But I also knew that, fair as it is – the Parks report totally exonerated me and my government – there was no way I could get out from under it." Harcourt knew he would have to quit but, as he explained, "his moment" would not arrive until after the party had dealt with its initial anger and sense of betrayal. He also decided to wait until the media was finished its feeding frenzy; abandoning ship in the middle of the hysteria would have sent the false message that it was media pressure, not the issue itself, that had forced him out of office. After all he'd been through, Harcourt was not about to give the "scrum of the earth" – as he light-heartedly referred to the press gallery – that kind of satisfaction.

In any case, the premier knew that the media's focus on NCHS was bound to shift from Dave Stupich – perpetually unavailable for comment – to members of his own government and other NDP players. First there was attorney general Ujjal Dosanjh, a former party vice-president and member of the executive when the *Democrat* received money from NCHS. Dosanjh was never implicated directly in the transactions – on the advice of a lawyer, he had withdrawn from any involvement. But his admission that he was at least partly aware that something was foul in the town of Nanaimo (and not just the pulp mill at Harmac) made him yet another suspect in the minds of the media. Then there was Elizabeth Cull, whose handling of the report back in June was once again raised as an issue of credibility. Cull had already been accused of lying about what she knew of the report's contents when Ron Parks first delivered it to her; now she was forced to dismiss accusations that she had misled the public by suggesting there was no connection between the party and the tainted funds of NCHS. Indeed, Cull appeared to dig herself an even deeper hole with her comment of October 13: "From all the evidence we have, that is still holding true."

Even the NDP's union "friends and insiders" were suspect in the days following the Parks report's release. According to the media, a

$500,000 loan by the BC Government Employees Union that ended up going to an NCHS subsidiary through another union, constituted a form of cover-up. A front-page article in the *Sun* described the loan as a "donation" and accused the BCGEU of deliberately concealing the money by "funnelling" it through the IWA.

"This was not a donation, as the Vancouver *Sun* suggests," said BCGEU president John Shields, in a prepared statement the same day. "Regular monthly interest payments were made to the BCGEU, and the loan was repaid in full in 1984. It was a legitimate and profitable real estate investment. There was nothing inappropriate about it, nor did Parks find there was anything inappropriate about it." Days later, Shields said that former BCGEU general secretary John Fryer misled the union executive by failing to inform members that the loan would end up at NCHS. "Why someone would want to scapegoat me, I don't understand," Fryer told the *Sun*. "At no time was there any suggestion that the BCGEU wanted to invest in Nanaimo Commonwealth."

Then there was Dave Barrett. The 69-year-old former premier suffered a major public relations setback when his long-awaited political memoirs, *Dave Barrett: A Passionate Political Life*, just happened to be published during the same month the Parks report was released – ensuring that his book tour would be dogged at every step by annoying questions about NCHS. Barrett, whose contempt for reporters was legendary, initially shrugged off his tormentors with a rhyming jingle: "*Alleg*ations have been made, no *charg*es have been laid, and I have *no* further *comm*ent" – sometimes repeating himself six or seven times until the reporter gave up. But he finally met his match in Prince George December 4 when he was ambushed by a talk show radio host. Barrett repeated his jingle until the host cancelled the interview without a single question about Barrett's book. During the commercial break, the two got into a loud argument and Barrett stormed out of the studio, calling the host a "fucking asshole." (The former premier was somewhat more cooperative the next day, however, when he arrived for his scheduled appearance on CKNW's Rafe Mair Show. "Is the D.B. me?" he said, responding to the famous initials in the Parks report. "It is absolutely possible and probable. But it is very likely and very possible … that money was raised either at a banquet or fundraising, for

Nanaimo Commonwealth Holding Society.")

Finally, there was Vancouver-Fraserview MLA Bernie Simpson, the party's former fundraiser. Simpson, a lawyer who had helped raise millions of dollars for Ethiopian relief in the 1980s, had frequently been congratulated by the party for his fundraising efforts. During the late 1970s and early 1980s he was a liaison between the NDP and business, organizing receptions and accepting corporate donations – some of which ended up in the NCHS bank account. "Obviously I'm not in cahoots with Dave Stupich on this," Simpson told the *Sun*. "My role was to collect the funds and turn them to him and I assumed at the time that they would be distributed for purposes they were intended."

But the problem, according to many in the party, was that Simpson was not supposed to be raising corporate donations in the first place. According to a 1978 resolution of the BC New Democratic Party, corporate donations were prohibited, "except for those from small businesses [privately held and Canadian-owned] who support the principles and policies" of the NDP. And even those were subject to approval by the provincial executive. While many New Democrats were embarrassed and scandalized by the revelation that Simpson had violated this policy, the easygoing MLA was initially blasé about it all. "I did raise corporate donations and many of those corporate leaders, who were the pillars of our community at that time, asked that these be anonymous. The reason was that they were being intimidated by the former Social Credit administration for even associating with the NDP." Having been caught in the act, Simpson not only defended himself but offered a direct challenge to the policy (and therefore, the party itself): "I challenge anybody to show me that a government [sic] is compromised by taking corporate donations. Just like I don't believe a government [sic] is compromised by taking donations from environmental groups." Basically, Simpson was telling his critics that corporate donors shouldn't have to be traditional allies of the NDP in order to give money; obviously, if they're giving money now, they must be supporters, right? (His argument, of course, depended on the assumption that donations are offered without strings attached.)

That logic didn't sit too well with Svend Robinson. The Burnaby-

Kingsway MP, fresh from conceding defeat to Alexa McDonough at the federal NDP leadership convention, returned to BC and launched a blistering attack on the Parks report finding and Simpson's admission. Robinson not only condemned the party for allowing this violation of policy to occur, but called for Simpson's expulsion from the party. Some of his comments in the media prompted Simpson to launch a defamation of character lawsuit against the Burnaby-Kingsway MP. In subsequent party meetings, the two New Democrats − symbolic of the party's ideological split − passed each other in the same room on several occasions, but avoided eye contact.

As all this was occurring, Harcourt was facing the inevitable media calls for his own resignation, or that of Elizabeth Cull and the provincial executive. On October 19, one week after the RCMP raid of provincial NDP offices, Harcourt attended a nine-and-a-half hour meeting with caucus in which cabinet ministers and backbenchers alike condemned the party's 1993 payment to NCHS as "a disgrace" and argued over what should be done about Bernie Simpson and corporate fundraising. The understatement of the day went to Cowichan-Ladysmith MLA Jan Pullinger, a director of NCHS: "We have the sense that something from the past has come up and kicked us in the head."

The following Sunday, Harcourt attended a meeting of the provincial executive in which party president Patrice Pratt offered to resign. Her offer was turned down. "We're not going to scapegoat people just to scapegoat people," the premier told reporters, emerging from a gruelling eight-hour session at the Biltmore Hotel. Instead, Pratt would draft a letter of apology to the party's 20,000 rank and file members, explaining what went wrong, and Harcourt would launch an internal review of the provincial party through a "renewal commission". Pratt, already under fire from the media, took the heat for another week until she finally came up with the promised letter, following which she was ridiculed for understating the obvious. ("You have probably been hearing about the report of the Parks Inquiry," she begins, prompting readers to wonder how many party members had been living under a rock for the past ten days. Later, she admits that "by failing to advise Premier Harcourt of our decision to repay funds to NCHS in 1993, I made a mistake," and concludes by telling members: "I know you share my sadness in events of recent days.")

Throughout most of these events, Harcourt held firm to his all-for-one-and-one-for-all approach. As long as he was premier, he said, no cabinet minister or party advisor would be sacrificed on the altar of political expedience. As far as Harcourt was concerned, the media was "reinforcing the testosterone school of political leadership" by constantly demanding that he fire someone. "They're not seeing that I have a distinct style of leadership," he told the author. "I'm stubborn about it, I haven't varied from it for 25 years, and it works. It brings people together, it gets results. It doesn't leave a lot of bruised and battered people who then seethe with revenge."

For the most part, Harcourt was right. Whatever was said to him behind closed doors, by the caucus at large or the so-called "Gang of Six" (Clark, Cull, Sihota, Miller, Petter, MacPhail), the premier could always depend on a united front when the cameras were rolling. There was at least one cabinet minister, however, who may have been seething with revenge for at least two years. Housing minister Joan Smallwood, demoted from social services in the 1993 cabinet shuffle when she fought with bureaucrats over a crackdown on welfare fraud, had been marginalized ever since when it came to the big decisions. Smallwood's supporters respected her guts and determination as an advocate for the poor who never strayed from the NDP's traditional socialist principles; her critics thought she was a pompous and inflexible moralizer, fond of using language like "right-thinking people." Even after her demotion, however, Smallwood's support on the left of the party gave her sufficient clout to criticize the government on its handling of social and moral issues. Thus, when the Parks report prompted the internal soul-searching by caucus, Smallwood surprised no one by speaking out. When she met privately with Harcourt on October 23, the premier expressed confidence in his housing minister. The feeling was not mutual, however. Having examined her own conscience about NCHS and found herself untainted, Smallwood decided that the premier wasn't expressing enough angst about it all. "He has to be seen to be wrestling with the issues," she told one interviewer. Instead, she explained, Harcourt was "acting as if it were business as usual." Smallwood's criticism centred around the delay of the Parks report's release, and the premier's decision not to advise cabinet of its contents. "We should not have been caught off guard without anything to say." Did she think that Harcourt had failed the leadership test? "I have grave concerns – yes," she told reporters the day after her meeting with the premier. Reading these comments in the paper the next day, Harcourt didn't hesitate over his next action. It is standard practice in parliamentary politics that when a cabinet minister publicly questions the leadership of a premier or prime minister, the cabinet minister gets fired. But when Harcourt announced his decision to drop Smallwood from cabinet on October 26, the news was treated as yet further evidence of the premier's inability to deal with the NCHS fallout. Harcourt was forced once again to deny that he himself would resign, and Smallwood was characterized as the noble martyr.

On November 6, Harcourt introduced the internal party renewal commission he had promised two weeks earler. Skeptics saw this solution as a typical NDP exercise in damage control ("When in doubt, strike a committee") about as useful as rearranging deck chairs on the *Titanic*. But Harcourt, as usual, expressed confidence in the process. Headed by former Saskatchewan NDP premier Allan Blakeney, the commission also included former United Church of Canada moderator Rev. Robert Smith, former student activist Michelle Kemper and long-time party member Millie Canessa. "They all expressed strong commitments to changes within the NDP that will ensure that nothing like the NCHS occurs again within the NDP or involving the NDP," said the premier.

But none of Harcourt's public optimism about the renewal process could alter his initial impression, after reading the Parks report, that his leadership was finished. By the end of that same week, on November 10, an Angus Reid poll commissioned by the *Sun* and BCTV told the story: support for the NDP, which had come to within ten percentage points of the Liberals in a September poll, had plummeted to its lowest levels in nearly two years. Support among decided voters had dropped six points in two months to only 24 per cent – less than half the support for the Liberals at 49 per cent. While the NDP was way ahead on the environment, forestry management and social issues, the

Liberals led on the economy, managing the budget, managing land claims and even "providing honest and trustworthy government." Finally, the Liberals held an 18-point lead on the question of who would do the best over-all job of governing BC. Worst of all for the premier, Harcourt's personal approval rating had fallen to 29 per cent, with a full 50 per cent "strongly disapproving" of his leadership. "It suggests I'm a lightning rod and I expected that," he told reporters. "I expect that will change in the future."

Indeed, it would. The following Wednesday, November 15 – four years and ten days after being sworn in as premier – Harcourt announced that he would resign as soon as a new party leader could be chosen. Within days, the party selected the weekend of February 16, 1996 for the leadership vote. By resigning when he did, Harcourt avoided a possible confrontation at the November 18 NDP provincial council meeting. Instead, the suddenly relaxed premier was greeted with a standing ovation. With his decision to quit, Harcourt the pragmatist immediately shifted his role from beleaguered boss to senior campaign manager, rallying the troops for the coming election. "If we're going to have a chance to get reelected, where the focus isn't on the past, then a new leader is necessary."

As for his own future, Harcourt didn't appear too worried. Several months before his resignation, the premier had hinted that his days in politics might be numbered. "I'd like to do a couple of terms to complete [the NDP's 48-point platform], but I've got another life," he told the author in May 1995. "I can go to other things. I have no interest in federal politics. None. Zip. But internationally, working with the Asian Development Bank, the UN, helping developing countries with sustainable forestry and land use practices – I can get excited about that."

Race to the Polls

IF ONE WERE TO JUDGE THE NDP'S PERFORMANCE IN OFFICE purely on the checklist of its 48-point election platform, it hadn't done too badly. It's hard to imagine what other party could have come

up with a land use model for the province that brought so many conflicting players to the same table. The CORE process may not have
ended the war in the woods, but it prepared BC for the inevitable
growing pains of future economic development brought on by the crisis in our ecosystem. As for the treaty process, one shudders to think
what kind of rhetoric may have filtered from the attorney general and
premier's office, had the Liberals or Reform Party been in power during the Gustafsen Lake dispute. The NDP, for all its haggling with
Ottawa over cost-sharing arrangements on the Nisga'a negotiations,
refused to cave in to the rampant fearmongering and anti-native sentiment that all too often characterized the commentary surrounding
roadblocks, occupations and other disputes involving native people
in BC from 1991 through 1995. Aboriginal land claims and self government are facts of life in BC, and so far the NDP has been the only
party with the patience and political will to allow the treaty process to
work.

Things were generally better for women and minorities under the
Harcourt New Democrats: pay equity, affirmative action programs,
choice on abortion, funding for assault centres and child care, and an
amended Human Rights Act were campaign promises the NDP managed to fulfil – although the party suffered a credibility problem with
its get-tough stance on welfare, with its reductions for single employables and three-month residency requirement for new welfare recipients, announced in the fall of 1995. The government also delivered on
its promise to get tough on polluters, passing a variety of laws to clean
up the environment; increased spending on infrastructures, focusing
on better public transit, highways and ferries to bring the system up
to date after years of neglect by the Socreds; resisted the right wing
trend toward privatized health care; and revamped post-secondary
education to provide more training in the skilled trades.

Ironically, the revised conflict laws and new freedom of information
legislation got the government in trouble on several occasions, but
provided the province with a better system of checks and balances for
the behaviour of future legislators. Notwithstanding continued criticism of Elizabeth Cull's bookkeeping on the botched Bonneville
hydroelectric power deal, the government also satisfied the right's

expectations to balance the budget over the business cycle, and the economy remained vibrant throughout the NDP's term. Housing starts and retail sales were up and small businesses were doing well, despite an organized revolt against what was probably the fairest new labour code possible and an Employment Standards Act that improved the rights of workers.

By the end of 1995, however, there was still much work to be done. The education system was experiencing growing pains, and the NDP was under increasing pressure from teachers concerned about the effect of cutbacks on school district budgets. The economy appeared to be heading for a downturn, and the next budget – which promised to be a tough one – would be announced in the midst of bargaining with hospital workers. The treaty commission had yet to produce a single land claim settlement. And even as the NDP was congratulated for saving the 107,000-hectare Stein Valley (finally ending a more than decade-long campaign), there were murmurings from the forest industry that the government's job strategy would fall way short of expectations. What new NDP leader would be willing and able to take on these challenges?

As 1996 began, the only declared candidates was Jack McDonald, a funeral director from Port Alberni who was a political unknown. Kamloops MP Nelson Riis, considered a favourite because of his complete lack of involvement with the NCHS scandal, bowed out of the race early. Several of the cabinet heavyweights also counted themselves out, including Dan Miller and Moe Sihota. Joy MacPhail also declined, citing "family considerations" (meaning, presumably, her relationship with BC Federation of Labour president Ken Georgetti). Elizabeth Cull, wounded by the controversy surrounding her handling of the Parks report, took herself out of the running early in the new year. Joan Smallwood, recently fired by Harcourt, declared her interest early although she was considered a longshot. Moderates like Ujjal Dosanjh and Paul Ramsey were also considered possibilities, but neither was willing to jump into it early.

A few days into the new year, veteran backbench MLA Corky Evans entered the contest, as did another longshot, party activist Donovan Kuehn. However, the quiet but unmistakable consensus was that cabinet would ultimately unite behind Glen Clark. The ambitious Clark appeared to have as many enemies as allies in the party, but most agreed that the articulate young minister had definite leadership qualities. Arrogant, ideological and shamelessly partisan, Clark was considered one of the few candidates nasty enough to handle a dirty election campaign by Gordon Campbell. Given the right-wing shift in popular opinion that had already swept the Bob Rae New Democrats from office in Ontario, Clark appeared to be a logical choice to unite the party's traditional supporters, attract more youth to the party and prevent a similar result from occurring in BC. Mike Harcourt's moderate approach may have been the ideal tonic for the post-Vander Zalm years, possibly the more pragmatic manner to reintroduce NDP philosophy to the public after sixteen years in opposition. But in the tougher, meaner economic climate of the mid-1990s, it was quite possible that the more hard-line approach of a "pitbull" like Clark would go much further with voters looking for an alternative to Gordon Campbell. And the party was anxious to avoid the divisive battles of 1984 that resulted in a leader, Bob Skelly, who was incapable of igniting the public imagination.

Nattering Nabobs of the Left

ONE OF THE UNKNOWN VARIABLES IN THE NDP'S ATTEMPT TO win a second term was the party's standing among traditional supporters. There wasn't much doubt about rank and file unionists. The BC Federation of Labour, of course, was solidly behind the NDP, regardless of who led it. The same could be said for the IWA, despite the growing pains of the CORE process and the party's embrace of environmental concerns. And the health care unions, heading into bargaining, were unlikely to abandon the NDP unless the new leader was going to adopt a Mike Harris approach to the budget. Among other traditional leftists, however, the NDP could not assume unconditional support. Despite its record – or perhaps because of it – the NDP continued to be maligned by leftist intellectuals who once grudgingly supported it. According to one critic, "contemporary

Marxists" were troubled by the NDP's recent embrace of "lifestyle issues like adoption, homosexuality [and] abortion". The party's move toward coalitions with "special interest" or social activist groups appeared to be "part of the perennial search for dissatisfied classes and destabilizing forces within the capitalist juggernaut," wrote longtime New Democrat and Simon Fraser University professor Paul Delany, in the summer issue of *Vancouver Review*. Instead of empowering the NDP and interest groups, the coalition model had mired both sides in "a lugubrious soap opera of political co-dependency" – reducing the governing party to a mushy, neo-liberal shadow of its former self.

Delany and many of his fellow academics were dismayed by a perceived anti-intellectualism in the NDP. Why was it, he asked, that social democratic parties in other countries were willing to support research departments and independent left wing thinktanks, while the NDP wasn't? Delany also bemoaned the use of cliched rhetoric like "slash and burn" and "Howe Street millionaires", at the expense of profound analysis or strategy. Other critics on the left complained that the Harcourt regime didn't hire enough quality people for the bureaucracy, or had cast its net too far to the east instead of settling for homegrown New Democrats. And of course, there was ongoing concern about the party's embrace of deficitphobia, and its willingness to buy into anti-welfare hysteria.

These criticisms were valid, but they didn't offer a lot of solutions when it came to the actual details of governing. What, for example, did "contemporary Marxism" mean in the mid-1990s. Would the NDP have dealt with the war in the woods by siding with IWA workers, at the expense of the environment? Would it have tried to win a fight with doctors during the BCMA lobby in 1993? What kind of partnership, if any, would it have developed with the business community, or with BC's trading partners in the Pacific Rim? And would it have dismissed aboriginal rights as just another "lifestyle issue"?

The issues that British Columbians were dealing with in 1996 required far more creative, compassionate and innovative solutions than the left had been able to produce in recent years. Delany's lament for coalition politics was a typical refrain of the whining, nostalgic babyboomer left that abandoned the NDP in droves after 1991 – preferring to criticize it from the margins. In the so-called "perennial search for dissatisfied classes," the professorial chattering classes of "contemporary Marxism" were surely the most dissatisfied.

For a better example of an NDP government with its head in the sand, left wing critics of the Harcourt years would do well to consider the fate that befell the Bob Rae NDP in Ontario. The Rae New Democrats managed to horrify their left wing supporters by seeking the wisdom of the right-wing C.D. Howe Institute on how to deal with the so-called "debt wall". The Ontario NDP abandoned a campaign promise to nationalize auto insurance; imposed public service wage rollbacks that overrode thousands of existing collective agreements (the so-called "social contract"); caved in to multinational drug companies by accepting the elimination of compulsory licensing on pharmaceuticals; extended incorporation rights to all health professionals (something Conservative and Liberal governments in Ontario managed to resist for 25 years); and put gay adoption rights to an ill-fated free vote in the legislature, leading to the proposed bill's defeat. Compare these results to similar circumstances in BC, and the Harcourt NDP's commitment to socialism looks pretty solid.

And those weren't the only differences between the Ontario and BC New Democrats. Unlike Bob Rae, whose party was stunned by its election victory in 1990, Mike Harcourt expected to win power and had some idea what he wanted to achieve once he got there. As NDP leader, he had a career of civic activism to build on; Rae had only theories. And unlike Rae, Harcourt was fortunate enough not to be burdened by a body of written work that could come back to haunt him once he was premier.

The young Bob Rae was a campus intellectual whose articles and essays expressed a variety of socialist sentiments the middle-aged Bob Rae would casually dismiss once his party came to power. Harcourt never had to worry about such a turn of events, because he never claimed to be anything but a moderate liberal in the first place. Therefore, any allegiance to social democratic principles by such a leader as Harcourt would have to be considered a plus. And, true to Stan Persky's assessments of him in 1980 and 1989, Harcourt as NDP leader appeared to be every bit as progressive as Harcourt the Vancouver mayor. It's not something he was willing to brag about when addressing business luncheons or the board of trade, but Harcourt's moderate approach had remained basically the same from the day he assumed the NDP leadership in 1987.

"I've always had some reason why I was [in politics], some change I wanted to introduce," he once told the author, not realizing these words would provide his own political epitaph. "I've always thought you have to be anchored in a set of values, and those values lead to a vision of your community ... which is not something that just sort of got written by a PR firm to throw out to the investment circle. I've always wanted to have a positive vision and have people come in behind that vision or plan, whether it's the city or provincial level. And that, I think, can really sustain you: if you're there to do something, to improve your community, to make it better than when it started – if you're there for that reason, you can endure the nicks and cuts and injustices."

IT WAS A GOOD RULE OF THUMB FOR HIS EVENTUAL SUCCESSOR, whoever that would be. Whether that vision would be enough to defeat the Gordon Campbell Liberals, however, was another question altogether. British Columbia likes to think of itself as the rebel of Confederation – independent thinking, bound neither by colonial tradition nor the latest trends of Central Canadian thought. In 1996, the province had a unique opportunity to resist the fashionable – to reject the neo-conservative economics of deficit fetishism, depart from the trendy ideas of Ontario and Alberta and, for the first time in its history, re-elect an NDP government.

It promised to be an interesting year.

NOTES

The epigraph is from *The Anatomy of Power* by John Kenneth Galbraith

1. April Fool

The description of Fantasy Garden as "a wasteland of uninventive hucksterism" is from *Vander Zalm: From Immigrant to Premier* by Alan Twigg, p. 141.

An outburst like the one comparing BC's justice system to Nazi Germany was not uncommon during Vander Zalm's political career. The premier's reputation for non sequiturs and hyperbole caught the attention of a Vancouver publisher, Arsenal Pulp Press, which produced two volumes of *Quotations From Chairman Zalm* for posterity.

In his letter to Vander Zalm, Tan Yu dismissed the investigation entirely, referring to it as the "unnecessary controversy" of Ted Hughes alone. Tan Yu turned down the conflict of interest commissioner's every request for an interview, even his offer to travel to Taipei.

"*Breach of Promise* was by no means the only critical assessment of the Vander Zalm years." Two earlier books published about the Vander Zalm Socreds were *Fantasyland: Inside the Reign of Bill Vander Zalm* by Vancouver *Sun* reporters Gary Mason and Keith Baldrey, and Stan Persky's *Fantasy Government: Bill Vander Zalm and the Future of Social Credit*.

2. Mikey Milquetoast

Volrich vs. Harcourt for the TEAM mayoralty nomination is from *The House that Jack Built: Mayor Jack Volrich and Vancouver Politics* by Stan Persky, p. 25.

"To give Harcourt his due" is from *The House that Jack Built*, p. 209.

"A reasonably typical Yuppie" is from *Fantasy Government*, p. 111-112.

"I don't understand people who get stand-offish" is from "Crusading lawyer became political star by appealing to moderates," in Vancouver *Sun*, October 18,

1991.

The background concerning Bob Rae is from *Rae Days: The Rise and Follies of the NDP* by Thomas Walkom.

The six candidates in the 1984 NDP leadership contest were Skelly, Vickers, King, Dave Stupich, Margaret Birrell and Graham Lea.

"In a single ten-second sound clip" is from *Fantasyland*, p. 66.

"A diamond right under their noses" is from "NDP split over Skelly exposed," Vancouver *Sun*, October 24, 1986.

Mike Harcourt's comments, beginning with "I never accepted that," are from an interview with the author.

"The unions were in Solidarity for what they could gain" is from "The Civilized Revolution" by Gordon Wilson in *Political Affairs* by Judi Tyabji, p. 41-42.

Description of Gordon Wilson as "more a double-breasted suit kind of guy" is from "A long upstream struggle against political currents and party dams," Vancouver *Sun*, October 18, 1991.

The Jack Kempf situation comments are from "Kempf goes independent as alternate rebuffs Socreds," Vancouver *Sun*, October 5, 1991.

The CBC debate was supposed to be carried by BCTV and UTV as well, but BCTV was committed to showing a Toronto Bluejays baseball playoff game that night. The station asked CBC to move the debate to October 7, but was refused.

Comments on accuracy of BCTV polling are from "NDP challenges BCTV pollsters," Vancouver *Province*, October 16, 1991.

NDP relationship with VSE from "The VSE and the NDP," Vancouver *Sun*, October 12, 1991.

3. Retooling the Shop

Regarding the number of seats in the BC legislature, with the redrawing of electoral boundaries, the total number of seats in the legislature rose from 69 to 75.

The overhead Kieran comment is from a Harcourt interview with the author.

New Democrats and the red warning light is from "People's trust will have to be earned," Vancouver *Sun*, November 7, 1991.

Harcourt's trip to Japan is from "Japan trade first target of premier," Vancouver *Sun*, November 18, 1991.

"Glen came into my office" is from the author's interview with Mike Harcourt.

"The books were so cooked" is from "How BC plunged into sea of red ink," Vancouver *Sun*, March 12, 1992.

Supreme Court Justice Coultas made reference to Peter Dueck's remark about people with AIDS in the case of *Persons With AIDS Society vs. the Minister of Health, the Minister of Social Services and Housing, the Director of Human Resources, and the Crown*, in 1989.

Kathy Sanderson's comments on the budget are from "Business barks at tax bite," Vancouver *Sun*, March 27, 1992.

Comments about Industrial Relations Act are from *Fantasyland* by Mason and Baldrey, p. 155.

BC as "an unnerving version of south Africa" is from "A double whammy from government," Vancouver *Province*, June 2, 1987, quoted in *Fantasy Government* by Persky, p. 123.

Bill Tieleman's comments about sectoral bargaining and the labour code were made in an interview with the author.

Sihota's comments beginning "We had a mandate" "We worked very hard on anti-scab" and "What a bunch of crap" are from an interview with the author.

Sihota's quote "If we were to compete with them" is from "NDP headed for failing grade on labour code," Vancouver *Sun*, January 18, 1993.

Sihota's description of the premier's backroom bargaining skills, and his remarks about Brian Mulroney's ego, are from an interview with the author.

Mel Smith's comments are from "BC's piece of the pie," Vancouver *Province*, July 12, 1992.

Vaughn Palmer on gender equity in the Senate is from "Why British Columbia's No is unique in all the provincial denials," Vancouver *Sun*, October 27, 1992.

Stan Persky on Harcourt's problems with the Charlottetown Accord is from "Pricked premier bleeds," Vancouver *Sun*, September 26, 1992.

"For the first time he has a serviceable text" is from "Harcourt speech fired up Yes furnace," Vancouver *Sun*, October 15, 1992.

Brian Mulroney's abuses of power, contempt for the electorate and abandonment of fiscal responsibility were cited by Peter C. Newman in his 1995 book *The Canadian Revolution* as major factors in the Canadian public's disenchantment with the political process and its shift from a culture of deference to one of defiance.

"We've had some tough challenges" is from "New labour code, constitution big issues for returning MLAs," Vancouver *Sun*, October 20, 1992.

4. "New Directions ... Same Old Turf

Explanation of Established Programs Financing Act is from "Social Services and 'Restraint'," by Robin Hanvelt in *False Promises: The Failure of Conservative Economics*, edited by Robert C. Allen and Gideon Rosenbluth, p. 246.

Gordon Austin's comments on HEU contract demands are from the *HEU Guardian*, June 1992, p. 10. Ironically, Austin was later fired by the HLRA and subjected to an RCMP investigation for questionable spending habits and alleged misappropriation of funds.

Chris Chilton testified about the list of hospitals to be closed when he was being interviewed by auditor George Morfitt regarding his role in the awarding of contracts to NOW Communications.

Regarding the HLRA vote on the job security agreement, under the HLRA constitution, the deal could only pass with a two thirds majority.

"They should have known that administrators wouldn't like it" is from Jean Greatbatch's interview with the author.

Doctors' reactions to the NDP 1992 budget are from "Specialists riled over income capping," Vancouver *Sun*, March 28, 1992.

Vaughn Palmer's comments on Bill 14 are from "Sledgehammer law smashes MDs' pensions," Vancouver *Sun*, March 31, 1992.

Jim Nielsen's comments on the NDP's battle with doctors are from "Doctors' dispute testing NDP mettle," Vancouver *Sun*, July 3, 1992.

"We had to make a lot of tough decisions fast" is from Victoria *Times-Colonist*, May 20, 1992.

John Pifer quote is from "Doctors deserve nothing less than fair treatment," Penticton *Herald*, June 8, 1992.

Cull's accusations that doctors were fearmongering appeared in "Doctors' unfounded claims frightening seniors—Cull," Victoria *Times-Colonist*, June 26, 1992.

"Count on it" is from "Health care haggling," Vancouver *Sun*, August 20,1992.

Arun Garg's response to Nanaimo communiqué is from "BC ratifies deal," *The Medical Post*, October 5, 1993.

"It was the wrong approach" is from the author's interview with Mike Harcourt.

5. Strange Bedfellows

Brian Kieran's description of Liberal caucus is from "Comedy of errors ends in a mixed blessing," Vancouver *Province*, October 20, 1991.

"But when it came to Howe Street heavyweights" and Gordon Wilson's refusal to accept a cheque with strings attached, are from *Political Affairs* by Judy Tyabji, pp. 123-124. Wilson confirmed for this book that the donor was Cadillac Fairview.

Information on Judi Tyabji's background comes from *Political Affairs*.

Description of ex-Socreds moving to Liberal Party, and comments by Jack Heinrich, Floyd Sully, and Kristian Arnason are from "Here come Campbell's Liberals," *Pacific Current*, November 1994.

6. The Premier in the Plexiglass Bubble

"It wasn't that we weren't carrying out what we said we were going to do" and Harcourt's comments on the politics of personality are from the author's interview with the premier.

Bill Tieleman's remarks about BC political leaders are from an interview with the author.

"There's always this fear that I have" is from Ken Georgetti's interview with the author.

Mike Harcourt discussed deficit reduction as a left-wing concept in an interview with the author.

The Wasserlein and Fleming quotes are from "Eastsiders skeptical about tax revolt," Vancouver *Sun*, April 7, 1993.

"I think the media tends to listen to powerful, vested interests" is from "Despite negative vibrations, strategists say scheme okay," Vancouver *Sun*, April 1, 1993.

"Awful—that's how I felt" is from "MLA Marzari was target when budget hit homes," Vancouver *Sun*, May 21, 1993.

"My biggest concern was that we were losing public confidence" and his comments about Skills Now are from Mike Harcourt's interview with the author.

Tom Perry's expressed his praise and reservations about Skills Now in an interview with the author.

Georgetti and MacPhail appeared to keep their promise to avoid conflict of interest. When cabinet discussions began regarding a proposed Vancouver waterfront casino project, MacPhail pulled herself out of every meeting in which the issue came up. This was because Georgetti was a director of Vancouver Land Corporation (VLC), the union-backed company that was a partner in the $1 billion project.

"I think Premier Harcourt took a real risk" is from Moe Sihota's interview with the author.

7. Brazil of the North

"The market needs political direction" is from an interview in *UNESCO Courier*, September 1990, pp. 4-9.

Moe Sihota's comments about the NDP's environment policy are from an interview with the author.

Report on the fall meeting of the green caucus is from "Harcourt denies green fight," Vancouver *Sun*, November 27, 1989.

The formation of the BC Round Table on the Environment and Economy was covered in "Connaghan heads 31-member body on environment," Vancouver *Sun*, January 16, 1990.

Remarks of Haskell and Chow are from "Turning sour," Vancouver *Sun*, January 4, 1992.

Kennedy's guest column was called "Logging Clayoquot will strip province of its natural beauty" and ran in the Vancouver *Sun* of February 20, 1993.

The five undisturbed watersheds were the last of ninety watersheds on Vancouver Island.

Bob Bossin's comments are from a letter to the editor in the Vancouver *Sun*, March 31, 1993.

Stephen Hume's comments on the Clayoquot announcement are from "Paradise Lost," Vancouver *Sun*, April 17, 1993.

"We have said no moratorium or veto to anybody" is from Mike Harcourt's interview with the author in May 1995.

Boycotts were not always successful. Mike Harcourt won a significant victory when he invited Egon Klepsch, president of the European parliament, to view BC logging practices firsthand. Klepsch, after meeting with BC forestry, government, and native leaders, said that a European boycott of Canadian forest products was highly unlikely.

The description of preparations for the war in the woods is from "A global war with Cold War techniques" and "Logging foes hoping for 1,000 to join blockades," both from the Vancouver *Sun*, June 30, 1993.

"It's an ignorant bum rap" is from "US news story on Clayoquot called an ignorant bum rap," Vancouver *Sun*, July 21, 1993.

George Watts's comments are from an interview with the author.

Harcourt's remarks on confronting Greenpeace protesters in Europe are from an interview with the author.

David Anderson's comments on Clayoquot are from "Now Chretien backing off Clayoquot," Vancouver *Sun*, October 28, 1993.

"Could this deal have less to do with a voluntary commitment to native justice..." is from "Here's a word a politician should never use," Vancouver *Sun*, December 15, 1993.

"When people go back and look at the Clayoquot decision" is from the author's interview with Mike Harcourt.

8. Sustainable Province

Moe Sihota's comments throughout this chapter are from his interview with the author.

Peter Bentley's July 19, 1989, letter was quoted in "Canfor boss floating plan to counter anti-everythings," Vancouver *Sun*, August 11, 1989.

The "green chain" was a low-tech, manual labour production process that was common in most sawmills before high-tech machinery arrived in the 1980s. When fresh, or 'green' lumber was sawn, it used to come out onto a 'chain' conveyor belt to be sorted manually. Most of these jobs have been rendered obsolete by automatic sorting systems.

Geddes Resources was also owned by Toronto-based Northgate Explorations Ltd. (40 percent) and by Cominco Ltd. (20 percent).

Stephen Hume's questions about Windy Craggy are from "Shangri-La," Vancouver *Sun*, May 7, 1993.

Description of Windy Craggy announcement is from "Windy Craggy deal worth $104 million," Vancouver *Sun*, August 19, 1995.

Ts'yl-os, or Ts'il?os (pronounced Sigh-loss) is the Indian name for Mount Tatlow, a Chilco Lake mountain with legendary and spiritual significance for the Nemiah.

The Cariboo forest industry was already in trouble. A ten-year harvest of areas infested with pine beetles was coming to an end, and a provincewide review of cutting rates had recommended significantly reduced rates for the region.

Cobb and Wallace's reactions to CORE report are from "Fear of forest job loss spurs strong grassroots protests," Vancouver *Sun*, August 25, 1994.

A discussion of Rafe Mair's anti-KCP campaign is in "Broadcaster Rafe Mair's broadcasts led fight against Alcan," Vancouver *Sun*, January 24, 1995.

Harcourt's remarks about the environmental and financial reasons behind the cancellation of KCP and about the angry crowd in Kitimat are from his interview with the author.

"CORE was not the IWA's favourite vehicle" is from Gerry Stoney's interview with the author.

9. Giving a Hundred and Eleven Percent

The Vancouver *Sun*'s April 1, 1995, story on native land claims was titled "Staking Claim" and ran on pages A1, B1 and B2.

Terry Glavin's comments on the "124 summers" since Confederation are from "Roadblocks to reconciliation," *Georgia Straight*, July 7-14, 1995.

"Few Indian communities have either the population or the economic wherewithal" is from "Land claims, 1: Calm down," Vancouver *Sun*, October 4, 1994.

The Royal Proclamation declared that Indian nations or tribes of North America were owners of "all the lands and territories lying to the westward of the Atlantic watershed"; lands within these territories were not to be settled unless the aboriginal inhabitants agreed to surrender them in treaties.

The description of the new relationship between government and native peoples is from the BC Claims Task Force Report, released June 28, 1991.

George Watts's comments in this chapter on the NDP and native concerns are from an interview with the author.

Regarding the six stages of the treaty process, by the end of the 1994-95 fiscal year, most of the 43 native groups who had filed a statement of claim were at the early negotiation stage. Only seven were ready to begin negotiating a framework agreement.

Angus Robertson's comments are from "Natives claims may be right, Victoria believes," Vancouver *Sun*, December 15, 1994.

Comments of Wendy Grant and Brian Smith are from "Land claims drawing attention of business," Vancouver *Sun*, September 10, 1994.

"The treaty talks are no more secretive than the resource-management meetings" is from the author's interview with Terry Glavin.

"We got this confidentiality agreement" is from the author's interview with Ken Georgetti.

Harcourt's description of Jack Weisgerber and the Mount Currie blockade is from the June 6, 1995, debate in the legislature, quoted in "Blockades won't work, A-G warns," Vancouver *Sun*, June 7, 1995.

Regarding the Craig Bay Estates cemetery, the government was in an awkward position because there are likely thousands of undiscovered burial sites like this one throughout the province. Cabinet had already confronted the issue two years earlier, when the bones of a woman, dating back at least 200 years, were found on a lot owned by Moe Sihota. Sihota, who lived in the Victoria suburb of View Royal, made an agreement with the local Songhees band to have the remains removed from his property under native supervision and reburied at the band cemetery.

The government bought fourteen acres of land and created a green space for the entire community. The appropriateness of this action became apparent later, when an ethnographic study revealed that the remains were likely not those of Nanoose band ancestors but of the Pentlatch (now extinct) or the Qualicum people.

"It's up to the courts" is from "Sihota dismisses use of force to end Native blockade to Apex," Vancouver *Sun*, November 18, 1994.

Gordon Gibson's views on the land claims negotiation process appeared in "Indian deals now immoral," Vancouver *Sun*, July 7, 1995.

Joe Gosnell's comments about Melvin Smith are from an interview with the author.

Information on the Upper Nicola Band blockade is from "Masked faces reflect new level of tension in relations," Vancouver *Sun*, June 7, 1995.

"The difficulty with this approach" is from "Treaty process is alive and well," Vancouver *Sun*, June 7, 1995.

"Harcourt wanted to face [land claims] head on" is from Terry Glavin's interview with the author.

10. Beancounters of the Left

Information about BC's economic situation after the Socreds is from "NDP facing a tough situation, BC economists told," Vancouver *Sun*, November 13, 1991.

Gideon Rosenbluth's comments on the NDP's economic subcommittee are from an interview with the author.

Vaughn Palmer's comments about Clark's response to the Socred deficit are from "For answers, Clark reaches far to the right," Vancouver *Sun*, January 9, 1992.

"[It was] highly unlikely that increases in government deficits" is from "The Political Economy of Deficit-Phobia," by Gideon Rosenbluth, in *False Promises: The Failure of Conservative Economics*, edited by Robert C. Allen and Gideon Rosenbluth, p. 62. The reference to Third World dictators is from the same book on page 72.

Harcourt's description of deficit cutting as "almost a game" for the Socreds is from an interview with the author.

Michael Goldberg's remarks about increased welfare premiums are from "Welfare recipients increasing in BC.," *Globe and Mail*, February 7, 1995.

Reactions to Harcourt's welfare crackdown are from "Premier's 'deadbeat' epithet criticized," Vancouver *Sun*, September 24, 1993.

"That was unfortunate" is from Harcourt's interview with the author.

Harcourt described his alternative to welfare in an interview with the author.

Mervin Harrower's comments are from Kathy Tait's "Matters of the Heart" column in the *Province* of June 18, 1995.

Thomas L. Friedman's article about Moody's credit ratings, "Don't mess with Moody's," originally appeared in the *New York Times*, and was reprinted in the *Globe and Mail* of February 27, 1995.

"If you compared, year by year, the budgeted deficit" and Gideon Rosenbluth's comments about foreign bonds are from his interview with the author.

"It acknowledges the gravity of the...deficit/debt problem" is from "Canada reaches a crossroads," Winnipeg *Free Press*, February 18, 1995.

Mike Harcourt and Bill Barlee's comments about the NDP's long-range plan are from interviews with the author.

Stephen Hume wrote about retail sales under the NDP in "As the register receipts show, an NDP government sells," Vancouver *Sun*, April 28, 1995.

"Whatever its method of accounting" is from "Mr. Harcourt's hopes," *Globe and Mail*, January 21, 1995.

11. Friends and Insiders

The quotation from Jeffrey Simpson's *Spoils of Power* was cited by conflict of interest commissioner Ted Hughes on page 25 of his decision regarding *Weisgerber and Emerson vs. Harcourt*, April 17, 1995.

"The New Democrats have shown great reluctance" is from "NDP strangely mum on Port Alberni," Vancouver *Sun*, November 28, 1994.

"The business community has never had the access to government" is from Mike Harcourt's interview with the author.

Ken Georgetti's reaction to the "nineteenth cabinet minister" tag is from an interview with the author.

The July 14, 1994, *Sun* editorial on Bamberton was called "Bamberton project a study in dithering."

"We got slowed down" and Ken Georgetti's comments about the Seaport Centre casino project are from an interview with the author.

Cliff Andstein's reaction to the casino is from "Casino Reality," *Pacific Current*, August/September, 1994.

"The people of Vancouver don't want this thing" is from "It's high time casino aces cut their losses," Vancouver *Sun*, July 28, 1994.

Mike Harcourt spoke about how the freedom of information legislation may have caused difficulties for the NDP in his interview with the author.

Connie Munro's 1990 comment about Social Credit insiders was quoted in "Munro has labored hard to haul in perks," Vancouver *Sun*, January 12, 1995.

"Because of the decisions of Jim Dorsey and Connie Munro" is from "WCB reforms 'scared' business: Chair's style forced resignation," Vancouver *Sun*, December 19, 1994.

It was important that Connie Munro's car fit into her garage for safety reasons. Because some members of the public blamed her for the fact that 70 percent of all compensation requests are rejected, she believed she would be safer if she could keep her car off the street.

"It's very easy to do a funny story on 1-900 numbers" and Moe Sihota's other comments on FOI are from an interview with the author.

Johnson was a "failed NDP candidate" because he ran four times unsuccessfully in the federal riding of Vancouver Centre. His first campaign was as a twenty year old against Liberal cabinet minister Ron Basford. NDP candidates in Vancouver Centre were never expected to do more than provide a competitive, three-way race.

Harcourt was criticized during the 1991 campaign for adopting a slogan that Struble had already used in a Rhode Island Democrat's call for "a government as honest and hardworking as the people who pay for it."

In November 1994, Opposition critics began hounding Harcourt about the number of calls made from the premier's office to Struble's Washington, D.C., phone number. The impression was that the premier couldn't sneeze without phoning his American spin doctor for advice. But according to various sources inside the government, many of the calls were not business inquiries by the premier but "pillow talk" between Struble and the premier's communications consultant, Sheila Fruman. Harcourt, confronted about the rumour by a legislative reporter in May, responded, "Why don't you ask her?"

Ad agency executives' reactions to the NOW issue are from "Agencies 'treated fairly' by NDP," Vancouver *Sun*, March 9, 1995.

John Langford, Jim Nielsen and Jess Ketchum were quoted in "Conflict law being used as 'political terrorism,'" Vancouver *Sun*, March 17, 1995.

12. Trouble in Hub City

The author relied on dozens of news clippings for background on the NCHS scandal. The most comprehensive account can be found in "The Charity Scandal: How corruption killed the NDP's 40-year dream," Vancouver *Sun*, December 17, 1994.

Bill Duncan's comments about NCHS throughout this chapter are from an interview with the author.

Frank Murphy's discussion of the Gaming Commission's 1988 investigation of NCHS, and his denial that his letter to the commission had anything to do with Stupich's defeat of his son-in-law, are from an interview with the author.

Dave Stupich's comments in this chapter, other than those quoted in the Vancouver *Sun*, are from an interview with the author.

Correspondence between Stupich and Frank Murphy and Cliff Shoop and the NCHS audit committee, along with comments by Carl Bolton and Ronald Parks were excerpted from the Investigation of the Affairs and Conduct of Nanaimo Commonwealth Holding Society and Related Societies, by Ronald H. Parks, May 31, 1995.

Brian Smith's comments on NCHS, Dave Stupich and Elizabeth Cull are from an interview with the author.

"It's a bullshit issue", and Harcourt's other comments on Vaughn Palmer, Elizabeth Cull and calls for a public inquiry are from an interview with the author.

Allan Blakeney's comments on Elizabeth Cull's handling of the Parks report are from "Cull's actions puzzling," Vancouver *Sun*, December 9, 1995.

The Westray inquiry was an investigation into a fatal mine explosion in Nova Scotia in 1992. Susan Nelles was a nurse at the Toronto Hospital for Sick Children who was accused, but later acquitted, of administering lethal overdoses of digoxin to several babies who had died at the hospital under mysterious circumstances.

13. Digging for Bones

Stan Persky on pack journalism is from "Media ain't nothing but hound dogs," Vancouver *Sun*, April 6, 1991.

Jamie Lamb discussed Douglas Day in "Politically correct New Democrats abandon fort tradition," Vancouver *Sun*, November 23, 1994.

Description of Bill 33 as a law to "intimidate and silence" is from "Bill 33 is a government gag order," Vancouver *Sun* July 6, 1993.

"We were criticized, I think quite savagely and unfairly," is from Harcourt's interview with the author.

The *Sun*'s "Socreds were saints compared to NDP" article ran on April 28, 1994.

"There were not innocent, flirty types of come-ons," is from "NDP accused of offering coverup," Vancouver *Province*, April 6, 1995.

Edith Antonio's comments are from "Woman who lost money calls ex-minister's plight 'unfair and unjust,'" Vancouver *Sun*, May 6, 1995.

Hubert Beyer's musing on the BC Law Society's investigation of Moe Sihota is from "Sihota slimed, but colleague merely slapped by law society," Saanich *News*, May 16, 1995.

The electronic town hall conflict with the Canucks game was reported in "Sitcom without a laugh track," Vancouver *Province*, February 23, 1995.

"The format, in retrospect, was hopeless" is from the author's interview with Mike Harcourt.

Vaughn Palmer on the "long-promised trip to the woodshed" appeared in "How Mr. Morfitt may somewhat discomfit," Vancouver *Sun*, May 19, 1995.

Harcourt's reaction to newspaper coverage of the NOW scandal is from his interview with the author.

"We're not being journalists" is from "Now firm shafted by uninformed journalists," Vancouver *Sun*, March 11, 1995.

"There's absolutely no connection" and Bill Tieleman's other comments about NCHS and the Vancouver Commonwealth Society are from an interview with the author.

14. Membership Has its Privileges

The major Op-Ed piece that *Kitsilano News* reporter Russ Francis sold to the *Sun* for its September 4, 1993 edition was headlined "He's developing a problem". The article provided much of the background for the Moodie saga.

In an interesting coincidence, Northwest Sports Enterprises, former majority owner of the Vancouver Canucks (now known as Orca Bay), held major shares in BCTV and CKNW, the tv and radio station, respectively, which held the broadcasting rights to Canucks' games—and which also broadcast financial advice programs by Campbell's brother Michael.

Sid Tafler's comments on the Campbell/Moodie connection vs. the NCHS story are from "Campbell's scandal and the media's conflict of disinterest," *Monday*, January

19-25, 1995.

Gordon Campbell's May 1 comments to the *Sun* about Atlas Travel were quoted in "Campbell forgets he knew about Atlas Travel," Vancouver *Sun*, May 2, 1995.

"The abuse of office by Gordon Campbell is systemic" is from Mike Harcourt's interview with the author.

Michael Campbell was manager of *Equity* until September 1995, when he sued the magazine for nearly $172,000 in unpaid salary, expenses and freelance article fees, plus damages for *Equity*'s "failure to provide reasonable notice of termination" when his contract was not renewed.

The *Georgia Straight*'s comments on the BCTV/CKNW-Michael Campbell relationship appeared in the paper's "Straight Talk" column, April 21-28, 1995.

"It seems that it's all the same people" is from Ken Georgetti's interview with the author.

Libby Davies spoke with the author about Gordon Campbell's leadership style when he was mayor.

The *Globe and Mail* wrote about Gordon Campbell in "Campbell has scent of power about him," on July 17, 1995.

Shirley MacGillivray's split with Gordon Campbell was covered in "Liberal riding association president quits over alleged high-handed tactics of leader," Vancouver *Sun*, May 3, 1995.

"I think one of the things we're very lucky about in British Columbia" is from "Campbell has scent of power about him," in *Globe and Mail*, July 17, 1995.

Art Cowie's comments are from "Cowie quits politics after losing Liberal nomination in Quilchena," Vancouver *Sun*, November 28, 1995. Cowie's argument was a strange one, given his own dubious record of loyalty. Gordon Wilson, reached by a reporter for a reaction, couldn't help but derive satisfaction from the misfortune of the man who had worked so hard to dump him as Liberal leader in 1993. "It is interesting to see how the worm turns," said Wilson. "What goes around comes around."

"I've been talking about [debt reduction] since 1993" is from "Campbell dislikes being compared to Ontario premier," Vancouver *Sun*, October 8, 1995.

Epilogue: Picking Up the Pieces

Audrey McLaughlin stepped down as federal NDP leader in 1994, in the wake of her party's disastrous showing in the 1993 federal election.

Description of the BCGEU's involvement with NCHS is from two Vancouver *Sun* articles, "BCGEU hid $500,000 loan to Nanaimo society," October 16, 1995, and "Fryer blamed in loan deal," October 19, 1995.

Bernie Simpson's defense of corporate donations is from "Corporate donations not illegal, MLA says," Vancouver *Sun*, October 17, 1995.

Jan Pullinger's comment on the scandal is from "Angry MLAs attend caucus meeting," Vancouver *Sun*, October 20, 1995.

Paul Delany wrote about the NDP in "What's left?" *Vancouver Review*, Summer 1995.

BIBLIOGRAPHY

Allen, Robert C. and Rosenbluth, Gideon, eds. *False Promises: The Failure of Conservative Economics* (New Star, 1992)

Ehring, George and Roberts, Wayne. *Giving Away a Miracle: Lost Dreams, Broken Promises and the Ontario NDP* (Mosaic Press, 1993)

Kavic, Lorne J. and Nixon, Garry. *The 1200 Days — A Shattered Dream: Dave Barrett and the NDP in BC, 1972-75* (Kaen Publishers, 1979)

Leslie, Graham. *Breach of Promise: Socred Ethics Under Bill Vander Zalm* (Harbour, 1991)

Lisac, Mark. *The Klein Revolution* (NeWest Press, 1995)

Magnusson, Warren; Carroll, William K.; Doyle, Charles; Langer, Monika; Walker, R.B.J. *The New Reality: The Politics of Restraint in British Columbia* (New Star, 1984)

Mason, Gary and Baldrey, Keith. *Fantasyland: Inside the Reign of Bill Vander Zalm* (McGraw-Hill Ryerson, 1989)

McQuaig, Linda. *Shooting the Hippo: Death by Deficit and other Canadian Myths* (Viking, 1995)

Persky, Stan. *The House That Jack Built: Mayor Jack Volrich & Vancouver Politics* (New Star, 1980)

Persky, Stan. *Fantasy Government: Bill Vander Zalm and the Future of Social Credit* (New Star, 1989)

Persky, Stan. *Mixed Media, Mixed Messages* (New Star, 1991)

Pitsula, James M. and Rasmussen, Ken. *Privatizing a Province: The New Right in Saskatchewan* (New Star, 1990)

Smith, Melvin H. *Our Home or Native Land? What Governments' Aboriginal Policy is Doing to Canada* (Crown Western, 1995)

Twigg, Alan. *Vander Zalm: From Immigrant to Premier* (Harbour, 1986)

Tyabji, Judi. *Political Affairs* (Horsdal & Schubart, 1994)

Walkom, Thomas. *Rae Days: The Rise and Follies of the NDP* (Key Porter, 1994)

INDEX